The Ojibwa of Southern Ontario

The Ojibwa have lived in Ontario longer than any other ethnic group. Until now, however, their history has never been fully recorded. Peter Schmalz offers a sweeping account of the Ojibwa in which he corrects many long-standing historical errors and fills in numerous gaps in their story. His narrative is based as much on Ojibwa oral tradition as on the usual historical sources.

Beginning with life as it was before the arrival of Europeans in North America, Schmalz describes the peaceful commercial trade of the Ojibwa hunters and fishers with the Iroquois. Later, when the Five Nations Iroquois attacked various groups in southern Ontario in the mid-seventeenth century, the Ojibwa were the only Indians to defeat them, thereby disproving the myth of Iroquois invincibility.

In the eighteenth century the Ojibwa entered their golden age, enjoying the benefits of close alliance with both the French and the English. But with those close ties came an increasing dependence on European guns, tools, and liquor at the expense of the older way of life. The English defeat of the French in 1759 changed the nature of Ojibwa society, as did the Beaver War (better known as the Pontiac Uprising) they fought against the English a few years later. In his account of that war, Schmalz offers a new assessment of the role of Pontiac and the Toronto chief Wabbicommicot.

The fifty years following the Beaver War brought bloodshed and suffering at the hands of the English and United Empire Loyalists. The reserve system and the establishment of special schools, intended to destroy the Indian culture and assimilate the Ojibwa into mainstream society, failed to meet those objectives.

The twentieth century has seen something of an Ojibwa renaissance. Schmalz shows how Ojibwa participation in two world wars led to a desire to change conditions at home. Today the Ojibwa are gaining some control over their children's education, their reserves, and their culture.

PETER S. SCHMALZ is head of the History and Social Science Department at Walkerton (Ontario) District Secondary School. His earlier books include *Man in Society* and *The History of the Saugeen Indians*.

Peter S. Schmalz

THE OJIBWA
OF SOUTHERN
ONTARIO

University of Toronto Press

Toronto Buffalo London

© University of Toronto Press 1991
Toronto Buffalo London
Printed in Canada

ISBN 0-8020-2736-9 (cloth)
ISBN 0-8020-6778-6 (paper)

Reprinted in paper 1991

Printed on acid-free paper

Canadian Cataloguing in Publication Data

Schmalz, Peter S.
  The Ojibwa of southern Ontario

  Includes bibliographical references.
  ISBN 0-8020-2736-9 (bound). – ISBN 0-8020-6778-6 (pbk.)

  1. Ojibwa Indians – History.*
  2. Ojibwa Indians – Government relations.*
  3. Indians of North America – Ontairo – History.
  4. Indians of North America – Canada – Government relations.
  5. Indians, Treatment of – Ontario – History.   I. Title.

  E99.C6S34 1991   971.3'00497   C90-094505-2

This book has been published with the help of a grant
from the Social Science Federation of Canada,
using funds provided by the Social Sciences and
Humanities Research Council of Canada.

CONTENTS

ACKNOWLEDGMENTS

There are several persons who, through their help and encouragement, made this book possible. Over two decades, E. Palmer Patterson has fanned the flame of interest on coals that were losing their glow. My gratitude must also go to the numerous native people who shared their knowledge with me. Chiefs Vernon Roote, James Mason, Ralph Akiwenzie, and Joseph Akiwenzie stimulated my efforts to investigate the history of their people. Irene Akiwenzie often demonstrated the traditional generosity of the Ojibwa and proved that she was a great *nokomis*. My former students, Sue Stump and Tammy Jones, helped in gathering oral traditions. The superb editorial skill of Rosemary Shipton was essential to transform the manuscript into a book. And, because the research and writing was done at the same time that I was teaching full time, my family (Shirley, Michael, Lisa, and James) must receive my deepest gratitude for their cooperation. To all of you, *megwach*.

PREFACE

Today there are approximately 20,000 Ojibwas located on about three dozen small reserves scattered throughout southern Ontario.[1] Although they now represent a relatively small minority in the multicultural population, for almost the whole of the eighteenth century they were by far the most influential and numerous ethnic group in that part of the province. While their ancestors have been in contact with Europeans for over 350 years, no scholar has attempted to write a definitive work on the history of this particular group, which has commonly been placed within the Southeastern Ojibwa of North America. Indeed, there is not even a useful guide to determine the decisive turning points in their history. This is amazing considering that the Ojibwa of southern Ontario are the most numerous Indians in the province and that they played an important role not only in the history of Ontario but in the broader colonial struggle for North America as well.

This history is an attempt to examine the interrelationship between the Ojibwa of southern Ontario and the Euro-Americans from their first contact in the early seventeenth century through to contemporary times. While such a comprehensive study at this time may be bold in light of the limited scholarship that has been dedicated to the southern Ontario Ojibwa, it is hoped that it will stimulate greater efforts in this field, create some intellectual fermentation, and form a tentative framework to aid future scholars.

In a broad context, this history traces the rise, decline, and resurgence of the Ojibwa in southern Ontario. Chapters 2, 3, and 4 deal with the Ojibwa as successful warriors, fur traders, and especially diplomats during their time of ascendancy. Chapter 5 explains how they lost their power through a 'peaceful' conquest. Chapters 6, 7, and 8 are concerned with the government's mismanagement of their lands, the assimilationist policy, and the economy of their reserves. Chapter 9 examines the roots and characteristics of the Ojibwa renaissance.

The settlement of the Ojibwa in the southern part of the province has been shrouded in mystery ever since the immigration of the first European settlers to the region. Over the years the myth developed that the Ojibwa simply moved into a political vacuum created by the Huron-Iroquois wars, or that the French alone so weakened the Iroquois that the Ojibwa could take over the region unchallenged. Certainly the Ojibwa were forced to flee the Iroquois when the Iroquois dispersed the Huron, Neutral, and Petun in the 1650s, but in the last three decades of the seventeenth century they moved from the defensive to the offensive. Indeed, if oral traditions from the Mississauga, Ojibwa, Ottawa, and Iroquois are to be believed, there is some justification to say that the Ojibwa conquered southern Ontario and drove out the Iroquois. Interpretations throughout this book will be based on oral sources as well as on colonial records.

Little has been published which shows the involvement of the Ojibwa in the colonial struggle leading up to the conquest of North America by the English. From 1701 to 1759 the victorious Ojibwa enjoyed a 'golden age' in their new homeland. They were masters of the Great Lakes region and determined to a considerable extent the destiny of other aboriginal groups as well as Europeans who entered their territory. As the major middlemen in the fur trade, they could choose between the French and their newly acquired trading partners, the English, in establishing the cheapest and best source of trade goods. Since the Ojibwa were also being wooed as essential allies by both of the European powers in North America, economic considerations in the trade were often secondary. This was especially true of the French. At times, the French traded at a loss with the Ojibwa simply to retain them as military auxiliaries. The Southern Ojibwa were in an enviable position with their cheap trade goods, profusely distributed 'presents,' and abundant booty from battles against the English. The situation lasted as long as the French were pitted against the English in trade and in the colonial wars. It came to an end when the English finally defeated the French in the 1760s.

It has commonly been believed that the English victory over the French in North America was also a victory over France's Indian allies. This view requires considerable qualification in the case of the Ojibwa, who have never admitted to losing any sustained war. They see the Pontiac Uprising in 1763, or, as they call it, the Beaver War, from a different perspective. In their interpretation, the Ojibwa and their allies still had the power in the Great Lakes, although there was division among them. Some chiefs, such as Chief Wabbicom-micot of the Toronto area, wanted to accommodate the English, their only trading partner. Rather than any British military power, it was he, and others like him, who prevented the total destruction of all the forts in the Great Lakes. While some historians have considered the Pontiac Uprising as the last death rattle of the Great Lakes Indians, the results were at least temporarily in favour of the Ojibwa and their allies. There was no successful retaliation against them, even though the English had lost numerous forts and thousands of lives. In the years immediately after the wars, abundant presents were distributed to them, and a Royal Proclamation protected their hunting grounds. A shadow, however, loomed over them. Some Europeans considered liquor, more than fire and sword, the 'chemical' solution to the Indian problem.

In the period between the Beaver War and the War of 1812, major events shaped not only the destiny of the Europeans in America but the Ojibwa in southern Ontario. There was a substantial disin-tegration among the Ojibwa caused by increased warfare, disease, and especially the flood of liquor into the region. Division occurred between the Ojibwa who were in close proximity to the more south-ern trading posts such as Toronto and the 'back Indians' closer to Georgian Bay. While the southern group was rapidly losing its independence, military ability, pride, sobriety, and traditional customs, the northerners retained their way of life considerably longer. Violent and unscrupulous traders such as David Ramsay contributed to this disintegration. Indian administration by William Johnson did much to prevent a repeat of the Pontiac Uprising and, during the American Revolutionary War, to retain the alliance or at least neutrality of the southern Ojibwa. Ironically, it was the results of that war which did the most damage to the independence of the Ojibwas of southern Ontario. They had little choice but to welcome the United Empire Loyalists and the Iroquois into their lands as refugees from the conflict. False promises by the British and the need for a European ally were the deciding factors. Yet an alliance with the land-hungry colonists to the south was no viable solution for the Ojibwa. As the United States expanded westward in the last decades of the eighteenth century, the Ojibwa of southern Ontario became concerned not only for their kinsmen's land but for their own. At first they reluctantly participated in the battles to the south, and then became completely involved in the War of 1812 when they were forced to defend their own settlements. Many historians have recognized the role played by the Iroquois in this war, but few have given credit to the role played by the Ojibwa. While the Ojibwa were shedding blood with the English against the Americans, they were beginning to feel the negative aspects of permitting their white allies to settle in southern Ontario. Indeed, although the ungrateful Loyalists considered the Ojibwa wicked and thievish, there is more evidence to conclude that the Loyalists themselves deserved such adjectives. The British authorities promised that the white settlers would aid the Ojibwa, cooperate with them, and respect their wishes, but this benevolent attitude was not forthcoming. Ojibwa fisheries and hunting grounds were despoiled and the people were treated worse than dogs. The commonly accepted belief that the local Indians were handled judiciously and that tranquillity reigned between the two races is a myth.

The land surrenders in the closing decades of the eighteenth century and well into the nineteenth century also created a legacy of fables. Many of the agreements made by the British with the Ojibwa were unconscionable. The few that were agreed upon in good faith were later broken through government manipulation of band funds. Some authorities believe that, unlike the United States, war was prevented during the surrenders because the less aggressive Ojibwa were treated 'fairly.' This is not true. There was less demand in Ontario for land and the British used more devious means to obtain the surrenders. A policy of Indian removal, similar to the one in the United States, was attempted in Ontario. It failed for several reasons, but primarily because the Ojibwa themselves took the initiative in establishing sedentary villages based on agriculture.

Peter Jones on the Mississauga Ojibwa Reserve at the Credit River saw his people dying like leaves in the frost of fall. With the help of the Methodist church, he was instrumental in saving them by establishing model agrarian communities. The government assumed that similar Ojibwa settlements throughout southern Ontario would solve two of their major problems involving the Indians. First, such agricultural settlements would, they hoped, free the treasury from its financial obligations to the Ojibwa. Second, in the minds of some officials for a brief but decisive interval, there was a moral obligation to prevent the extinction of the native people. Not all of the elderly Ojibwa, however, agreed that an assimilationist policy was necessary for survival. Since many of the adults resisted cultural change, both residential and day schools were established for young Ojibwa. The major objective was to assimilate the Indian population into the Euro-Canadian society. Such a transition required adequate funding, cooperation, and superior leadership in both cultures. In 1860 when the British relinquished their control of Indian Affairs to the Canadian government, the assimilation experiment was considered a failure. While the Ojibwa survived, they became 'strangers in their own lands.'

They remained on their ancestral lands, nevertheless, and their population began to grow. Less than two decades after the British relinquished their responsibility, the Canadian government realized that the Indian problems would not be buried in the graves of the indigenous people. The Indian Act of 1876 consolidated the piece-meal legislation inherited from the British and a more assertive effort was made at assimilation using limited band funds. Separated from mainstream society, the native school system expanded under missionary guidance. The youth were correctly considered more malleable. They could be punished, and were, if they spoke the Ojibwa language. All communication with their parents in their indigenous language was discouraged. In contrast with the day schools on the reserves, the transition to the white mentality was more complete in the residential schools. Yet the schools did not prove to be the elixir that the Indian Department had anticipated.

Culture shock was tremendous for these young children, and some of them could not even communicate with their parents after spending five or more years in the institutions. Reserve-educated children coined the phrase 'Apple Indians' for those who had been educated in the boarding schools. They were considered 'red' on the outside and 'white' on the inside. Many were caught in limbo, since they were accepted fully neither on their own reserve nor in mainstream society. The limited facilities and funds available for residential schools dictated that most Ojibwa continued to be educated in their own communities. Their elders considered this a better solution to the problem than sending their children to residential schools.

Euro-Canadian Indian agents inspected the reserve day schools and generally controlled the political, economic, and social life of the communities. The grand council of the Ojibwa of southern Ontario met regularly every two years in an attempt to form a united front against the growing dictatorial power of the Indian Department and its agents. The council's influence was negligible, partly because of disenfranchisement and partly because of disunity in the organization which reflected divisions on many of the individual reserves. The influx of Ojibwa kinsmen, the Potawatomi, from the Indian wars in the United States did much to create this disunity. While the refugees were reluctantly accepted, they created both economic and social problems on the Ojibwa reserves of southern Ontario. Tribal unanimity was required in an attempt to counter the growing power of the Indian agents who, through patronage appointments, formed little dictatorships. In greater sympathy with the local farmers, fishermen, and lumbermen, the Indian agents did much to prevent economic progress on the reserves. Farming was the only acceptable occupation encouraged by the Indian Department. Yet the centralization of decision making retarded improvement on reserve lands that were, in most cases, not suitable for farming. Fishing and lumbering were discouraged and taken over by whites. The loss of the fisheries was especially decisive, since fishing formed the traditional backbone of Ojibwa economic survival. The very fact that the Indian Department limited its activities almost exclusively to the confined geographical areas of the isolated reserve lands dictated that the assimilationist policy would continue to be a failure.

The Ojibwa, like all colonial peoples throughout the world, were tremendously influenced by the two great wars of the twentieth century. No other ethnic group in Canada contributed a greater proportion of their men to the defeat of the enemy. The Ojibwa returning from the European battlefields showed a greater degree of militancy in their political organizations, which now demanded a fair share of Canada's wealth. A more sympathetic public would not tolerate the poor living conditions on the reserves. While material prosperity improved, the Ojibwa, in alliance with other native organizations across Canada, attempted to end the assimilationist policy in their schools and on reserves. After attaining the power to vote in 1960, they demanded greater self-determination in the social, economic, and political destiny of their people. While it is too early to determine the degree of success in these areas, there are signs that the Ojibwa are experiencing a renaissance.

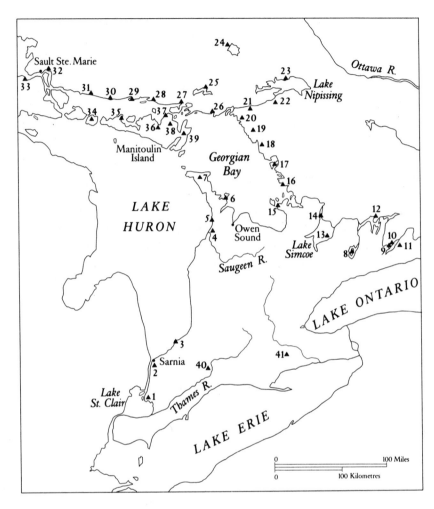

Many of the reserves listed here have been Ojibwa settlements for centuries:
1. Walpole Island 2. Sarnia 3. Kettle & Stony Point 4. Saugeen 5. Chief's Point
6. Cape Croker 7. Saugeen-Cape Croker hunting reserve 8. Scugog 9. Rice Lake
10. Sugar Island 11. Alnwick 12. Mud Lake 13. Georgena Islands 14. Rama
15. Christian Islands 16. Moose Deer Point 17. Parry Island 18. Shawanaga
19. Manetawan 20. Henvey Inlet 21. French River 22. Dokis 23. Nipissing
24. Wahnapital 25. Whitefish Lake 26. Mattagami 27. Whitefish River 28. Spanish
River 29. Serpent River 30. Mississagi River 31. Thessalon 32. Garden River
33. Bay Mills 34. Cockburn Island 35. Sheshegwaning 36. West Bay 37. Sucker
Creek 38. Sheguianda 39. Wikwemikong 40. Caradoc 41. New Credit.

The Ojibwa of Southern Ontario

1

INTRODUCTION
'We Are Not Brutes To Be Whipped into Duty'

The Ojibwa history of southern Ontario generally suffers from a combination of misunderstanding and neglect. In the early period of the French in Canada, there are few clearly defined sources dealing exclusively with the Ojibwa; beginning in the mid-nineteenth century, in contrast, there is a mountain of undigested archival sources. Added to this problem is confusion about the people who constitute the Ojibwa. Purist historians have shied away from examining the Ojibwa, whose very name seems to defy definition. One of the most knowledgeable scholars who investigated these people was E.S. Rogers, and his use of Ojibwa to define the Indians of that nation in southern Ontario will be employed throughout this book. This choice should be viewed, however, in the context of the etymological labyrinth which surrounds the Ojibwa.

The *Handbook of Indians of Canada* lists over one hundred different names for Ojibwa; indeed, the etymology of the word has not been determined to the satisfaction of many scholars. Almost all of the ethnic groups which came into contact with the Ojibwa gave them a different name; for example, the French called them Achipoue; the English, Chepawa; the Germans, Schipuwe; the Mohawk, Dewaganna; the Huron, Eskiaeronnon; the Caughawaga, Dwakane; the Sioux, Hahatonwa; the Fox, Kutaki; the Winnebago, Negatce; the Tuscarora, Nwaka; the Oneida, Twakanha; the Assiniboine, Wahkahtowah; and the Ottawa, Ojibbewaig. Trading partners such as the French not only varied the spelling of the name they designated for the Ojibwa, but had several other names for them as well.[1]

The diversity and complexity of tribal terminology was the result of several factors. Their country by the late eighteenth century encompassed an expanse of land from the eastern end of Lake Ontario westward to the vicinity of Lake Winnipeg in Manitoba and the Turtle Mountains of North Dakota. This was a greater range of territory than that of any other Indian tribe in North America. If these people belonging to the Algonquian linguistic family were asked to identify their nation, many traditionalists would respond by answering 'Anishinaubag' or 'men' in their tongue. This name, however, has not been generally accepted outside of the Ojibwa communities themselves.[2] The diversity of names which Europeans and other Indian groups gave the Ojibwa resulted from their loose tribal organizations, their policy of freely adopting other Indians into their communities, their close alliances, and particularly the early Europeans' ignorance of the extent of this numerous and widespread nation. The confusion is understandable considering that each of the many semi-sedentary Ojibwa bands was given a specific name related to geographical characteristics, band chiefs, totems, or cultural activities, at various locations throughout their territory.

The French first contributed to the confusion of terminology by referring to 'more than thirty different Nations that are found in these Countries' as Ottawa, since these 'traders' were 'the first to come down to our French settlements.'[3] The Ottawa and the Potawatomi had been united with the Ojibwa, according to tradition, and shared many of their cultural characteristics as well as their history. But there were many dissimilar groups in the territory, including the Fox, the Miami, and the Sioux. It is likely that Champlain met some of the Ojibwa-speaking people as early as 1615 on the east shores of Georgian Bay. In 1622 other groups were encountered by Etienne Brûlé and, by 1648, the mission of Saint Peter was established for the Indians of Manitoulin Island and the northeastern shore of Lake Huron. By the middle of the seventeenth century several groups, presumably Ojibwa, were identified by the French: the Marameg, Mantouek, Noquet, Saulteaux, Mississauga, Amikwa, Nikikouek, Achiligouan, Outchougai, and Ouasouarini. Because of the Iroquois attack from the southeast on the Huron and their Ojibwa allies, the Saulteaux, Nikikouek, Marameg, and Outchougai united for purposes of defence and, over time, became the people called Ojibwa. Additional Ojibwa-speaking groups were likely recruited when their enemy, the Sioux from the west, agreed to a non-aggression pact with them in 1679, thus ending for the Ojibwa a war on two fronts. The secure western front permitted a successful united effort against their more formidable enemies, the Iroquois Confederacy. As a result, expansion into what is now southern Ontario was made possible.[4]

The Ojibwa of southern Ontario date from about 1701, since it was not until that year that the territory between Lakes Huron, Erie, and Ontario was occupied by them. Prior to the period of expansion, their settlements were in the Georgian Bay area and on Lake Superior, especially the north shore. A major meeting place was at the falls of St Mary, between Lakes Superior and Huron. Here, large numbers of the 'food-gathering' Ojibwa got together each summer and fall to process huge quantities of fish – and, no doubt, to renew military alliances and further develop their cultural unity as well. The Indians at this location were the 'Bawa'tigo- winiwug' Ojibwa, whom the French called Saulteaux (people of the falls). About 1667 the French established a mission at the Sault to accommodate all the Indians in the area – the 'Mission to the Outchibouec' [Ojibwa?].[5] Contact with the French caused greater tribal unity. Hunting for food and furs became more efficient with the introduction of firearms, and there was more time to gather in large groups for trade and warfare as well as cultural activities.

A thorough understanding of Ojibwa culture in the pre-European contact period is difficult to obtain. No written records were made by those who lived within the culture at that time. Our knowledge, therefore, is based partly on the accounts of explorers, missionaries, fur traders, soldiers, and government officials. They wrote about these people often years after European cultural contact had taken place. Their accounts are biased, and are often misleading and incomplete. They incorrectly viewed the Indians as a static, un-changing people, rather than a people in transition. Yet in the first two centuries of contact a good case could be made from the existing European sources to indicate that the Ojibwa culture was evolving at a more rapid pace than the European. Unfortunately, no Ojibwa wrote about their culture and history until long after it had changed dramatically. Even then, the oral traditions they collected were written in the English language. This in itself was indicative of the European bias which had been thrust upon them.

Some appreciation of Ojibwa culture is essential to any understanding of Ojibwa-European relations over the past three centuries. Ojibwa oral tradition can be used to get away from an entirely Euro-Canadian ethnocentric interpretation. Although considerable change has occurred within Ojibwa culture, early native writers must be viewed as the essential reservoir of their tradition. The contemporary Ojibwa world view is a product of their cultural past. Any attempt to understand the southern Ontario Ojibwa must begin with an examination of their traditions – with the way they comprehend themselves, their fellow man, nature, and the spirit world. Only with this knowledge can we begin to understand the historical dynamics and cultural survival which sustained this ethnic group well into the twentieth century.

Ojibwa religion, or as Europeans put it, 'mythology,' has deeply interested anthropologists and other scholars for generations. The majority agree that the supernatural world dominated the way in which the Ojibwa viewed reality. Ojibwa tradition indicates that 'Keehe-munedoo,' the Great Spirit, 'told them how to act; and with this knowledge they think it would be wrong, and give great offence to their Creator, to forsake the old ways of their forefathers.' With this attitude, cultural change occurred only when their traditional responses failed to satisfy their need to survive. Radical change was required to adjust to the incursions of the Europeans, yet, as the eminent anthropologist Ruth Landes observed, 'they must yet resemble psychoculturally their forebears.'[6]

The precarious nature of subsistence through hunting as well as the uncertainties of warfare, which increased with the territorial demands for furs, put a great deal of emphasis on the individual Ojibwa's ability to control the supernatural. Both warfare and hunting required similar skills in the forest of the Great Lakes region. The hunter-warrior's speed, accuracy, concealment, endurance, and strength were attributed to the individual's understanding of the manitous and his ability to please them. This was in most cases practical, since a myriad of manitou spirits was found in the sky, hills, animals, birds, trees, lakes, rivers, and streams.

Knowledge of this natural environment was essential to survival. A successful hunter or warrior could brag among his peers of his exploits without seeming egocentric, since he was, in effect, praising his gods. No important expedition against an enemy or in pursuit of game would be conducted without the 'correct' ceremonies. The most scrupulous attention was also paid to the signs of the heavens, the flight of birds, and, above all, to the dreams and predictions of the *jos-so-keed*, priest or prophet, who accompanied the warriors, and who was entrusted with the sacred sack of medicine. However, 'in addition to the shamans, almost all the gifted individuals, those who excel in any walk of life, be it as hunter, fisherman, warrior, craftsman, etc., attain to a great degree of knowledge, much of which is associated with a high development of religious feeling and consciousness, for in their education a large amount of attention is fixed upon religious practices.' Indeed, 'religious education' was the foundation to every successful activity of life.[7]

Future events were predicted by those with the 'power' through dreams, which were often induced by fasting. An Ojibwa shaman gave the following account of the importance of fasting and dreams in his life:

When I reached the age of puberty, my father wished me to fast, that I might become holy; invincible and invulnerable in war; become like one of those about whom tales are told in the future. Thus I would be if I made special effort in my fasting. I would be 'blessed' with long life, he told me; I would be able to cure the sick; life would not be able to harm me in any way. No one would dare to be uncivil to me for fear of incurring my enmity. He pleaded with me to fast long and intently, for only then would the various spirits 'bless' me.

There was a hill near my father's wigwam called the Place-where-they-keep-weapons. It was a very high hill, steep and rocky. They said it was a very holy place. Within that hill lived spirits called Those-who-are-like children (i.e., Liliputians). There were twenty of them and they possessed arrows. My father [a very famous shaman] was in charge of these (i.e. some powerful manitoo had in his 'blessing' placed these under his control). When he wished to 'bless' a man, he would do as follows: He would take his bow and arrows in both hands and take the spirits around the hill into his wigwam (into the middle of the hill), where stood a stone pillar. On this pillar he drew the pictures of various animals. Then he danced around the stone and sang, and when he was finished, commenced to breathe upon it. Then he walked around it again, shot at it, and it turned into a deer with great antlers ... So I could do if I wished, and if I poured tobacco and fasted.[8]

Although secular and spiritual power were not inherited, the son of a powerful shaman stood a greater chance in obtaining such power if a 'special effort' were made. The shaman surrounded his son with conditions that practically made it certain he would be blessed by the same spirits. Continuity of leadership and a substantial following in wartime could be obtained in this way. Those who could induce an encouraging dream obtained the self-confidence necessary to follow in the footsteps of a famous father.

This was especially true with glory obtained in warfare. Another Ojibwa, living in the mid-nineteenth century, recorded the following tradition of an old chief in his military preparations for war against an enemy tribe:

He assembled all his warriors together, and, after informing them of the object he had in view, called them to him one by one, and inquired what they had dreamt of during their fast-days, and what munedoos they could rely on for assistance. Those who had had dreams, and those who had had none at all, he placed by themselves. All who had dreamt of wars, or things proof against the arrow, tomahawk, or bullet, he selected for the expedition. When he came to the last man and asked him what he had dreamt of, he replied ... 'ahnit,' that is, a spear. The chief asked, 'And what good will a spear do you?' [He replied,] 'As the point of the spear is proof against the arrow, tomahawk, and bullet, so is my body against all the shot of the enemy.' 'Very well,' said the chief, 'you shall go with me to the war.' The chief, with his select warriors, then left for the scene of action; and, after crossing a river in canoes, they fell upon the enemy, whom they soon conquered, destroying many of them. In all the battles they fought, not one of the old chief's party fell. The success and preservation of this war party was attributed solely to the aid of the manitoos obtained by dreams.[9]

The pantheistic belief in manitous not only prepared the Ojibwa for war but also protected him in battle. A Saugeen Ojibwa told of the tradition involving his ancestor who had 'powerful medicine.' While completely surrounded by the enemy in a battle, he was able to change himself and a fellow warrior into 'small turtles,' enabling them to 'creep under a log.' They later escaped to the Sauble River by changing into 'water snakes.' This is not an isolated account. Another Ojibwa tradition tells of an escape by canoe when a group of warriors was pursued by a strong war party. As the enemy were gaining on them, one of the warriors reached in his 'medicine bag' and 'pulled out an old pouch made of the skin of a Saw-bill, a species of duck. This he held by the neck to the water. Immediately the canoe began to glide swiftly at the usual speed of a Saw-bill; and after being propelled for a short time by this wonderful power, they looked back and found they were far beyond the reach of the enemy, who had now given up the chase.'[10] While these religious beliefs in metamorphosis were viewed by most Europeans as pagan nonsense, the psychosomatic effect on the power of the believer was substantial. For the Ojibwa, the self-fulfilling prophesy of an encouraging dream gave him great strength in battle; but for the European officers whose Indian allies depended on such dreams for motivation, it was most frustrating. A sustained campaign against the enemy often hinged on an unpredictable 'supernatural' experience. Peer pressure and political realities, of course, were likely to influence the dreams in which they had the greatest faith.

The famous American fur trader, Alexander Henry, gave one of the most publicized accounts of the importance of Ojibwa dreams. At Michilimackinac in 1763, the Ojibwa Wawatam presented Henry with 'a large present, consisting of skins, sugar and dried meat. Having laid these in a heap, he commenced a speech, in which he informed me, that some years before, he had observed a fast, devoting himself, according to the custom of his nation, to solitude, and to the mortification of his body, in the hope to obtain, from the Great Spirit, protection through all his days; that on this occasion, he dreamed of adopting an Englishman, as his son, brother and friend; that from the moment in which he first beheld me, he had recognized me as the person whom the Great Spirit had been pleased to point out to him for a brother; that he hoped that I would not refuse his present; and that he should forever regard me as one of his family.'[11] An Ojibwa dream had not only enriched Henry, it later saved his life in an Indian uprising when Wawatam prevented the other Ojibwa from killing his newly acquired 'brother.' It is interesting to speculate on the source of Wawatam's dream. Was it inspired by astute political insight and eventual economic gain? Certainly the replacement of the French by the English traders in the Great Lakes at the time made such a friendship most advantageous.

As long as the spirit world communicated with the Ojibwa through dreams, their resistance to Christianity was sustained. It is likely that 'good dreams' were inspired by a good life on Earth. Early missionaries in the Great Lakes region found the Ojibwa religion strong and resistant to change. The first few Christian converts involved the wretched in Ojibwa society – the deserted women, the sick old men, the diseased children, the blind, and the sexually maladjusted. [12] It was not until the mid-nineteenth century that Christianity made any serious impression on the Ojibwa, and this was mainly because of the widespread misery created by culture shock and the depletion of their food supply.

In traditional Ojibwa culture, every person had a guardian manitou who provided protection in battle, success in hunting, and identity within the group. Each person maintained a supernatural relationship without normally consulting religious leaders for guidance. In religious as well as civil and military matters, the Ojibwa retained a high degree of personal autonomy. Nicholas Perrot, who was one of the first to spend time among the Ojibwa, was shocked that 'the father does not venture authority over his son, nor does the chief dare to give commands to his soldiers.' Despite this individualism, there were persons who possessed extraordinary power gained from puberty visions. Such persons were able to command a substantial following when the group was threatened by challenges that went beyond the average individual's ability. A massive attack by a powerful enemy, for example, caused Ojibwa warriors to look for leaders who had a greater degree of power granted to them by the manitou. It was a pragmatic decision. Only after demonstrating unselfish leadership and ability in such activities as warfare did the individual gain any following for major campaigns. As the Jesuit Father Antoine Silvy observed in 1709, one became a chief only 'by the deeds he had done, by the friendships he struck when young and by the gifts he gives. Usually these chiefs are the worst clad of the tribe as they give everything to be liked.'[13]

The political structure of the Ojibwa tribe was both its strength and its weakness. As Vernon Kinietz, an authority on the Indians of the Western Great Lakes, stated: the 'Chippewa [Ojibwa] society was not highly organized. The tribe as a whole had no organization at all.' Indeed, 'the make-up of this tribe is very confusing.'[14] He was not the only ethnologist who shared this belief. George Irving Quimby spent only five pages on the Ojibwa in *Indian Life in the Upper Great Lakes* and failed to recognize them as the largest and historically most important tribe in the region. Only brief mention was made of their political organization in the decisive years, 1640–1760: 'There was no political leader for the whole Chippewa tribe, but there was tribal unity of sorts based upon ties of common language, kinship and clan membership. These ties cut across bands, helping to unify the bands into a tribal whole.'[15] Both Quimby and Kinietz believed that no leadership existed for all of the Ojibwa Nation, but this was only partly correct.

Evidence confirms that there was no continuous hereditary ruler or sustained elective leadership for all the Ojibwa Nation. Indeed, terms such as 'nation' have different connotations when they are applied to the Ojibwa and to European political entities. Among the Ojibwa, they are used to describe a common linguistic, cultural, and historical denominator, seldom a political one. A thorough understanding of the self-determination that existed among Ojibwa bands and individuals was almost beyond the comprehension of most Europeans who came into contact with them. Those who looked for continuity of leadership had little success. But this does not mean that no individual influenced the majority during various crucial periods of their history. The ethnohistorian Harold Hickerson concluded that 'the stereotype of Chippewa and other northern Algonquians as highly individualistic, hence non-cooperative, begins to crumble under the force of the descriptions of the period.'[16] The clan totems, the Feast of the Dead, and the Midewiwin societies contributed substantially to uniting the Ojibwa in a common bond during the early period, even though individual choice dominated their culture. Over an extended period of time, Ojibwa bands were not politically unified throughout the broad region they occupied, but they formed an alliance system that could assert itself in warfare against the Sioux and the Iroquois. Numerous Ojibwa bands representing the various clans gathered from hundreds of miles around Sault Ste Marie to participate in religious festivals, to renew their alliances, and to indulge in the consumption of large quantities of white fish which sustained them during their lengthy meetings.[17] Such meetings gave ample opportunities to potential leaders to form massive military units against their enemies.

Leadership could and did develop through consensus. As Peter Jones, the Mississauga Ojibwa, observed in considering the position of head chief, 'their influence depends much on their wisdom, bravery and hospitality.' Another Ojibwa, Kahgegagahbowh (George Copway), confirmed this belief: 'They would not as brutes be whipped into duty. They would as men be persuaded to the right.' He demonstrated how this was accomplished at a meeting of forty-eight chiefs from southern Ontario, when each was given an opportunity to speak at a grand council.[18] The vast majority of the group followed a leader only if they believed that the objectives were desirable and would benefit the whole community. A threatening external enemy, peer pressure, and individual conviction were among the few unifying forces. This was in sharp contrast with European political systems, which formulated policy from above and seldom took into consideration the wishes of individuals below. The Ojibwa could, and did, unite under a great war chief when the majority of the warriors saw the need for a sustained, unified effort – as they did against the Iroquois.

2

CONQUEST

'By the Power of the Great Serpent'

The expansion of the Ojibwa into southern Ontario in the last decades of the seventeenth century must be examined in the context of the fur trade and the related conflict between the French and the English colonial powers in America. That conflict created a system of native alliances that attempted to gain hegemony in the beaver-skin trade. Those Indian traders who would not conform to the wishes of the dominant aboriginal groups faced pillage, dispersal, or extermination. At the same time, those groups which did exchange furs for the coveted European goods greatly increased their material standard of living and their power.

The beaver pelts that were used in making the fashionable European hats could be obtained directly by trapping, or indirectly by trade or stealing from the enemy. The Iroquois chose stealing as the more risky but also the more lucrative alternative. All native groups recognized the superiority of European trade goods. Metal tools such as needles, knives, and hatchets were far more efficient than those made from bones and stone; iron and copper pots were more durable than those in bark or clay; cotton and wool blankets and clothing were a welcome complement to the skins of animals. Most important was the introduction of the musket. The European firearm revolutionized hunting and warfare in North America when it all but replaced the bow and arrow as well as the spear. Greater accuracy and distance could be achieved with this new weapon, which could not be manufactured by the indigenous people. Tribal warfare existed before Europeans began to settle North America, but the new military technology and the desire for European goods created an entirely different dimension to the conflicts. Within a few years, Samuel de Champlain established a French settlement at Quebec, the old site of Stadacona (1608); the Dutch settlers arrived at New Amsterdam where New York now stands (1611); and the Plymouth Pilgrims landed in New England (1620). The English colony grew rapidly and eventually replaced the Dutch in the New World, but France continued to be their strongest rival in the struggle for furs. In a trade environment that was hostile, indigenous allies were essential to success.

One year after the founding of Quebec, Champlain encountered the Iroquois at Ticonderoga. Although he was accompanied by only two other Frenchmen, he had an army of Algonquin, Huron, and Montagnais who encouraged him to attack the Iroquois. This was a momentous occasion, since he personally killed two Iroquois chiefs with his arquebus before the others fled in panic. It is possible that the Ojibwa were among Champlain's victorious allies. They were in close proximity to Huronia (now Simcoe County) and were trading partners with the Huron, who had 'long been at war [with the Iroquois] on account of many cruelties practiced against their tribe under colour of friendship. They said that, having ever since desired vengeance, they had asked all the Indians ... to come to meet the French for the purpose of making an alliance with them.'[1] This alliance was strengthened by Champlain's participation in other battles and his visit to the Georgian Bay area several years later.

Champlain was probably the first European to describe the Ojibwa who were located near the mouth of the French River in Georgian Bay:

We met with three hundred men of a tribe named by us the *Cheveux relevés* or 'High Hairs,' [Ojibwa] because they had them elevated and arranged very high and better combed than our courtiers, and there is no comparison, in spite of the irons and methods these have at their disposal. This seems to give them a fine appearance. They wear no breech cloths, and are much carved about the body in divisions of various patterns. They paint their faces with different colours and have their nostrils pierced and their ears fringed with beads. When they leave their homes they carry a club. I visited them and gained some slight acquaintance and made friends with them. I gave a hatchet to their chief who was as happy and pleased with it as if I had made him some rich gift and, entering into conversation with him, I asked him about his country, which he drew for me with charcoal on a piece of tree-bark. He gave me to understand that they had come to this place to dry the fruit called blueberries, to serve them as manna in the winter when they can no longer find anything. For arms they have only the bow and arrow.[2]

These scattered, semi-horticultural hunters and fishermen did not attract the same attention as the centrally located, sedentary Huron who quickly became the middlemen in the fur trade. French government and religious leaders could live much more comfortably in the large agricultural settlements of Huronia than in the scattered Ojibwa communities which were seasonably on the move.

Some Frenchmen, however, who had not become accustomed to the refined way of life in their homeland were more venturesome in America. Etienne Brûlé, for example, was sent by Champlain to learn the language of the Algonquin as well as the Huron. He became the first known 'Indianized' European among many who would follow him as interpreters destined to play an important role in the early days of the French colony and the fur trade. Brûlé did not leave any records, but it is generally accepted that he was the earliest European to travel into the heart of the Ojibwa country at Sault Ste Marie and possibly to Lake Superior. Such Frenchmen, visiting and living with the Ojibwa, encouraged trade and military alliances. They also laid the foundation for attempts at religious conversion.

The Jesuits made their way to Sault Ste Marie in 1640. They opened the Mission of Saint Peter in 1648 for the Indians of Manitoulin Island and the northeast shore of Lake Huron. The Sault in the pre-contact period had become a cultural, religious, and economic centre for the Ojibwa. The Jesuit Claude Dablin described the 150 Saulteur as having allied themselves with three other bands, numbering 550, who were living there in the mid-1600s. About 1000 others came to fish in the summer and to participate in religious and cultural activities such as the Feast of the Dead and gift giving. By the end of the 1640s the Jesuits had come into contact with most of the Ojibwa bands in Georgian Bay. Father Jérôme Lalement observed: 'Leaving them [the Huron] to sail farther up the lake

[Huron] ... to an island in this fresh water sea about thirty leagues long [Manitoulin] inhabited by the Outanuan ... After the Ami-kouai, upon the same shores of the great lake, are the Oumisagai, whom we pass while proceeding to Baouichbiouian – that is to say the nation of the people of the Sault, for in fact there is a Rapid, which rushes at this point into the fresh water sea.'[3] Seven years later other bands were added by the Jesuits to the list of known Ojibwa: 'The Eastern and Northern shores of this lake are inhabited by Algonquin Tribes, Outaouabamigouek, Nikikouch, Michisaguek, Paouitagoung – with all of which we have a considerable acquain-tance.'[4] Actually this acquaintance was somewhat limited. The Jesuits were not as successful in converting the Ojibwa as the Huron, but they had considerably strengthened the French commer-cial and military alliance.

This alliance brought the Ojibwa into sharp conflict with the Iroquois, the ancient enemies of the Huron. By the 1640s, hostilities had developed from fur-raiding war parties to full-scale attacks on large villages. As a result of a superior political organization and especially an ample supply of Dutch muskets, the Iroquois Con-federacy had a distinct advantage in the confrontation with the Huron Confederacy and their allies, the Ojibwa. George T. Hunt, in *The Wars of the Iroquois*, explained the lack of weapons among the French allies in terms of the high prices that the money-hungry monopolists charged. Recent scholarship, however, has shown that this conclusion ignores a fundamental difference between the French and Dutch colonists. While the Dutch had a strong bourgeois attitude that was motivated almost exclusively by risk-taking profits, the French did not. Few arms reached the Huron and the Ojibwa because the French feared that weapons in their hands would threaten the security of their vulnerable colony in New France. In addition, the Jesuits denied firearms to non-Christians, and distrib-uted them only sparingly to special converts at their baptism. Indeed, for a Christian to obtain a gun it was necessary for him to travel to Quebec or Trois-Rivières as a fur trader. As late as 1648 the number of Christian traders did not exceed 120, and this group probably represented the maximum number of Huron who were eligible to obtain guns. Since the Ojibwa were much less willing to give up their religious beliefs, it is possible that they had no firearms at the time. In contrast, as early as 1644 the Mohawk had 400 guns. With such fire power and other advantages as well, they had an immediate edge in any conflict.[5]

The Huron, along with the Petun, Neutral, and some Ojibwa, were forced from southern Ontario in 1649–50. If the Iroquois strategy was to divert the trade of the Huron into their own hands, as Hunt suggested, then the attack was too widespread and too severe.[6] In the following years, moreover, the Iroquois continued their attacks to the north and west into Ojibwa country. The Ojibwa had supplied furs to the Huron who had acted as middlemen in the trade. If the Iroquois simply intended to replace the Huron in that capacity, their continuing wars against the Ojibwa were defeating such an objective. Bruce G. Trigger's explanation comes closer to the truth:

The evidence thus supports the conclusion that the aim of the Iroquois was not to replace the Huron as middlemen in their trade with the north, but to intensify the warfare that they were waging against the Hurons and their neighbours to the point of dispersing them. In the short run, both the Mohawk and Seneca stood to gain by uniting their forces to attack the Huron and plunder their villages of all the furs and European trade goods that could be found inside them. In the long run, the Seneca stood to gain from the dispersal of the Huron, who hitherto had prevented their hunting and raiding parties from safely penetrating into the fur rich territories to the north ... With the Huron out of the way, the Seneca could hunt in central Ontario and raid the Algonkian-speaking peoples around the shores of Lake Huron [who were mainly Ojibwa] in the same manner that the Mohawk raided the Algonkin, Montagnais, and Abenaki. Because these northern hunting peoples were more dispersed than the Hurons, they were easier to attack and thus seemed to be a stable prey that the Seneca could continue plundering for a long time. The violent attacks that the Iroquois launched against the northern hunting peoples, as soon as the Huron were dispersed, thus were not a mistake, but an integral part of Iroquois strategy. This strategy aimed to provide the Seneca and the other western Iroquois tribes with a northern hinterland in which they could hunt and rob furs, as the Mohawk were already accustomed to do farther east.[7]

Although Trigger's conclusions are more reasonable than Hunt's, he makes two assumptions which future events proved to be false. First, these northern hunting Ojibwa were not easier to attack than the Huron, since they were not centrally located and could easily spread throughout the forests when attacked. The Ojibwa could carry on much more effective guerrilla warfare than either the Huron or the Iroquois because of their greater mobility and their ability to live off the land. Second, the attacks against the northern hunting people, although likely an integral part of Iroquois strategy, were definitely a major mistake. The failure of the Iroquois to respect the military capacity of the Ojibwa and to attempt diplomatic reconciliation with them resulted in a shift in the power structure of the Great Lakes area.

In the fifty-year period between 1651 and 1701, southern Ontario went through three stages of population shift. In the first stage (the 1650s to the 1670s), after the dispersal of the Huron and their allies, the area was used as an Iroquois hunting ground. In the second stage (the 1670s and 1680s), Iroquois settlements were established for the purpose of agricultural production as well as beaver hunting. As early as 1669 the Sulpicians, François Dollier de Casson and René de Bréhant de Galinée visited Tinawatawa, an Iroquois village (near Westover, Ontario), where they met Louis Jolliet and René-Robert La Salle. It was a small village in fear of being attacked, since the Ojibwa were still at war even though the French had concluded a peace. By the early 1680s there were at least a half-dozen Iroquois villages established on the north shore of Lake Ontario and into the interior, but the Ojibwa by this time had settled just north of the evacuated Huron Territory. The third stage, from the mid-1680s to 1701, involved the defeat and withdrawal of the Iroquois from most of southern Ontario.

The battles in the Ojibwa-Iroquois trade wars first began in the Georgian Bay area in an attempt by the Five Nations to force the Ojibwa into submitting to their dominance. Bacqueville de La Potherie, French Royal commissioner to Canada in the 1690s, is a major source for these events. Although his statistics involving the numbers in battle may be questionable, his chronological closeness to the time of the battles gives his account credibility. He remarked that the Ojibwa 'were the first to defeat the Iroquois, who to the number of a hundred warriors came to take possession of one of their

villages' near Sault Ste Marie. With a force of only fifty fighting men
and using arrows and tomahawks against muskets, they entirely
defeated the Iroquois war party. In 1653 a combined Ojibwa force
of 'Nikikouek, Mississaga and Saulteurs' defeated an Iroquois force
of 120 men north of Manitoulin Island. Only one of the enemy
escaped. The exploit brought such glory to the war chief that three
years after his death, when his son decided to honour him by taking
his name and giving a feast, 1600 warriors attended the celebration.
In January 1658 the Jesuit, Father Simon Le Moyne, reported that
an army of 1200 Iroquois set out against the Ojibwa and their allies
to get revenge. This was likely the force that the governor of
Montreal island, Nicolas Perrot, mentioned in his *Memoirs*. After
failing in an attempt to take a fortification built by the Huron, who
obtained refuge among the Ojibwa, they divided, half returning
home by way of Georgian Bay and the Toronto route. Somewhere
on the north shore of Lake Huron they were surprised and defeated
by a combined army of Ojibwa. Two years after Le Moyne reported
the attack, fur traders, Pierre-Esprit Radisson and Médard Chouart
des Groseilliers accompanied a flotilla of Ojibwa and their allies to
Montreal where they sold furs valued at 200,000 livres.[8] As a result,
the Ojibwa had muskets to meet the Iroquois on equal terms.

To break the enemy's hold on the western fur trade, the Iroquois
were compelled to continue their attacks against the Ojibwa, who,
Perrot conceded, 'they feared much more than the French.' He also
observed that the Iroquois set their minds on the destruction of the
Ojibwa, 'who of all their enemy were the most formidable.' Another
war party was sent out in 1662 to attack the central location of the
Ojibwa at Sault Ste Marie. One hundred Iroquois went above the
Sault and camped at the mouth of Lake Superior, five leagues from
the rapids. They were foolish enough to let their campfire smoke
drift into the view of the enemy. The Ojibwa gathered an equal
number of warriors and 'during the night made their approaches,
and posted themselves on a small but steep bank of earth, some five
or six feet high, at the base of which were the tents of the Iroquois,
who were sleeping very tranquilly. Their dogs, scenting the
ambushing Saulteurs [Ojibwa], were beguiled by a little meat that
was thrown to them, in order to prevent them from barking; and,
when the light of day began to appear sufficiently for discharging

their arrows with effect, the assailants uttered their usual war-cries.'
All were killed but the scouts, who made diligent haste to carry back
the dismal news to their people. Perrot was told that this was the
last time that the Iroquois dared to enter the heart of the Ojibwa
lands.[9]

In the first two or three decades after the dispersal of the Huron
in 1650, the Ojibwa fought a relatively successful defensive war
against the Iroquois. Their semi-nomadic way of life allowed them
to retreat from the fringe of their territory in the southern Georgian
Bay region to as far north as Keweenaw near Lake Superior, without
any major problem of food supply since they had basically a hunting
and fishing society. By 1670 they were again back on Manitoulin
Island where, in one season, they were reported to have killed 2400
moose, indicating a substantial Indian population there. By this time
they had thoroughly established themselves as the middlemen in the
fur trade with the French. The revengeful Huron among them, the
attraction of furs in the territory between Lakes Huron and Ontario,
the desire for cheap competitive trade goods with the English who
were entering the market, and the shorter and safer canoe routes to
the south were obvious reasons for their expansion into southern
Ontario.

The historical sources for the battles fought in the more southerly
part of Ontario are incomplete and based almost entirely on
aboriginal oral tradition. No Europeans seem to have participated in
the major confrontations. The ethnologist Harold Hickerson
observed that 'oral traditions reflecting definite historical associations
in the minds of members of cultures without written language may
provide strong insights into ... geographical movements of the recent
past.' He goes on to indicate the limitations, especially when a great
time gap is involved, but concludes that 'without field investigations
... no ethnohistory would exist.' Ethnohistorians have convincingly
shown the value of certain types of oral tradition in the reconstruction of the past, especially in pre-literate societies. Historians should
rely on oral tradition for historical events rather than for detail or
chronology. In general, people remember what they consider
important. Herodotus, the 'Father of History,' made extensive use
of oral tradition in his writing of the Persian Wars, and little would
be known of that great confrontation without his contribution. In the

Ojibwa-Iroquois war, the native groups did not completely lack physical records. Wampum belts and birchbark 'writings' would have recorded the events and especially the peace treaty. Henry R. Schoolcraft, the well-known scholar who married an Ojibwa, observed that 'of the existing branches of the Algonquin stock in America, this extensive and populous tribe [of Ojibwa] appears to have the strongest claims to intellectual distinction, on the score of their traditions, [since] ... these people possess the art of picture writing.' According to Methodist minister Peter Jones, the original treaty ending the struggle between the Iroquois and the Ojibwa, and the many confirmations, were recorded in wampum. There are simply too many similar Ojibwa accounts of the battles from various reserve areas to be ignored or easily discredited. Indeed, Ojibwa tradition was accepted as the truth by those who were the first to know them well. Nicolas Perrot admitted: 'I am limiting myself to an account of only such things which I have learned from the lips of the old men among the Ottawa tribes.'[10] While his approach was too limited for good historical writing, Perrot is still considered one of the most important sources of aboriginal history of the period.

In the 1680s the most powerful of the northern Indians, the Ojibwa, moved from the defensive to the offensive. Their aggression was made possible because their warrior population had increased as a result of the more efficient trade goods used in hunting. Attacks on the Iroquois occurred throughout southern Ontario. The trade war between the two groups may have intensified in this area as a result of the unsuccessful campaign by the governor of the colony, Marquis de Jacques-René Denonville, against the Seneca in 1687. Denonville was able to attract a large army of Ojibwa and their allies to the rallying point at St Clair, from where they moved on to rendezvous with the French army at Irondequoit Bay. While the Ojibwa ridiculed the French for simply 'warring on the corn fields' in a scorched-earth policy, they and their Indian allies were more belligerent on their own in the 1690s. Oral tradition gives us some insight into the events. Kahgegagahbowh (George Copway), a Mississauga-Ojibwa, recorded the following memories of the events from the elders in 1851:

The Ojibwas ... annually sent some of their number to trade with the

French at Quebec or Montreal. A party of these was waylaid and killed by the Iroquois. Threats of reprisals were treated by the latter with scorn. After a second party had been similarly attacked and slain, a council of nations was held, resulting in some of their chiefs being sent to confer with the Iroquois. The meeting was held at Saugeen [Southampton], and resulted in the Iroquois agreeing to pay a bale of furs for each man that had been killed and in addition granted permission to the Ojibwa to pass peaceably on trade trips to Montreal. This treaty held good for three years, when bands of Iroquois waylaid simultaneously several parties of Ojibwas returning from a trading journey. This happened in the fall of the year ... In the meantime runners were sent to the various allies in the coming war. In the month of May following, the combined forces gathered in two parties, one at Lake St. Clair and the other at Sault Ste. Marie, seven hundred canoes being there assembled. This latter party divided into two bands. One advanced on the enemy by way of the Ottawa valley, while the other proceeded to Penetanguishene. The Lake St. Clair division at the same time came up the east coast of Lake Huron to the mouth of the Saugeen River, where a fierce battle was fought with the Iroquois, who ultimately gave way and fled before the savage onslaught of the Ojibwa.[11]

The heads of the Iroquois were cut off and made into a pyramid, and the event became known as the Battle of Skull Mound. In the 1840s Copway, as a native Methodist minister, had close contact with the Ojibwa whose ancestors had settled at the mouth of the Saugeen River after the Iroquois defeat. The artist Paul Kane, while painting at the mouth of the Saugeen River in 1845, wrote: 'It is the site of a former battle-ground between the Ojibwa ... and the Mohawks. Of this, the mounds erected over the slain afford abundant evidence in the protrusion of the bones through the surface of the ground.'[12]

Copway's account agrees with Governor Denonville's observation that before the Ojibwa moved up the Lake Huron coast to Saugeen, they gathered at St Clair. Two battles occurred in that area, one on land and the other on Lake Erie. Historian George Laidler wrote that the Seneca were attacked and defeated in their canoes near Longpoint by the Wyandot, who had joined the Ojibwa after their defeat by the Iroquois in 1650. A battle must also have been fought on land according to John Graves Simcoe, who left the following record in 1793: 'From Dalson's we went to the mouth of the Thames [River on Lake St Clair], and, about twelve miles on, we saw the remains of a considerable Town ... where it is reported that a desperate battle was fought between the Chippewas and the Senecas, and that the latter were totally vanquished and abandoned their dominions to the conquerors. Certain it is, that the human bones are scattered in abundance in the vicinity of the grounds, and the Indians have a variety of traditions related to this transaction.'[13]

One tradition was given by Nimekance, chief of the Sarnia band in the early 1800s. According to his account, 400 canoes, each containing eight warriors, were involved in a two-pronged attack in the St Clair region. William T. Mitchell, who recorded the story, indicated that 'numbers of great burial mounds, filled with skeletons, Indian weapons, and ornaments, until a recent day attested the terrible slaughter.' The great chief, Nimekance, who led his people in the battle, died at the age of 107. He was buried in an Indian tomb on one of the great mounds, 'his people gathering from far and near to do him honor, and to add to the pomp of a great warrior's burial.' Mitchell states that he 'conversed with some of the native French who witnessed the imposing ceremonies.' In concluding, he observed that 'there are many evidences that indicate the story's general truth ... of the fact that the Iroquois were driven away and the Chippewas remained in possession as conquerors.'[14] It is most likely that such battles did occur, since the Ojibwa and their allies would not have left a large enemy village in the rear as they advanced to the mouth of the Saugeen.

According to the oral tradition of the two reserves in the Saugeen area, Cape Croker and Chippawa Hill, there were numerous confrontations in their territory. In the weeks following the Battle of Skull Mound, their tradition indicates that battles occurred inland, along the shore and on the islands of Georgian Bay and Lake Huron in the vicinity of the Saugeen (Bruce) Peninsula. The Iroquois lost in a conflict on the clay banks (in Walkerton), on Indian Hill near the Teeswater River, and at Wadi-weediwon (Owen Sound). Three hundred warriors were defeated in an entrenched position on the northwest side of White Cloud Island in Colpoy Bay, the island taking its name from the victorious Ojibwa chief. Moreover, weapons of war have been found a few miles away on Griffith Island

and at Cabot's Head, where tradition indicates another victory occurred. In the Fishing Islands, north of the mouth of the Saugeen River, Red Bay received its name from the condition of the water after the Mohawk were defeated there. Skull Island in the Georgian Bay was also given its name from the remains of the vanquished. Kahkewaquonaby (Peter Jones) in his *History of the Ojibway Indians* wrote in 1864: 'There they fell on a large body of the Nahdoways [Iroquois] who had been dancing and feasting for several nights, and were so exhausted as to have sunk into a profound sleep the night on which they were killed. The island is called Pequahkoondebaymenis, that is, Skull Island, from the number of skulls left on it. In one of my tours to the north I visited this island, and lodged on it for a night. Its present appearance indicates a place frequented by Indians, the smoothness of its surface being well adapted for a great Indian dance.'[15]

Copway gives us no details about the Ojibwa army which moved along the Ottawa River. This major canoe route to Montreal had been one of the most important battle zones in the trade war. Native sources in the area indicate, however, that the Iroquois were also defeated in this more northerly region. Edwin G. Higgins, in collaboration with the Ojibwa of the Whitefish Lake Indian Reserve, No. 6, recorded accounts of numerous skirmishes along the Mattawa River. Moreover, the daughter of a Hudson's Bay factor, living in Gogama in the first decade of the twentieth century, remembers playing with human bones on the shore of Lake Minisinaka. She was informed by local Ojibwa that the skeletons were the remains of the Iroquois who were defeated by them.[16] No Iroquois villages would have been attacked in the northern area along the canoe route to Montreal, since it was too dangerous for any substantial Indian settlements to be established there at the time.

It is most likely that the Battle of the Blue Mountains was fought near Penetanguishene shortly after the attack by the St Clair division. About the same time as Copway wrote his account, Frances Assiginack of the Wikwemikong Reserve recorded his version of the events:

Early in the spring the Ottawa braves and their allies gathered at the command of their chief, Sahgimah, at the old trysting-place of the lake, the

Blue Mountains, near Penetanguishene to watch for the expected approach of the invading Iroquois. The Ottawa and Ojibwa had gathered from their headquarters at Manitoulin Island and from as far west as Lake Superior; their kinsmen, the Saugeens, had also come from the Saugeen River, as well as help from the Indian villages of Wadi-weediwon [Owen Sound] and the Beaver River [Meaford]. When word arrived from near Rice Lake that the Mohawk war party was coming by the Lake Simcoe route, final preparations to meet the invasion were immediately launched.

Swift messengers were despatched west and north for all available warriors to hasten to join their chief at the sign of the serpent (the chief's livery), at the Blue Mountain. It was then that the final contingents came through from Saugeen and Owen Sound.

The attacking party soon had the Mohawk camp completely surrounded. Just as the first gleams of sun-rise came over the eastern side of the Blue Mountains, the fierce war hoops of the Ottawa rang out from the shrubbery and brush of the hillside. The attackers fell upon the terror stricken and almost defenseless Iroquois with gun, tomahawk and ax. But for the arresting hand of Sahgimah not one Mohawk of the surrounded force would have been taken alive.

'No,' said the wily Ottawa strategist, 'by the power of the Great Serpent we shall not slay these craven Mohawks; we shall use them as messengers to go home to bring the news of what a Mohawk defeat means on the shore of our lake of the Ottawas. Let us first array our glorious battlefield so that it may be well remembered. Let us cut off the heads of all the dead enemies and mount them on poles with faces turned towards our lake, then let these men go home and tell their kindred.'[17]

Assiginack, a war chief of the Ottawa, was from a family with a proud military tradition. His father had fought in the War of 1812 and he himself was made an interpreter and orator for the Indian Department for his heroism. This honour alone cannot give credibility to the accuracy of the military accomplishments of his ancestors, yet a comparison of the Battle of the Blue Mountains with the account given by Perrot of the battle near Sault Ste Marie exposes remarkable similarities in military tactics, even though the time span between them is almost 150 years. Both battles involved a surprise attack; they occurred just as the sun was rising; the attacks came from raised ground; a couple of Iroquois were permitted to take the message of defeat to their people; and the bodies were mutilated to demonstrate the hatred they had for their enemy. What makes the account convincing is that it can be integrated with Copway's record of the Battle of Skull Mound. Their forces both gathered in the spring. The Sahgimah division went to Penetanguishene; the St Clair division attacked the Iroquois at Saugeen and Wadi-weediwon and defeated them. Sahgimah was waiting for the Iroquois to come down the Nottawassaga River (the coming-out-place of the Iroquois) and was in a position to call on the St Clair division from Saugeen and Wadi-weediwon. Moreover, the commander at Fort Michilimackinac, Antoine de Lamothe Cadillac, considered Sahgimah as the leader most feared by the Iroquois, and his name is found throughout the colonial documents of the period. Possibly in honour of this great chief, southern Ontario at the time was given his name, 'Saguinan.' [18]

While the Ojibwa and their allies had gained control of the land in and immediately south of Georgian Bay, the rest of Ontario to the south remained a stronghold of the Iroquois who had settled there. The most valuable contribution to our knowledge of the battles in this area was made by 'Paudash, son of Paudash, son of Cheneebeesh, son of Gemoaghpenassee to the Ontario Historical Society' in 1905. This unique published source has been neglected by almost all historians of Ontario's Indian history, yet the four generations of oral tradition going back to Gemoaghpenassee place the account close to the events. Cheneebeesh lived to be 104 years old and Paudash, his son, died at the age of seventy-five in the year 1893. All were chiefs of the Mississauga-Ojibwa. Paudash remarked: 'I am glad for the sake of the memory of the Mississauga ... to hear of this revival of interest in the Mississaugas, who do not appear in history or in the records of this country as much as they deserve from the importance of their deeds in war.' [19]

Since this account is the major source of the conquest of southern Ontario, it deserves to be quoted at length. Paudash's traditional explanation for the battle of Skull Island in lower Georgian Bay agrees with Jones's account, but Paudash indicated that after a 'great slaughter' the Iroquois were compelled to retreat. He continued: 'The Mississaugas then advanced up what is now the Severn River to Shunyung, or Lake Simcoe, stopping at Machicking, which means fish fence, at the narrows between Lake Simcoe and Lake Couchiching, in order to get a supply of food. There they received reinforcements, and making preparations for a campaign, divided into two parties.' While waiting at Lake Couchiching, one of the Ojibwa, most likely a medicine man, made a rock painting predicting the defeat of the Iroquois. After this reassurance, the main body of the army

proceeded along the portage ... to Balsam Lake; the other party went south to Toronto. After various skirmishes the Mohawks continued their retreat down the valley of the Otonabee, or Trent, to where they were settled in numerous villages along the River Otonabee, and on Rice Lake. They made their first real stand at Nogojiwanong, which was the original name of the town of Peterborough, meaning the place at the end of the rapids; Katchewanock, above the present village of Lakefield, meaning the beginning of the rapids. A sharp skirmish took place here upon what is now known as Campbelltown ... After great preparation, an attack was made by the Mississaugas, both by land and water, and the Mohawks were driven, after the battle, in which no less than one thousand warriors were slain, down Rice Lake to what is now known as Roche's Point. Great quantities of bones and flint arrow-heads are found at the site of this battle, even to this day. At Roche's Point there was a Mohawk village, in front of the former site of which is a mound in the shape of a serpent [Sahgimah's livery] ...

The Mohawks fought well, but the Mississaugas were just as good. An attack having been made upon this village, the Mohawks then fled to Quegeeging, or Cameron's Point, at the foot of Rice Lake, where great numbers of weapons and bones have since been found, and were again fiercely attacked by the Mississaugas, who compelled them to beat a further retreat down the river to Onigaming, the famous carrying-place ... from Lake Ontario into the Bay of Quinte, and from there into their own country. The Mississaugas rested at Onigaming, and waited for the detachment from Toronto to join them. Before pursuing the main body of the Mohawks further, after the attack at Cameron's Point, a party of the Mississaugas went up country to a lake called Chuncall [Moira Lake], in Madoc, north of Trenton, where a party of Mohawks dwelt, and wiped them out.

Near the Bay of Quinte on an island called 'Mississauga' or 'Fighting Island' a company of Mohawk were also attacked and defeated, their remaining skeletons giving ample evidence of the battle. Paudash's account of the battles in his area are to some extent confirmed by one of the first pioneers, Colonel Samuel Strickland, who, 'in his explorations of the County of Peterborough, found near the Otonabee River the field that gave the Mississaugas lordship of Rice Lake and Stony Lake, and the other lakes beyond.'

The Mississauga continued their attack into the Iroquois country south of Lake Ontario. In 1699 Dekanissore and Cagenquarichton, chiefs of the Iroquois, reported to Albany that the Ojibwa were attacking them in their own 'castles.' But why did the one division of the army go south from Lake Simcoe to Toronto and then join the other at Onigaming? Peter Jones gives us the answer in his chapter on the 'Wars of the Ojebways.' A battle was fought at Burlington Bay 'where the Government House formerly stood. Near to this place a mound of human bones is to be seen to this day; and also another at the north end, close to the residence of the late Captain Brant. Besides these, there are traces of fortifications at short distances along the whole length of the beach, where holes had been dug into the sand and a breastwork thrown round them. They are about twenty or thirty feet in diameter, but were originally much larger.'[20] The sweep of the Ojibwa through southern Ontario destroyed the Iroquois villages and fortifications as well as a considerable number of their warriors.

The oral tradition of the Iroquois defeat is not confined to Ojibwa, Ottawa, and Mississauga accounts. The Huron, who had fled for protection to the Ojibwa after the destruction of Huronia and later joined them in their attacks, also retained the oral tradition of the result of the war. Peter Clarke in his *Origins and Traditional History of the Wyandotts* indicated that in 1775 some Seneca appeared to instruct the Wyandot that they were subject to the Iroquois. The Wyandot then called for the oldest man in the town to describe how in the early years of his life he saw the great battles in which the Wyandot and the Ojibwa crushed the Seneca. Then a wampum belt was produced to confirm the account. Clarke indicated that the Seneca 'sullenly' withdrew from the meeting. The tradition of those who had been defeated is even more convincing. The *Iroquois Book*

of Rites was composed a decade or two after the final battle. The
Onondaga chant records the lowly state of their people: 'Woe! Woe!
Harken ye! We are diminished! Woh! Woh! The cleared land has
become a thicket. Woh! Woh! The cleared places are deserted. They
are in their graves – They who established it.' Horatio Hale
expressed the Iroquois oral tradition of the war: 'The contest was
desperate and destructive. Many sanguinary battles took place, and
great numbers of warriors fell on both sides. On the whole the
balance inclined against the Iroquois.'[21] Although understandably
laconic, the accounts of the vanquished do not differ greatly from
those given by the victors.

An anonymous French map of southeastern Ontario, c. 1680,
indicates the villages that were probably destroyed by the Ojibwa.
There were two villages at Burlington Bay, which account for the two
'mounds of human bones' observed by Jones. There was also a village
at Toronto, which was flanked by two other settlements some distance
away. In the Rice Lake area several other Iroquois 'castles' were
located. The seven major villages from east to west were Ganneious,
on Napanee Bay, an arm of the Bay of Quinte; Quinte, near the
isthmus of the Quinte peninsula; Ganaraske, at the mouth of the
Ganaraska River; Quintio, on Rice Lake; Ganestiquiagon, near the
mouth of the Rouge River; Teyaiagon, near the mouth of the Humber
River; and Quinaouatoua, on the portage between the western end of
the lake and the Grand River. One historical geographer estimates the
population of these villages at about 5000. La Potherie recorded the
Iroquois tally of their losses. They admitted 'that ten cabins,' meaning
villages, had been destroyed. This could account for the great decrease
of 1500 Iroquois warriors by 1701.[22]

After these battles the Ojibwa replaced the Iroquois in southern
Ontario. Some French cartographers were not aware of the new
occupation. As late as 1755 maps of southern Ontario incorrectly
placed the *Iroquois du Nord* in the area, thereby adding to the
confusion among historians about the time in which the Ojibwa took
possession. It is possible that some Ojibwa were living in southern
Ontario before the conquest of the late seventeenth century.
Champlain's map indicates that there were four villages of Algonquian, called Hontagounon, on the north shore of Lake Ontario as
early as 1612.

The effects of these battles, without the direct participation of the French, were to force the Iroquois to sue for peace. In reporting to the commissioners of Indian affairs in Albany on 30 June 1700, the Five Nations admitted: 'We are come here with a lamentable complaint that the Dowaganhaes or Far Indians [mainly Ojibwa] have now again killed many of our people at their hunting [in southern Ontario]. The French themselves declare they will not take the hatchet out of the Dowaganhaes' hands till we come and submit to the Governor of Canada and make peace with him ... The French might as well be in open war with us as to set their Indians to war upon us continually.' The hatchet symbolized the military supplies provided by the French, whose contribution to defeating the Iroquois seemed to be limited mainly to that capacity. In 1695 Kinonge, a chief of the Ojibwa, was asked by Governor Frontenac to direct his people's energies against the Iroquois, promising arms and provisions. Kinonge responded: 'All of our young men are gone on the war path, and they will be very glad to find on their return wherewithall to continue.' Ample military supplies were provided. By 1699 the Five Nations constantly complained to Albany about the loss of lives at the hands of the Ojibwa, who were not only attacking them in their hunting grounds but also in their villages south of Lake Ontario. It was mainly the French arms in the hands of the Ojibwa and their Indian allies which forced the Iroquois to seek peace.[23]

The peace talks, which involved negotiations for several years, were finalized in the treaty of 1701. Historian W.J. Eccles concluded from his study of French documentary sources that 'it had been only by the exercise of great adroitness, patience and knowledge of the Indian mentality that [Governor] Callières had finally succeeded in bringing these long-drawn-out negotiations to a most successful conclusion.' Were the *French* successful? It has also been stated that an 'outstanding aspect of this peace settlement was that, although the Iroquois fangs had been drawn, they were still strong enough to act as a barrier between the French allies and the English of New York, thus ensuring that the fur trade of the up-country tribes would continue to pass through Montreal rather than through Albany.' Yves F. Zoltvany would disagree. In 'The Problem of Western Policy under Philippe de Rigaud de Vaudreuil (1701–25)' he concluded: 'In the ten years after the peace of 1701 the Ottawa [including the Ojibwa], Huron and Miami began to trade directly at Albany. The Iroquois barrier was breached.' The American Colonial Records support Zoltvany's stand. As early as 1700 Governor Bellomont of New York advised the Iroquois to cooperate with the Ojibwa and their allies since 'their continual warring upon you will in a few years totally destroy you.' In a memorial of two French bushmen to the Earl of Bellomont, there was a promise that in the month of September 1701, thirty French fur traders and 'ten or twelve of the principal Sachems of the Ottawa [mainly Ojibwa] Nation' would come to Albany. The French records confirm the Iroquois acceptance of this trade with the English as early as 1708. The Iroquois informed Henri de Tonty, the Sicilian soldier of fortune at Fort Frontenac, that the Mississauga and Sauteur should not be discouraged from trading with the English. In return for the Iroquois Confederacy's recognition of their occupancy of southern Ontario and for an 'open path' to Albany, the Ojibwa offered peace. The Five Nations, in their enfeebled state, had no alternative and they accepted.[24] In these negotiations, the Ojibwa and the English won, and the French and the Iroquois lost.

The establishment of a fort at Detroit by Lamothe Cadillac at the conclusion of the war with the Iroquois has often been used to symbolize the 'victory' of the French over the Five Nations. It was assumed by some writers that Cadillac 'removed' the Ojibwa from Michilimackinac to southern Ontario by establishing the post. There seems to be more evidence to conclude that since many Ojibwa had settled in southern Ontario and could control the Iroquois aggression, Cadillac could safely establish a fort there and have a better chance at controlling the northwest fur trade from that location. Denonville admitted that the posts 'cannot harm the Indian enemies.' It is obvious from the conferences at Albany in 1701 that neither the English nor the Iroquois wanted the French to establish a stronghold at Detroit, but the Ojibwa in the area prevented either one from stopping the construction. The fort could stand in the way of the Iroquois, preventing them from gaining access to their beaver hunting grounds in southern Ontario. Since the fort supplied the Ojibwa with a ready source of weapons, little more was required. Indeed, it was the Mississauga-Ojibwa with their allies, the Ottawa and Potawatomi, who prevented the fort from falling when it was under siege in 1712. The impotency of the Five Nations caused them to deed their lands in Ontario, already conquered, to the English with the frustrated hope that the English could win them back from the Ojibwa. But the English had no desire to remove the Ojibwa. Indeed, they sent men such as Samuel York among the Ojibwa to encourage them to trade at Albany rather than at Montreal. The close proximity of the Ojibwa to the English centre of trade was a definite advantage to both, and 'a mighty blow to the French.'[25] Cadillac's establishment of the fort at Detroit contributed to this trade by drawing more Ojibwa to join those already in the south. In this respect the fort was a great boon to the Ojibwa and the English, of dubious value to the French, and a recognition of Ojibwa power by the Iroquois.

   Territorial acquisition has traditionally been a sign of conquest and the Ojibwa-Iroquois wars are no exception. Although a treaty had been made between the warring parties in 1701, the Ojibwa in the first decade of the eighteenth century, without the consent of the French, continued to attack the Iroquois in order to keep 'the path to Albany open' and to entrench themselves in southern Ontario. The Iroquois reported the establishment of sixteen new 'castles' of the three Ojibwa nations, including the Saulteur, Mississauga, and the Ottawa. By 1702 some Ojibwa were located at two of the most important trade locations, Toronto and Fort Frontenac. Because the Ojibwa were seasonally on the move throughout the conquered territory, it is not until 1707 that there is direct Euro-Canadian evidence of more substantial settlements; for example, at Chippewa Creek near Niagara. By 1720 they were firmly established throughout southern Ontario. Europeans had located the Ojibwa at Kente, the Toronto River, Matchedach, St Clair, and at the head of Lake Ontario by 1736. Undoubtedly they were also located north of these points. It was not until 1755 that the first map designated southern Ontario as the 'Country of the Missesagues,' and by 1768 twenty-five Ojibwa villages were located in southern Ontario. In 1784 the British had to pay the Ojibwa £1180 for land on the Grand River in order to settle the Iroquois displaced by the American Revolution.[26] It was only natural that to the victors went the spoils of war.

   The evidence presented here should have a revisionist impact in several fields. First, for Iroquois specialists, the defeat of the Five Nations by other Indians must call into question the traditional belief in their invincibility in forest warfare. Second, for scholars of the New World, there is evidence that the Ojibwa, not the French, determined much of the policy in the Great Lakes. Third, for historians of early Ontario history, a new chapter may be added. Fourth, for anthropologists, the belief that the Ojibwa never successfully united for any length of time in a common effort requires a re-examination. Finally, students of Ojibwa history should find that nation of much greater importance in influencing the destiny of the colonial struggle not only in Canada but in North America as well.

There seems to be adequate evidence to conclude that the Ojibwa claim to their driving the Iroquois out of Ontario is worthy of consideration. The various oral traditions fit like a well-constructed jigsaw puzzle, one piece complementing the other to make almost a full picture. Many of the Euro-Canadian and English colonial records contribute to the belief in the Ojibwa tradition, which is also enhanced by numerous Iroquois and Huron accounts. The lack of chronology and specific death counts in each battle is the major weakness.

Archaeologists and anthropologists could contribute a great deal to solving some of these problems. J.V. Wright, in 'A Regional Examination of Ojibwa Cultural History,' indicated that a flintlock mechanism, dated 1720, was located at the Shebishikong Site near Parry Sound. If this type of research were expanded, much could be learned about the Ojibwa battles. Eleven additional Ojibwa sites were examined northwest of Shebishikong, but unfortunately for this study they did not involve locations where battles had occurred. Archaeologists seem to have shown little or no interest in this area of Ojibwa history because of the relatively limited information that could be gained compared with earlier Iroquois sites or other Indian settlements. A close examination of an undisturbed battle site could possibly reveal the number killed, the types of weapons used, the year of the battle, and other information that would confirm or reject the Ojibwa claims to their victories.

Anthropologists could also contribute to solving this complex puzzle in Ontario's early history. R.W. Dunning in *Social and*

Economic Change among the Northern Ojibwa, Ruth Landes in *Ojibwa Sociology*, and Paul Radin in 'Ojibwa of Southeastern Ontario,' as well as others, have added considerably to historians' knowledge of Ojibwa cultural change and interpersonal relations, but the recording of Ojibwa tribal wars with the Iroquois has been almost totally neglected. The great events in the Ojibwa heritage are still retained in the minds of elders, and much can be gained from tapping this reservoir of knowledge. Bruce Trigger observed in 'Indians and Ontario's History' that 'during the past several decades, the role accorded to native peoples in studies of Canadian history has been changing rapidly. This has happened as a part of dramatic alterations in the general perception of native people and their role in Canadian society. Although many professional historians are still reluctant to recognize it, these changes have also been bringing about major alterations in the nature of what is recognized as being historical research.'[27] To obtain conclusive physical and oral evidence in this area, historians must work closely with anthropologists and archaeologists.

3

THE GOLDEN AGE
'Our Warriors Make the Earth Tremble'

After the conquest of southern Ontario in 1701 and until the fall of New France in 1759, the Ojibwa in the Great Lakes region experienced a 'golden age' of trade, presents, and plunder. With the advantages of competitively priced European goods, gifts from their allies, and war booty, the Ojibwa were in an enviable position. Both the English and the French in America vied for the coveted furs which these Indians and their allies could provide. This competition forced up the price of pelts to such an extent that the trade was sometimes conducted, particularly by the French, more for retaining their Indian allies than for profit. When the trade was disrupted by blockades resulting from the wars, however, serious problems temporarily developed with the Indian allies of the European powers in America. The Ojibwa demonstrated that their alliance with the French was in no way carved in stone. It could shift, and at brief times did, to the English. Their diplomacy was focused on retaining their middleman position in the fur trade, between the two European powers and native groups to the north and southwest of southern Ontario. This was no mean task. Interference by the Iroquois and other peoples continued to cause minor frustrations, but their white allies required even greater diplomacy. As long as the French were pitted against the English, the Ojibwa were treated with respect and sought as friends in trade and in war.

The price of furs was a major factor in Ojibwa-European relations. During the first half of the eighteenth century a growing number of Ojibwa began to look upon European trade goods as a necessity rather than a luxury. While these foreign products facilitated hunting, trapping, fishing, fighting, and domestic activities, the native people became so dependent on them that at times they caused tragic results. This was particularly true of the more isolated Northern Ojibwa. As early as 1718, when Captain St Pierre arrived at Madeline Island to revive the fur trade after a twenty-year absence of licensed traders, he discovered starving, ragged Indians who had forgotten the traditional skills of making stone, bone, and wood substitutes for worn-out iron and brass weapons, tools, and utensils. This was not an isolated case. By the middle of the century even the Ojibwa in the Lake Superior region had become completely dependent on these goods for their well-being. Alexander Henry, for example, personally observed Indian suffering caused by the curtailment of trade: 'On my arrival at Chagoueming [Chequamegon], I found fifty lodges of Indians there. These people were almost naked, their trade having been interrupted' by war. At a council meeting, Henry was informed by the chiefs that unless he supplied them with trade goods on credit, 'their wives and children would perish; for there was neither ammunition nor clothing left among them.'[1] Muskets, metal knives, hatchets, kettles, and other European goods had irreversibly changed the subsistent economy of the Ojibwa. As a result, the price and supply of trade goods were major factors in determining who would be the European trading partners. The Southern Ojibwa, in contrast, did not suffer from scarcity since they were accessible to both the French and the English.

In addition to obtaining cheap trade goods, the Ojibwa expected the Europeans to respect and attempt to understand their culture. These were added factors which determined where the Southern Ojibwas would take their furs and with whom they would make their military alliances. In this context the French Canadians had a definite advantage over the English. The Ojibwa had gained a strong attachment to the free-spirited French fur traders, the *coureurs de bois*, by the beginning of the eighteenth century and this relationship continued to be entrenched throughout the period under consideration. A century of contact and especially intermarriage fused an alliance between many of the Ojibwa bands and the French, who often lived in the Indian villages. Unlike the English, it was a common practice for a French fur trader to take an Indian wife, thus establishing a vested interest in the native community.[2] Competitively priced English products could not entirely eliminate this influence.

Marriages between the French and the Indians also began to erode the influence of the English over the Iroquois. Historian Frank H. Severance thoroughly documented the importance of Euro-Indian marriages in shaping alliances and trade agreements involving the Seneca. The Joncaire family, among the Seneca, for example, was a decisive element in establishing the French fort at Niagara, and substantially contributed to the periodic neutrality of the Iroquois during the last half-century of French rule in Canada. Adopted Frenchmen among the Indians often became influential, as did a few of the British. Major Robert Stobo of the Virginia Regiment observed in his memoirs that, as a young Scottish prisoner of the Mississauga, he was held in such high regard that they 'conferred upon him the honour of the Mississauga Indian nation. The ceremony of the installation he had not declared, but the badge of this order he can never go without, for it is pricked on the foresides of both thighs, immediately above the garter, in form something like a diadem; the operation was performed with some sharp fish-bones dipped in a liquid which leaves a blackness under the skin which never wears off.'[3] Yet neither Stobo nor any other influential person at the time seems to have resided among the Ojibwa to represent the British interest. For the French, a policy of adoption into every acceptable Indian village did much to strengthen trade relations as well as mutual understanding and peace in the Great Lakes region. While the English made some headway with the Iroquois, the French were most successful with the Ojibwa. In neither case did this mean that the European dictated the policy of the band in which he resided. His voice was simply heard in council and sometimes respected.

Peace, at the time, was like a fragile canoe in a rapid, rocky river. Keeping the path open to Albany and retaining southern Ontario as their exclusive hunting grounds required constant vigilance on the part of the Ojibwa in the opening decades of the eighteenth century. At first, the Iroquois were concerned that English goods would become dearer as the Ojibwa became more involved in that trade. In an attempt to avoid conflict, the Ojibwa requested the English to

exclude the Five Nations from Albany while they were trading
there. Confrontations, however, were often unavoidable. In 1705 a
group of Ojibwa attacked a Seneca hunting party near Fort Frontenac, killing several and taking many more prisoner. This was in
retaliation for the death of one of their chiefs killed by that nation.
The French took the Iroquois side in this particular dispute in
demanding that the prisoners be returned. The Ojibwa responded
by setting fire to a barn at Fort Detroit, a sign of dissatisfaction
with their French allies. But the French had the upper hand at the
time. Without French powder, balls, and guns, they would soon
suffer defeat, especially if the French and the Iroquois combined to
prevent them from obtaining arms and munitions from the British.
The Ojibwa and their allies bowed to the French, who forced them
to return thirty Seneca prisoners and prevented the Michilimackinac
Ojibwa from renewing hostilities with the Iroquois. Governor
Rigaud de Vaudreuil, who did not trust the Iroquois, observed that
any greater punishment of the Ojibwa 'would be useless since they
are the major force keeping the Iroquois in check.'[4] Nevertheless,
such control by the French prevented independent action by the
Ojibwa, who could only achieve greater self-determination by
extending their trade with the English.

This was soon accomplished. Ojibwa trade with the English
increased and became less erratic. At times the 'Mississagues and
Amikoes returning from their hunting around Lake Erie' even traded
with the Iroquois for English goods. By 1708, the Mississauga who
were settled at Lake St Clair had acquired a wampum belt from the
Iroquois allowing them to pass peacefully through their country to
trade directly with Albany. The Iroquois, recognizing the equality
if not the superiority of the Ojibwa, must have found some way to
benefit from this trade, possibly by charging a toll for passing over
their lands. They not only accepted but encouraged the trade: 'We
have told you [English] that we have not only permitted ye Far
Indians to come through our County to trade in this Town [Albany]
but set our agents thither to invite them and required them to tell
the Far Indians that they should have goods very cheap. We
therefore desire that the Traders may be ordered to let the Far
Indians have good penny worths, rather cheaper than we of the Five
Nations have it ourselves, which will be the only means to draw

them and to induce them to come hither.'[5] French reports of the great number of Ojibwa flotillas heading to Albany confirm the fact that the Iroquois had consented to the trade and were forced to accept the wishes of the Ojibwa, their potentially most dangerous enemy, to pass through their lands. This trade, of course, was diametrically opposed to the wishes of the French.

The Ojibwa and their allies also demonstrated their independence from French control by starting a war with the Fox Nation, a French trading partner, and drawing the French unwillingly into the conflict. Sahgimah, the great war chief of the Ojibwa, was insulted by some Mascouten allies of the Fox when they called him a coward. To avenge the insult, he, with a Potawatomi chief named Makisabi, headed a party of a hundred warriors who slaughtered over two hundred Mascouten near the St Joseph River. Some Mascouten fled to their Fox allies at Detroit for protection, but the Ojibwa pursued them and, on the way, attracted more allies who brought their force to around six hundred men. Jacques-Charles Dubuisson, commander at Fort Detroit, attempted to prevent Sahgimah and his allies from continuing the attack, but 'he met with a fierce refusal.' He reported, in fact, that he was compelled to provide the warriors with powder and ball which were used to destroy a thousand men, women, and children, mostly of the Fox Nation located on lake St Clair. The Fox and their allies retaliated by making it unsafe for any Frenchman in the territory west of Lake Michigan for most of the period up to 1737.[6] While the immediate cause of the war was the insult given to Sahgimah, the long-term goal was to prevent the Fox from taking furs directly to the French. In achieving this result, the Ojibwa increased the value of their trade.

Ojibwa commerce with the English also expanded. A major concern of the French was to retain their existing trade and expand it if possible. The paramount problem became the flow of furs to Albany. Although a fort was built at Detroit at the turn of the century, it did not prevent the Ojibwa from crossing Niagara from the Toronto portage and other locations on the north shore of Lake Ontario on their way to Albany. The French assumed that the establishment of a fort at Niagara would stop most of the Ojibwa trade with the English. The simultaneous construction in 1720 of trading posts at Niagara, Toronto, and the Bay of Quinté, in addition to the older Fort Frontenac, informed the English that the French intended to close Lake Ontario to their rivals. Colonel Peter Schuyler complained that 'the French settle and secure those passes through which the Five Nations usually go to hunt and the Far Nations [Ojibwa] come to trade at Albany; and I am of the opinion we must justly prevent these mischiefs since those very Lands have been given ... to the Crown of Britain' by the Iroquois. The early colonial records of William Johnson indicate that the Iroquois deeded southern Ontario to the English, but only after the Five Nations had been driven from the region by the Ojibwa and their allies.

After these efforts of conquest, the new settlers had no intention of letting the French block their way to Albany. Indeed, the attraction of English trade goods was so strong that it had even divided the Ojibwa. As Sahgimah explained to the Albany English and the Mohawk: 'We have always endeavoured to go to Corlaer [Albany] and Quiber [Oswego] but we heard from a Nation called Aghsiesagechrone [Mississauga of southern Ontario] who endeavored to hinder us and told us many evil stories concerning you ... but we resolved to come and see.' Sahgimah then gave a calumet or ceremonial pipe to the Mohawk, who were with the English and formerly their greatest enemy, and asked to become united with them in a friendly trade alliance. The Ojibwa promised the English that they would keep the trade a secret from the French. Sahgimah and his band were given two hogs, several bushels of peas and corn, ninety loaves of bread, twelve blankets, eighteen shirts, and twenty-six gallons of rum.[7] No guns were distributed, but the Ojibwa were still impressed by the English. Moreover, if the Mississauga Ojibwa of southern Ontario were conspiring to exclude their northern brothers from the English trade, they were not about to let a few French forts stop their own trade from going there.

By 1725 it was clear that the Ojibwa and their allies were avoiding the French trade. During a voyage to the posts in the lower Great Lakes, Charles Le Moyne de Longueuil, governor of Montreal, encountered over a hundred canoes of western Indians going to and coming from Albany. Many were Ojibwa from southern Ontario. As a result, the four French posts were economically depressed. From 19,297 livres in 1724, the value of their trade fell to 9151 livres the following year. The only solution to the problem was to lower the price of goods in the French king's posts on Lake Ontario in order to retain the trade. To the great advantage of the Ojibwa, French profits began to shrink and almost disappear.

In addition to the Ojibwa, some of the French voyageurs also took their furs to Albany. English prices for furs were occasionally lower than those offered by the French because of the fur-trading licences required by the French and because the English restricted trade goods from entering Canada during war time. As a result of greater competition and overhead costs in the Great Lakes region, the French were periodically forced to trade their goods for the Ojibwa furs at a loss. Their most desired object was to establish a monopoly by destroying the Oswego trade. This could be accomplished, they reasoned, because the Ojibwa and their allies would not extend their journey by several days if they could get the same goods, at the same price, at the French trading stations established among the Ojibwa. Their assumption was correct.

The English traders retaliated. By purchasing 200 trading canoes from the Ottawa and Mississauga, the Albany merchants contributed substantially to the natives' wealth in 1725. Some of these canoes were thirty-three feet long and each could hold about three tons of trade goods. The English were now in a position to take 600 tons of merchandise to aboriginal groups in their own territory. The results were immediate. In 1726 Niagara, Frontenac, and Toronto showed a profit of only 2382 livres because the English were bold enough to trade within ten leagues of the French forts. This action cut profits by more than half and temporarily destroyed the French trade advantage among the Ojibwa.

In 1726 Longueuil took 100 soldiers to Niagara, mainly to patrol the lake and to stop the English canoes from going up the Toronto route to trade. French voyageurs passing through Lake Ontario were commanded to follow the north shore from Frontenac to Niagara. If found near Oswego, the English trading post, they were liable to seizure and confiscation. This did not deter some. Joseph La France, the son of a French fur trader and an Ojibwa woman, successfully ran the blockade, but in 1736 when he attempted to get a trading licence, he was refused on the grounds that he had been selling brandy to the Indians. This alienated him from the French, along with his Ojibwa friends and relatives, since he was not alone in considering alcohol a necessary trade article. Rather than chance being arrested in the south, he decided to transport his furs to the English at distant York Factory on Hudson Bay. In 1742, with a large band of Ojibwa, his brigade was one of the first to go from Michilimackinac to York Factory.

The Ojibwa of southern Ontario, in contrast, were not compelled to make the same drastic change. Their diplomacy with the French was quite open. They asked them 'to supply their wants, under promise that if their request be granted, they would drive off the English from that quarter and have no dealings with them; if refused, they would be under necessity of inviting them thither.'[8] But the French were not always able to supply their wants at low prices, especially when European wars interfered with transportation across the Atlantic.

In the context of the fur trade, the War of the Austrian Succession (1740–8) had its influence on the Ojibwa of southern Ontario. Colonial warfare began in 1744, ending almost thirty years of relative peace. The English fleets scoured the seas and captured French merchantmen in large numbers. Indian trade goods grew so scarce by 1745 that the governor of New France offered trade licences free, but no one would accept them. The Indian allies could only interpret this shortcoming as a major weakness of their European ally. The reason for the Ojibwa's allowing the French in their lands almost ceased to exist. The Ojibwa were displeased with the dramatic rise in prices on those goods that did get through, and conspiracies against the French spread throughout the west. This indicated that France's Indian allies were only interested in allowing the Europeans into their lands if the trade goods were cheaply supplied in adequate quantity.

The Ojibwa still had three possible solutions to their immediate problem. The life-preserving goods could be obtained from the English, but their trade goods were also expensive and in short supply because the merchants were afraid to enter the Indian country during the war. Another alternative was to pillage the French canoes and aid the English directly or indirectly in the war. Or they could satisfy their material needs by going to war with the

French against the English, from whom they would obtain the spoils of war. All three alternatives were used by various bands, indicating that the Ojibwa were unable to come to a consensus and present a unified front as they had done in their war against the Iroquois.

Many Ojibwa and their allies joined the French in their war against the English in 1745–6. Numerous small war parties were equipped and sent out with a Frenchman, who made certain that they attempted their objectives rather than going directly home. Some thirty-one Ottawa from Detroit, fifty Potawatomi from Green Bay, fifty Ottawa from Michilimackinac, eighty Ojibwa from Lake Nipissing, and sixty-five Mississauga from Toronto, and other warriors each made several attacks against the English who were located on the frontier.

The Ojibwa Nation, however, did not unanimously support the French in the war. Those in British interest 'were active among all the tribes on the Ohio and even on the Illinois. According to Chabert [a French officer], there was formed a far-reaching league against the French, achieved and cemented by English wampum-belts "to induce them" – the tribes – "to lay violent hands on all the French scattered about in the different posts of this country."' The French traders were in such great fear of their Ojibwa 'allies' that in some years 'no trading expeditions set out from Montreal, and the trade between the Canadian lakes and Louisiana was carried on almost exclusively by *coureurs de bois*, deserters from both colonies.'9 This fear was certainly justified.

In 1747 Iroquois interpreter Louis-Thomas Chabert de Joncaire was informed by a Seneca at Fort Niagara of a plot involving some Ojibwa on their way to Albany. He reported: 'On this information, having taken with me twenty Iroquois, I hastened to notify the commandant of that place [Niagara], that he might keep the soldiers from going out. I next went with a reinforcement of 15 Frenchmen from the garrison to overtake the Saulteaux [Ojibwa] deputed for the English. I caught up with them in the second day's march, took them by surprise, and carried them all prisoners to the fort. They confessed the plot, after two days in prison. *In order to manage their people carefully, they were set free*, on their promise that they would turn against the English who had won them over. In fact, they killed several of them.'10 Chabert had lived among the Ojibwa as well as the Seneca and his influence on both was considerable. As a French officer, he was not able to punish the Ojibwa conspirators in the traditional manner of flogging or death. Their killing the enemy was acceptable retribution. The informant role of the Seneca is understandable. Undoubtedly, the Seneca participated in exposing the plot and capturing the Ojibwa ambassadors in order to sustain Iroquois neutrality in the war. An English-Ojibwa alliance would have destroyed this neutrality since the Iroquois formed the geographic centre between the two nations. Chabert was an adopted member of the Seneca and any attack on him and the French at Niagara could have expanded to include the Seneca in a war against their most feared enemy, the Ojibwa. While Chabert was successful in preventing some of the Ojibwa from cementing a military alliance with the English, ill-feelings against the French were so strong that not all plots could be defused so simply.

In a speech to Governor George Clinton at Albany, some Mississauga Ojibwa and their allies stated that they were determined to 'destroy the Fort at Yaugree [Niagara], for they saw a sort of Witches about the said Fort always keep the Path foul and dirty, and for that reason they have resolved to make it clean.'[11] A few of the Ojibwa had obviously been prevented at Niagara from taking their furs to Albany. But to destroy the fort at Niagara required not only the full support of the Ojibwa and their allies but also the neutrality, if not the aid, of the Seneca and the English. There was no unanimous agreement among the Ojibwa on the proposal, and they were 'opposed by others of their tribe' in their desire to destroy the French forts. At this time, lack of unanimity prevented the Ojibwa from formulating a long-range, consistent, and productive foreign policy. Moreover, only some of the Mississauga-Ojibwa on the north shore of Lake Ontario had any faith in the English as potential allies.

In a report by the Marquis de la Galissonière, commandant general of New France, to Count de Maurepas there was evidence of a great deal of confusion on the part of the French as well. The French-Indian alliances were seriously shaken. It was no longer reasonable to consider the Ojibwa as neutral, and certainly not as a dependable, united force against the inroads of the English. La Galissonière was informed by Longueuil at Detroit that some of the

Miami had defected and all the Huron were won over by the English. The Huron had killed five Frenchmen at Sandusky. Throughout the northwest, at various locations, bands of Saulteau, Mississauga, and Ottawa participated in killing and pillaging the French. Some were killed at the Ottawa village 'between Detroit and Missilimackinac; others at Chibaouinani (La Cloche), by some Mississaugas; others at Grosse Isle, near Missilimackinac and even at Missilimackinac, also the voyageurs were robbed and maltreated at Sault St. Mary and elsewhere on Lake Superior.' It was impossible for the French to know who was friend or foe among the Ojibwa and their allies.[12]

Five Ojibwa, who had attacked the French and pillaged the canoes, were captured by Longueuil. One was killed, one committed suicide by cutting his throat, and the other three were put in irons. One of the prisoners, a relative of the Saguinan chief, Achaoualina, was to be returned after the chief had demonstrated his loyalty by attacking the English. But while being transported by canoe, the three Indian prisoners with manacles on their feet killed the eight French soldiers and escaped without any help. The French, even when they had some Ojibwa in captivity, did not have adequate control over them.

The French obviously could not control and maintain their Indian allies by force. The only solution to this chaotic situation was a compromise, but with the Ojibwa essentially getting their own way. To save face, the French had to demand the arrest of the murderers and the return of the plunder. They added the threat of totally cutting the trade if these two demands were not met. The Saguinan band sent in two hostages, claiming that they could not locate the murderers. The French replied that pardon would not be granted to the Mississauga and the Saulteaux until they made due submission by surrendering the guilty; and that any Huron entering the Detroit Fort without a pass would be put to death. Such threats had little effect on the French Indian 'allies,' with the possible exception of cutting off trade.[13]

The major problem facing the Ojibwa in relation to the French during the colonial wars was the price of trade goods. La Galissonière clearly understood this situation when the war in Europe ended with the Peace of Aix-la-Chapelle in 1748. It was not simply a case of scarcity causing high prices because of the war. He criticized the system of leasing the trading posts to the highest bidder: 'This has caused these leases to reach prices much above what had previously been demanded from the officers. The purchasers have therefore thought that they have the right to draw as much profit from them as possible, without any regard for the disadvantages which might result. Price of merchandise at the posts had risen enormously, with the result that those who had secured the contracts have brought the Indians to the point of despair and reduced them to going to Chouaguen [Oswego].'[14] French commerce was interfering with colonial diplomacy. The solution was to give up the detrimental system and to return to *congé* licensing, thereby lowering prices and attracting the Indians back to the French trade. *Congés* were granted to needy families that were not expected to gouge the Indians. Since it was essential to become competitive with English traders, this system of licensing was reintroduced to the satisfaction of the Ojibwa. Nevertheless, it was not a perfect system and considerable damage had been done to the French economic and military alliance with the Indians.

The French found it difficult, if not impossible, to determine the fidelity of their Indian allies, 'to know who was good or bad.' In the last year of the war their loyalty was put to the test by requests to organize raiding parties against the English. Some of the Ojibwa of southern Ontario proved their friendship in this way, whereby they not only obtained war booty, but were equipped by the French to obtain it: 'Twenty Mississagues from the head of Lake Ontario [Toronto] have come to Montreal to see the Governor; they have promised fidelity, and assured us that they had no participation in the bad Belts that have been distributed. Sixteen of them have demanded to go on an expedition for which purpose they have been fitted out. Sieur Lungy Foutenelle has been given to them as a commander.'[15] The 'loyalty' of some Ojibwa was also confirmed by Captain Pierre Caude de Pécaudy de Contrecoeur, who reported that the group at the Toronto post had 'prevented evil designs that were concocting.' But not all the Indians at that location were loyal: 'Three strange Indians, from *Fond du Lac* [Toronto] went ... to the Illinois Country, with a message from the English, in the name of the Iroquois, Hurons, Abenaquis, Pouz and Outaoas and all the

Ouabash Tribes, inviting the Illinois to abandon the French, otherwise they were dead men.' The lack of unanimous Ojibwa support for the French in the Toronto area was still evident some years after the war. In 1752 the storekeeper there wrote to Jean-Baptiste Jarret de Verchères, commandant of Fort Frontenac, who reported 'that some trustworthy Indians have assured him that the Saulteaux, who killed our Frenchmen some years ago, have dispersed themselves along the head of Lake Ontario, and seeing himself surrounded by them, he doubts not but they have some evil design on his fort. There is no doubt, my Lord, but 'tis the English who are inducing the Indians to destroy the French, and that they would give a good deal to get the savages to destroy Fort Toronto, on account of the essential injury it does their trade at Choueguen [Oswego].'[16] Fear that the Toronto Ojibwa would attract their allies to the English in great numbers worked to the advantage of the Ojibwa generally. The strategy induced the French to be generous in the fur trade and liberal in the distribution of presents, particularly in equipping war parties to fight the English.

Numerous small bands of Ojibwa continued to be supplied with equipment to fight the English. Ninety Ojibwa and their allies from Detroit and Michilimackinac requested to be organized into a war party against the New York frontier. They had previously killed French fur traders. As a result of their pledge to fight the English, Chief Achoabmet, who had given himself as a hostage, was released, and his band received valuable equipment to obtain the spoils of war. Under such advantageous conditions, Mikinac, an Ottawa chief, and thirty families from Saguinan gave assurance of their fidelity. These war parties were not isolated cases. Several dozen Ojibwa incursions were sent out repeatedly from these locations.

In return for the support that many Ojibwa gave in the war, the French made a serious effort to compete with the low prices at Oswego. Personal gain had to be submerged in the interest of the colony. The high cost of trade goods meant at the very least the loss of Indian allies. The French were able to reduce costs by selling 'lighter, more merchantable and cheaper hollow-ware than usual,' but they found 'it difficult to compete with the English cloths.' In 1749 an order was issued to the commandants at Frontenac, Niagara, Toronto, and Detroit to see that traders and storekeepers charged the same prices as the English at Oswego. As a result, the English policy of winning the Ojibwa to their side by offering cheaper trade goods was temporarily countered.[17] To the Ojibwa in the Great Lakes region, the War of the Austrian Succession had been a trade war in which they were victorious in the various battles.

Although the war had ended in Europe in 1748, it continued in North America, especially in the contested region of the Ohio Valley. Throughout the 1740s the English had greatly enlarged their trade, attracting the Miami and other French allies to a trading post which became known as Pickawillany (Piqua, Ohio). The French could not let this go unchallenged. The first two attempts to destroy the English trade in the Ohio met with failure because the French could not get the active support of the Ojibwa. Since the expeditions involved an action against the Miami, led by La Demoiselle (also called Old Briton or Memeskia), the southern Ojibwa 'near Detroit would not permit the raiders to pass through their territory, saying that the Miami had intermarried with them and that they would not consent to an attack upon their relatives.' To convince the Ojibwa to attack the Miami and the English in the Ohio required a Frenchman with a cultural understanding of the Ojibwa and family relations among them.

Charles-Michel Mouet de Langlade was admirably suited to the task. The son of a French trader, his mother, Domitilde, was the sister of Nissowaquet, chief of one of the four major Ojibwa bands near Michilimackinac. As a child he had accompanied the Ojibwa and their allies on an important and successful raiding party, where he acquired the reputation of having 'a special protecting spirit.' Langlade was able to convince the Ojibwa to attack the Miami in 1752 when he arranged a 'dog feast to appeal to their savage bravery and by this means succeeded.'[18] Undoubtedly his knowledge of the Indian way of raising a war party was important, but his family ties at Michilimackinac encouraged the Ojibwa there since they, in contrast with the Ojibwa in southern Ontario, had fewer relatives among the Miami. Moreover, the opportunity for plunder was great, particularly for the more northerly Ojibwa who had not established any strong trade agreements with the English.

In 1752 Langlade, at the head of 200 or 250 *coureurs de bois* and

Ojibwa from Michilimackinac, killed La Demoiselle and twenty of his followers, took five or six British traders prisoner, and swiftly retired with a vast amount of goods, 'estimated as worth three thousand pounds.' British influence in the region crumbled, as half a dozen other nations whose allegiance to the French had become shaken sent war parties against British traders.[19] Many Ojibwa flocked to the French flag. Nevertheless, this action did much to promote greater British retaliation against the French and their allies.

Three years after his success at Pickawillany, Langlade led a larger group of Ojibwa and other allies to defend Fort Duquesne against a massive British attack. The French had 72 marines, 146 Canadians, and 637 Indians, while the advancing British army under Edward Braddock had about 1500 combatants aided by thirteen pieces of artillery. Langlade claimed that he planned the decisive ambush that led to the defeat of Braddock at the passage of the Monongahela. Certainly his Ojibwa were more useful than the marines, who were not accustomed to forest warfare, and the Canadians, who were, according to Guy Fregault, 'unfortunately only children.' As early as 1729 the age limit for the cadets, who were in every major engagement, had been reduced to fifteen. The British troops in red uniforms and heavily loaded with equipment and supplies had little chance against the Indians. As one of the British remarked, 'You might as well send a cow in pursuit of a hare as one of our soldiers ... against naked Indians.' After the battle many British soldiers admitted they had not seen a single adversary during the whole day. But the enemy had seen them. Losses were staggering, with 977 killed or wounded while the French lost only twenty-three. 'For years gold and silver coins, garments of broad-cloth and velvet, chased and engraved weapons, and even books and letters were to be found' among the Ojibwa and other Indian allies of the French. Almost 1000 rifles, a great quantity of munitions, 100 oxen, and 400–500 horses made up the plunder shared by the Ojibwa[20] – the greatest spoils obtained by the Ojibwa in any battle to that date. Both the Ojibwa and the Potawatomi first acquired horses around this time, and the French victory at Fort Duquesne determined to a considerable extent the side which many Ojibwa favoured in the Seven Years' War which began only months later.

The Anglo-French struggle for empire in North America had been going on in the Great Lakes region long before the decisive war broke out in 1756. In the final confrontation the French still feared the Iroquois and threatened to 'let loose all the Upper Nations [mainly Ojibwa] on them' if they were found among the English soldiers. The Iroquois claimed they would remain neutral in the conflict. At a council in 1757 attended by the French and the Iroquois, an Ojibwa chief threatened their ancient enemy: 'We notify you to be faithful to the speech you have just solemnly delivered. If you falsify it, we will make a sacrifice of you and your bloody body will reproach you for your lack of faith. I am but a young chief; you see me now accompanied by few warriors, but in the spring the number of our warriors will make the earth tremble.'[21] The Iroquois had maintained their neutrality with the French ever since the treaty of peace in 1701, with the exception of the Mohawk who, on several occasions, conducted minor raids against them. The French, in retaliation, engaged in limited and successful skirmishes with the Iroquois. Some of the Seneca were even won over to the French side and actively participated with the Ojibwa against the English. Gaiachoton, the Seneca chief and diplomat, for example, was part of the Indian force which met and routed Braddock. The Ojibwa relationship with the Seneca probably led William Johnson to state that 'Nockkie, a great Sachem of a Castle of the Mississaugas who lives on the North side of Lake Ontario, and belongs to the Chippawa Confederacy ... [represents] a very numerous people, allies of the Six Nations.' In the first month of the Seven Years' War a combined band of the Mississauga and Seneca killed fifty Englishmen near Fort Cumberland on the Ohio River. In the same year a French report indicated that 'the Upper Nations appear to be well disposed towards us, and as yet nothing but neutrality is perceptible among [most of] the Six Nations.'[22]

Liberal presents, cheaper trade good, the promise of abundant plunder, and French family ties won many of the Ojibwa bands to the French side in this final war between the English and the French in North America. The French told the Ojibwa they had much to lose by not actively participating against the English. An effective propaganda campaign by their European allies convinced many Ojibwa that the British wished to destroy them and take over their lands, while the French only wanted trade with them. The expanding population in the Thirteen Colonies and the removal of the Indians along the Atlantic seaboard seemed to confirm their fears.

In a war conference in 1756 between Governor General Pierre de Rigaud de Vaudreuil and his Indian allies, some Ojibwas requested: 'Father, we are famished, give us fresh meat; we wish to eat the English; dispatch us quickly.' In the following year, after being equipped, several war parties were sent against the enemy. A number of reports to the war office show the extent of their success: 'The domiciliated Mississauga of Presqu'isle have been out to the number of ten against the English. They have taken one prisoner and two scalps and give them to cover the death of M. de St. Pierre'; or 'The Potawatomi near Detroit have killed in the current war [1756] 120 English.'[23] The Ojibwa participated in numerous raids by small war parties and in attacks against well-established English forts.

The English fort at Oswego (Chouaguen) had for decades been a threat to the French fur trade and to the Ojibwa-French alliance. It must have been an agonizing decision for the southern Ontario Ojibwa to agree to attack this solitary British stronghold on the Great Lakes since it had provided them with cheap trade goods and increased the value of furs they sold to the French. The fort, moreover, was located almost in the heart of the Six Nations' settlements. Yet fear of the Ojibwa 'staggered the Iroquois,' according to William Johnson, the British superintendent of northern Indian affairs in 1756. He admitted that 'it is true the French do more with their Indians than we can do with ours and many reasons might be assigned for it. Besides they have many more Indians than we have.' One major reason for the Ojibwa attack was the use of propaganda by the French. An English soldier, Thomas Butler, reported that the Ojibwa were told by the French that the English spread smallpox among them when they distributed presents. By wearing the English goods, the Indians would immediately die. The severe epidemic which occurred in 1755 seemed to confirm such statements since 'multitudes had died at Niagara.'

The French plan of attack on Oswego began by cutting off

supplies to the fort. As Frégault observed, 'most of the raiding bands came from Niagara and Toronto, and they were relentless.' One Mississauga war party was sent to Oswego by M. Duplessis, commandant at Toronto, while their families moved to Niagara for protection and provisions. Captain François Pouchot, during the construction of fortifications there, observed how the Indian women attempted supernaturally to aid their men who were at war:

These women assembled every evening to 'make medicine,' one old woman singing, the others replying in chorus. It was reported in the fort that these women were working a spell of some supernatural sort, in accordance with ancient forms of their people, and the French officers from the fort went out to the scene of the strange ceremony and looked on. At the end of six or seven days, they inquired why they made no more medicine, when an old woman replied that their people had beaten; that she had juggled and that they had killed many people. An officer who knew these juggleries [prophets], wrote down the spot, the day that she designated, and when the party returned, he questioned the Indians and prisoners, whose answers confirmed the old woman's account.[24]

The Southern Ojibwa and their allies played a significant role in the capitulation of the only English fort on the Great Lakes. Lt-Col. Littlehales, compelled by 'the fear of falling into the hands of the Indians,' decided to surrender to the French.

In the summer of 1757 over 1000 Ojibwa and their allies rallied to the French flag for an attack on Fort William Henry. For this purpose, ninety southern Ojibwa gathered at Toronto. In his generally excellent book, *Toronto during the French Régime*, Percy J. Robinson indicated that this band of warriors conceived the idea of pillaging the French fort there in spite of the fact that it belonged to their friends. He supposed that the supply of brandy stored in the fort proved too great a temptation for their loyalty. It is more likely true that the commander of the fort, Joseph de Noyelle, did not treat the warriors with the respect they considered their due when they were going to war. For their long journey and battle, the Southern Ojibwa traditionally expected to be given food, clothing, arms, ammunition, and liquor. But the French fort at Toronto was in short supply, as were all French posts during the winter of

1756-7.[25] With the destruction of Oswego, all the Indians in the area of the Great Lakes had to depend on French goods which, during wartime, were limited since England controlled the seas. The Indians had been promised abundant and cheap goods for their participation in the destruction of Oswego. While this scarcity contributed to the eventual weakening of Ojibwa support of the French, it temporarily proved to be an added incentive to fight in order to pillage the English. Fort William Henry was no exception.

The defeat of Oswego played a major role in attracting a great many Ojibwa to the battle at Fort William Henry. As Montcalm observed, 'all Indians of the Upper Country are most strongly attached to us; this owing principally to the fall of Choueguen [Oswego].' They had little alternative if they wished to obtain the European goods which had become necessities of life to them. After Fort William Henry had capitulated, however, no proper provisions were made for the Indians to obtain the spoils of war. In what became known as a 'massacre,' the Ojibwa ignored the pleas of the French troops and helped themselves. They 'took possession of swords, watches, hats, and coats. They even tore the shirts from the backs of officers and soldiers before finally scalping their owners.' As Louise Phelps Kellogg observed: 'The Indians were sent back to their homes under a cloud of disapproval by their [French] commanders.'[26] The French officers should have realized that the Ojibwa would react in this manner: the French themselves could not supply them with trade goods; Indian military ethics sanctioned such actions; and the almost exclusive object of Ojibwa participation in the war was to obtain booty.

The siege of Fort William Henry marked a turning point in the colonial war. It was also a turning point in the 'Golden Age' of the Ojibwa. Famine, the lack of supplies, and the spread of disease combined to weaken the Ojibwa as well as their French allies. By 19 May 1758, New France was almost reduced to starvation: 'Nothing is more melancholy or more afflicting than the actual condition of this Colony, after having passed a part of last autumn and winter on a quarter of a pound of bread per person a day. We are reduced these six weeks past to two ounces.'[27] Having no food themselves, the French were unable to sustain the Ojibwa warriors in the field. Even if the Indians had been able to trap for furs instead of participating in the war, they would not have been able to purchase their much needed supplies. To symbolize their need for French support, if their role in the war were to continue, some Mississauga-Ojibwa at Fort Niagara 'offered bloody scalp-locks in exchange for food and powder.' In their weakened condition, smallpox spread rapidly among them. The intensive contact with the Europeans during the campaigns seriously exposed the Ojibwa to the 'white man's disease,' since smallpox was rife in English ranks as well as among the French. The Ojibwa at Michilimackinac experienced an unprecedented epidemic of such virulence and proportion that the priest's register presented a dismal list of burials all through the autumn and winter of 1757–8. Many Southern Ojibwa deaths were also reported at Niagara, Toronto, and Frontenac. The French military admitted that 'this was a real loss to us.'[28] Although there are no complete statistics on Indian deaths by disease or in battle, the colonial reports give the impression that more Ojibwa were killed by smallpox than by English bullets. This might have been the determining factor in the destiny of France in America.

By 1758 it was impossible for the French to rally any substantial number of their Ojibwa allies in the defence of Fort Duquesne. Three years earlier they had been successful in defeating Braddock, but at that time their Indian allies were healthy and well supplied. François Le Marchand de Ligneris, the new commander at Fort Duquesne, had only 130 Indians in the field against an advancing army of 7000 men, including 2000 able Virginians. Although the fort contained 1200 French soldiers, they could be supplied for only eighteen days. This was not considered sufficient to withstand a siege. The viable solution was to burn the fort and retreat. News of the French defeat spread quickly. The Menominee at La Baye (Green Bay) were the first to react by killing eleven Frenchmen and plundering the warehouse containing scarce and high-priced goods. When they attempted to regain their French alliance the next year by offering expiation for their crime, two of the guilty were put to death by the French in the governor's presence. The historian Severance considers this the first time that capital punishment was used by a governor against his Indian allies. The Menominee had admitted their guilt, but claimed they were driven by the need for

European goods. They took the murderers to the French, but not to have them put to death. The French could never have brought them 'to justice' themselves. Traditionally, Indians expected to repent by taking English scalps at least to the number of French killed. During wartime, this alien European justice was a diplomatic blunder that no Frenchman with knowledge of Indian culture would make. It failed to impress the Ojibwa and the other Indians who were allies of the Menominee.

The English capture of Fort Frontenac was an obvious sign that the Ojibwa alliance with the French was crumbling. Joseph M. de Noyan, commander of the fort, received information from a scouting party of four Mississauga that a well-armed longboat was reconnoitring along the north side of Lake Ontario. The Indians successfully captured it and took two papers which indicated the pending English attack. But the Ojibwa did not come to the defence of the fort. Lt-Col. John Bradstreet landed within a mile of the fort without any opposition, and, when the nine sailboats that were the entire French fleet on Lake Ontario were captured in the harbour, the fort surrendered at once. The irreplaceable wealth of stores and ammunition, intended to strengthen Fort Duquesne and to fit out the long-planned attack on the Mohawk Valley, were taken or destroyed. These stores were valued at the considerable sum of 800,000 livres and should have been previously dispersed among the Ojibwa for the protection of the fort. Most important, the major means of supplying Forts Toronto, Detroit, and especially Niagara was all but cut off. Lack of military supplies made it almost impossible for the Southern Ojibwa to mount an offensive in the battles to come. A desperate appeal went to Versailles for presents to distribute to the Indians during the autumn, but they were not forthcoming.

The defence of Forts Niagara and Toronto was extremely important if the French wished to retain their western Indian allies. With the fall of Fort Duquesne, they had lost many of their Indian friends in the Ohio Valley. In fact Owiligaska (alias Peter Spelman), a German living among the Shawnee, proposed to William Johnson that he could 'get some Indians and take Toronto away from the French.' This would not have been a difficult undertaking since there were fewer than two dozen French soldiers there and the local

Ojibwa would likely not have protected them because of the way they had been treated by the commander. Niagara, rather than Toronto or the other lesser forts in the Great Lakes, however, was the major prize desired by the English, since its capitulation would cause all of the other surrounding forts to fall. William Johnson had a personal interest in its destruction because it greatly interfered with his fur-trading profits. He knew, however, that it was futile to attempt to take the fort without the consent of the Iroquois and the Southern Ojibwa. The Chenussio, a subgroup of the Seneca, and a band of the Ojibwa controlled the Niagara portage. They had both been lukewarm allies of the French and were about to play a major role in the future of the fort. If they could be won over to the English cause, Niagara would fall without difficulty.

The commander at Niagara, Pierre Pouchot, was the major cause of his own demise. Not wanting their enemies to take advantage of their shortage of Indian truck, he stopped the Southern Ojibwa and the Chenussio from attempting to cross the Niagara pass in search of an English market. These Indians lacked clothing, ammunition, guns, snare wire, and other necessities for their well being because French promises of cheap and plentiful supplies were not being kept. When Johnson called a meeting at Canajoharie, then, most of the Ojibwa and Seneca were willing to come and listen.

On 11 April 1759 sixty Chenussio arrived at the meeting place and informed Johnson that 'the Tionontaitis, the Miamis, the Shawnees, the Amikwas, the Chippewas and the Missisaugas, all western tribes long in alliance with the French, were, in response to Sir William's belt of invitation, on their way to make an alliance with the English if the English would trade with them.' Among the last of these three groups were a majority of the Ojibwa from Southern Ontario. Johnson was delighted with his success, for he had worked hard the year before in bringing about the defection.[29] Not only were the Iroquois abandoning their long-held neutrality, but the powerful Ojibwa were willing to listen to his proposal of alliance.

Johnson's 'family' relationship with the Iroquois for several years provided him with the experience required to win the confidence of most Indians. He fed them well, distributed abundant presents, treated them to liberal proportions of rum, and conducted a war dance. For the Chenussio this was likely unnecessary since most of them had previously planned on pillaging Fort Niagara. The Southern Ojibwa were uncertain. Some still wished to remain loyal to the French and a few were willing to join the Chenussio, but most at least indicated their neutrality. This was all that was needed to shift most of the Iroquois to an active support of the English. They no longer had to fear a devastating attack by the formidable enemy that had dropped them to their knees in the 1690s and moved into southern Ontario.

Governor General Pierre de Rigaud de Vaudreuil reacted immediately when he was informed that Niagara was threatened. He summoned troops from the Illinois and from Detroit, with instructions to gather at Presqu'ile on Lake Erie. He added: 'As these forces will proceed to the relief of Niagara, should the enemy besiege it, I have in like manner sent orders to Toronto to collect the Mississagues and other natives, to forward them to Niagara.' He was not very optimistic since he also commanded: 'If the English should make their appearance at Toronto, I have given orders to burn it at once and fall back on Niagara.' It was soon burned.

On 30 June the formidable English force of 2200 soldiers and about 600 Indians, mostly Iroquois, advanced with cannon from Oswego to Niagara. They landed four miles from the fort without Ojibwa opposition. In the fort there were only 486 French soldiers, some Seneca who were friends of the Joncaire family, and Indians from the Head of the Lake (Burlington). The Iroquois asked the few Ojibwa and the Seneca to leave before the battle commenced since they feared that they might anger those nations by accidentally killing one of them. Most of them acquiesced to the Iroquois request as the English cannon inched closer to the fort. This was not to be a battle in which Ojibwa fought Iroquois. That contest had been settled fifty years earlier.

The gathering warriors at first seemed to indicate that such a confrontation was about to take place. On 12 July, 400 French and 1000 western Indians had assembled at Venango with the intention of attacking Fort Pitt, but a message arrived directing them to relieve the besieged Fort Niagara. Severance observed that their movements 'showed not only lack of generalship, but of the craft and caution in which these wilderness warriors were supposed to excel. It is not recorded that they even sent scouts in advance.' A similar army had destroyed Braddock's much superior force in 1755, but such a victory was not to be repeated. The fact that the Iroquois and Ojibwa were not willing to fight each other probably accounts for the Ojibwa's 'warning' the enemy of their advance. Certainly they had always prided themselves on a surprise attack, but did they want this to be a surprise? Severance attributed the English victory to Johnson's ability and French stupidity, but he failed to consider the strategy of the Indian allies.

The Ojibwa and Iroquois had agreed not to go to war against each other. Many of the 1000 Indian allies of the French were Ojibwa, and the 900 Indian allies of the English that Johnson finally attracted were mainly Iroquois. The French, moreover, had not kept their promise to both groups to provide a plentiful supply of cheap trade goods at Niagara and had attempted to prevent them from trading with the English. As a result, it was discovered later, the Ojibwa and the Iroquois agreed before the battle not to kill each other. In addition, the Ojibwa were not inclined to fight the English for a fort that had frustrated many of them. As one account of the battle explained: 'It is said all the Indians but the brave Mohawks stood neuter the first onset the enemy made, to see, it is thought, which way the scale would turn; for I believe it was imprinted in their mind the French were invincible. As soon as they found to the contrary, and that the French gave way, it is said but a yard of ground, they fell on them like so many butchers.'[30] The Indians were certainly aware that the French were not invincible, especially without their Ojibwa allies. The Indian strategy was obvious. The object was to lure the French into a trap without any Indians getting into their line of fire by accident. One account indicates that only 350 of the 1000 French Indian allies participated in the battle. Another source states that most of the Ojibwa, after sending the delegation to the Iroquois, refused to return to the French force. In foolish frustration, before all of their Ojibwa allies abandoned them, 'Aubry and de Lingery waved their swords, called to the Indians, and ran toward the enemy. But the war-painted horde vanished into the forest, leaving with their French allies "only thirty of the most resolute."'[31] There is no record of any Ojibwa being killed in this battle, but it certainly was a slaughter for the French. Estimates of those killed ranged from 200 to 500, and of those captured, 100 to 120. Since Niagara had failed to serve its intended purpose of supplying sufficient trade goods for the Indians in the lower Great Lakes area, the Ojibwa and Iroquois were drawn together in an effort to destroy it or at least permit it to be destroyed. As a result, they achieved their objective of opening up trade with the English, with the bonus of plundering the fort without any serious loss of their lives.

Pouchot surrendered to Johnson on 25 July 1759. Unlike most egocentric European generals at that time, Johnson attributed the victory to the Indian allies. Immediately after the Niagara defeat he started to hold councils with the local native groups, many of whom were from southern Ontario. An Ojibwa chief from Toronto, Tequakareigh, came to the fort within a week of the French capitulation. Johnson's lengthy interview with this chief indicates the importance of the meeting:

With a string and two belts of wampum I bid him welcome and shook him by the hand. By the second, which was a black belt, I took the hatchet out of the hands of his and all the surrounding nations; recommended hunting and trade to them, which would be more to their interest than quarrelling with the English, who have ever been their friends, and supplied them at the cheapest rates with the necessaries of life, and would do it again, both here (Niagara) and at Oswego, provided they quitted the French interest. This I desired he would acquaint all the surrounding nations with. A black belt, the third and last, was to invite his and all other nations living near them, to repair early next spring to this place and Oswego, where there should be a large assortment of all kinds of goods fit for their use; also recommended it to them to send some of their young men here to hunt and fish for the garrison, for which they would be paid, and kindly treated. Told them at the same time that I would send some of my interpreters, etc., with him on the lake to the next town of the Mississagas, with whom I desired he would use his best endeavours to convince them that it would be in their interest to live in friendship with the English, and that we had no ill intentions against them, if they did not oblige us to it. To which he (Tequakareigh) answered, and said it gave him great pleasure to hear our good words, and was certain it would be extremely agreeable to all the nations with whom he was acquainted, who, with his, were wheedled and led on to strike the English, which he now confessed he was sorry for, and assured they never would again; and that should the French, according to custom, ask them to do so any more, they would turn them out of the country. He, at the same time, begged earnestly, that a plenty of goods might be brought here and to Oswego; and there they, as well as all the other nations around, would come to trade; and their young men should hunt for their brothers, whom they now took fast hold of by the hand, and called upon the Six Nations, who were present, to bear witness to what he had promised.[32]

Johnson gave Tequakareigh clothing and 'handsome presents to carry home.' Then he took a large French medal from the chief's neck and gave him an English medal as well as a silver gorget. Soon after, 150 Ojibwa delivered two English prisoners taken at Belle Famille. Since there was no evidence of punishment but only rewards, Johnson's treatment of the Ojibwa was a clear indication that he did not assume they had been defeated with the French and that he wanted them as allies in trade as well as war. While Tequakareigh did not represent all of the Ojibwa in southern Ontario, his views were likely held by most. George Croghan, deputy superintendent of Indian Affairs under Johnson, met with two other southern Ojibwa chiefs on 7 August 1759 and buried the hatchet 'under a large pine tree that it may never be found more.' Only one small band of Southern Ojibwa was resolved to retain its alliance with the French, according to an English prisoner who escaped to Fort Pitt. This was possibly 'the domiciliated Mississaugas of Presqu'isle [who] followed the French to Detroit. The Nations of Detroit, with a very good grace, have taken charge of a certain number of Frenchmen whom they have supported in this winter camp by hunting.'[33] It was reported as late as 24 June 1760 that some Ojibwa were killing Englishmen near Niagara and at the mouth of Chenandas (Chippewa Creek, Ontario). Nevertheless, if the English were willing and able to trade honestly and regularly with the Southern Ojibwa, most of that nation were willing to let them replace the French in the lower Great Lakes area without fear of resistance from the majority of the natives there.

The capitulation of Niagara ended the Southern Ojibwa's active participation in the Seven Years' War. These warriors likely played a minor role in the decisive battles in the east, since the Great Lakes area and the trade there were their major concerns. The shifting strategy in the last few years of the war indicated a degree of disunity and confusion among the Ojibwa. Forces beyond their control were determining their destiny. They were forced to move from an enviable position with two eager European trading nations bidding high prices for their furs to only one, first the French (with the destruction of Oswego) and then the English (with the capitulation of Niagara and the other lesser forts). In seeking the Ojibwa as allies, both European powers had been forced to lower the price of their trade goods during the first half of the eighteenth century. This created a golden age of trade for the native people of the Great Lakes. As the colonial struggle for America intensified and goods became scarce and expensive, the French Indian alliances crumbled. The war booty from pillaged forts and pioneer homesteads sustained the Ojibwa for a time, but as Indian families began to suffer from lack of supplies and smallpox the alliance with the French evaporated.

There was never any binding 'patriotic spirit' or loyalty that inspired the Indians to fight for the kings of France. The European forts in the Great Lakes were tolerated for only one reason – cheap trade goods. Whenever they failed to serve this purpose, French forts and traders were not protected by the Ojibwa against their enemies. Indeed, they were attacked. Frenchmen who had gained respect through their being assimilated into native bands sometimes upset this general principle; for example, Langlade, who convinced the Ojibwa to drive the English out of the Ohio Valley, and Joncaire, who swayed the Southern Ojibwa and the Seneca in their destruction of Oswego. Pitting the English against the French was preferable to the destruction of either one. Participation in the war temporarily gained European goods and satisfied the warrior's urge to prove himself, but the elimination of one European power drove the price of furs down in the trading posts of the victorious nation since there was no other foreign competition. This was undoubtedly understood by the Indians. A complete and decisive victory of one of the European combatants over the other was neither anticipated nor desired. For over a century the English had periodically been fighting the French in America. Why should this end with the

Seven Years' War? The Ojibwa likely did not comprehend the full impact of the fact that England was the ruler of New France at the end of the war, but the reality would soon be felt. Was there any military reason after 1760 for the English to treat the indigenous peoples as independent, sovereign 'nations' now that they were not needed as essential allies?

An Amikwa Ojibwa, possibly the first drawing of an Ojibwa, c. 1700

While the French portrayed their Indian enemies, the Iroquois, as frightful and warlike (left), their allies, the Ojibwa, were pictured as attractive and peaceful.

The Ojibwa victory over the Iroquois as portrayed on a birchbark box in the collection of the Royal Ontario Museum. The design on the box, which is made with porcupine quills, is taken from a rock painting near Lake Couchiching. According to Mesaquab (Jonathan Yorke of the Rama Reserve), a Mohawk is being clubbed by one Ojibwa while the other stands by with a musket, likely symbolizing the pincer attack on the Five Nations.

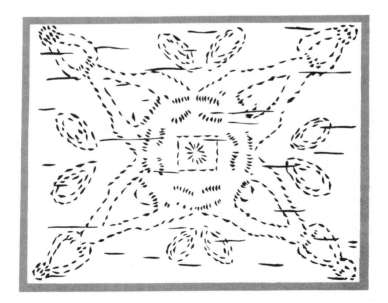

Wampum was used as a mnemonic device.
This wampum is a deed of land given
to M. Piche by the Saugeen in 1818.

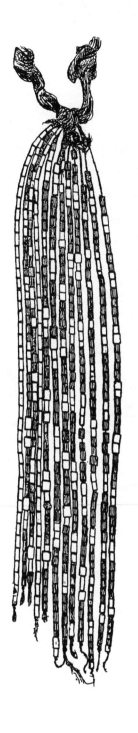

OPPOSITE

Birchbark biting design. The origin of the
cutout pattern is thought to go back to the
'toothmark' or old bitten patterns that
Ojibwa women marked on birchbark with
their teeth. To make a pattern, thin bark
was folded in two or more layers and a
series of dots was impressed with the eye
teeth. The folding of the bark caused a
duplication of the design, giving symmetri-
cal patterns.

Present giving at Wikwimikong, Manitoulin Island, 1840s

Kahgegagahbowh, George Copway, was the first North American Indian to write a history book.

An Ojibwa woman, 1880s

Chief Nawash,
at this point blind and crippled,
had fought in the War of 1812.

George Kaboosa and his son, 1880s

Ojibwa of Garden River Reserve, 1901

Ojibwa chief

Ojibwa north of Lake Nipigon

An Ojibwa camp

Ojibwa with a child on a carrying board

Garden River band in Hiawatha pageant

Ojibwa in traditional dress

In 1860 Nahnebahwequay (Catherine Sutton) was the first Indian woman to present Ojibwa grievances to Queen Victoria.

Mrs Peter Jones, wife of the first chief at Cape Croker, 1800s

Reverend John Sunday, Shawundais, an Ojibwa who took Methodism to the western tribes in the 1840s

Chief David Wawanosh of the Sarnia Reserve, 1880s

Francis Assikinack,
educated at Upper Canada College,
1860s

Captain Thomas G. Anderson

4

THE BEAVER WAR
'You Have Not Yet Conquered Us!'

The Seven Years' War ended with the defeat of the French in America, but their Indian allies had not been conquered, nor had they been included in the European peace negotiations between Britain and France. How would the dominant European power on the continent treat the Ojibwa of southern Ontario now that the Indians could no longer count on the French for military supplies and trade goods? The well-being of the indigenous people of the Great Lakes had been sustained by the competitively priced trade goods which they obtained in exchange for furs. Their strength lay in pitting one power against the other and in surviving off the land by hunting and fishing in a territory that amply satisfied their needs. Their aboriginal way of life depended on a diplomatic and ecological balance. Both appeared to be threatened as the British took over the forts in the Great Lakes. There seemed to be only two viable solutions to the problem of the British advance – accommodation or war. Since there were advantages and disadvantages in both options, the individualism which was characteristic of the Ojibwa dictated that the choice of one over the other would not be unanimous. Conditions in the Great Lakes, however, led to a military confrontation that was more serious than any other in the history of Ojibwa-European relations in North America. The Indians called it the Beaver War, but it is best known as the Pontiac Uprising.

Throughout the Seven Years' War the Ojibwa had not been in a battle which they themselves had lost. This was not true of the French. Gradually the Ojibwa came to understand that their erstwhile ally had been decisively defeated in America. Most of the

Ojibwa felt they could simply shift their alliance from the French to the English. This belief in their own power was clearly stated by Minavavana, an Ojibwa chief, to one of the first English fur traders among them after the war: 'Englishman, although you have conquered the French, you have not yet conquered us! We are not your slaves. These lakes, these woods and mountains were left to us [the Ojibwa] by our ancestors. They are our inheritance; and we will part with them to none. Your nation supposes that we, like the white people, cannot live without bread – and pork – and beef! But, you ought to know, that He, the Great Spirit and Master of Life, has provided food for us, in these spacious lakes, and on these woody mountains.'[1] Minavavana was convinced that as long as his people could live off the land by gathering food they could not be defeated. Little did he know that the fear of starvation would stalk the dark side of his children's dreams.

Minavavana's conviction was shared by most Ojibwa. For generations, however, they had fought their wars aided by Europeans who supplied them with musket, ball, and powder. Clothing and food were often provided by the French in longer campaigns against the British, especially during siege operations. Only the Master of Life knew how formidable the Ojibwa could be without such aid in a war against a European power.

Unwittingly, Jeffrey Amherst, commander-in-chief of the British forces in America, was about to test their strength. His dislike of and contempt for the Indians are amply reflected in his journals. In writing to William Johnson, who had keen insight into the native mentality, Amherst reiterated his Indian policy: 'Service must be rewarded; it has ever been a maxim with me. But as to purchasing the good behavior either of Indians or any others, [that] is what I do not understand.' In another letter to Johnson, after hearing about a plot at Detroit in 1761, he foolishly stated: 'I know their Incapacity of attempting anything serious, and that if they were rash enough to venture upon any ill Designs, I have it in my power not only to frustrate them, but to punish the delinquents with Entire Destruction.' Neither Amherst nor any other British government official knew the population or the military potential of the Ojibwa at the time. The Ojibwa, as well as many other Indian nations, permitted Europeans and their forts in the territories because of the benefits they derived from them. The Indians expected military officers and traders to make a liberal distribution of presents as a form of rent for the posts and a toll for passage through their country. Gifts of liquor, equipment for hunting, and, increasingly, clothing and food demonstrated to the Indians the 'respect' that the Europeans had for their nations. Indeed, the Ojibwa did not look upon such expressions of friendship as simply 'presents' but as a form of tribute. Amherst failed to understand Johnson's maxim: 'Presents make Indian friends.'

Johnson considered it 'absolutely necessary' to give ammunition and numerous other gifts to the Indians if the British expected to secure their friendship. In anticipation of his first grand council with about 2000 western Indians, Johnson prepared a list of goods to be distributed. Amherst objected to spending over £1845 at the meeting, but for the time being he acquiesced to Johnson, who claimed that there would be trouble with the Indians if there were any reductions.

The rapid occupation of French forts by the British and the attitude of British soldiers towards the Indians created a great deal of distrust and suspicion among the inhabitants of the Great Lakes. Johnson, in the grand council at Detroit in the fall of 1761, was questioned by local Mississauga about the number of troops and cannon that were coming into their lands. Since the French had been defeated, the Indians reasoned, there was no need to man the old fortifications or to build new ones. Johnson temporarily placated them and some other Ojibwa with liquor, beef, clothing, ammunition, and other provisions, and added that he would send them a blacksmith by the next fall. He even 'swapped his gun with a Chippewa Indian for his French gun' and gave the Indians at Presqu'isle a keg of rum to drink to the English king's health. In addition, Wabbicommicot, chief of the Mississauga in the Toronto area, was the privileged dinner guest of Johnson and Major Henry Gladwin. Others were treated almost as well. An Ottawa Indian whose horse had been killed by soldier David Lutts was given in payment a gallon of rum, two blankets, two pounds of powder, four pounds of ball, and a promise of another horse. This gift was made after Lutts had been punished with 100 lashes, and under threat by the wronged Ottawa that if he were not given a horse, he would kill all of the horses and cattle belonging to the British fort. Not all Indians received such a substantial redress for their grievances. The Seneca allies of the Ojibwa suffered more and received less consideration. Members of the Detroit garrison stole a keg of rum and four Seneca horses, shot a warrior in the breast and arm, and killed another at Venango without cause. Johnson's reaction to these complaints showed an uncharacteristic lack of diplomacy. He had four men whipped in public for stealing, but failed to give the customary compensation to the relatives of the injured warriors. Moreover, the Seneca were all refused presents and given only enough ammunition to hunt on their way home. Johnson recorded in the *Detroit Journal*: 'I returned their own wampum, to show them I paid no regard to what they said, which greatly staggered them all.' While some of the Indians were well treated, most were insulted. By 19 March 1762 Governor Burton of Montreal found it necessary to issue a warning to his troops to treat the Indians with humanity.[2] The insults continued.

The animosity of the American regulars who occupied the forts in the Great Lakes is understandable but not justifiable. Many of their friends and relatives had suffered as a result of Ojibwa raids on frontier settlements during the war. No satisfaction had been achieved against them on the battlefield because of their elusiveness. Little imagination is required to understand the soldiers' enmity when the Ojibwa presented white women as prisoners held for ransom. One English woman, for example, was given up after the war only when the Ojibwa family 'received fifteen pounds of powder, eight bars of lead, a blanket, a petticoat, a pair of leggins, and a shirt.'[3] While the soldiers viewed this with anger, such payments for hostages were part of the Ojibwa tradition and considered legitimate spoils of war.

The traders from New York often caused as much discontent among the Ojibwa as the soldiers. Their trading methods frequently digressed from the accepted norms established by the Ojibwa with the French. A Mississauga child was kept by a trader's wife, Mrs Vandreisin, for example, as a pledge of security for the unpaid trade goods they were given. When the Indians brought their furs in payment and asked for the child, she lied by saying she could not find him. On hearing the Mississauga complaint, Johnson remarked that such treatment simply confirmed what the French had told the natives, 'that we look upon them as our slaves or Negroes.' Mistrust of the Indians prevented many novice British traders from extending credit. During the French period, it had been customary for the French to supply trade good on credit to the Indians, who unfailingly made their payments in furs at the end of the hunting season. Another breach of etiquette involved liquor. As La Rochefoucault-Liancourt observed: 'It is a circumstance, worthy of notice, that an ancient French law, enacted at the time, when Canada belonged to France, prohibited any rum to be sold to the Indians by the agents on pain of the galleys. Hence originated the custom ... of giving it away.' Most British traders could not understand the utility of giving away the rum, and they distributed it freely only as a method of intoxicating the Indians so they could 'over-reach them with more facility in the intended business.'[4] After the Indians became sober and found they had received few or no trade goods for their winter furs, they justifiably felt cheated. British trade among the western Indians, in contrast to the French, was characterized by more of a capitalist and entrepreneurial spirit, being almost completely profit-oriented. Johnson correctly observed that the French often 'took care to cultivate a good understanding with the Western Indians, which the safety of their colony and their ambitious views of extending their boundaries, rendered indispensably necessary; to effect this, they were at an immense expense in buying the favour of the Indians.'[5] French trade goods were diplomatic tools. British trade had exclusively one objective – to fill the pockets of a few mercenary merchants. Many Ojibwa saw the British traders as a necessary evil in their society, but did they have any choice?

An examination of the trade goods bartered at the posts of the lower Great Lakes in 1722–3 and the distribution of presents by Johnson at Niagara in 1761 gives ample evidence of the Ojibwa's growing dependence on an increasing variety of European products. Blankets, ready-made shirts of cotton and linen, cloaks of flannel and serge, and woollen leggings and mittens had all but replaced leather and furs for all members of the family. Cloth, ribbons of various colours, beads, thread, lace, gilt and mock-silver trimming could be worked with metal scissors, sewing thimbles, and needles, and these implements replaced wood, bone, and stone tools. The Indian

women could design their own native costumes with this new
technology in considerably less time than that required to work the
skins by traditional methods. Indeed, it is possible that the women
encouraged the trade more than other members of the family. Their
preparation of food was greatly facilitated by iron axes for gathering
firewood, steel for striking fires, metal knives for cutting meat, and
brass and copper kettles for cooking. Life was also made much easier
for the men who provided the food. Bows and arrows were replaced
by muskets and ball, which were more accurate at a greater distance.
Copper wire made trapping animals more dependable, and metal fish
hooks and spears as well as European fish lines and nets considerably
increased the harvest from lakes and streams. The Ojibwa's physical
appearance was changed by European clothing, rings, hawk bells,
paint, and razors. Their religious ceremony of smoking expanded
into a common social activity as large quantities of pipes and tobacco
became available, and liquor brought escape from rigid cultural
restrictions. While the Ojibwa could do without the luxuries, they
increasingly required European goods to obtain their basic food
supplies.

The British traders who went among the 'almost naked' Indians
after the Seven Years' War were viewed by the Ojibwa as representatives of the British crown. Unfortunately, many were unfit for
such an ambassadorial role. Most were novices in the Indian trade
and interested only in making a substantial profit. Even Alexander
Henry, the first recorded British trader in the Upper Great Lakes,
refused to supply merchandise and ammunition to 200 warriors from
L'Arbre Croche in 1762 in exchange for fifty beaver-skins on credit.
He soon corrected his error, however, and became successful in the
trade. Most did not.

Some of the men in the Indian trade set very bad examples and
failed to gain any respect for the British in the eyes of the Indians.
Ferrall Wade was one of the few semi-literate traders who could
communicate in writing his disgust at the habits of his fellow trader.
Writing from his Toronto trading post, he had this to say about his
constantly intoxicated partner: 'I would not know wheather he was
blessed with a tounge or not. When the [Southern Ojibwa] Indians
come atrading not a word will he say to them without its Extorted
from him I then say why dont you Welcome the Indians its All the

same I am Obliged to Stammer to them, In short he does not know what we are about, or the price of a single knife on the Whole he is One of the Most Lazy, Indolent Young fellows I ever saw, the whole Winter he sate at the fire side with his Elbow on his knee & his Chin on his hand picking his nose without speaking a Word he has wore a shirt 13 or 14 weeks without Changing & the Whole time I dont think he Ever Washed, when he took his shirt Off the Man showed it me it was swarmed with lice.'[6] It was reported that he required a pint of rum before he got out of bed in the morning. Such examples created neither friendships nor respect between the indigenous people and British traders at this critical time.

The greatest fear among the Ojibwa was the threat the Europeans posed to their food supply. They fully understood that, as settlers advanced, the Indians were forced to withdraw. As early as the 1760s there were about sixty families of white settlers in what became known as Windsor, Ontario, but these were French who respected the customs of the local Ojibwa. They gave the Ojibwa part of their crops as payment for the use of the land. The British approach was different, as exemplified in an Indian complaint to Johnson in 1762: 'Some of our people were lately repairing a fishing wear (where we have fished time out of mind for our support) ... when an officer came up and forbid us, telling us he would order his men to break down what we had made. We did not think it hard while our brothers and we shared alike; which was the case when the former officer commanded there: but the present officer acts an unbrotherly part, which we hope will be taken notice of, and prevented for the time to come.'[7] It was this fear of losing their means of support that also caused the Ojibwa to object to houses being built by the British in the Niagara area. Encroachment on their food supply was justly considered by the Indians a matter of life and death.

Johnson reported to Amherst as early as 22 June 1761 that 'something not right is a brewing and that very privately among them.' Amherst's response was to cut off presents, especially ammunition and arms, which he claimed they had 'in abundance.'[8] Thomas Hutchins, who was sent among the Indians in 1762, reported that the Ottawa, Potawatomi, and Ojibwa were very displeased that presents were not being distributed. He observed: 'I always found in Private Conversation that they were not so well satisfy'd as I could have wish'd as they were disappointed in their Expectations of my not having Presents for them and as the French had always Accustomed themselves both in time of Peace, and during the late War to make these People great Presents three or four times a Year, and always allowed them a sufficient Quantity of Ammunition at the Posts, they think it very Strange that this custom should be so immediately broke off by the British, and the Traders not allowed even to take so much Ammunition with them as to enable those Indians to kill game sufficient for the Support of their families ... It is with the greatest difficulty that the Officers [of the posts] can keep them in good humour.'[9] Johnson reported to Amherst that some 'distant' Indians had even died on their way to Niagara because they lacked ammunition to kill game for their subsistence. The breaking point came for many of the Ojibwa and their allies when a new policy was introduced which limited the supply of ammunition available to traders and thus threatened many families with starvation. The British had broken the unwritten contract which permitted them to live in the Indian territory and move safely through it.

In 1763 the general discontent erupted into open warfare in what became known as the Pontiac Uprising. Francis Parkman substantially contributed to popularizing the idea of a conspiracy led exclusively by Pontiac, the myth of a one-man leadership of the Great Lakes Indians. While Pontiac's heroic role was successfully questioned by Howard H. Peckham, the myth still lives on in less scholarly works.[10] Pontiac did not have the absolute power attributed to him. Indeed, many Indians rated his true stature below that of other Ojibwa chiefs at the time. The part played by leaders such as Wabbicommicot in the war is much more complex than most authors have indicated, if they considered him at all. He and other Ojibwa were not the puppets of an all-powerful head chief. Among the leaders, however, there was a unanimous desire to establish a workable relationship with the British.

The Ojibwa had not been faced with so serious a problem for over half a century. Pontiac obviously comprehended the impact of the British victory and played an important part in the formation of an active alliance to deal with it, but many other chiefs were involved and some even opposed his leadership and saw alternatives to military action. His cultural background undoubtedly played a part in attracting the Indians to his cause, but his precise cultural affiliations are not clear. Nineteenth-century Ottawa tradition indicates that Pontiac's mother was Ottawa and his father Ojibwa. Two other accounts, by Henry Conner, a United States Indian interpreter, and Henry R. Schoolcraft, an Indian agent, stated that Pontiac's mother was Ojibwa.[11] Almost all sources agree that there was a genetic connection with the Ojibwa. Such a blood relationship would account for his having some support among the Southern Ojibwa, but he certainly did not have the unquestioned loyalty of all of them.

On several occasions Wabbicommicot, the most powerful chief in the Toronto area, opposed Pontiac and those who advocated war against the British. Some might say that he even acted as a spy for the British. He reported to a British trader at Toronto in the winter of 1762–3 that Luc de La Corne (also known as La Corne Saint-Luc) had earlier sent a message to the various nations promising that a French fleet would arrive and retake the country. With the continuing presence of hostile Franco-Spanish troops on the Mississippi, Canadiens firmly expected liberation. Their enthusiasm spread to the Indians of the Great Lakes. Wabbicommicot warned the trader that the Indians would go to war against the British in the spring. He obviously wanted to prevent the confrontation by giving the British a chance to eradicate the grievances. Had all the Ojibwa bands met and come to a common agreement, his message would have been an inexcusable breach of trust since surprise attacks had always been their greatest weapon. He strongly disapproved of a military solution, but although he was considered by Johnson 'ye Chief Man North & West upon Lake Ontario and so far upon Lake Erie as ye big [Grand] River,' he could not 'dictate' to his people.[12] This was likely not the first time that Wabbicommicot had informed the British about the pending uprising. On 28 September 1762 Amherst received intelligence from 'An Indian of good character amongst all the Western Nations' who informed him 'that there was a great Council held at the Ottawey Town Above D'Troit this Summer by the Chiefs and Principal Warriors of the Wyandotts, Cheapwas, Ottawas, and Poutauwautimies and some other Tribes who lived amongst those Indians on Lake Superior, above Mechelemackinac and Fort La Bay; that this council was kept a great Secret from all Indians Except those of the greatest note amongst their Nations, that Two French men came down with the Indians who came from above Mechelemackinac in Indian Dress; and that as soon as it Broke up, Deputies of the Indians were Sent to the Twightwes, Ouia-tanons, Kickaupoose, and Pyankishaws, and other Tribes Settled on the Wabash ... This Man Says I may depend upon it that they were Meditating Something Against Us.'[13]

The attack was to come the next spring 'when the frogs began to speak.' Late in May 1763 Wabbicommicot appeared at Niagara demanding rum and threatening that he would not be responsible for the consequences if he were refused. This action, according to historian Jane E. Graham, 'had clearly been forced on him by pressures within his tribe, for he added the personal opinion that the British were more generous than the French and he again warned that trouble was afoot.'[14] He was not the only informant. The chiefs of the Miami delivered a war belt to Ensign Robert Holmes which had been sent to them by the 'Shawanee' Nation in the winter. They demonstrated their loyalty by informing the British officer that they 'were not to let this belt be known ... and then we were all to Rise & put the English to death all about this place [Fort Miamis] and those at the other place.'[15] While there was ample evidence of pending disaster, the arrogant Amherst failed to take it seriously. He had no respect for the Indians' military ability.

Wabbicommicot prevented most of the bands in the Toronto area from joining Pontiac's struggle against the British, but he was the exception among the Ojibwa rather than the rule. Only one other unnamed Ojibwa chief in southern Ontario maintained a neutral stand. The remainder were mostly active participants in attacking British traders and forts. Chief Sekahos, who was the leader of the warriors in the Thames River region, strongly assisted in the movement against the British. He commanded 170 Mississauga Ojibwa who not only participated in the siege of Detroit but also captured eleven traders at the mouth of the Grand River. Three barges of much-needed military supplies fell into Ojibwa hands. Wasson, chief of the Ojibwa of Saginaw Bay, brought 250 warriors to besiege Detroit, and also attacked some smaller forts to the south.

At Detroit there were considerably more Ojibwa than Ottawa under the leadership of Pontiac. While his attack on the fort was poorly planned and executed, the Ojibwa to the north were immediately victorious.

The Ojibwa in the more northerly part of southern Ontario were much less willing to accept the British as the dominant Europeans in the Great Lakes region. In contrast, the Ojibwa on the shores of Lakes Ontario, Erie, and Huron, having traded with the British as well as the French for almost a generation, were divided in their loyalties. Indeed, some were so greedy for British trade that they had discouraged their Ojibwa allies to the north from communicating with the British. As a result, the Ojibwa around Michilimackinac did not forget their warriors who had been killed by the British in the Seven Years' War. Revenge, not reconciliation, was the theme of their battle songs, as illustrated by Chief Waub-ojeeg:

On that day when our heroes lay low, lay low,
On that day when our heroes lay low
I fought by their side, and thought, ere I died,
Just vengeance to take on the foe,
Just vengeance to take on the foe.

On that day, when our chieftains lay dead, lay dead,
On that day, when our chieftains lay dead,
I fought hand to hand at the head of my band,
And here on my breast have I bled, have I bled,
And here on my breast have I bled.

Our chiefs shall return no more, no more,
Our chiefs shall return no more,
Nor their brethren of war, who can show scar for scar,
Like women their fates shall deplore, deplore
Like women their fates shall deplore.

Five Winters in hunting we'll spend, we'll spend,
Five winters in hunting we'll spend,
Till our youth, grown to men, we'll to the war lead again,
And our days like our fathers' will end, will end,
And our days like our fathers' will end.[16]

In less than five years their young warriors were ready again to follow their chiefs on the warpath against the English.

Over four hundred Ojibwa warriors gathered at Michilimackinac in the spring of 1763. The garrison was well armed. Ninety privates, two subalterns, and the commandant probably could have withstood their force if the officers had been alert behind the walls of the strongest fort in the Upper Great Lakes. Captain George Etherington was warned on several occasions about the intentions of the Ojibwa. He foolishly disregarded their advice, however, and was not aware of the passionate hatred that the head chief, Minweweh, had for the English.

On 2 June 1763 Minweweh organized a surprise attack on Fort Michilimackinac under the guise of a baggataway (lacrosse) game. Alexander Henry explained the stratagem:

The game of baggataway ... is necessarily attended with much violence and noise. In the ardour of the contest, the ball ... if it cannot be thrown to the goal desired, is struck in any direction by the adversary. At such a moment, therefore, nothing could be less liable to excite premature alarm, than that the ball should be tossed over the pickets of the fort, nor that having fallen there, it should be followed on the instant, by all engaged in the game, as well the one party as the other, all eager, all struggling, all shouting, all in the unrestrained pursuit of a rude athletic exercise. Nothing could be less fitted to excite premature alarm — nothing, therefore, could be more happily devised, under the circumstances, than a stratagem like this; and this was, in fact, the stratagem which the Indians had employed, by which they had obtained possession of the fort, and by which they had been enabled to slaughter and subdue its garrison.[17]

Of ninety troops, about seventy were killed and the remainder captured.

Minweweh made a much more dramatic and successful attack on Fort Michilimackinac than Pontiac mounted against Fort Detroit. Minweweh's famous lacrosse-game ploy is possibly the best known and most sensational of all Indian victories. Had Minweweh been willing to take his warriors to Pontiac's aid, the siege at Detroit might have been successful. Why did he not? Possibly Minweweh was insulted by the actions of the Ottawa at L'Arbre Croche. If the uprising was mainly instigated by Pontiac, 'the Ottawa Chief,' the members of this group to the north were most uncooperative and unsympathetic. One hundred Ottawa forcefully took the British prisoners of Michilimackinac away from the Ojibwa 'to save their lives.' The Ojibwa were 'confounded at beholding the Ottawas espousing a side opposite to their own' and alleged that of all the Indians, the Ottawa of L'Arbre Croche alone were at peace with the British. This was untrue. The Ottawa were mostly disgusted with the Ojibwa for not including them in the attack on the fort and they refused to join the Ojibwa under Minweweh in continuing the war. Thus, when Pontiac's ambassadors requested them to aid in the Detroit siege, they refused.[18] Yet this was not the only reason why Detroit remained intact.

Wabbicommicot could also be considered the 'savior of Fort Detroit.' The fort's commander, Henry Gladwin, was extremely demoralized by the defeat at Bloody Run in which almost two hundred men were lost. By 1 October 1763 his garrison had flour for only three weeks. Moreover, one hundred Miami from the headwaters of the Maumee had arrived to aid Pontiac. At this crucial point, and against the wishes of Pontiac, the Toronto chief asked Gladwin to meet in order to end hostilities. Finding such a divided council, half the Miami immediately parted. In three meetings, 11, 12, and 13 October, 'the powerful old chief laid the groundwork for a general peace.' Such was Wabbicommicot's influence with the nations that on 14 October the Ojibwa turned in six prisoners as evidence of their desire to end the war. Three days later the Potawatomi under Ninivois, the Ojibwa under Wasson, and even some of the Ottawa under Manitou gathered for a peace council with the fort's commander. The Indian war was all but over.[19]

Wabbicommicot had both humanitarian and personal economic reasons for wanting to end the war. He was a friend of Gladwin, who had treated him well and had even shared his dinner table with him. Possibly Wabbicommicot's relationship with Gladwin was similar to Wawatam's friendship with Alexander Henry. Both saved British lives. In a conference with General Thomas Gage, who had replaced Amherst, and Daniel Claus, Johnson's son-in-law, the Toronto chief demonstrated his neutrality and pacifism:

The message consisted of a large String and a Belt of about 2000 Wampum, by the former he expressed his great Concern on account of the present unhappy Disturbances about Detroit, etc., and that he abhorred and detested it and therefore had since the Beginning kept out of the way in the Environs of Cataracqui [Kingston], that at the same Time he was thereby reduced to the greatest distress for want of Necessaries being brought among them, and therefore requested & implored the General [Gage] to let ye Trader La Farge alias Tawaniawe the Swegachie interpreter, who used to supply them heretofore with Necessaries come to his Village this Season that they might not be prevented from this Winter's Hunt for want of Ammunition, etc. – Belt.[20]

Gage was conciliatory. Besides, as a witness of Braddock's ignominious defeat, he displayed a much greater respect for the fighting ability of the Indians. Indeed, Gage had been critical of Amherst's unrealistic suggestion of pursuing scalping parties. 'I despair,' he wrote, 'of any of our parties composed of Rangers only even coming up with the Indians; as none have yet done it in the many pursuits after them since my arrival in this country.' In the current war the equivalent of one-and-a-half British regiments had died or been captured, as had at least two thousand civilians. Gage was justifiably conciliatory. He arranged for Wabbicommicot's delegation's armaments to be mended and he gave them some ammunition, tobacco, and rum along with a good-conduct passport. He was aware, however, that the Mississauga Ojibwa had participated in the war and he was therefore unwilling to send traders among them. Wabbicommicot understood that peace must come before the traders would be permitted into the Great Lakes. Although the Indians had lost considerably fewer men than the British – about eighty to ninety in the Detroit area – the deaths and the lack of trade goods were sufficient 'to open their ears' to peace talks.

In the winter of 1764 plans were made to have a Grand Indian Council at Niagara with all of the warring nations. Johnson, who was to be the British representative, admitted that 'it is our Misfortune that the Indians know too well their own Strength and that it is not in the power of the English alone to punish them effectually.' He even had misgivings about his own safety: 'Straggling Delaware, Mississagaes, etc. who all know of my intended Journey, and are greatly Irritated against me, might be induced to way lay me.'[21] Nevertheless, he arrived at the 'great carrying place' without any threat to his life.

Wabbicommicot was only one of twelve Ojibwa chiefs who attended the conference during the period from July to August 1764. Over two dozen other nations were present, making an impressive total of more than two thousand Indians, 150 of whom were women and children. The predominance of men indicated the uncertainty of the peace talks. Few of the major war chiefs were present since they and 300 warriors had gone up the Miamis River with Pontiac. It is likely that the civil chiefs took charge of the negotiations.

Wabbicommicot, after showing Johnson a pass and certificate from Major Gladwin, spoke with a black belt containing five circles of white wampum which possibly indicated the number of peaceful bands he represented: 'Brother – On my hearing of a Disturbance at Detroit, I went there and found the Indians in that Quarter drunk [killing the British], whereupon I used all my Influence to disperse them, which I effected: – that is the reason of your not Hearing from, or seeing me, and of my leaving my Castle [at Toronto] ... I return you many thanks for the Kindness now shewn us, by allowing us a little Trade.'[22] Wabbicommicot was unwilling to say much more because he did not want to 'add to Johnson's troubles,' but what he said was significant. His claim to having dispersed the hostile tribes in the Detroit siege was not contradicted. Obviously the British respected his actions and owed him a great deal. After thanking the old chief, Johnson produced a belt with a figure representing Niagara's large house and fort, with a road running through it, and with two men holding it on each side. This belt symbolized the commencement of peaceful trade and the treaty ending the half century of war between the English and France's Indian allies. Johnson then asked Wabbicommicot and his people to resettle at their old place of abode near Toronto and to keep a careful eye on the area and protect it. Obviously some hostility still existed. The Seneca had killed almost one hundred soldiers at the great carrying place about a mile below Devil's Hole, and Johnson was calling on the Ojibwa, their ancient enemies and conquerors, to prevent any repetition of this carnage. Wabbicommicot felt highly honoured, and accepted. Sir William then gave medals to him, his

elder brother Estawabey, and his brother-in-law Weynakibio. His
head warriors were also given medals and gorgets, as well as a liberal
supply of goods and rum. The Ojibwa of the Toronto area were
greatly pleased with the preferential treatment shown to them by the
British king's representative.

Johnson's strategy at the conference was obvious. He hoped to
divide the nations, pitting one against the other. In order to show
their loyalty and have trade restored, the warriors were commanded
by the British to participate in a punitive expedition against the
groups that remained hostile. Those who consented received an
ample supply of presents. His tactics were only partly successful. In
August 1764 over 500 Indians set out with John Bradstreet to attack
the Delaware and Shawnee who, along with Pontiac, had not been
to the peace conference. Nevertheless, no more than fifty Ojibwa
participated, possibly because Wabbicommicot did not give his
sanction. Such a military solution to the problem was bound to fail,
mainly because the sympathies of Indian allies were not in the
campaign. Yet the action did serve the important purpose of dividing
the Indian alliance. The final solution to the problem could not be
found in forest warfare, and reconciliation was required.

In the following year, Johnson determined to eliminate Pontiac's
influence through peaceful means. The Ojibwa played a major role
in his plan. In speaking at a general Indian council held at Johnson
Hall in the Mohawk Valley, New York, Johnson announced: 'I
intend to Send a Message to that turbulent Fellow Pondiac by our
brethren the Chippawaes, who have a few days ago signified to me
their good disposition towards Us, & their resolution of maintaining
Peace with the English, & of keeping the Communication to their
Country good & open, so that Trade may be carried on to our
Mutual advantage, as I flatter myself, I can't have as better opportunity than by those People ... [I requested the Ojibwa to] bring
Pontiac to me here & I will plainly point out to him his Interest, &
that of his Nation, & shew him how blind he is to Suffer himself to
be directed & led by the Nose, by a handful of poor Ignorant
People living in so remote a Corner of the Country, that they can
know nothing of what passes in ye World.'[23]

Wabbicommicot was given a large quantity of wampum with
which to make the belt he was to take to Pontiac. Then he spoke on

behalf of his nation: 'Brother Johnson, I have with the utmost attention listened to Your Words & those of the Six Nations etc., and assure You it gives me & my People ye utmost pleasure to find Every thing so peaceable in these parts, & so strict an Union between You & yr. brethren, & I wish it may ever last. For my part I have received a Meddall & Colours [a British flag], etc. from You last Year at niagara, which binds me so to You. Nothing can alter my resolution, be assured I shall communicate without delay what you desire to ye neighbouring Nations, also to *Pondiac, who I think will pay regard to what I shall Say to him, should he not to Yours.*'[24] Wabbicommicot believed that he alone could accomplish what a British army or the powerful words of Johnson could not achieve. He was correct. In 1765, when war threatened to break out again at Detroit because of the death of two soldiers, the Toronto chief enlisted the aid of Kinisshikapoo, a Southern Ojibwa chief. Kinisshikapoo's help was imperative since he had been 'the person who took ye Traders Battoes in 1763 & killed Wendall,' a British trader. Wabbicommicot's influence caused Kinisshikapoo to prevent more bloodshed and to confess to Johnson: 'I acknowledge I have been drunk myself [warlike against the British] which I attribute to this French Medal [taking it off], but notwithstanding, I had always a great Esteem for it I have resolved to give it up since it has made me drunk ... I came here with my Brother Wabbicommicot, to assure you of my fixed resolution to observe & follow your Advice ... (He then delivered up a large French Medal which was later exchanged for a British one).'[25]

In less than two months, the Toronto chief was also successful in pacifying Pontiac, whom the British considered the major war leader. After several preliminary meetings with Johnson's subordinates, Pontiac stood before the British leader of Northern Indian Affairs and addressed him, not on equal terms as 'brother,' which the Toronto chief used, but as 'father.' Nevertheless, he generally spoke as an equal and was treated as a friend rather than an enemy. Johnson seems to have given complete satisfaction, since Pontiac said: 'You have been so good as to bury everything that was or might be disagreeable to us.' There was no evidence of *surrender* on Pontiac's part. In fact, he and most of those who had participated in the hostilities were eventually rewarded with an abundant supply of trade goods, as well as promises that the conditions that led to the war would be corrected. Johnson told the Ojibwa that the British 'have no designs either on your Libertys or possessions. All they require is to live at peace with you, & carry on Trade with the Several Nations. The garrisons are necessary for the Security of Goods & Stores, & will not Affect you, nor will his Majesty Suffer any of his Subjects to oppress you, whilst you live in friendship with him.'[26]

The eminent historian Howard Peckham concluded in 1947 that the Pontiac war 'proved that savages could not defeat civilized men or hold back their settlement of a rich land hunted on by aborigines. Henceforth, the Indians would have to live *with* the white man and adjust themselves to his way of life. From this date the real tragedy of the Indian begins, for he could neither perceive the meaning of Pontiac's *defeat* and thereby prepare for the inevitable change nor obtain an honest and sympathetic policy from the alien government. Indian independence was a lost cause, its banner snatched from Pontiac. The Indian way of life was doomed. Steadily and relentlessly they would be pushed from place to place, generation by generation.'[27] In retrospect, such conclusions seem to be partly correct from the American perspective of the time; but a considerably different interpretation may be given from the contemporary Indian perspective, especially with regard to the future of Indians in what became British North America. First, it is open to question whether the Indians were 'defeated' in this war. Many Southern Ojibwa did not participate in the battles, and those who did were in the most part successful in their campaigns. Indeed, many more lives were lost by the British than the Indians. Second, it is far from being clear that the Indians wished to drive the Europeans from the Great Lakes, and it is likely that they had neither the desire nor the objective of total victory in mind. The object was not to 'defeat civilized man,' but to come to some working relationship with him.

By 1763 an uncomfortable marriage between the European and the Indian had been made and it could not end in divorce. This relationship had periodically broken down and there had been separations in the past, but economic necessity on the part of the Indian had kept the marriage largely intact. By the end of the Seven Years' War the Indian-European relationship had dramatically changed; the French had lost Canada and there was no alternative but to deal with the British. The Indians of the Great Lakes region had punished the Europeans in the past for not conforming to their notion of fair trade and occupancy. They were simply repeating a well-established response in the Pontiac war. It differed from past actions mainly in magnitude. Experience had shown the Indians that the European seemed to respect only force. In 1763 force was again temporarily successful. The Ojibwa and other nations began to receive an abundant supply of presents that had been cut off by Amherst; and they forced the British to establish a policy that at least on the surface was sympathetic to their needs. In addition, there was no substantial and successful military retaliation for the many deaths caused by the Ojibwa and their allies. Indeed, the British, through Johnson, gave many indications that they had been the cause of the conflict and were willing to restore generous trade relations and protect the Indian territory from white encroachment. Most important, their rights to the land had been guaranteed by a Royal Proclamation.[28] The Indians were depending on the honesty and integrity of the British. They had no choice.

Could the words of the British be trusted? There is ample evidence in the military correspondence of the period they could not. There was much frustration over the fact that the hostile Indians could not be punished for the depredations they had caused. The Indians had taken eight forts (St Joseph, Miami, Michilimackinac, Green Bay, Presqu'isle, Le Boeuf, Sandusky, and Venango), and only three remained (Detroit, Niagara, and Pitt). The areas west of the Alleganies, moreover, had been purged of their inhabitants. As late as 1770 Guy Carleton reported that there were only thirty families settled beyond the mountains. The frontiersmen had suffered greatly and wanted vengeance. Since they could not get at those who had caused the devastation, they attacked peaceful Indians who had nothing to do with the Pontiac Uprising. The Conestoga Indians, for example, were massacred in the winter of 1763 by the Paxton Boys, a mob of Pennsylvania settlers. Frontiersmen such as these felt that Indians, instead of receiving presents, should be subjected to extermination. When a convoy carrying such goods neared Fort Loudoun on 7 March 1765, it was attacked by two hundred settlers with their faces blackened. Under such rebellious conditions, British policy and promises to the Indians were difficult to uphold.

Even the military establishment, unable to defeat the Indians in forest warfare, proposed germ and chemical warfare to destroy their foe. In June 1763 Sir Jeffrey Amherst suggested to Colonel Henry Bouquet at Fort Pitt that blankets be infested with smallpox and distributed to the Indians as presents. Bouquet responded that he would try. A few months later, smallpox is known to have played havoc with the enemy groups. Peckham, drawing on William Trent's journal, stated that the smallpox epidemic was attributable not to Bouquet, but to Captain Simeon Ecuyer, who gave the Delaware chiefs two blankets and a handkerchief from the smallpox hospital. Bernhard Knollenberg in 'General Amherst and Germ Warfare' claims that some British officers might be charged with what Parkman called a 'detestable' intent. But execution of the intent is not supported even by circumstantial evidence, and there is no indication that the British had a policy of eliminating the Indians through disease. Another alternative, proposed by Major Gladwin, was chemical warfare: 'The free sale of rum will destroy them more effectually than fire and sword.' There is more evidence to indicate that this became the government's method of dealing with potential uprisings. In 1761 traders had been forbidden to carry, sell, or give strong liquor to the Indians, but on 27 April 1763 Bouquet was calculating the expense and equipment required for 375 packhorses to carry 18,000 gallons of liquor to Fort Pitt. Again, given the social disintegration caused by alcoholism among the Indians, it is possible that there was an unwritten policy in this regard following the peace and the resumption of trade.

Although Johnson liberally distributed liquor as much as the other Europeans, he had a certain degree of respect for the Indians, especially the Iroquois. His relationship with the influential Mohawk Molly Brant resulted in an understanding and sympathy for the Indians that few Europeans possessed. As superintendent of the northern Indians, he was the most influential European in contact with the indigenous people, especially after Amherst was replaced by Gage as commander-in-chief of North America in the critical year of 1763. Johnson was the officer most responsible for preventing a useless attempt at retribution for the almost 2500 deaths resulting from the Indian uprising. Fortunately, after his death in 1774 his methods of dealing with the Indians were carried on by his son John and his sons-in-law Guy Johnson and Daniel Claus. Johnson in 1764 was concerned with the growing misconception among British officials that the Ojibwa and other Indians considered themselves 'subjects of the crown.' In writing privately to Gage, he attempted to clarify this point:

You may be assured that none of the Six Nations, Western Indians, etc. ever declared themselves to be Subjects, or will ever consider themselves in that light whilst they have any Men, or an open Country to retire to, the very Idea of Subjection would fill them with horror – Indeed I have been Just looking into the Indian Records, where I find in the Minutes of 1751 that those who made ye Entry Say, that Nine different Nations acknowledged themselves to be his Majestys Subjects, altho I sat at that Conference, made entrys of all the Transactions, in which there was not a Word mentioned, which could imply a Subjection, however, these matters ... seem not to be well known at home [in Britain], and therefore, it may prove of dangerous consequence to persuade them that the Indians have agreed to things which are so repugnant to their Principles that the attempting to enforce it, must lay the foundation of greater Calamities than has yet been experienced in this County, – it is necessary to observe that no Nation of Indians have any word which can express, or convey the Idea of Subjection.

This letter to the commander-in-chief exposed several factors which were and would be important in the lives of the Southern Ojibwa. First, the Indians did not have the same understanding as Europeans of the word 'subjection.' Therefore, what had been written down in the treaties, such as their being 'subjects of the crown,' had not been clearly comprehended by the Indians. In the eyes of the Indians they had given little in these grand councils, but in the eyes of the British they had given a great deal. Such misunderstanding would continue to be a major problem for generations to come. Second, after one of the worst Indian wars against the Europeans in the history of North America, Johnson admitted that greater calamities could occur in the future if the indigenous people were treated as 'subjects.' If the average fur trader, the soldier at the posts, the government official, and especially the pioneer had had the empathy, humanity, and understanding that Johnson demonstrated, it is possible that serious cultural clashes could have been avoided in the future. The Southern Ojibwa and other Indians could and did trust Johnson, but he had considerably less control over his people on the frontier than the chiefs had over theirs. Was Pontiac correct when he confided in M. de St Ange, commandant at the Illinois: 'The English are the most cruel of enemies, with whom there is no guarantee for any conventions they might enter into as to what regards their country and who conceal their resentment until they would have an opportunity to satisfy it'?[29]

During the first few decades after the Pontiac Uprising the British made a study of concealing their resentment. The last thing they wanted was an expensive Indian war. Accommodating the Indians was the keystone of the military and Indian departments during the postwar period. No protection was extended to any settlers who crossed into the Indian Territory. Indeed, it was government policy to let Indian customs prevail in such cases rather than British law. The proclamation of 1763, involving the protection of Indian lands, could not be easily enforced by the British on the frontier. For the time being, the Indians were permitted to drive settlers off their land with impunity.[30] In this context, the Beaver War had been successful, but storms loomed on the horizon.

5

THE PEACEFUL CONQUEST
'We Have Melted Away Like Snow'

Before the Pontiac war there seemed to be a serious effort on the part of the government to control, if not eliminate, the distribution of liquor to the Indians. After the war, rum flowed freely and increasingly became the main method of appeasing (if not destroying) Indian militancy. It was the indispensable product sold by the uncontrolled traders who multiplied among the Southern Ojibwas, eroding their will to resist. The highest officials in the Indian Department made their fortunes through the trade in spirits, even though they knew they were weakening Indian morale as well as their physical and intellectual fiber. Alcoholism in itself, however, was not the primary problem but a symptom of a much deeper and broader social upheaval involving their growing lack of control over their own destiny in the last half of the eighteenth century. While they had not been militarily defeated in the Pontiac war, the events in 1763 dramatically demonstrated that the English had become the only source of the supplies which had become absolutely necessary for their existence.

Ironically, the Beaver War had been fought because the English were parsimonious in the distribution of presents, but in the end those presents, with too much liquor and too little ammunition, almost resulted in the disintegration of the Ojibwa as a people. Factionalism increased and they no longer could unite for an adequate length of time to solve a common threat to their well-being. Even throughout southern Ontario, Ojibwa disunity occurred. This was partly a result of cultural diversity caused by the European trade. The degree of dependence on trade goods was not the same for every band. Those near the trading posts on the north shore of Lake Ontario showed more signs of cultural disintegration than the isolated bands on Georgian Bay.

Those who were most influenced by the negative aspects of European encroachment were the first to show resistance. Shortly after the Pontiac war, settlers again began to flow into the Ohio Valley. Many of the Ojibwa and their allies attempted to stem the tide by participating in two major confrontations: the War of Independence and, finally, the War of 1812. A basic cause of the American Revolution was the frustration experienced by settlers as a result of the Royal Proclamation of 1763 which restricted their movement into the Indian country. During and especially after the revolution, the 'Westward Movement' increased in intensity and speed. This caused those Indians who had been weakened by the Americans to flee farther west and particularly into southern Ontario, where they were welcomed by their Ojibwa allies. The United Empire Loyalists, also allies of the Ojibwa, came in great numbers too and were permitted to settle among them. These Loyalist guests proved to be their worst enemy. However, pioneer encroachment did not influence all of the Southern Ojibwa negatively at the same time. It took over half a century before most of the Ojibwa hunting and fishing grounds were threatened. When their very homeland became inundated by this multitude which consumed their natural resources, the Southern Ojibwa could do little but accept the foreign power.

The colonial conflict involving the Anglo-Saxons continued after the establishment of the United States. While neither the British nor the Americans could claim victory or would admit defeat in the War of 1812, this was not true of the Ojibwa of southern Ontario. By the end of the war, nothing remained of Tecumseh's confederacy, which aimed at collectively defending their lands. The Southern Ojibwa bands had been some of the strongest supporters of the confederacy. Nawash, the head chief south of Georgian Bay, pronounced its epitaph in 1814: 'Since our Great Chief Tecumtha has been killed we do not listen to each other, we do not rise together. We hurt ourselves by it.'[1] With such division, confederacy lands could be taken without any British war of expansion. It was a peaceful conquest.

By 1780 the fur trade had not only rendered the Mississauga of the Lake Ontario region dependent on the white man, it had also divided the Southern Ojibwa into 'back' and 'lake' Indians. The back Indians could be described as those less-assimilated Ojibwa who lived north beyond Lake Ontario, and the lake Indians as those more assimilated Ojibwa who lived in close proximity to the European traders and soldiers in the Lower Great Lakes. The former were better protected from, less pampered by, and less dependent on Europeans than the latter. The degree of difference varied according to their willingness to accept the Europeans, their distance from them, and the intensity of contact with them. In retrospect both groups, from the 1760s on, should have surmounted their differences, tried to gain back some of their self-sufficiency, and made a common front to resist the complete loss of their territory.

For the Ojibwa on the north shore of Lake Ontario, such actions seemed impossible. The extent to which the lake Ojibwa had become dependent on the European is well illustrated in a speech by chief Wabbicommicot to Johnson:

Brother, I hope you'll excuse our appearing in this dress, as our poverty prevents us from coming before you in a better; you may observe the Days are now clear, & the Sun burns bright, therefore, I should be very glad to wear a hat to defend me from its heat.

Brother, I have tried several times with my Hands to catch fish for my living but found it would not answer; therefore I should be glad to have a Spear to kill them with; I am likewise prevented from hunting by reason of my Guns being broke.

Brother, I have discovered a fine Tree which I should be desirous to cut down for firing, but for want of an ax I am necessitated to make a fire at its roots in order to burn it down.[2]

At the time, those who were fearful of the Indians wished that all of them required such a reliance on the British. Under such beggarly conditions there was obviously little that they, as enemies, could do. On 17 July 1767 the Toronto chief visited the Indian agent, Norman McLoud, at Niagara, 'but was so drunk that no one could understand him' until two days later.[3] The following year he was dead. This was likely indicative of the alcoholism which had begun to spread in a devastating manner among some of the Ojibwa of southern Ontario. Undoubtedly, alcoholics made poor warriors as well as poor hunters.

Such behaviour was not typical of the back-country Ojibwa. When Nanebeaujou, one of the great chiefs of southern Georgian Bay, visited Ferrall Wade, the trader at Toronto, on 22 September 1771, he called Monoghquit, the chief who had replaced Wabbi-commicot, to a grand council. The latter arrived with twenty of his warriors. The principal chief, who 'had made' Monoghquit a sachim of the Toronto Indians, admonished him in no uncertain terms. First, he called the Toronto chief and his people slaves of the British, and indicated that the foreigners must despise them since they did not hunt for their furs like they, the back-country Ojibwa did. They begged rum from the visiting Indians from the north and drank at the post with the white men rather than take the liquor to their village to drink among themselves, which was the Ojibwa custom. Nanebeaujou criticized them particularly for stealing six kegs of rum from two traders and demanded that they be repaid. When they indicated that liquor had caused their bad behaviour and that in their weakened state they were greatly afraid of their former enemy, the Seneca, he said they were fools and 'women.' He reminded them that if they were in danger they could come to his people where he would provide them with corn and protect them against the Seneca. In the meantime, since it was September, he told them to go to their hunting grounds. They hung down their heads, admitted that they had been wrong, and complied with his commands. Such condemnation of one chief by another in the company of their warriors, and especially a European, was extraordinary. It called into question, moreover, the generally accepted belief that the Ojibwa villages maintained total autonomy.[4]

Monoghquit's embarrassing confrontation exposes a great deal about the cultural revolution that his people were experiencing. It is obvious that those Indians in southern Ontario to the north of Toronto differed considerably from those on the lake. The former seemed to have retained their relative independence, pride, strength, integrity, customs, and sobriety which the latter were rapidly losing as a result of more intensive contact with the traders and soldiers nearby. The lake Ojibwa stayed near the forts and trading posts, which supplied them with food in exchange for gathering wood and other odd jobs. They traded single pelts, especially, for rum. In contrast, the back Ojibwa, around Lake Simcoe and southern Georgian Bay, made infrequent trips to the posts, usually in the spring and fall, and traded with large quantities of furs. As a result, the degree and intensity of contact with the Europeans and exposure to alcohol created dramatic cultural differences among the Ojibwa. This difference in acculturation became evident to the casual observer as the eighteenth century drew to an end. Lady Simcoe, the wife of the lieutenant governor, described the back Ojibwa as 'extremely handsome with a superior air,' similar to figures painted by the old masters and speaking in the stately style of the ancient Greeks or Romans. They had no great longing for liquor. The Ojibwa around York (Toronto) and Kingston, however, she described 'unwarlike, idle, drunken and dirty.'

For most Ojibwa, relations with the whites in the late 1760s and 1770s were almost exclusively with traders. The majority of them were 'the very scum off the earth, and their treatment of the Indians was such as hardly to be suitable for description.'[5] Fur trader David Ramsay, for example, caused the greatest discontent among the Southern Ojibwa.

Ramsay's relations with the Southern Ojibwa exemplify both the life of the Ojibwa and their interaction with the Europeans at that time. Two divergent oral traditions, one by the Indians and the other by the European settlers in Ontario, have been recorded involving his activities. One account will be pitted against the other in an attempt to determine the ways in which each viewed the past.

The major incident involved several Ojibwa being killed in 1772 by Ramsay near Kettle Creek, not far from present-day Port Stanley on Lake Erie. The pioneer tradition of the events was given by Mrs Frederick Mabee, one of the first settlers at Turkey Point in 1793. She stated that 'the Indians, nine in number, seized Ramsay's liquors and other goods, and after becoming crazed with "fire-water," bound Ramsay hand and foot and determined on burning him alive. The attack was made in the night, and before the preparation for the burning was completed, the savage spirit succumbed to the liquid spirit of Christian civilization, and they decided to wait until morning. Eight of them stretched out in a drunken snooze around the fire, and the ninth was detailed to guard the prisoner. On this occasion Ramsay was accompanied by his nephew – a mere lad, whom the savages did not molest. During the night the boy secured a knife and severed the thongs which bound his uncle; and when thus freed, Ramsay made short work in sending his drunken captors to the "happy hunting ground," and made good his escape.'[6]

This tale of a 'pioneer hero,' protecting his property against overwhelming odds of 'savages,' is in sharp contrast with the Ojibwa tradition. The Mississauga Peter Jones recorded their interpretation of the events: 'I have been informed by some of the Indians, that on one occasion Ramsay was with a small party of Indians on the shore of Lake Erie. Ramsay had some rum which the Indians demanded; on being denied, they took and tied him hand and foot, and then took his fire-water, and having freely drank, all became perfectly helpless. Ramsay then got an Indian to untie him, after which he took a hatchet and killed all the adult Indians on the spot. He afterwards surrendered himself to the authorities, such as there were in those days, and was allowed, according to Indian custom, to make an atonement for his crime, by paying the relatives of those he killed a certain amount in goods and rum.'[7]

The major contrast between these accounts is that Jones does not say (as the English source does) that the Ojibwa were 'savages' intent on burning Ramsay. Indeed, it was the Indians, not his nephew, who released him. Moreover, Ramsay's refusal of rum was an unpardonable breach of forest diplomacy. It has already been noted that the distribution of free rum and presents was a well-established tradition which permitted Europeans to move into the Indian country. Both accounts, however, are incomplete and lack the true horror of Ramsay's actions, as the records of his own account reveal.

In Ramsay's declaration at Niagara on 15 May 1772, he confessed that on the night of the full moon in March on Kettle Creek he not only killed a man, Wandagan, but two women as well. He also kidnapped two of their children, one about twelve years old. In April he was discovered by some Ojibwa near Long Point after lying to them by saying that the children with him were English. He was tied and placed by the fire. He then escaped and killed four adults and a child. In both cases he claimed he was defending his life and property. Johnson, who read Ramsay's full report and spoke to the Indians involved, believed that the slaughter was not in self-defence. He concluded that 'the Murder of two Women and Child, and the *Scalping* them afterwards is inexcusable and the Circumstance of his being able to do all this, is an evident proof that he was not in the danger he represents, & that the Indians were too much in Liquor.'[8] In a letter to Frederick Haldimand, temporary commander-in-chief, Johnson indicated that scalping by Indians was always considered a declaration of war. He also observed that 'the few Acts [of murder that the Indians] committed compared with what they suffer are nothing, especially when we consider that they are [considered] a People without Laws or Authority and that we pretend to both, tho as they say we Manifest neither.'[9] Johnson would be the first to admit that the Ramsay affair was a perfect example of a white man, not an Indian, being a 'savage.' Indeed, this incident was so serious that some Ojibwa considered Ramsay's scalping a declaration of war by the British on their nation.

There was great fear that this atrocity would result in a general Indian war in the Great Lakes if the correct action was not taken. The Ramsay murders occurred among the band of Ojibwa who had been hostile to the British in the Pontiac Uprising. They were not within the jurisdiction of the famous peacekeeper, Wabbicommicot, whose people had been loyal and helpful to the British for over a decade. The relatives and friends of the murdered Ojibwa formed a band which lived on Kettle Creek, less than fifty kilometres from the Thames River. The principal chief of the Thames, therefore, had some jurisdiction over the band in question. During the Indian War in 1763 the head chief was Sekahos, who had gathered 170 warriors, including the Kettle Creek band, to aid in the attack on Lieutenant Cuyler at Point Pelee, to destroy Wilkins's reinforcements at Pointe aux Pins, and to lay siege to Detroit with Pontiac. War belts again passed among the Ojibwa in 1772. Ferrall Wade, Johnson's trading partner at the Toronto post, informed his patron that about eighty Ojibwa men, with women and children, had come to him, indicating 'how sore there hearts was at Losing so Many people.' From his Indian friends there he received disturbing intelligence that some Ojibwa were going to Lake Erie to take revenge, but they would not 'bloody' Lake Ontario. He gave them rum and a considerable number of presents in an attempt to distract them. His actions were only partly successful. Some Mississauga-Ojibwa went to Lake Erie 'fully Determined to Cut off any English they Can Meet,' but a delegation also went to Johnson Hall in an attempt to settle the problem peacefully. Wade advised Johnson that a war would be inevitable without his taking speedy measures by meeting with them personally. He, himself, was taking no chances since he quickly moved to Fort Niagara for protection. [10]

Johnson took the Toronto trader's advice. In a conference with the offended Ojibwa he said that the affair was the 'private act of a villain' and not the accepted policy of the British. He gave them 'a Valuable present with provisions, & a battoe to carry them back.' This included twenty gallons of common rum. The 'present' was in addition to the £50 of goods given to them at Toronto by Johnson's trading partners. He then instructed Major Etherington to send troops to Detroit and Niagara, and to have the commander of Niagara send the prisoner Ramsay down to Montreal for trial. The superintendent of northern Indian affairs believed that the trader 'deserves Capital punishment.' Retaliation by the Southern Ojibwa was expected and, as a precaution, all traders were called into the military posts and not permitted to leave until they were given the word. Not being satisfied by what he had accomplished with the delegation that spoke with him at Johnson Hall, Sir William went to Niagara to appease all the Ojibwa chiefs. His opening words to them set the tone: 'It was with great Concern that I heard from Amenibijou and the rest of your People, that so many of your Nation have been lately killed by one of ours. – The General who Commands all the Kings Army and all the English are much enraged at it.' Again presents and rum were distributed to the Ojibwa to 'cover the graves' of the slain.

Word of the Indian deaths spread quickly to many nations, often in exaggerated form. The Caughnawaga in Quebec knew of the tragedy before 3 July 1772, and by then the death count had expanded to ten. Such fabrication created problems for the Indian Department. The Huron were requested by Captain Stephenson at Fort Detroit to deliver one of their warriors who had killed a trader at Sandusky, but they responded by saying they would wait to see what the English did with Ramsay. They added that most of these murders were caused by the intoxication of the Indians and it was the fault of the English who provided the rum. It was difficult to overcome such logical arguments, as Johnson admitted. By 27 August 1772, however, he could say that 'the murder of the Mississauga by the Trader would have proved of immediate Ill Consequence, but for my Interposition.'[11] It cost the government dearly in presents to prevent an uprising.

It is important to note that the Ojibwa chief, whose granddaughter was killed by Ramsay, did not request Johnson to enforce capital punishment for the murders: 'We don't Desire the Death of the man Who has murdered our friends much less that of Any Englishman, but rest Entirely on your Interposition in this affair.' He was most anxious, however, to know Johnson's decision on the matter and provided him with a messenger, their 'greatest' warrior, Messekias. Johnson, nevertheless, felt that such cruelty should be punished by death, but he had his doubts whether there could be a fair trial. Knowing there would be great sympathy for an Indian killer in New York, he sent Ramsay to Montreal, but even there Johnson did not 'think he will Suffer, had he killed a Hundred.'[12]

Why was the death sentence not insisted upon by the Southern Ojibwa? Peter Jones has already provided us with one reason – it was Ojibwa tradition to atone for a death by paying the relatives in goods and rum. This was also implied by the Indian relatives who expressed their desire to Johnson through their speaker: 'I hope You don't think that we have Anything bad in our hearts on account of our faces being Coloured black, we assure You we have not, & that they are as white as Snow, it is for want of paint that we have painted black.' Blackened faces were a traditional sign of mourning which Johnson understood. The apology for not having white paint was simply a polite way of asking for goods to 'cover the graves' of the dead. Their request was abundantly successful, as we have seen. However, Johnson's political mind provided an additional explanation: 'The Indians may not desire him to be punished, to avail themselves thereof whenever they Murder any of our people.' It is no wonder that Johnson wanted to see British justice rule, but unfortunately his prediction was correct about the trial. Ramsay received no punishment in the courts, partly because the prosecution provided no Indian witnesses.[13]

Ramsay, while in prison, bragged about his murders and indicated that once he was released he would repeat the action. He may have been successful. When John Long was in the Michilimackinac area in the late 1780s, he heard from the local traders of 'an extraordinary escape which a Mr. Ramsay and his brother had from a tribe of the nation of the Poes, in their way to St. Joseph.' The account is similar in some respects to the murders committed in southern Ontario. Ramsay was captured, tied up, cut loose, and killed several Indians too drunk to protect themselves. There are several details, however, which differ from the account of the murders in 1772. Ramsay was 'dragged out of his canoe, and carried on shore,' and permitted to make his 'death-feast' and a speech. Later the commanding officer at Michilimackinac congratulated him on his fortunate escape. Was this a repetition of his earlier homicidal act or was it simply a new version of his murders in southern Ontario? Donald Smith, who thoroughly researched the subject, failed to note Long's account, but simply indicated that Indians unsuccessfully attempted to take revenge on Ramsay. The homicidal trader must have sufficiently 'atoned' for his crimes, since he later was accepted among the southern Ontario Ojibwas. However, one of the sons of those whom he murdered did not forget. After failing in an attempt to kill Ramsay in 1794, he was suspected of being one of those Ojibwa who killed four people in the new settlement on Lake Erie. He was caught wearing clothing from one of the dead persons and put on trial, but later acquitted. Johnson had indicated that vengeance was often committed on the innocent many years after. The Ramsay affair vividly demonstrates the type of Europeans that the Southern Ojibwa had as 'models of civilization,' and the difficulty of bringing British law to southern Ontario in the last half of the eighteenth century.

One may conclude in spite of the violence that the realities of the Indian administration in the Great Lakes were fulfilling the objectives of the white pioneers. Amherst considered the Indians 'only fit to live with the Inhabitants of the Woods being more nearly allied with the Brute than the Human Creation.'[14] He, and many others, saw no place for such 'brutes' in a civilization that was rapidly expanding westward into their territory. Extermination, not reconciliation, was his policy. But a military solution was found to be both expensive and ineffective. Major Gladwin's proposal of free trade in rum, 'more effective than fire and sword,' was proving to be the final solution. Major Henry Basset at Detroit in 1773 reported that 'the Chiefs complain much of the intention of the English to kill all their young men [with liquor], it prevents their hunting, by letting such quantities of spirits go out amongst them, and hurts the trade very much, for instead of that Poison when they return from their winter, they would purchase blankets, shrowdings etc. The Chiefs declare they loose more of their young men by Rum than they used to do by war, & I imagine from what I can learn, are discontented.'[15] The free supply of rum by unscrupulous traders destroyed the power of the Ojibwa and their allies without creating any great expense on the part of the government in loss of soldiers and money.

Violent acts, including murder, were common in the Great Lakes during the last decade of Johnson's Indian administration, but they were more likely to involve Indians killing their own people while in a drunken state. The vast majority of cases involving even whites never saw the courts. Unimplemented regulations did exist: 'Trading with the Indians was only permitted under the Cannon of the Forts and before the Governor of a province granted a trading license he made the Trader enter into Bond to Obey all Instructions sent by the superintendent.' In the instructions it was not considered good policy to get the Indians drunk and then take all their furs. In 1767 alone over seven hundred men in 121 canoes entered the Great Lakes with over £38,964 sterling in merchandise. There were considerably more illegal traders, such as Ramsay, who had no permission at all to trade. The results, reported at Fort Niagara, were not uncommon. Ojibwa came to the post 'naked and destitute of Everything, having Sold their Skins at Toronto for Rum.' Johnson was in charge of Indian relations in the Great Lakes area, but his hands were often tied by colonial governors who were petitioned by the fur-trade lobby: 'The general regulations of trade attempted to be carried into execution by the superintendents are asserted in these petitions to be ill-suited to the particular circumstances of the several provinces, and to serve rather to clog the trade with useless and vexatious restrictions than to remove the evils of which complaint has been made.' The regulations were ineffective, and illegal trade practices continued beyond the canon of the forts. [16]

Toronto was no exception. Although Wabbicommicot in 1767 brought in those traders found in his jurisdiction and had them arrested at Niagara, the nefarious trade continued. Three years later Ferrall Wade and his translator, Peter Keiuser, did a lucrative business in stiff competition at the same location. They arrived with trade goods consisting 'almost entirely of rum.' They were likely knowledgeable about the regulations that had been established six years earlier, when prices had been set. For one beaver an Indian was to receive one of the following: a ruffled shirt, a blanket, a roll of gartering, 300 wampum beads, one pound of vermillion, a steel beaver trap, a bed gown, twelve silver broaches, or a gallon of rum. Few, if any, heeded the regulations. On first arriving at Toronto, Wade traded a gallon of rum for '18 Musquash skins, 1 fisher, 1 Deer Skin, 1 pr. of Deer Skin Stockgs, a Verry fine Salmon, with half a Dozen Eels.' He was considered very honest by the local Indians, who informed him when he was in danger. It is astonishing to find that Wade and Keiuser were partners with, and outfitted by, Johnson, who had established the rules of trade which he and his associates were disregarding.

This 'free-trade' environment existed because the British military officials saw no need for an effective government policy to keep the Indians as allies, as had been the case in the wars between the English and the French in America. Johnson had no weapon but persuasion while crimes and retaliation went on unchecked. The numerous English traders had little understanding of the Indian mentality. One, for example, while drinking with the Ojibwa, held his head down and dared them to kill him, 'which the Indian readily complied with.'[17] Under such conditions, the loyalty to the British, the contentment of the various Ojibwa bands, and the degree of tranquillity in the Great Lakes depended to a considerable extent on the acceptability of the local English trader. Each band of Indians and each trader determined the law 'or lawlessness' among themselves. Because of this situation, the unity of the Ojibwa Nation was not enhanced. These various bands, therefore, were less prepared to withstand the impact that would hit them in the last decades of the eighteenth century.

With the Quebec Act of 1774 and the death of Johnson in that same year, the Ojibwa were no longer able to determine their own destiny in southern Ontario. In the following year the American Revolution began. British Indian policy, which attempted to prevent the westward movement of settlers, played no small measure in bringing about that confrontation. The immediate events of the revolutionary war were not conducted in the Great Lakes, however, and the Ojibwa were able to control their degree of participation in it. Their military involvement was considerably less intensive than that of the Six Nations but more active than the Moravian-Delaware who mainly remained pacifists because of the missionaries among them. The Ojibwa of southern Ontario were most fortunate in that they were not geographically located in the middle of the conflict. While most remained neutral, some Ojibwa expressed their willingness to join the British side as early as 1776 and fought under Captain William Caldwell. Other tribes wished to avoid the conflict, but could not. The Six Nations and the Delaware did not share the geographic isolation of the Ojibwa and suffered greatly. Since the three Indian nations – the Iroquois, Delaware, and Ojibwa – would eventually have their destinies intimately intertwined in southern Ontario, a brief explanation of the Indians' role in that war is required.

'One of the most confused polemical aspects of the War for American Independence concerned the decision by the British and Americans to employ Indian warriors as combatants.'[18] Most Indians preferred to remain neutral, and some delighted in the fact that their English enemies were killing each other. Both the British and the Americans eventually put great pressure on the Indians to join their respective side in the war. The British were much more successful, especially with the Six Nations, because of their experienced Indian Department, their years of distributing presents, and their claims that they were attempting to hold back the pioneers from Indian lands. The Ottawa, Chippewa, and Potawatomi were attracted to the British flag under the leadership of Chaminitawaa, who shared in the distribution of 17,520 gallons of rum in 1779 at Detroit alone![19] The Americans, nevertheless, were more skilful in fabricating Indian atrocity stories to gain support in the Thirteen Colonies against the British. Such inflamed propaganda and unjust American retaliation influenced the southern Ojibwa to join the British.

The so-called Massacre of Wyoming in 1778 was considered the greatest atrocity committed by the British and their Indian allies in the war. Egerton Ryerson in *The Loyalists of America* (1880) thoroughly examined the accounts. Two of the American interpretations stated that the massacre was 'a mere marauding, cruel, and murderous invasion of an inoffensive and peaceful settlement ... the inhabitants, men, women, and children, were "indiscriminately butchered" by the 1,100 men, 900 being their Indian allies.' Ryerson, after thoroughly researching the topic, was convinced that only soldiers were killed in battle and that the accounts 'published by the Congress party were of the most exaggerated and inflammatory character, containing the grossest misrepresentation, and doing the greatest injustice.'[20] After the battle of Wyoming, the Seneca especially were interested in destroying farms and crops, but with some justification other than simply retribution. The 75-square-mile area was 'their' land and had never been surrendered or paid for by the 6000 Wyoming pioneer squatters in the valley. It was considered the best Seneca hunting ground. Aside from the land question, the Seneca had more recent causes of irritation. The settlers of Wyoming had seized a peaceful party of their nation, put them in prison, and later killed and scalped two men and a woman. It was these Seneca, likely with some southern Ontario Ojibwa, that made up the party of 300 Indians and 200 rangers who killed 227 Americans, but refrained from killing women and children in the so-called Wyoming Massacre.

Admittedly, the Indians took the scalps from the dead soldiers. This action was used by the Americans to create an elaborate propaganda message in order to convince their own people of the cruelty of the British allies. When the Seneca villages were later overrun by the Americans, the latter claimed that they found a message with eight large packages containing the scalps of 43 Congress soldiers, 98 farmers killed in their houses, 97 farmers killed in the fields, 102 farmers burned alive and tortured in various ways, 88 women, 193 boys, 211 girls, 122 mixed but containing 29 infants' scalps. The message indicated that these were to be sent to the king of England. Such fictitious reporting did much to create a tremendous hatred in the minds of most Americans for all Indians, and contributed substantially to the growing belief among some of them that 'the only good Indian is a dead Indian.'

In the hysteria which followed, the Americans in 1779 attempted to exterminate the Six Nations after the Wyoming defeat. The Americans, with 6500 men, were as unsuccessful in taking Iroquois lives as Frontenac's invasion of their lands had been a hundred years earlier, but the destruction of their forty towns and 160,000 bushels of corn was complete. General John Sullivan, the American commander of the expedition, lost forty-two killed or missing and three wounded, while the Iroquois lost five with three wounded. Sullivan's 'victorious troops amused themselves by scalping the dead, and in two cases actually skinned the bodies of Indians from the hips downward, to make boot tops or leggings.' Five thousand famished Iroquois were forced to take refuge at Niagara. With the British already short of rations and war matériel, it was difficult for the Six Nations to continue the war. Indeed, some of their officers, such as Guy Johnson, compounded the problem by embezzling funds. The government auditors indicated that he was in collusion with the local merchants: 150 rifles were debited against government accounts when the entry should have been fifty, and 1156 kettles were charged to the king when the number should have been 156. Under such conditions, the Six Nations were eventually forced to seek protection on Ojibwa land in southern Ontario.

The case of the Moravian Delaware was considerably different. These Christian Delaware were peaceful and retained almost a complete neutrality throughout the war, while the Iroquois had conducted several campaigns against the Americans. Colonel David Williamson, leading 160 incensed American militia, appeared to approach the Delaware town of Gnadenhutten on the Muskingum River peacefully. There he found the famished people busy salvaging corn before they left the location, which had become a dangerous war zone. Williamson and his soldiers

assured them of sympathy in their great hunger and their intention to escort them to food and safety. Without suspicion, only thankful that they need not perish in Sandusky [where the main body of their tribe had gone for safety], the Christians agreed to go with them and after consultations, hastened to the Salem fields to bring in their friends. The militia relieved the Indians of their guns and knives, promising to restore them later. The

Christians felt safe with these friendly men whose interest in their welfare seemed genuine.

Too late they discovered the Americans' treachery. Once defenseless, they were bound and charged with being warriors, murderers, enemies and thieves, having in their possession horses, branding irons, tools, axes, dishes, all articles used by whites and not common to Indians. [These of course were purchased for them by their missionaries.] After a short night of prayer and hymns ... twenty-nine men, twenty-seven women, and thirty-four children were ruthlessly murdered. Pleas, in excellent English, from some of the kneeling Christians, failed to stop the massacre. Only two escaped by feigning death before the butchers had completed their work of scalping.[21]

The survivors of the Moravian mission fled to Detroit where they had previously established good relations with the sympathetic Ojibwa and English. They too would soon move to southern Ontario, along with the Iroquois, and spread the news of the atrocities committed by the 'Long Knives.'

While the Moravians' religious belief prevented them from retaliating, no such restrictions held back the Southern Ojibwa. The Americans, elated by the ease with which they had accomplished their foul deed of murder, declared their intention to march against Sandusky to repeat their actions there. Their intention became known at Detroit. Caldwell, with his company and the lake Indians, was ordered to march to the assistance of the Indians at that place. His 70 rangers, 44 lake Indians, and 150 Wyandot of Sandusky were reinforced by McKee's 140 Shawanese. They were able to kill 250 of the 500 mounted riflemen, most of whom were involved in the massacre.[22] The relatively small number of Southern Ojibwa participating in this campaign is indicative of their general neutrality in the American Revolution. However, the impact that these warriors had on the majority of Ojibwa must have been significant.

The massacre of ninety Moravians, two-thirds of whom were women and children, and the retreat of almost all of the Iroquois Nation, the Ojibwas' most formidable traditional enemy, must have caused extreme fear and confusion among the Ojibwa of southern Ontario. The diabolical actions of the frontiersmen and the military power of the new republic fully demonstrated the formidable powers opposed to their way of life. They likely believed, with much justification, that what had happened to those nations could soon happen to them. Under such conditions they were willing to accept any Indian support, even from the Iroquoian-speaking peoples who sought refuge among them.

The first to seek refuge were the Six Nations. They came as a defeated people, having been driven out of their homeland. More than any other event in the revolution, Sullivan's expedition had broken the power of the Iroquois. As Ryerson stated, possibly with only some exaggeration, 'all the devastations of settlements, burnings, and slaughter committed by the "Tories and Indians" during the whole war shrink into insignificance in regard to extent of territory, the number of inhabitants and towns, the extent of cultivated farms and gardens, when compared with General Sullivan's one vast sweep of ruin and misery.' The fleeing 5000 Iroquois had been forced to live off the rations at Niagara for the duration of the war. Other refugee loyalists were also putting an enormous pressure on the fort, which had to supply 20,000 rations per day. Since the 'scandalous' peace treaty that ended the war in 1783 made no provisions for the British Indian allies, land had to be provided immediately for their well-being. The Iroquois chose to settle in the area from which they had driven the Neutral in 1650 and from which they had been driven by the Ojibwa at the end of the seventeenth century. Some chose the Bay of Quinte, but most moved to the Grand River.

At first some dissident Mississauga-Ojibwa were unwilling to receive them because of the friction that might result. After further consideration, however, the Ojibwa chief, Pokquan, announced that since 'we are [all] Indians ... and are bound to help each other ... we are happy to hear that you intend to settle at the River Oswego [the Grand River] ... and hope you will keep your men in good Order, as we shall be in one Neighbourhood, and to live in friendship with each other as Brethren ought to do.'[23] Pokquan obviously believed that even his ancient Iroquois enemies, since they were 'Indians,' were preferable to having European settlers in his lands. He hoped they could provide mutual protection. Joseph Brant, chief of the Six Nations on the Grand River, had a much better understanding of the Europeans than any other Indian at the time, and some Ojibwa were willing to give his people land if Brant would join in protecting them from white encroachment. Pokquan's chieftainship, however, did not include all of the lake Indians of southern Ontario. There were at least three others: Nanibizure (Swan), Wabicanine (Eagle), and Minaghquat (Duck). There is no evidence to indicate that all of them were involved in the decision to permit the Iroquois to settle among the Ojibwa of southern Ontario.

The Iroquois proved to be very questionable allies in the following decades. It is likely that the Ojibwa were to some extent willing to grant land to the Six Nations, but for their exclusive use. Joseph Brant put their 675,000 acres (six miles deep on each side of the Grand River), to a different use. Within a few years he had sold or leased 350,000 acres to white settlers. Although Brant attempted to help the Ojibwa in their land transactions with the government, he was unsuccessful. The Iroquois failed to give substantial support to them in times of crisis. Indeed, this may have led to open hostility between the two groups in the closing decades of the eighteenth century, if one can trust John Long's account of an event which took place near Kingston: 'When I was at Cataraqui [Kingston], the capital of the Loyalist settlements in Canada, a party of Mohawks and Messesawgers accidentally met, and having bartered their skins and peltry with the traders, sat themselves down to drink the rum their merchandise had produced. As the liquor began to operate ... a dispute arose and a Messesawger Indian was killed, and his heart taken out, which the Mohawks intended to have boiled, but they were prevented by a gentleman who accidentally passed by their hut, and prevailed upon them to give it up.'[24] Such hostilities as this could account for the Mississauga, Peter Jones, claiming in the mid-nineteenth century that 'there still is a smothered feeling of hatred and enmity between the two nations; so that when either of them comes within the haunts of the other, they are in constant fear.' In these crucial years, unanimity and cooperation between the two groups would have done much to improve the declining influence of the Southern Ojibwa as well as the Iroquois.

The Delaware were even less helpful. On 12 April 1792, eight years after the Six Nations settled in southern Ontario, the Moravian Delaware moved from their temporary home near Detroit and founded a settlement at Fairfield, far up the Thames River. They, like the Iroquois, had been over-run by settlers in the Ohio valley, and, 'in an effort to get away from Indian war parties and white rum-peddlers,' they moved to what was then a remote part of southern Ontario. Captain Thomas McKee suggested the Fairfield location to the Moravian missionaries and made arrangements with the local Ojibwa. They soon seem to have replaced the Ojibwa in supplying Detroit with products such as maple sugar and berries, but they were most generous when needy local Ojibwa came to their settlement for food. Being pacifists, they were of no military use to the Ojibwa, but as sedentary farmers they, as well as the Iroquois, set an excellent example of the type of life that the Southern Ojibwa would soon be compelled to live.

The Six Nations and the Moravian Delaware who settled in southern Ontario were neither sufficient in numbers nor strongly inclined to aid the Ojibwa and their allies in the struggle for independence against the great wave of Americans flooding into the Ohio valley. As in the Seven Years' War, the peace negotiations following the American War of Independence did not seriously consider the Indians. As a result, in 1783 nineteen Indian nations in the Great Lakes area and to the south united in a defensive alliance so that if one were attacked, all would come to its aid. In 1791, when the Americans crossed the Ohio River, which had been established as the boundary before the American Revolution, over a thousand warriors were ready to push them back. Yet many of the southern Ontario Ojibwa were at first reluctant to join the Indian Confederacy, Lieutenant-Governor John Graves Simcoe observed, since they were 'principally living within the British Line' and were not directly threatened.[25] The Six Nations among them also refused to send warriors. There was some fear that while the Ojibwa warriors were away fighting to the south, their families at home would be attacked by the Iroquois or abused by the militia.

By 1794 scalps and war belts were being sent to the Lake Indians in an attempt to shame them into fighting. A few months later, as 'a consequence of some superstitious circumstances,' the Ojibwa Nation was 'unanimously determined on War.' They attempted to persuade the Moravian Delaware to join them in battle, but without success. By 5 July the Ojibwa were the most active warriors in an attack against the advancing troops of General Anthony Wayne's army. In the first successful confrontation, the Macinac and Lake Indians 'completed their belts,' having taken many scalps and prisoners. But the lack of food and ammunition prevented their continued participation. After killing a patrol of almost three hundred men, they had foolishly attempted to storm a fort, which resulted in the loss of sixteen or seventeen warriors and as many wounded. This was considered a great loss to them in warfare.

Smallpox as well continued to take more lives than the American bullets. At Chicago alone fifty Ojibwa died of the disease. While the warriors returned home, the chiefs stayed to watch the movements of Wayne's army so that if the warriors were needed, they could be called. This proved to be a major error. By September, Wayne claimed a victory at the Battle of Fallen Timbers, where at nearby Fort Miami the British refused to aid their Indian allies. In greatly exaggerated form, Wayne bragged in the peace talks with the Western Indians that 'in return for the *few drops* of Blood we lost upon that occasion, we caused *Rivers* of yours to flow.' Since the British supplied only small quantities of food and ammunition, and no soldiers, in this campaign, their Indian allies could not succeed. Resentment grew. In the battle of Tippecanoe several years later the same problem of supply existed, but at that confrontation the Indians lost only twenty-five to the American's hundred.[26] These battles have been traditionally considered victories by American historians.

Because the British did not participate as active allies in the Indian war against the Americans, there was fear that the Ojibwa would turn on the United Empire Loyalists in Ontario. In a letter to Lord Dorchester on 18 June 1786, Simcoe explained that the Southern Ojibwa 'deserve the utmost attention ... nor is their power to be slighted since tho' they are not numerous themselves in this part of the country, they can draw to a head very formidable numbers from Lake Huron, etc.'[27] Fear of the Ojibwa often dominated British Indian policy at the time, but it was not fear of the Southern Ojibwa alone since their population had dramatically decreased.

Their numbers continued to decline mainly as a result of liquor and the 'whiteman's disease,' smallpox. A devastating epidemic swept the Indian communities of Lake Simcoe in 1793 and, in a matter of decades, the Indian settlements were greatly reduced in numbers and in strength. The population of the Mississauga on the north shore of Lake Ontario, for example, had declined from about 500 in 1788 to 191 by 1827. The contagious diseases were likely spread by the numerous United Empire Loyalists who entered southern Ontario after the American Revolution.

William Canniff traced this Loyalist population growth in southern Ontario. The refugees from the United States and the soldiers who settled during the period 1783–5 were estimated at 10,000. When Quebec was divided into Lower and Upper Canada (Ontario) in 1791, the population of Upper Canada had grown to about 20,000 and, during the War of 1812, it reached about 70,000. In the Midland District, the white settlers outnumbered the Indians seventy to one by 1817. The ratio of whites to Indians in southern Ontario was likely the same.[28] Indeed, as early as 1785 the white Loyalists possibly equaled the Ojibwa population in the province, even if the Indian Loyalists, the Six Nations, are included.

The 'General Returns of Militia for the Province of Upper Canada' in 1794 indicated that over 5000 soldiers could be mustered. In the same year, all the Indians in the southern Great Lakes would have had difficulty in matching such a force. For food gatherers, who lived chiefly by hunting and fishing, southern Ontario was slowly becoming an unenviable habitation. Had the settlers been generous to the owners of the land and respected them as equals, the Ojibwa transition to a new way of life would have been less difficult. But generosity was lacking. One southern Mississauga chief in 1820 told the English: 'You came as a wind blowing across the great Lake. The wind wafted you to our shores. We ... planted you – we nursed you. We protected you till you became a mighty tree that spread thro our Hunting Land. With its branches you now lash us.'[29]

Certainly the British recognized the colonial potential of southern Ontario as a haven not only for Loyalists but for immigrants from Britain. The English authorities did not discourage the Indian wars in the Ohio valley because they acted as a protection against American expansion into the province. What, specifically, were those 'branches' that lashed the Ojibwa? The major problem was the way the Loyalists treated the Indians and their land. Fear of starvation was the major concern. Not only were the settlers shooting deer, bear, and game birds by the thousands, but their fisheries were also threatened. No Indian location was held sacred near a Loyalist settlement. The government was made aware of the problem and acted in 1797 by a 'Proclamation to Protect the Fishing Places and the Burying Grounds of the Mississaugas.' It was ineffective. Kineubenae, an Ojibwa chief at the Credit River, complained nine years later that a settler was building a weir to catch salmon on their way upstream to spawn and that the river was becoming so polluted 'by washing with soap and other dirt, that the fish refuse coming into the River as usual, by which our families are in great distress for want of food.'[30] Laws to prevent such abuses were only operative if the vast majority of the population were willing to abide by them. They were not. The Ojibwa became 'outlaws' in their own land. Loyalists, recently forced from the American territories, 'avowed the opinion that a white man ought not in justice to suffer for killing an Indian; and many of them ... thought it a virtuous act to shoot an Indian at sight.'[31] Prejudice against the Indian was inseparable from the attitude that the settlers had towards 'paganism.' Since a non-believer could not take an oath in the courts, the redress of grievances could not be legally obtained by Indians in this manner. The Indians also failed to utilize the courts because capital punishment and prison sentences were alien to the Indians' culture. They advocated some form of payment to the victim's family or, if not satisfied, retaliation in kind by them. La Rochefoucault, in travelling through Upper Canada in 1795, observed that 'the colonists, by their mean and barbarous policy, teach the Indians to despise them.' As a result, many attempts to legislate protective laws for the Indians of southern Ontario were ineffective.

Because of bias against Indians in general, conflict began the moment the Loyalists arrived to re-establish the farms that the revolution had forced them to abandon. How did the Indians expect to be treated by the Loyalist settlers whom they first welcomed as friends into their lands? The Ojibwa were misled by Indian agents and by early Loyalist pioneers, as Quinipeno, a Mississauga chief, complained: 'Colonel Butler told us the Farmers would help us, but instead of doing so when we encamp on the Land they drove us off and shoot our dogs and never give us any assistance as was promised to our old Chiefs. Father – The Farmers call us Dogs and threaten to shoot us in the same manner when we go on their land.'[32] There was a firmly anchored distrust of all Indians in the minds of many Loyalists. When sheep, horses, or cattle became lost or torn to pieces by wolves, the Indians were the first to be accused. In contrast, when the deer, game birds, and fish were poached from the Ojibwa reserves by the whites, the latter claimed that nobody owned them. As a result, in less than fifty years wild life all but disappeared near the most populated centres.

The negative impact of Loyalist settlements was evident in the appearance of some Ojibwa. La Rochefoucault described those in the environs of Kingston as 'the filthiest of all the Indians, I have hitherto seen, and have the most stupid appearance. They are said to live poorly, to be wicked and thievish, and men, women and children all given to drinking.'[33]

There is more evidence to indicate that the non-Indians in Ontario were the ones who were 'wicked and thievish.' Resentment against the British grew in 1794 among some of the Southern Ojibwa because the British failed to support them in their campaigns against the American expansionists and because of encroachment on their lands. There were reports of discontent from several locations. Augustus Jones, the deputy surveyor, was told at Lake Simcoe 'that during his survey ... some Chippawas and Missassaugas came and inquired of Wapinose, a Mississago [who was aiding the whites], the business of the Surveys – Wapinose made answer that he came to open a line for the benefit of trade, and that both parties would find the advantage from it in a short time. The Chippawas and Missassaugas then said they had no knowledge of the sale of those lands and at length began a dispute with Wapinose for accompanying the Surveyor. Wapinose said he was very sensible of the same, but that surveying did not take the lands from them; however, in order to end the dispute he gave them a belt about the value of 7/6 Halifax Currency.'[34] This incident clearly illustrated the division among the Ojibwa and the fact that chiefs alone did not have the power to surrender lands. Often 'on paper' they gave away much more than they intended.

Repercussions to settlers were sometimes unpleasant, as William Bond explained: 'Three Missassaugas or Chippewas came to the man he had left upon his lot making an improvement (about twenty miles in the rear of the town of York), and robbed him of all his provision, and even the shirt from off his back.'[35] Trouble also occurred on the Thames River, where the Ojibwa told the surveyor that their lands were never sold. The surveyor responded by saying that 'he then told them that Wabaconoing had already ceded the land. They made answer that Wabaconoing or the Indians of the [Ontario] Lake have no right to those lands, and that he was an old woman: that his land did not extend beyond the Grand River. A short time after they told Wapinose and Pokaton [Ojibwa chiefs] that the English were nearly as bad as the Americans in taking away their lands, and in consequence of which they would take cattle where they could find them, in lieu of Deer ... The British were but few; that the Americans were very numerous, and that the Americans would soon cut them off, or in plain terms, exterminate them.'[36]

The weakness of the British was demonstrated by their withdrawal of troops from Detroit, Niagara, and Michilimackinac in 1796 as a result of the Jay Treaty. This action caused Lord Hawkesbury to caution Lord Grenville: 'If the Indians felt they had been deserted by the British, the Indians will charge us with Treachery. They may massacre all the English now settled among them, and the war which they now wage against the Americans may be turned into an Indian war against us.'[37] Could a major spark of discontent unite the Ojibwa in an attack against British Canadians?

The murder of Wabakinine, the head chief of the Credit River band, would answer that question. As Donald Smith has aptly observed: 'The most important event in Wabakinine's life was his death, and the story of his violent end and its consequences helps dispel the traditional belief that relations between whites and Indians in Upper Canada were generally harmonious.'[38] Just before his death, 'Wabegonne sent an Indian named Mechaguese to inform the Indians at River Thames to be on their guard, for their Father, the English, was going to send a party of soldiers with Captain Brant's people to destroy them and all the Indians on Lake Huron. The Indians at River Thames sent a messenger to Lake Huron, named Nesguance who told them to be on their guard, for their Father the English was going to destroy them.'[39] The message seemed credible since relations with the British had been strained and the Six Nations had already demonstrated that they were willing to promote white settlement in southern Ontario. Their long loyalty to the British certainly made it unlikely that they would side with the Ojibwa in their struggle against white encroachment in the province. Five Ojibwa chiefs met with Captain Shank at Niagara on 22 May 1796 to determine if the information was true. They were told it was false. Notwithstanding, by the fall of that year their head chief had been killed by a British soldier. Peter Russell reported:

it appeared that the Indians having sold salmon at York had got drunk with the money and one of your Excellency's Regiment (McKewen) having given a dollar and some rum to the Chief's sister to induce her to grant him certain favors came after dark when the Chief was asleep under his canoe opposite Berry's, and took the Squaw from thence to a little distance. This being perceived by Wabikanyn's wife she roused her husband and told him the Whites were going to kill his sister upon which he got up and staggering from under the canoe half asleep and half drunk. A scuffle ensued between him and McKewen who knocked him down and left him senseless on the ground. The women making a great noise at this brought thither the other Indians who carried the Chief and them over to the Peninsula and removing early the next morning to the River Credit he died in the course of that day.[40]

Wabakinine's wife, who was the sister of a powerful chief, died several weeks after her husband. The Ojibwa believed that this was 'in consequence of the ill treatment she had received from the whites.' McKewen was put on trial but released, as usual, for lack of evidence. War belts were passed among the Ojibwa and their allies.

The principal chief of the Ojibwa of Lake Huron, a man who was held in high regard by all his people, was 'much displeased at the murder of one of their Chiefs by the white people' and 'it was his wish to open a war against the English to get satisfaction.' He indicated that he had 'at the place of his residence, a great number of warriors, that he could bring out at his command.' As late as 12 October 1798, Paqua, a Mississauga Ojibwa who had sided with the Americans, attempted to get the southern Ontario Ojibwa to join the United States and France in an attack on the English 'to revenge

Wabakanyne's death.'[41] There was much talk, however, but no action.

What prevented the Ojibwa from attacking the English? There were several factors. The relationship between the Indians and the Loyalists was not completely negative. Whereas in the past there were only a few traders in Ontario buying furs, with the coming of the Loyalists there were numerous demands for many Indian products, not just furs. In the early years food supplied by the Ojibwa was very important to the survival of the Loyalist communities. Since the natives were more familiar with the country, a variety of surplus game and fish could be traded, including large quantities of maple sugar, berries, Indian corn, baskets, and canoes. Such a demand continued as white settlements expanded north, but those Ojibwa in the immediate vicinity of the Loyalists began to feel the scarcity of forest and lake products. Those Indians more distant from the settlements did not feel the same pressure and benefited from the white settlers to the south of their lands. Inherent in this economic disparity was an element of disunity among the Indians. Those natives who had their land close to the settlements were threatened, those who were farther away were not.

Another factor contributing to disunity was that some groups in southern Ontario, especially the Six Nations, were not willing to retaliate against the British because they had been their allies for a number of years. Brant, the would-be protector of the southern Ojibwa, used the Wabakinine crisis to his own personal advantage. He threatened to join the Ojibwa if his land sales were not legalized by the government. When the government acquiesced, the Iroquois remained loyal and the Ojibwa lost a powerful ally. Against the British alone, the Ojibwa could be a formidable enemy, and they even made threats of attack against the Six Nations. But a united force of Loyalist militia, the British army, and the Iroquois made the Ojibwa threats all but meaningless. Moreover, the many disappointments and false rumours for almost half a century convinced the Ojibwa that the French would not return to help them, and alliance with the Americans was out of the question since the numerous recent atrocities committed by the 'Long Knives' convinced most of them that, in siding with the English, they had chosen the lesser of two evils. Better the devil they knew than the one they did not. The events that occurred in the first two decades of the nineteenth century confirmed their belief.

The American threat of attack on Upper Canada in the war of 1812 united most of the Ojibwa, British soldiers, Loyalist settlers, and Iroquois in southern Ontario in a defence of their homelands. The Six Nations were slower than the Ojibwa in taking up arms against the Americans. This greatly concerned General Isaac Brock, who believed that 500 militia had deserted the ranks to protect their families from a possible Iroquois attack. Similarly, the Iroquois wished to remain at home to protect their families from a feared attack by the reluctant militia. In contrast with the Iroquois, most of the Ojibwa, who could more easily remove their families out of danger, acted immediately. While the Six Nations remained neutral in the first few decisive months of the war, the Ojibwa and their allies made significant contributions which resulted in Captain Roberts's easy capture of Fort Michilimackinac on 17 July, the successful engagements of Brownstown on 5 August, the victory at Magauaga on 9 August, and, most important, the capture of Detroit on 16 August.

The early capitulation of Michilimackinac was decisive in attracting the Ojibwa and their allies to the British flag. John Baptist Askin, the Indian interpreter, believed that 'without the Indians we never could keep this country, and that with them the Americans never will take the upper posts, for let them send forward as many men as they will, if we employ the ... Indians we can have equal number, which is more than is wanted, for in the woods where the Americans must pass one Indian is equal to three white men.'[42] Askin was very active in sending war parties of 'Missisaugay and Lacloche Indians' to York. He reported to Captain Duncan Cameron that 'every Indian that can bear arms along [lake] Michigan and Huron from Saginaw Bay to Matchedash are going to exert themselves in driving away if possible these scoundrels that have harassed them so long.' He explained one problem which had a deep cultural significance. In contrast with the Ojibwa on Lake Ontario, those 'in the interior of the country [the Georgian Bay area] always have the guns of their deceased relations deposited in their graves, which deprives the rising generation from benefiting by them.'[43] This symbolized a deep cultural gap between the Northern and Southern

Ojibwa since it involved a basic religious belief that was radically changing in southern Ontario. This did not prevent the impressive 'British' victory at Detroit, however. They captured some 2500 American soldiers, thirty-three pieces of ordnance, and the town and fort of Detroit. It was achieved not so much by Brock's 700 white soldiers, regulars, and militia, but by his 600 Indian allies. Small wonder Brock wrote to Provost, 'When I detail my good fortune, Your Excellency will be astonished.' It was not the fear of Brock's regular troops, but the Indians that caused the commander at Detroit to capitulate with his superior force. In Brock's demand for the surrender of Detroit, he stated: 'It is far from my intention to join in a war of extermination, but you must be aware, that the numerous body of Indians who have attached themselves to my troops, will be beyond control the moment the contest commences.' The commander at Detroit was led to believe that Brock had 5000 Indians with him. There were considerably fewer. In fact, while the Ojibwa from the Thames River area participated, the hundred Ojibwa warriors from the St Clair River arrived the day after the capture of Detroit. Nevertheless, Brock willingly admitted that, without the aid of the Indians, 'it could never have been so easily achieved.'[44]

Not all British officers were as willing to give the Ojibwa and their Indian allies justifiable credit for their victories. The Battle of Beaver Dam is a fine example. Mary Agnes FitzGibbon in supporting her relative, a British officer involved in the American defeat, quoted Tennyson's lines:

A lie that is all a lie can be met and fought with outright,
But a lie that is half a truth is a harder matter to fight.

She went on to say: 'The fact of including the forces under De Haren with the small detachment under FitzGibbon's immediate command in his report to the General, leaves ... the impression that the combined forces were present when the negotiations between Colonel Boerstler and the British were entered into – not, as was actually the case, that they arrived *after* the American general had surrendered at discretion to FitzGibbon.'[45] The person who received the surrender was considered more important than those who achieved the victory. The one was not synonymous with the other. Much heated debate revolved around who actually accepted the surrender rather than the more significant facts of successful participation. It was assumed that both went hand in hand, but this was not so. The Indian view of this battle is that no British officer achieved the victory over Colonel Boerstler, as the *Journal of John Norton* reveals: 'In this, the account of the Indians differs from that of the Forty Ninth [Regiment of Lieutenant FitzGibbon] – the Latter say, that the White flag was not hoisted by the Enemy, until they arrived, – The former insist that it was, – & that resistance had ceased, – but both concur that only the Indians, with a few Scattered Militia Men, had been engaged. The number amounted to two hundred and Eighty men from the Village of Caghnawague, – Kaneghsatague & St. Reges, – about one hundred from the Grand River, and about sixty Chippawas & Messisagas.'[46]

This view was 'unofficially' confirmed by FitzGibbon himself several years later when he admitted that 'with respect to the affair with Captain Boerstler, not a shot was fired on our side by any but the Indians. They beat the American detachment into a state of terror, and the only share I claim is taking advantage of a favorable moment to offer them protection from the tomahawk and scalping knife.'[47] By this time FitzGibbon had become a hero. The glory stolen from the Ojibwa did much to create the public image that they were cowards. Unfortunately, the Ojibwa left no personal records of their detailed participation in this battle or in the War of 1812 in general. Most of the official British and American documents, moreover, make relatively few references to the activities of specific groups of Indians.

The Southern Ojibwa fought with Major James Givins, agent at York for Indian affairs; Captain Matthew Elliott, superintendent of Indian affairs; and Major John Norton, an Indianized Scotsman adopted as a chief into the Six Nations. Elliott was illiterate and could not record the numerous battles he fought with the aid of the Ojibwa. While Norton left a journal of his activities in the war, it was naturally biased in favour of the Iroquois. Yet he did give credit to 'a brave young Man, – a Chippawa Canadian of the name of Langlade' who, 'with thirty Ottawas from Michilimackinac and about thirty or forty Chippawas & Miessisagas was slightly wounded in the arm' in a harassing expedition against the Americans.[48] There are other scattered accounts of the active participation of specific individual Southern Ojibwa in the war. The principal chief of Lake Simcoe, Musquakie (Yellowhead), with about fifty Ojibwa warriors, was reported to be severely wounded in the defence of York (Toronto) in 1813. It was he who was responsible for holding the Ojibwa of southern Ontario loyal to the British in the War of 1812. Nawahjegezhegwabe (Joseph Sawyer), later chief of the Credit River band, supported the crown in the battles at Detroit, Queenston Heights, and Lundy's Lane. Head chief Nawash, from the Saugeen Territory, also contributed substantially to the defence of southern Ontario. He was rewarded with the full red-coated military dress of captain and a pension, but only one record seems to be available to indicate his specific contributions. This involved a struggle among British officers in an attempt to attract his warriors to their detachments. Indians farther to the southwest also participated. Nimekance, chief of the Ojibwa in the Sarnia area, was with General Sinclair in most of his campaigns. Shinguaconse, chief of the Garden River band near Sault Ste Marie, fought with Brock. A little more is known about the great chief Blackbird (Assiginack) of the Manitoulin Island.

Chief Blackbird first came to notice during the War of 1812 and may have taken part in the first battle involving the capture of Michilimackinac in 1812 and one of the last battles at Prairie du Chien in 1814. There is some evidence to indicate that at both battles the Ojibwa and their allies were instrumental in helping to achieve victory. Blackbird and Captain Elliott led a number of warriors 'to Niagara peninsula where they bolstered British strength after the battle of Beaver Dam and in 1813 participated in a number of skirmishes at Frenchtown, Fort Meigs (near Perrysburg, Ohio) and Fort Stephenson (Fremont, Ohio).' Their participation was enthusiastic. The British commander, Henry Procter, blamed Elliott for failing to prevent the Indians from killing American prisoners. On 18 July 1813 Blackbird was informed by the superintendent about this complaint in a Grand Council at Ten Mile Creek. Blackbird's speech on behalf of the Ojibwa and their allies is worthy of quoting at length, since it is one of the few times that their views of the war were recorded.

At the foot of the Rapids (the Grand Rapids, Michigan) last spring we fought the Big Knives [Americans], and we lost some of our people there. When we retired the Big Knives got some of our dead. They were not satisfied with having killed them, but cut them into small pieces. This made us very angry. My words to my people were: 'As long as the powder burnt [the fighting continued], to kill and scalp,' but those behind us came up and did mischief [by shooting the Indians after the surrender]. Brother, last year at Chicago and St. Joseph's the Big Knives destroyed all our corn. This was fair, but, brother, they did not allow the dead to rest. They dug up their graves, and the bones of our ancestors were thrown away and we could never find them to return them to the ground. Brother, I have listened with a good deal of attention to the wish of our father. If the Big Knives, after they kill people of our colour, leave them without hacking them to pieces, we will follow their example. They have themselves to blame. The way they treat our killed, and the remains of those that are in their graves in the west, makes our people mad when they meet the Big Knives. Whenever they get any of our people into their hands they cut them like meat into small pieces. We thought white people were Christians. They ought to show us a better example. We do not disturb their dead. What I say is known to all the people present. I do not tell a lie. Brother, it is the [Ojibwa] Indian custom when engaged [in War] to be very angry, but when we take prisoner to treat them kindly.

Brother, we do not know the value of money [being offered for prisoners]; all I wish is that our people receive clothing for [giving up] our prisoners. When at home we work and hunt to earn those things; here we cannot. Therefore, we ask for clothing. Brother, the officer that we killed, you have spoken to us before about. I now tell you again, he fired and wounded one of our colour, another fired at him and killed him. We wished to take him prisoner, but the officer said 'God damn' and fired, when he was shot. That is all I have to say.[49]

Blackbird obviously participated in numerous campaigns in which his warriors were not treated with the same respect given by the Americans to the British troops. In the minds of some British officers, Blackbird and his warriors had created a most favourable impression of their military ability. A board of British officers substantially recognized the important role in the war played by the Ojibwa and their allies. They recommended the following annual pensions: to a seriously wounded chief, $100; to a seriously wounded warrior, $70; to a family of a chief killed in action, a present of $200; to the widow of a warrior killed in action, a present of $170. In addition, $5 was given to a warrior for each prisoner brought in alive. This is the first time in the history of Indian wars that the individual native participants received systematic compensation for their specific losses.

Certainly a thorough examination of the Ojibwa in the War of 1812 might reveal that they, rather than the Six Nations, made a greater contribution to the defence of Canada since they entered the conflict sooner. Military historians such as G.F.G. Stanley, however, give full credit only to the Iroquois: 'If Canadians are disposed to think about the War of 1812 ... they cannot fail to recognize that it was during the critical years of this war, 1812, 1813, when British troops were few in number and Britain was still heavily engaged upon the continent of Europe, that Iroquois Indians, both from Grand River and Caughnawaga, helped preserve their country's independence.'[50] The same could be said for the Ojibwa, who had considerably less reason than the Iroquois to defend British subjects in Canada.

The War of 1812 was a turning point in the history of southern Ontario Indians since it was the last time they participated in a colonial war on the side of a European power. In the Treaty of Ghent (1814) the war was treated as a stalemate between the Americans and the British, but in actual fact the Ojibwa and their Indian allies had lost. Their bitterness was expressed by Head Chief Ocaita on Drummond Island on 7 July 1818:

Though many of our young men were mixed with the earth [killed in battle] we were happy, and took to your chiefs [the British officers] the hair of a great many of the heads of your enemies; and tho' we were enjoying ourselves and everything going on well, we were astonished one morning to hear by a little bird [messenger], that you had buried the Hatchet and taken our enemies by the hand ... My heart now fails me. I can hardly speak. We are now slaves and treated worse than dogs. Those bad spirits [the Americans] take possession of our Lands without consulting us, they deprive us of our English traders. They even tie us up and torture us almost to death [flog them]. Our chiefs did not consent to have our lands given to the Americans [in the treaty], but you did it without consulting us; and in doing that you delivered us up to their mercy. They are enraged at us for having joined you in the play [war] and they treat us worse than dogs. We implore you to open your ears to listen to our Grievances, fulfill your promises that we may be released from Slavery, and enjoy the happiness we did previous to the War.[51]

The promises to protect 'their' land, however, were not seriously considered in the peace talks.

Posterity had also robbed the Ojibwa of their brave contributions. In the minds of the setters of Upper Canada, their participation in the war was ambiguous, as a traveller to Canada observed in 1821: 'The Indians are feeble and useless allies, but dangerous enemies. They were of little benefit to us during the last war, being under no discipline or subordination; and generally taking to flight at the commencement of an action, and returning at its termination, that they might plunder the dead of both armies. However, had they been hostile to us, they might have done incalculable mischief; for their intimate knowledge of the woods, their talents for ambuscade, and the unerring fire of their rifles, would enable them to harass and weaken an enemy, without incurring almost any risk themselves.'[52] This was likely the way in which the militia justified taking credit for victories while still recognizing the military 'talent' of the Indians. It simply is not logical to say that the Indians could be 'useless allies' at the same time that they were dangerous enemies. Indeed, it was not the Indians so much as the regular soldiers who often 'took flight at the commencement of the action.' In the battle of Moravian Town, for example, Tecumseh stood to fight while the British fled. It is clear that the wars fought by the Ojibwa created a certain amount of fear in the minds of the settlers and prevented them from pushing their Indian neighbours too far.

The period from 1764 to 1814 involved a traumatic revolution of Ojibwa life in southern Ontario. The English traders, in contrast to their predecessors, the French, appeared to be less generous, more avaricious, and considerably lacking in any understanding of Ojibwa culture. The traders ceased to be an extension of the government's diplomatic arm, as they had often been before the conquest. The British crown, represented among the Indians by William Johnson, acted as a somewhat effective and generous distributor of presents, especially liquor. This countered many of the atrocities of the independent traders. As a result, many Ojibwa sided with the British against the colonists in the American revolutionary war. British protection was extended mainly to the Iroquois, however. The Indian Department was less sympathetic to the well-being of the Ojibwa after Johnson's death, and the relatively peaceful United Empire Loyalist 'invasion' of Ojibwa lands came after the English traders. Promises were made that if the Loyalists were permitted into southern Ontario, they would improve the well-being of the Ojibwa. The peaceful acceptance of the rapid settlement of Indian and white Loyalists along the north shore of Lakes Erie and Ontario was typical of the way the Ojibwa comforted their defeated allies. There had been a similar experience over 100 years previously when the Huron fled north as refugees to be accepted by the Ojibwa. In contrast, the displaced English did not share the Huron's appreciation and respect for the generosity of the Ojibwa. The Loyalists' promises of cooperation and peaceful coexistence were soon broken.

After 1776, the Americans were the major European enemy of the Ojibwa. In their attempt to keep the Americans out of their allies' territory in the Ohio valley, the Ojibwa of southern Ontario were unsuccessful, mainly because of the massive influx of settlers and soldiers, but also because they could not depend on the British for substantial aid. The influx of the United Empire Loyalists and 'Feathered Loyalists' into southern Ontario created a dilemma for the Ojibwa. On the one hand the British government demonstrated some support and gave many promises; on the other, they took their lands. Although the Ojibwa were greatly frustrated in their homeland, at least the British were distributing an abundant supply of presents and attempting to give some form of compensation for the dispossession of their lands. The death of Tecumseh in the War of 1812 and the disintegration of the confederacy sealed the fate of the Southern Ojibwa. The hunting grounds that remained in their territory would be taken from them, thus radically changing their lives forever. It was government Indian policy, rather than any benevolence on the part of the settlers, which prevented substantial retaliation by the Indians.

Years after the war, one of the Ojibwa chiefs, Shinguaconse, reflected on the events that had taken place: 'When your white children first came into this country, they did not come shouting the war cry and seeking to wrest this land from us. They told us they came as friends to smoke the pipe of peace; they sought our friendship, we became brothers. Their enemies were ours. At the time we were strong and powerful, while they were few and weak. But did we oppress them or wrong them? No! And they did not attempt to do what is now done ... Father. Time wore on and you have become a great people, whilst we have melted away like snow beneath an April sun; our strength is wasted, our countless warriors dead.'[53]

6

THE SURRENDERS
'You Have Swept Away All Our Pleasant Lands'

Over a period of about one hundred years, from the 1780s to the 1880s, the Ojibwa of southern Ontario surrendered almost all of their lands and began to live on reserves. The major cessions covered three distinct chronological periods and geographical areas: 'Between 1781 and 1806 Britain acquired the waterfront along the St. Lawrence River, Lake Ontario, the Niagara River, Lake Erie, the Detroit River, Lake St. Clair and the St. Clair River. In the decade after 1815, the Crown arranged several large purchases which opened up a second line of settlement, behind the first range of surrenders, to accommodate the rather heavy influx of post-war immigration. After 1830 four major and two smaller "agreements" saw the Indians agree to settlement on the Bruce Peninsula, the Manitoulin Island and the north shores of Lake Huron and Lake Superior.'[1] It is true that millions of acres changed hands in southern Ontario without any bloodshed. Yet the southern Ontario Ojibwa were willing to fight and die with their allies in the Ohio valley in an unsuccessful attempt to retain the lands for their friends there. Why did they not defend their own lands against the British expansion in southern Ontario?

The conventional wisdom in answering this question was established by historians such as William Canniff in *The Settlement of Upper Canada* (1869): 'The Mississaugas [Ojibwas] being a race of naturally peaceful disposition, the settlers never had any reason to fear them, even had the Canadian Government, like the American, forgot to recognize the rights of the natives, and owners of the soil. When under the influence of liquor they might assume a mock heroic character to intimidate women and children, in order to get something; but no attempt was ever made to disturb the settlers.'[2] Although some of the Mississauga Ojibwa refrained from joining Pontiac in his war, it has already been thoroughly demonstrated by their numerous battles that they were far from having a 'peaceful disposition' in the past. If the answer does not lie here, is it that they were treated fairly in their land transactions, as Canniff implies?

Certainly by comparison with the United States, the British government was less sanguinary in its land dealings with the native people in the period under consideration. During almost the whole time in which the British were peacefully taking over southern Ontario, the Americans were fighting wars of extermination against the Indians in their territories. The Ojibwa of southern Ontario, who participated in an unsuccessful attempt to stop the American westward movement, were certainly aware of the contrasting treatment. This to a considerable extent influenced their attitude towards the surrenders. A greater number of uncontrolled American settlers, assisted by a powerful army, moved into the Indian territory while their elected representative, sensitive to democratic public opinion among the white voters, stood by and did nothing to protect the Indians; in southern Ontario, in contrast, fewer settlers demanded land under the British government, which was more impartial and less sensitive to public opinion in Canada. This does not necessarily confirm the traditional beliefs in Euro-Canadian society that the British government was 'liberal,' 'honourable,' and had a 'fair regard for their treaty rights.'[3]

There were two rationales in the minds of the officials who attempted to resolve the Indian land problem, and these were on most occasions diametrically opposed to one another. One rationale, which was 'idealistic,' gave the Indians a legal right to land, while the other, which was 'realistic,' took that right away. The document which recognized the Indians' exclusive control over their lands was the Royal Proclamation of 1763. It contained the statement that 'no private person was to presume to negotiate as land-purchase for the Indians, but if at any time any of the said Indians should be inclined to dispose of the said land the same shall be purchased only for us [the Crown], in our name, at some public meeting or assembly of the said Indians *to be held for that purpose* by the government.' This idealism, of allowing the Indians a legal right to their own lands, had a realistic purpose at the time of its inception. As Allan G. Harper noted: 'The purpose of Indian administration in the seventeenth and eighteenth centuries had been to keep the Indians in peace and alliance with Great Britain ... to secure the safety of the settlements from attack, and to use the natives, when necessary, in the conflicts arising among the warring sovereignties in the New World. The treaties which Great Britain made were but means to these ends.'[4] The need for Indians as allies, or the fear of them as enemies, decreased when the possibility of hostilities in America declined and the white settlers greatly outnumbered the Indians. The purpose of the Proclamation of 1763 had ceased to be a benefit to Britain shortly after the War of 1812, but the principle continued to be law.

Settlement in southern Ontario began well before the British Proclamation was announced. As early as 1754 there were thirty-four French families located in what became the Windsor border region. After the Indian war of 1763 this region seemed to be temporarily open to land speculation. Several Englishmen as well as Frenchmen obtained 'free gifts' of land from the local Indians, ironically even from Pontiac. As late as 1780 William Macomb received land from the Ojibwa 'on the south shore between Riviere a Pins & Stoney Point running into the woods three leagues' and the 'price' was 'in consideration of good-will, love and affection.' For a similar consideration, the Labadie family acquired land 'from Stoney Point to Rivière La Tranche [the Thames] and 150 acres deep; next to MaComb's land.' Eight years later even relatives of the Indian Department were involved in the land 'grab.' James Allan, Wm. Caldwell and J. Caldwell obtained from the local Ojibwa '11 miles by six miles north of Lake Erie, beginning at lot 1 of land already inhabited by planters,' but they were willing to pay 'three bushels of Indian corn annually or value thereof for 999 years renewable.' Without the crown being involved in the transactions, their grants should have been illegal, but most were confirmed legally later. The surrender period obviously started off in a chaotic setting.[5]

The first surrender involving the British government in southern Ontario came in 1764. William Johnson, in an effort to punish the Seneca for their participation in the Pontiac War and to facilitate the transportation of goods, demanded and received a surrender of a tract of land on both sides of the Niagara River. The Seneca, however, did not have the right to part with the tract on the west side of Niagara since the Ojibwa claimed it. In 1781, when the Ojibwa were allies of the British in the American Revolution, it was 'legally' surrendered by four of their chiefs: Nanibizure, Missisaga, Wabicanine, and Minaghquat. They were expected to surrender the almost sixteen square miles as a demonstration of their 'loyalty' and, in return, they received a 'handsome present,' likely of trade goods.[6]

This first surrender set several standards by which the Proclamation of 1763 would be put into effect. First, the British obviously recognized the Indians' rights to the land. Second, the indigenous people, who were assumed to own the land, were called together to consider a surrender. Third, only the chiefs, rather than all of the adult males, signed the treaty. Fourth, the surrender was considered a test of loyalty. Fifth, the area ceded was vague, since no survey of the land had been taken. Sixth, some compensation was given to the Indians. And last, those government officials, military officers, and traders who knew the Indians well, and had in some cases fought with them and gained their confidence, represented the British in the surrenders.

From the British point of view this system of Indian land cession was almost ideal. The land was piece by piece taken over by the use of presents, which were necessary anyway to keep the Indians as allies. Land was obtained at a small expense. The use of 'friends of the Indians,' many of whom were respected missionaries or long-standing traders such as John Rousseau, created a feeling of trust and honest dealing. The surrenders served a dual purpose, as Simcoe reported to George Clinton: 'I beg to Observe, that should my Plan be adopted and *London* made the seat of Government, a small tract of land must be purchased ... of the *Chippewas*, and under the Circumstances of the Country I should think this a fortunate Event, as in the management of this business, I make no doubt I should be able to conciliate this Powerful Tribe (of whom no purchase has been made) by a trifling Expense to the King's Interest, and the benefit of the Colony.'[7] Land was obtained and British loyalty was enhanced by each of the early transactions, since the loss of land was not immediately comprehended but the presents were greatly appreciated.

British officials recognized that the Indians who signed the first surrenders did not understand the full impact of the treaties. They admitted that one hundred townships could be purchased in the early period for the same price it would likely cost them for ten townships later. It is important to observe that a policy of 'civilizing' the Indians during the land-transfer period was diametrically opposed to colonization. One government official remarked: 'It certainly cannot be in our interest to promote their improvement until the land is taken from them.'[8] Peaceful Indian land cessions were obtained not so much because the Ojibwa feared the British but because of the subterfuge employed. Indeed, it was mainly the British fear of the Indians which was the dominant motivating force behind the legal recognition of Indian rights to the land.

From the Indian point of view at the time, the early negotiations which permitted the settlers to enter southern Ontario were fair, if the word of the British could be trusted. Individual Ojibwa bands were told in the negotiations that they would be permitted to fish and hunt in their old locations as before. They would be protected from the encroachments of the settlers, who would help those Indians who wished to learn the art of farming. Indeed, they were promised that even blacksmiths and doctors would be provided for their benefit. While some verbal agreements were kept, most were not. Robert Surtees has thoroughly demonstrated the disadvantage to the Indians in not receiving all of the promises made in the treaties.[9] The land surrender in the Lake St Clair region, called the Chenail Ecarté (Sombra Township), is an excellent case in point. Superintendent Thomas McKee explained at a council involving thirteen Ojibwa chiefs that the king wanted this area 'not for his own use, but for the use of his Indian children and you yourselves [the Chippewa] will be as welcome as any others to come and live therein.' The Ojibwas willingly agreed to accept such a surrender for £800 in trade goods. Why would they not? Being at war with the Americans, they could make ready use of 772 knives, 278 pounds of gunpowder, 2100 pounds of shot and ball, and twenty-six rifles. In addition, the distribution of 3456 tobacco pipes is indicative of the number of warriors whom the British hoped to please. Domestic needs were not overlooked, since items such as 333 kettles and 1498 blankets were included. These distributions kept the Indians loyal to the British and antagonistic towards the Americans. But this newly acquired area was not reserved for the Indians; later it was 'simply opened to white settlers.' In such a move, the British had achieved two goals. They provided the Ojibwa with the means to protect southern Ontario from American expansion and they opened the area to peaceful British settlement. The Ojibwa, nevertheless, while being pleased with the liberal distribution of military and domestic goods and with the British concern for the displaced Ojibwa allies, were not aware that they were surrendering the land for white settlement. Several years later as the European pioneers took up this land, the protesting Indians were shown the written document which contained their totem marks. The treaty made no reference to the land as an Indian settlement. By this time the Ojibwa had considerably decreased in power and a successful military campaign against the English was out of the question. It was this type of Machiavellian diplomacy which permitted the early peaceful settlement of southern Ontario.

Most scholars have argued that in the early surrenders the indigenous people were not aware of the full impact of their land cessions. They correctly argue that the Indian cultural perspective considered the land much like the air we breath – given to all, but not specifically 'owned' by anyone. The Ojibwa's ignorance of the European concept of landholding, however, should not be considered the paramount reason for easy dispossession in southern Ontario. For well over a century the Southern Ojibwa had visited the highly populated centres in the British as well as the French colonies. They had not only communicated with the Indians who had been dispossessed, but they had also seen the negative effects of white settlement on the environs. They were even aware that the Iroquois wars as early as the 1650s were partly caused by the depletion of game which to some extent had resulted from the westward movement of settlers. Rather than cross-cultural ignorance of land use, it was a need for trade goods, a feeling of trust, a certain degree of loyalty, and especially the lack of alternatives which made the cessions relatively successful.

This is not to say that the Indians fully comprehended the 'written' terms of the treaties. It is likely that there was not one Ojibwa who could read or write before the first quarter of the nineteenth century, much less understand the legalistic terminology found in the treaties; and by this time most of southern Ontario had been ceded to the crown. Indeed, many of the early treaties were not only filled with complicated jargon, but were also ambiguous, incomplete, and, as Surtees expressed it, 'sloppily concluded and occasionally badly recorded.'[10] There are more than a few examples of such documents.

Three basic problems may be found in the early treaties as well as some later ones. First, the description of the land involved was frequently vague or entirely missing. Second, the land cessions of one band often included the territory of several other bands. And third, some Indians even surrendered land that they did not possess at all. A few examples will demonstrate the problem.

Robert Prescott, governor in chief of Canada, in a letter to Peter Russell on 9 April 1798 complained that 'the land purchased from the Missisaugos was most undoubtedly in an awkward predicament' since some of the treaties did 'not express a single Boundary.' A frantic attempt was made to clarify the situation by interviewing those who were involved. The interpreter, Nathaniel Lines, who was a witness to the negotiations, stated that a 'blank deed' was signed by all parties. This was the famous 'Walking Treaty' or, as some called it, the 'Gun Shot Treaty.' Captain W.R. Crawford claimed he had negotiated the surrender with the Mississaugas on 9 October 1783 for the land 'from Toniato or Onagara to the River in the Bay Quinte within eight leagues of the bottom of the said Bay, including all of the Islands, extending from the lake back *as far as a man can travel in a day*.'[11] When Alexander Aitkins attempted to survey the area, he found that the Ojibwa were unhappy not only with this treaty but with others made in the area as well. Further treaties were made in an attempt to correct the error. But years later even Captain T.G. Anderson of the Indian Department still maintained that, of the area under consideration, there remained unsurrendered 'a hundred miles of the richest farm land in the province.' By 1923 this 'farm land' included 'almost half of the City of Toronto, to say nothing of Whitby, Oshawa, Port Hope, Cobourg and Trenton.' The Ojibwa at Alnwick, Rice Lake, Mud Lake, and Scugog were finally given $375.00 each for this land. One scholar, who analysed the implications of the Gun Shot Treaty in detail, concluded: 'If the federal ministers, civil servants or the commissioners felt any qualms in abandoning the interest of their wards in this conflict of interest, none showed any remorse – then or later.'[12] The Ojibwa of Matchedash Bay also signed a blank deed and were treated in a similar fashion. In the late eighteenth century, however, when the Indians were not yet considered 'wards' of the state, this problem could have been corrected much more easily, if greater care had been taken in defining the boundaries in the surrenders.

British officials were often confused about which specific Indian band rightfully owned the land. In a letter from Simcoe to Dundas on 20 September 1793, he lamented: 'The Messissagua Indians, who are the original proprietors of the Land, which has been sold to Government, make great Complaints of not having received the presents which they stipulated when they sold the Lands. Colonel Butler upon my inquiry, told me this originated from a mistake of Sir John Johnson's who had given the Presents to the wrong Persons.'[13] While Johnson was familiar with the Iroquois and their language, neither he nor those in the Indian Department at the time had a clear knowledge of the Ojibwa and their language. Confusion resulted. This did not prevent the government from surveying the land from Lake Simcoe to Matchedash. The party, however, including Augustus Jones who was aided by Chief Wapinose, encountered some difficulty. A band of Ojibwa stopped the survey on the grounds that the land had not been surrendered. Wapinose admitted that he was 'very sensible' of the fact that a surrender had not been conducted, but he was convinced that this was just an opening of 'a line [road] for the benefit of trade, and that both parties would find the advantage from it in a short time.'[14] The disgruntled warriors acquiesced only when Wapinose presented them with an expensive wampum belt. No other action was taken.

Surveyor General D.W. Smith sent Alexander Aitkin to Matchedash Bay the following year to lay out a road with one lot on each side. Settlement was obviously intended. Smith's instructions to Aitkin were more detailed in how he should treat the Indians than how the survey should be done. Difficulties were expected. Aitkin was cautioned to 'do away if possible, all Jealousy & discontent (should any exist) among the Indians, relative to these purchases.' This was to be achieved by wooing George Cowan, a local trader who had the trust and confidence of the Ojibwa. Cowan was to be given 'as much Lands as he shall require, not inconsistent with public purposes.' Furthermore, Cowan was to be put in charge of giving rum & a few trifling things to the principal Men among the Indians.' In addition to the land grant, he would be handsomely rewarded for his cooperation. Aitkin was informed to 'tell Mr. Cowan, that he is to be paid, well, for his trouble; the Rate per Day, must be arranged between ye, it being certain, however, (to use His Excellency's Expression) He must have, *almost* what he demands.'[15] Bribed with both money and all the land he wanted, it must have been most difficult for Cowan to respect his long friendship with the local Ojibwa, especially since the government had obviously divided the Indians on the land issue. Government officials would use subterfuge if necessary to extricate themselves from an embarrassing situation.

The surrenders involving the Lake Simcoe Indians were so confused that Simcoe decided to consult one of the band's chiefs. After showing Chief Yellowhead a 'sketch' of the land which Russell 'understood' to be surrendered, he asked the chief's view. Yellowhead responded: 'If you white people forget your transactions with us, we do not. The Lands you have just now shewn to us belongs to you; We have nothing to do with it; We have sold it to Our Great Father the King, and was well paid for it. Therefore make your mind at easy. There may be some of our young people who do not think so; They may tell your people that the Land is ours, but you must not open your ears to them, but take them by the arm and put them out of your houses.'[16] Much weight was put on this statement by Russell's superiors, since no new surrender was found necessary as a result. British authorities often assumed wrongly that one man, a head chief, had the authority to sign away the land of the majority. At the time, democracy did not exist in Britain, and in Canada the concept was 'tainted by Americanism.' Certainly it was not in the nature of Ojibwa culture to delegate such authority. Yellowhead's statement could be interpreted as an expression of great honesty or some might even say foolishness. Undoubtedly, as the chief admitted, there were some who believed that they had not surrendered the land in question.

There were obvious cases where individual band members

consented to surrenders of land which they did not possess. Chief Mynass, who had assisted Crawford in his surrenders with the Ojibwa in 1783, was a prime example. Mynass indicated that the land he personally possessed ran from the Gananoque River to the Toniato Creek (renamed Jones Creek) just below present-day Brockville, extending from the St Lawrence to the Ottawa River. A total of eleven townships may be said to have formed this land which Mynass unscrupulously sold. As an authority on these surrenders noted, it was 'an enormous chunk of land to take from a single chief' who claimed the land had been granted to him by the French.[17] In payment, he and his family were to be clothed each year throughout their lives. The British benefited considerably from this transaction, especially since Mynass died shortly after the surrender. His claim was considered valid by the authorities. Again, persons such as Crawford, while being acquainted with the Iroquois, were often ignorant of the Ojibwa language, customs, and landholdings. As a result, it was difficult but not impossible at the time to determine what specific band owned a particular territory. A special effort was made only when resistance was encountered. The process of settlement was usually gradual, taking several years to 'fill up' the back townships which supposedly had been surrendered. The time gap between surrender and settlement was often decisive, since many of those involved or those who should have been involved were dead when the legality of the transaction was called into question. The written agreements in almost all cases took precedence over the Indian's oral tradition, especially when they were to the advantage of the settler.

In addition to providing the United Empire Loyalists with land, British officials in the pre-1812 surrenders were conscientiously attempting to please the Ojibwa at least to the extent that they would remain neutral, or possibly act as allies, in time of war. Fear of an Indian uprising (similar to Pontiac's) haunted officials such as Lieutenant-Governor Simcoe, though, by the late eighteenth century, the Ojibwa in Ontario were most likely far outnumbered by the white population. A relatively accurate census of the Ontario Indian population was not available to government officials until the mid-nineteenth century, however, and fear of the unknown prompted British caution. Although there was much bungling in the early application of the Royal Proclamation of 1763, considerable effort was made to give it token recognition. Yet, as fear of the Americans gradually receded after the War of 1812 and as settlers increasingly outnumbered the Indians, the indigenous people were looked upon in the treaty negotiations more as 'savage children' than as 'brothers.'

The controversy between those who believed the Indians had a right to the land and those who felt they did not likely goes back to the first contact between Indians and Europeans. As the fear of the Indians in southern Ontario decreased, however, the debate was resolved mainly in favour of dispossession. Those who supported the Indian claim were represented by missionaries such as the Methodists, evangelical organizations such as the Aborigines' Protection Society, and various philanthropic groups and individuals. They were opposed by the land speculators, those who advocated 'progress,' and especially the farmers and the would-be farmers, all of whom were convinced that the Indians had no rights to the land as hunting grounds.

Those who advocated dispossession without compensation expressed the belief, first judicially stated by Emeric de Vattel as early as 1758, that groups using the land for hunting and fishing 'cannot be held as real and lawful taking possession; and when the Nations of Europe, which are too confined at home, come upon lands which savages have no specific need of and are making no present and continuous use of, they may lawfully take possession of them and establish colonies in them.'[18] By 1845 this had become the philosophy of some members of the Legislative Assembly of Upper Canada: 'The unsettled habitation in those immense regions of Canada cannot be accounted a true and legal possession, and the people of Europe, too closely pent up at home, finding land of which the savage had no particular need, and of which they made no actual constant use, were lawfully entitled to take possession of it and to settle it with Colonies.'[19] This Eurocentric perspective failed to take Indian culture into consideration, especially in relationship to landholding. Specific Ojibwa families had an exclusive right to hunt and fish in specific geographical areas, and any Indian encroaching on that land could suffer death as a result. Moreover, each family needed approximately one square mile to subsist by foodgathering, whereas European farmers required considerably less land for subsistence. If the majority of Ontario farmers had had their way in the first half of the nineteenth century, it is likely that the Royal Proclamation would not have been enforced at all.

Why were the rights of the Ojibwa to their lands considered valid after their power had waned? One scholar has argued that by then the precedent of recognizing Indian title had been well established in law and that they were 'buttressed briefly by the philanthropic impulse which affected imperial policy' in the decisive years of the 1830s and 1840s.[20]

The most important territory still owned by the Ojibwa in the early 1830s was over 2 million acres of land in the Saugeen Peninsula and watershed. A detailed analysis of the ten surrenders involving these 'Saugeen' Ojibwa over a period of fifty years (1836–86) demonstrates an increasing sophistication in the Ojibwa's understanding of the value of the land, the way in which they were aided by missionaries and philanthropic groups, and the attitudes that they had towards the transactions. Unlike almost all the previous surrenders, the Saugeen cessions reveal the views of missionaries and a great variety of individuals, including the Indians themselves, several of whom have left their own records of the events.

Of the ten surrenders, the first in 1836 was by far the most important since it involved about 1.5 million acres. The next surrender came fifteen years later. It included 4800 acres. The following ten years saw the ceding of three parcels of land in the Indian (Bruce) Peninsula. Of these, the 1854 surrender was the largest, involving about 450,000 acres. The other two surrendered tracts included the villages and farm lands of Nawash (1857) and Colpoy Bay (1861). The former took in 10,000 acres; while the latter, ceded four years later, involved 6000 acres. In the last twenty-five years of the surrender period the majority of the islands off the coast of the Saugeen Peninsula were relinquished. This occurred mainly in the years 1885 and 1886, and involved several thousand acres. These lands were bound on the east by a line drawn from the present town of Arthur to Cape Rich on Georgian Bay; on the south, a line from Arthur to Lake Huron (north of the Home District); on the west, Lake Huron; and on the north, Georgian Bay. This was considered at the time some of the most valuable farm land (and later tourist land) in Canada.[21]

The first surrender of the extensive Saugeen watershed must be

examined in the context of another surrender at the time involving
Manitoulin Island. Both surrenders were to serve a dual purpose in
1836. On the one hand, they would enable the lieutenant-governor
of Upper Canada, Sir Francis Bond Head, to solve his pressing
financial problem with the Reform party. The grievances of the
party's supporters could be removed substantially by providing a
considerable number of acres for settlers or speculators. The land
payments, although small, would be sufficient to free Head from
local political control. On the other hand, Head assumed that the
'Indian problem' could be solved by grouping as many native people
as possible in one remote area.

Head saw a sharp contrast between the Indians in the Georgian
Bay area and those farther to the south who lived in small settlements near the growing towns and cities. In the northern part of the
province, he claimed, the Indian 'breathes pure air, beholds splendid
scenery, traverses unsullied water, and subsists on food which,
generally speaking, forms not only his sustenance but the manly
amusement, as well as occupation, of his life.' He stated that death
by consumption (tuberculosis) and other diseases had almost
exterminated the Indians who had come into contact with civilization. His conclusion was that 'civilization is against the Indian's
nature and they cannot become civilized.' As a result, Head thought
that it was only just to move the Indians to an isolated area. While
he was distributing presents to 1500 Indians on Manitoulin Island in
1836, he obtained a surrender from sixteen Indians, including F.B.
Assikinack, so that the islands could be made 'the property (under
your Great Father's control) of all Indians whom he shall allow to
reside on them.'[22]

Many Ojibwa in southern Ontario could see the advantage of
having their own land on which they would have no 'white'
interference, a place where they could live their lives, with their own
customs, free from the evil influence of 'fire-water' and 'white man's
diseases.' Certainly many Indians were suffering from the flow of
Europeans into their ancient homelands.

Head's conclusions seemed to have a degree of validity. Some of
the more Europeanized Ojibwa substantiated his view of the
suffering Indian. In the year in which Head was acting to put his
Manitoulin project into effect, one of the first literate Southern

Ojibwa, Peter Jacobs (Pahtahsega), wrote a letter which was published in the New York *Christian Advocate*. Since it gives a native overview of Indian conditions on the north side of Lake Ontario at the time, it is worthy of a lengthy quote:

Dear Brother: I take this opportunity to give you a paper talk; and if you think it is worthy of a place in the columns of your paper, you will please give it. When I was about fifteen years of age I used to think that the white man did us a great [dis-] favor in bringing the fire water into North America, which has ruined our great and powerful nation of Chippewas, both their bodies and souls. And this fire water has caused the tears of many orphans and widows – and it caused them to become beggars, and to live upon the liberality of their friends ... they were very numerous and powerful. But let me ask, Where are they now? They are not to be seen sir. The fire water that the white man brought has cut them down to their graves like as the scythe does the grass ... In about the year 1818 there were a great many hundreds of Indians of Kingston, Upper Canada, and at Belleville and Rice Lake. And they were all unhappy drunkards. I was well acquainted with these tribes of Indians. And in 1829 I do think there were not more than half the number; for they were dying very fast every year. Some of them were stabbed, some were shot, some were toma-hawked, some were drowned, some were burned, and some were frozen to death. And thus we were going to destruction at a great rate ... Let me tell you a little more of the evil of the fire water: my father and mother died when I was very young, in drinking the fire water to excess. Here the fire water has made me fatherless and motherless. My sister and brother-in-law then took me to bring me up. But in a short time they died also in drinking the fire water to excess. My sister was frozen to death on a drinking spree, on new year's day ... And in about one year from this time one of my sisters, in a drunken spree, was struck with a club on her head by her husband, which caused her death. And in the same year my brother was tomahawked in a drinking spree, at Montreal. Thus the fire waters have left me without father or mother, and without brother or sister in the world.[23]

Unfortunately, Jacobs himself became 'constantly bedevilled by heavy drinking and sank into poverty and oblivion.' His tragic life was not an isolated case. Another Ojibwa, Chief Joseph Sawyer

(Nawahjegezhegwabe) from the Credit River band, was sold at the turn of the eighteenth century by his father for a bottle of liquor.[24] Henry Gladwin's prediction to Amherst in 1764, that the Indians may be destroyed by the free sale of rum, 'more effectively than by fire and sword,' seemed to be coming true. It was no surprise to find some Indians advocating an isolationist policy in sympathy to some extent with Head's Manitoulin project.

Kahgegagahbowh (George Copway), from the Rice Lake area, was another Ojibwa who saw the ill effects of living in too close proximity to white settlements, but he suggested a solution. He advocated the establishment of a 150,000 square mile Indian territory where 100,000 Indians could be exposed to 'the cause of Education and Christianity.' Under a white governor the 'well educated' Indians, such as he, would administer the territory. Copway's idyllic dream of a great Indian reserve never materialized.[25]

Head's plan did succeed, however. The British Colonial Office accepted his analysis and proposal at face value. Almost simultaneously Lord Glenelg, the colonial secretary, received a storm of protest from some educated Ojibwa, Canadian Methodists, British Wesleyans, and the influential and newly formed humanitarian organization, the Aborigines' Protection Society. Fresh from their victories over British slavery, the English philanthropists were well seasoned in effective lobbying. T.F. Buxton, chairman of the Select Committee on Aborigines, and D. O'Connell, with about sixty members of parliament, drew Glenelg's attention to the plight of the Ojibwa. Dr T. Hodgkins, president of the Aborigines' Protection Society, and the Rev. R. Alder of the Wesleyan Mission Society spearheaded the campaign to prevent removal. They stated that Head had taken 3 million acres of arable land from the Ojibwa of Upper Canada and left them with 23,000 'barren islands.' The Rev. J. Evans of the Lake St Clair mission and the Rev. E. Ryerson of the Credit River mission testified on the progress that had been made by the Ojibwa in the southern Ontario Indian settlements. The two native missionaries, the Rev. John Sunday and the Rev. Peter Jones, also gave evidence in personal interviews with Glenelg, who recognized them as living examples of the success of the Methodists in southern Ontario. Many chiefs, such as Ishtonaquette of Lake St Clair, had signed petitions against removal. They argued that Head's report might have been valid ten years earlier, before the Methodists had successfully converted many Indians, but it was not valid in 1836. A major, undeniable argument was the fact that the 'Christian' Indians were increasing in numbers on their farmlands in southern Ontario, while the 'pagans' were decreasing on their hunting grounds. Dr Hodgkins indicated that removal in the United States had been tried but was unsuccessful. He concluded that 'we should ameliorate them in the situations in which they have already fixed themselves and render them auxiliary to the improvement of others more remotely situated.' Head's pessimistic reports to Glenelg were discredited. One scholar has described them as a 'cynical decoy,' 'a heretical view,' and 'unscrupulously deflecting attention from his clever political scheme' of using the Ojibwa lands of southern Ontario to fight the democratically stimulated Reform party.

The protests partly achieved their object. Instead of forced removal, the Indians were to be entrenched in their claims to the land. They were to be granted deeds registered in the normal system of the provincial register, 'as valid and secure as their white neighbours.'[26] But would this victory prevent the blatant injustice of forced surrenders?

In the important case of the 1.5 million acre Saugeen surrender, the protest had no retroactive effect. This last large surrender in southern Ontario created a bitter controversy because there were no specific references to traditional compensation and because those who signed the surrender had a limited, if not dubious, right to the land. To the Ojibwa, moreover, it was much more serious to surrender 1.5 million acres to the Euro-Canadians than to cede the Manitoulin Islands for the general use of the Indians who wished to move there.

Head stated in the treaty document: 'I now propose to you that you should surrender to your great Father the Sauking Territory you at present occupy, and that you should repair either to this island or to that part of your territory which lies on the north of Owen Sound, upon which proper houses shall be built for you, and proper assistance given to enable you to become civilized and to cultivate land, which your Great Father engages for ever to protect for you from the encroachments of the whites.'[27] The treaty involving this large tract of land was signed by seven white men and only four Indians. There is ample evidence to conclude that this treaty was illegal. Since a grand council had not been called specifically to implement a land sale, Head's actions were violating both the Royal Proclamation of 1763 and the Additional Instructions of 1794, both of which required prior indication of intent. Moreover, not all those Saugeen who had a right to sign were present, and those who were resisted the surrender. While Head asserted that they 'cheerfully gave up this great tract of land,' a different interpretation was given by Joseph Stinson, general superintendent of the Wesleyan Missions, who had been an eyewitness to the proceedings:

Sir Francis wished the Indians to surrender the whole of that territory to him; they declined; he endeavoured to persuade them, and even threatened them, by telling them that he could not keep the white people from taking possession of their land, that they (the Indians) had no right to it only as hunting-grounds etc. They told him they could not live on the Munedoolin Island, that they would not go there, that they wanted land that they could call their own ... The council of the Saugeen Indians separated. About an hour or two after, Sir Francis called them together again, renewed his proposals, persuasions and threats. The Indians refused. Sir Francis then proposed that if they would surrender to him the territory adjoining the Canada Company's Huron tract, he would secure to them and their children the territory north of Owen Sound ... and build them houses on it from the proceeds of the sales of the territory ... To this purpose ... the poor Indians did readily accede with tears in their eyes.[28]

All of the Saugeen were 'disgusted with the transaction' but one of their subchiefs, Jacob Medegwaub, signed because he was 'influenced by the fear of offending his Excellency.' He was not vested with the power to do so.

The Saugeen had anticipated such a move by the government and they had agreed that no person should have the authority to cede the Saugeen Tract without the sanction of a general council and the concurrence of the hereditary and acknowledged chief. The Wesleyan Methodists indicated in their annual report of 1837 that neither the council nor the chief had met with Head. A year after the surrender this was also confirmed in a petition to the government by Joshua Wawanosh, the hereditary head chief. In an enclosed letter along with the petition, Wawanosh's closing statement read, 'Your

Red children will continue to pray to the Great Spirit to make you wise, strong, happy and useful.' The prayers were partly successful. Support came from other sources. The illegal treaty was a great concern to the Rev. James Evans who had been at the surrender and had unwittingly signed the treaty as a witness. When he was informed of his mistake, he immediately took action by sending a letter to a member of the House of Assembly for Upper Canada. He detailed the injustice, indicating that by rights of heredity the Saugeen Territory was the property of

Joshua Wawanosh, the Chief residing at the St. Clair. His father & grandfather were the acknowledged chiefs according to the testimony of William Jones, the Government Agent at this place, who informed me that others of the Indian Agents are as well acquainted with this fact as himself. This Chief, finding it necessary to reside at the St. Clair, appointed as temporary chief Jacob Medegwaub who resided at Saugeen. In 1836 His Excellency visited the Munnedoolin Island where he found the said Jacob Medegwaub and there effected a purchase in behalf of the Crown of the greater part of the best of the Territory including the whole of the Indian improvements with their houses, chapel and Wesleyan Mission House – the land cleared and under cultivation amounting to perhaps not less than 300 acres ... There is no doubt that he [Wawanosh] is the Hereditary and acknowledged chief, as the Indians at this place, at Lake Simcoe, at Coldwater River, at Muncey Town on the Thames, at the Credit and even those at Saugeen, who signed the document obtained by His Excellency, acknowledge.

As a further proof of the nonvalidity of the title procured in behalf of the Crown, a letter will be found in the office of the Indian Department, signed by the Chiefs from the Credit River, Muncey Town, St. Clair and Saugeen, if I mistake not, in which the late Governor Sir John Colborne was informed that no person has authority to transfer the said lands unless in a council of all the Chiefs, not even then without the consent of Wawanosh ...

I can assure you that Wampum has been passing from body to body demonstrating the existence of those feelings of dissatisfaction and resentment, which, if allowed to rankle in those savage and proud hearts where they at present find a place, may ere long lead to such events as may prove detrimental to the peace and dangerous to the lives and property of our fellow subjects; and expose those, who thus provoked to unjustifiable excesses to a more speedy extinction than under more favourable treatment.[29]

The Saugeen were threatened with the loss of not only their extensive hunting grounds but also their 300 acres of cultivated fields, houses, and church. Injustice, personal guilt, fear of an Indian uprising, and the possible retaliation resulting in the 'extinction' of the Indians concerned motivated Evans to attempt a reversal of Head's surrender. He joined Wawanosh to 'resist the measure to the utmost of his ability.'[30]

Chief Superintendent James Givins responded to the head chief's petition by saying: 'It does not appear that Wahwahnosh has proved himself entitled to have been consulted previously and that his consent was necessary to its validity.' The next month, however, Givins sent £25 to Wawanosh in an attempt to placate him, but the bribe was unsuccessful.[31]

In the next year the Ojibwa gained powerful allies in England. The Aborigines' Protection Society was informed about the plight of the Indians in Upper Canada. They petitioned Lord Durham, who had recently been appointed to investigate the rebellion in the province. They objected to the government's attempts to 'dispossess' the Indians 'of their most valuable reservations in Upper Canada ... In particular,' they emphasized, 'we would most urgently but respectfully solicit, that the measures to which we have alluded, and which have for their object the virtual expulsion of the Indians from their reservations, may be forthwith abandoned, and the steps which have as yet been taken in reference to them retracted.'[32] In the 1836 surrenders involving the Manitoulin Islands and the Saugeen tract, as well as lands near Kingston, the Bay of Quinte, Amherstburg, London, and Lake Simcoe, there were no 'retractions.' The Rebellion of 1837 dictated that the will of the white people, especially for cheap land in Upper Canada, had to dominate. Nevertheless, the combined pressure of the Aborigines' Protection Society in England, the Wesleyan-Methodists, and the Indians achieved a certain degree of success.

The government *Report on Indian Affairs in Canada* in 1847 admitted that the isolation of Indians was generally recommended because of its convenience to the white population rather than from any philanthropic views for the ultimate benefit of the indigenous people. The report also conceded that 'the Indians had a strong veneration and affection for their old haunts and considered it a disgrace to abandon the "bones of their ancestors," while the faith of the Crown, and "every principle of justice" was opposed to their compulsory removal.'[33] While government officials were not prepared to reverse their decisions on the coerced surrenders, they were willing to listen. The Saugeen, in order to communicate with the department, were forced to by-pass their angry and uncooperative Indian agent, T.G. Anderson. He objected to any compensation for the cessions. Instead, they petitioned the secretary of state to retain at least their village and their cornfields at the mouth of the Saugeen River, and especially to obtain remuneration for the 1.5 million acres of land taken from them. With the aid of their philanthropic allies, they were partly successful. The land north of the Saugeen River, which contained their village, was excluded from the surrender, but they lost their 300 acre cornfield to the south of the river. This loss of cleared land was a retrogressive step, since agricultural activities were Indian adaptations to the European presence. They were also granted some additional legal protection for the remaining reserve lands. A Royal Deed of Declaration was issued in 1846 stating that they and their descendants were to 'possess and enjoy' the Saugeen (Bruce) Peninsula. They were also given a £1200 annuity.[34] The small yearly payment had replaced the customary single distribution of presents in the surrenders. While the compensation for such a large tract of land was small, $3\frac{1}{2}$ pence per acre, the deed to their 450,000 acre peninsula seemed to be a strong fortification against a repeat of the 1836 expropriation. Although the results of this struggle were a compromise, the fact that the Ojibwa of southern Ontario were not all being forced to give up their holdings in the heavily populated areas to be driven onto the Manitoulin Island was a major achievement. Moreover, the Saugeen Peninsula was retained by the Indians and could act as a haven for those who 'wished' to retreat there. In this respect, the Ojibwa had won at least a temporary victory. Still, would the many legal guarantees prevent the Saugeen Peninsula from being swallowed up by land-hungry settlers?

It would not. While many Ojibwa and their allies from all parts of Canada West (Ontario) and the war-torn American frontier were moving into the Saugeen Peninsula, a road and a settlement allowance half a mile wide were being cut through their territory from Owen Sound on Georgian Bay to Southampton on Lake Huron.[35] Some Ojibwa who settled in close proximity to the old portage saw some utility in the road construction, but its main purpose was to accommodate the rapidly growing Euro-Canadian settlements on Lake Huron and Georgian Bay. Unfortunately for both the Indians and the settlers, the government permitted land speculators to buy the acreage; as a result, road construction was curtailed for over two decades. This was likely a patronage move to satisfy party supporters and gain financial support from influential contributors. Indeed, the 4800 acre road surrendered in 1851 and sold 'for the benefit' of the Indians was only a preliminary attack on the peninsula. Three years later the major confrontation would come, one that involved the last large Ojibwa hunting ground in southern Ontario.

A substantial indigenous population could still live on the peninsula, subsisting on their traditional diet of game and fish. Individual Indians and bands regarded it as a place of refuge should the pressing white population to the south became intolerable. Anderson and Peter Jones, the leading Mississauga missionary, encouraged the Southern Ojibwa to use the Saugeen Peninsula as their homeland. At a grand council in Orillia in 1846 Anderson promised that 'the Government will secure, by writing, such lands as the Indians repair to, with the consent of the government.' With Jones's aid, he also obtained the permission of about a hundred Indian representatives to build industrial schools at Owen Sound, Alnwick, and Munsee Town.[36] One-quarter of their annuities for a period of twenty-five years, however, was to go towards construction and support of the institutions. The planned industrial school at Owen Sound would aid those going to the Saugeen in their adjustment to the expanding white communities. The hereditary owners of the peninsula were receptive to their suffering kinsmen who fled to the Saugeen lands in an attempt to escape the detrimental influence of culture shock. The Saugeen Peninsula, therefore, was important to all of the Ojibwa of southern Ontario.

There were others who also looked upon the territory with envy in the mid-nineteenth century. The famine in Ireland, the skyrocketing population growth in England, and the displacements caused by the agricultural revolution combined to create an exodus of British immigrants to Canada West (Ontario). The 'responsible' government, introduced into Canada by Lord Durham, dictated that the cry for land would be heard. It was expected that the poor British immigrants would provide cheap farm labour if they could not purchase the lands themselves. Even though numerous promises were made to protect Indian lands, the settler squatters were considered by the government as an 'uncontrollable force of ... natural law.'[37]

Pioneer land hunger was out of control at the time. L. Oliphant, superintendent of Indian affairs, reported a frightening situation to Governor General Elgin in 1854:

They [the pioneers] threatened, in my presence, to settle upon the Indians' reserve [Saugeen] in defiance of the Government. The general principle that Indian concessions are beneficial alike to the Indian and the white, was here merged in a more important consideration. So keen was the struggle for land, that a surrender of the territory for the purpose of sale, appeared the only method by which the property of these tribes could be conserved to them. It therefore became an obligation upon the Indian Department to spare no pains in endeavouring *to wring from those whom it protects*, some assent, however reluctant, to the adoption of the only means by which this object could be achieved. That there should be some disinclination existing on the part of a partially civilized community to cede for ever those lands which formed the hunting grounds of their fore-fathers ... is to be expected.[38]

Oliphant, in attempting to 'wring' an assent to the surrender from those whom he was appointed to protect, was not being heartless or cruel. At the time it was almost impossible to prevent squatters from settling on Indian lands in the more remote parts of southern Ontario. An erosion of Indian lands in this way could have resulted in bloodshed and possibly no compensation at all to the Indians for the loss of their hunting grounds. Needless to say, this does not justify the many promises that the British made to protect their lands. Oliphant was also correct when he said the Indians would be disinclined to part with their last great territory in southern Ontario.

Even those who had spent a long and intimate period among the Indians could not obtain the consent of the Saugeen. Anderson, in great frustration, finally resorted to threatening them: 'After talking all day yesterday and nearly all last night, on the subject of your reserve, you have concluded not to cede your land to the Government ... You complain that the whites not only cut and take your timber from your lands, but that they are commencing to settle upon it, and you cannot prevent them, and I certainly do not think the Government will take the trouble to help you ... The Government, as your guardian, have the power to act as it pleases with your reserve.'[39] Under such threats, the Ojibwa continued to argue that they wanted to retain the lands for their children and for many of those Indians who had expressed a desire to live among them. Anderson's credibility with them had previously been destroyed. In the 1820s he had established a large Indian settlement at Orillia for the Indians in 'perpetuity,' but it had been taken away from them to permit the expansion of the white town. On that same site in 1846 he had again promised the Indians that they would have a large reserve, the peninsula, protected from white encroachment. In 1854 he was still making false promises in Owen Sound, an expanding white settlement that did not contain the Indian residential school that they were promised. Anderson's attitude was that they should be 'compelled by their Guardians' to remove. He proposed a policy to his superior, Oliphant, that all the Indians who interfered with the advancement of settlement in southern Ontario should be forced to 'secure civilization that would result from their removal and consequent concentration.' His dictatorial philosophy was exposed when he complained that the affairs of the Ojibwa were 'governed by the voice of the people [not the chiefs alone], hence the difficulty experienced by the Indian Department.' The method of removal that he advanced was to distribute their annuities from land sales only to those at the proposed isolated reserves. Since these annuities were essential to the survival of those Ojibwa suffering from culture shock, the program undoubtedly would have resulted in a massive movement. Anderson's solution clearly reflected the wishes of most pioneers at the time.[40]

Fortunately, it did not become the policy of the Indian Department. Oliphant was prepared to use devious means to obtain a surrender, but not compulsion. He met personally with the Saugeen after Anderson's failure and was partially successful. Using the Indian Department's traditional policy of divide and rule, he obtained the signatures of those in debt, those who had a weak claim to the land, those who feared white encroachment, and especially those interested in farming. Although this treaty signed the death warrant for traditional methods of Indian subsistence in southern Ontario, its terms indicated a tremendous advancement in the Ojibwa's ability to negotiate. Indeed, it was the best surrender obtained by any Indian group in Canada up to that date.[41]

In 1854 five large reserves and the numerous islands along the Saugeen Peninsula were excluded from the almost half-million acres which had been ceded to the crown. Two of the largest reserves exempt from the cession were in close proximity to the growing pioneer settlements of Owen Sound and Southampton. They represented a major concession on the part of the government as well as the tenacity of the Ojibwa. According to a clause in the surrender agreement, the great extent of ceded land was to be sold by the government to settlers at a public auction for the benefit of the Indians. With the tremendous demand for land, the expectations of a substantial income for the Saugeen was soon realized.[42] The way in which the government handled the Saugeen trust funds resulting from these sales determined the extent to which the surrender satisfied the needs of the recipients.

Surrenders involving the loss of hunting grounds could be explained in terms of farmers making greater utilization of the land, but the removal of the Ojibwa from their villages and cultivated fields could not be justified with the same rationale. The expulsion of four Indian bands from their villages and farm lands in southern Ontario illustrates the problems created by the Indian Department which frustrated their own policy of 'civilizing the Indians.' The villages were located at Coldwater and the Narrows, at the mouth of the Credit River, and on Colpoy Bay and Nawash, immediately north of Owen Sound.

Unlike the other three villages, the Coldwater settlement was established as an experiment by the Indian Department in 1830 for the purpose of teaching the Lake Simcoe Ojibwa the utility of a sedentary farming life. Anderson, who was put in charge of the project, gave a detailed report on the progress of the settlement:

It is now Five Years since, by the Direction of your Excellency, I undertook the Settlement and Civilization of Three Tribes of Indians at Coldwater and the Narrows of Lake Simcoe, numbering about 500 Souls. The Tribe under the Chief John Aisance, and that of the Potaganasus under Chief Ashawgashel, were fixed at Coldwater, whist the Tribe under Chief Yellowhead were settled at the Narrows.

It will be necessary to look at the past Condition of these people and compare it with the present ...

Prior to the Year 1830 these Tribes had become much demoralized from their long Residence near White Settlements.

They were in the constant habit of drinking spirituous Liquors to excess; not one of them could read or write; and they scarcely knew any thing of Religion.

Their Hunting Grounds were exhausted, their Government Presents were exchanged for Whiskey, they were in Debt to all the Traders, and unable to obtain more Credit, and thus were constantly in a State bordering on Starvation.

Their Suffering and Misery were strongly marked in their personal Appearance and the Condition of their Wigwams; the latter, imperfectly made, and very insufficiently supplied with Fuel, could scarcely be said to afford shelter to the ragged and emaciated Frames of the elder Indians, whilst the wretchedly diseased Appearance of the Children spoke still more forcibly of the Intoxication and Want of Food of the Parents.

[Now] ... each Indian with a Family has a little Farm under Cultivation, in which he raises not only Potatoes and Indian Corn, but also Wheat, Oats, Pease, etc.; his Wigwam is exchanged for the Log House; hunting has in many Cases been altogether abandoned, and in none appears, as formerly, to be resorted to as the only Means of Subsistence ... About 500 acres in the Whole have been cleared and are under Cultivation, and it is very gratifying to observe this Year that many of the Indians are, of their own Accord, and unassisted, erecting Log Barns and Stables ...

I must not omit what I consider highly in their Praise, that, although obliged frequently to submit to irritating and extremely unjust Treatment on the Part of the neighbouring White Settlers, no Indian has, during the whole Period of my Superintendence, been complained of for any breach of the Laws.[43]

The Lake Simcoe Ojibwa were doing extremely well in their transition from food gatherers to sedentary farmers, according to Anderson, who certainly had a wealth of experience in his half-century contact with them. In his report, however, he noted threatening signs for this budding farm community, particularly from the nearby Europeans. In the same year in which Anderson gave his glowing report, the Indian settlement, 'surrounded by the white population,' was forced to move. Progress for the whites took precedence over progress for the Ojibwa. The bands scattered to more isolated areas in the Saugeen territory – Rama, Beausoleil Island, and Snake Island. A considerable number of them moved to Colpoy Bay in the Saugeen Peninsula where they again built houses, cleared the land, and even established a sawmill. In 1861 pioneer pressure again forced them to move. At Cape Croker, where the land was unfit for cultivation, they were not disturbed. These expulsions from the 'progressive' settlements were far from being isolated cases.

The Credit River band experienced the same problems as the Lake Simcoe Ojibwa. Their chief, Joseph Sawyer (Kawahjegezhegwabe), had been pressured by Head to move to Manitoulin Island, but he responded: 'Now we raise our own corn, potatoes, wheat; we have cattle, and many comforts, and conveniences. But if we go to Maneetoolin, we could not live; soon we should be extinct as a people; we could raise no potatoes, corn, pork, or beef; nothing would grown by putting the seed on the smooth rock.' Head had difficulty responding to such a logical argument since his overt policy was to make farmers out of the Indians. With great tenacity, the Credit band held out until 1847, but their numerous petitions to government to protect their lands from white encroachment failed. One scholar observed that 'only when the government's intention not to give them secure title to their reserve was made clear did Sawyer and his council consider leaving the Credit River.'[44] The squatters were taking over their lands for nothing. At least the government was willing to pay something. Ironically, in 1847 most of the band were forced to move to the fertile lands of the Grand

River which they had over half a century earlier ceded to their former enemy, the Iroquois.

Ten years later, several well-established Indian settlements came under attack by the encroaching white setters north of Owen Sound. This fertile Nawash Reserve contained substantial frame houses, barns, and church, as well as many cleared acres. In addition to the indigenous Ojibwa, Indians from southern Ontario and Quebec were also located on the 10,000 acre settlement. The expanding towns-people of Owen Sound demanded their removal. As their missionary lamented, they were pressured by economic necessity: 'Though they have many thousand pounds [from their land sales] in the hands of others, yet very little is at their own command.' They each received about $10 per year, which required most of them to beg for a living. Some of the 'less progressive' members of the band agreed to a surrender of their 10,000 acres in 1857 and moved north to the more isolated and less fertile Cape Croker, but an agreement was made to sell their Nawash lands at public auction for their benefit. In addition, houses were to be built for them to replace the ones they had established at Nawash. Such a removal was diametrically opposed to the Indian Department's stated policy of 'civilizing' the natives and to the attempts by some of the more 'progressive' Indians to assimilate into white society.

After the British relinquished control of Indian affairs to Canada in 1860, hundred of acres continued to be carved off the Ojibwa reserves in southern Ontario, not only for farm land but also for the expansion of towns and cities as well as roads. Several bands tenaciously and successfully held onto at least a small portion of their ancestral holdings. In the southwestern part of the province, five reserves remain at Walpole Island, Sarnia, Kettle Point, Thames River, and the Grand River. To the east, eight settlements still exist at Golden Lake, Curve Lake, Rama, Hiawatha, Alderville, and Georgina Island. On the Bruce (Saugeen) Peninsula only four reserves remain. In the least fertile area around Georgian Bay may be found the most numerous settlements of Ojibwa, about two dozen reserves in all.[45] There was some pressure to surrender these pockets of Ojibwa culture, but it met with little success. The demand for land in the east lessened as the movement west opened up agricultural land for pioneer farmers.

7

EARLY RESERVES
'We Must Go Begging'

As the Ojibwa relinquished their millions of acres in southern
Ontario, they either retained small areas, usually on rivers and lakes
which had traditionally been their summer camps, or purchased or
were permitted to settle on small tracts isolated from the more
populated European settlements. Unauthorized white persons were
discouraged from living among the Indians in these geographical
areas set aside for the exclusive use of Indians. This policy, initiated
by the British and continued by the Canadian government, evolved
into the Indian reserve system as we know it today. The reserves
were established to convert the Indians from heathens to Christians
and from hunters to farmers. Schools were built in an attempt to
accelerate the cultural transition, and some children were sent to
residential schools to isolate them from parental influence.

The system was not entirely without merit since the natural
environs of the southern Ontario Ojibwa were transformed to such
an extent by the Europeans that a radical cultural transformation was
also necessary for survival. The transition could have been made less
traumatic if the Indians had been treated fairly by those government
officials who claimed to be looking after their well-being and
financial interests. As wards of the state they had inadequate political and legal power. Some non-Indian humanitarians at the time
considered full citizenship as the solution to the 'Indian problem,',
but the Ojibwa unanimously rejected it. On the surface, enfranchisement seemed to have advantages, including the right to vote, the
opportunity to hold political office, and the ability to borrow money.
But with full citizenship Indians also had obligations: they were

forced to live off the reserves, they had to pay taxes, and their homes would be lost through unpaid debts. The terms of the enfranchisement act did more to create isolation than to achieve its main objective of assimilation.

Once the Indians outlived their usefulness as allies in the War of 1812, two major problems faced the government. First, there was a strong desire to eliminate the expense of the Indian Department which had grown enormously during the war years. The annual budget for Indian affairs had risen from £60,000 in 1811 to at least £125,000 in the last year of the war. During the war, £350,000 were required for presents alone. These costs had been unavoidable if the Ojibwa and their allies were to be well equipped and maintained in the field, but in peacetime the department found them difficult to justify. About one-fifth of the normal annual expenditures was paid for the purchase of Indian lands, but the remainder was considered a 'gratuitous waste' by the British. There was some fear of repercussions should these presents be withdrawn, however.[1] The second and related problem facing the government was the lowly 'uncivilized state of paganism,' which was still the lot of most Indians. As we have seen, by the 1820s the traditional means by which the Ojibwa survived in southern Ontario were extremely limited and were diminishing at a rapid rate. Humanitarians such as William Wilberforce, Henry Thornton, R. Barclay, and the Rev. J. Owen concluded as early as 1806 that 'Among the valuable Institutions which have been formed by British liberality, for meliorating the condition of mankind in distant parts of the world, it cannot [but] be regarded as [a] matter of surprise and regret, that not one has yet been projected for extending a similar advantage to the numerous native Indians of North America.'[2]

The government project of civilizing the Indians was undertaken partly for humanitarian reasons, but mainly as a method of weaning the Indians from the public purse. This colonial objective was to be accomplished, at least among the Southern Ojibwa, in one generation. It failed. Over a hundred years after the commencement of the program the Indians still retained much of their culture and even more of their dependence on government finances. Their tenacity to retain their identity was sustained at great cost. An examination of the reserve system as the framework of the civilization programs contributes a great deal to understanding the failure to assimilate the Ojibwa into white society.

In Ontario, the first attempts at civilizing the Ojibwa had not been by the government. Indeed, the Indians' understanding of the white man's ways, especially in landholding, was discouraged during the surrenders of the late eighteenth and early nineteenth century for obvious economic reasons: their knowledge of European land values would only raise its price. It was a non-British religious sect which first attempted to acculturate the Ojibwa in southern Ontario. Christian Frederick Dencke, a Moravian Brethren, established an evening school for 'six single men and youths' who taught each other European trades in the winter months of 1800–1. This was most likely the first venture of its kind in Upper Canada. Dencke used Joachim and Tobias, converted Delaware on the Thames River, to speak to the Ojibwa and convince them of the benefits of a sedentary missionary settlement:

It is true we live better than you. We have cows, which give us milk and butter, and pigs which give us fat and meat. We live together at one place, have large plantations, raise much corn, and so always have enough to eat for ourselves and our children. Formerly we did not so live, we also were continually wandering about, but now since we have teachers who instruct us in the Word of God and the great words which save us for eternity, and also give us instruction for improving our outward [material] condition ... we obey them and do well in consequence.[3]

Some Ojibwa were convinced, but most were not. Although a new settlement was begun, traditions were still too strong since there was not yet the economic compulsion to change their ways. Their gods still seemed to favour them. Four hundred whitefish could be caught in the St Clair River with one dip of the nets. The power of the shaman, Siskiboa, dominated the settlement, and the early attempt at civilizing and Christianizing the Ojibwa in the St Clair area failed. Nature, however, did not provide wild game in all parts of southern Ontario at the time.

In the York (Toronto) area the opportunity for living by hunting and fishing was decreasing rapidly, and the cultural foundation of Ojibwa life was threatened. During the War of 1812, for example,

Chief Kineubenae (Golden Eagle) gathered some warriors about him and told them

of his fast in which, through the grace of unseen spirit power, he had obtained protection against arrows, tomahawks, and even bullets. And he would demonstrate this gift. He took a tin kettle and, with some difficulty on account of his age, walked a short distance away from the circle. As soon as he raised the kettle up before his face a warrior was to fire, and Kineubenae would collect the bullet in the kettle. The marksman, like the others, believed in Kineubenae's 'medicine' and he fired. The chief instantly fell. The band, to their horror, found that 'the lead went into his head and [had] killed him on the spot.' That one bullet did more than kill a respected leader; it shook the faith of many Mississaugas in their traditional way of life.[4]

Golden Eagle had initially welcomed the settlers, but by the end of his life he accused them of treating his people 'like dogs.' He admitted that the 'young Men & Women have found fault with so much [land] having been sold,' but he understood that the pioneers' encroachments on the food supply of wild game and fish could not be prevented.

The need for dramatic economic improvement among the Ojibwa situated in close proximity to the white settlers in Upper Canada was urgent, and some transition to the European way of life was imperative. The rapid influx of settlers along the coastal waters of Lake Ontario was destroying the traditional native economic base. The population growth of York well illustrates their dilemma. In 1799 the whole district around York had only 224 white inhabitants; in 1826 the town itself had a population of 1677; and in 1830 it had increased to 2860; by 1845 the city had mushroomed to 19,706. This large population made it impossible for the Ojibwa to subsist by hunting and fishing. In 1841, 132 barrels of fish passed through the Welland Canal; by 1844 the number had increased to 1754 barrels. Traditionally, fish had been one of the most important means of subsisting, but commercial fishing was destroying the Ojibwa's livelihood. Several reserves presented petitions to the government objecting to white encroachment on Indian fisheries. They had no effect. Deer and other wild animals also decreased in numbers as the lands were cleared for farms. Pioneers also supplemented their food supply by hunting and fishing, yet the Ojibwa were threatened when they trespassed on the farm lands which had been their source of food. Half-starved Indians could be found in most Upper Canada towns at the time. They attempted to find work and sold such items as baskets, maple sugar, handicrafts, and fish. Many of them were reduced to begging for food. Annuities from land sales and government assistance prevented mass starvation,[5] but it became obvious to some Ojibwa that a major degree of adjustment was required through education.

Various missionary societies were eager to supply funds and teachers, and the catalyst needed to begin work among the Ojibwa was found in the person of Kahkewaquonaby (Peter Jones). His father, Augustus Jones, was of Welsh descent and his mother, Tuhbenahneequay, was the daughter of Wahbanosay, a chief of the Mississauga. He had been raised by his mother in Ojibwa customs until he was fourteen years of age, but then he was educated formally in his father's culture. His conversion to Christianity at a Methodist camp meeting was significant not only for religious reasons but also for the future education of Indian children. William Case, the minister at the camp meeting, exclaimed: 'Glory to God, there stands a son of Augusta Jones, of the Grand River among the converts. Now is the door open for the working of conversion among his nation!'[6] To the Methodists who emphasized the virtues of hard work and the reading of the Bible, conversion and an English education were almost inseparable.

With the aid of the Methodists, Peter Jones began to establish the first schools and churches among the Ojibwa in 1824. Because of his strong emphasis on 'improving' the conditions of his people, Jones's secular educational work ranged from teaching reading and writing English to practical lessons in 'how to plough, buy seed potatoes and oxen.' At first he received little aid or encouragement from the government or the Church of England, since the Methodists and their education were considered tainted with anti-British and pro-American republican ideas. Even though Anglican-Methodist relations were strained, however, Jones established a school for Ojibwa at Davisville on the Six Nations Reserve, which had been the exclusive missionary field of the Church of England.

Peter Jones had partly received his education on the Six Nations Reserve and he had close family relations there. Thomas Davis, a Mohawk chief, gave up his own house to be used by Jones as a temporary school. As the new school was being built, about one hundred Mississauga adults, hoping that their children might receive the advantages of education, pitched their tents nearby. Both Peter Jones and his friend, the Rev. Seth Crawford, supervised the construction, and soon they had many Ojibwa students.[7]

Among the students was Kezigkoenene (David Sawyer), son of the chief of the Credit River band. His education with Crawford began on a formal basis when he was about fourteen years old. In 1826 the whole band moved to the mouth of the Credit River, where a new mission school was established. Sawyer continued his education there and benefited considerably from his studies. He and Jones became the first ordained native Methodist ministers in Canada. They held positions as teachers, interpreters, writers, and preachers on several reserves in the province. Their ability in both cultures is clearly expressed in the numerous letters and reports they sent to the Methodist Home Office and government. The British education they received was far superior to that of the average pioneer in Upper Canada.[8]

Another Ojibwa, Kahgegagahbowh (George Copway), also received an excellent education in the 1820s. He was one of the first students at the Methodist institution on Rice Lake, and he had the Rev. James Evans, later known as the inventor of Cree syllabics, as his teacher. Working as an interpreter and schoolteacher, Copway spent the winter of 1834 at Kewawenon Mission on the south shore of Lake Superior, and the winters of 1835 and 1836 at La Pointe, Wisconsin. His intellectual talents were recognized by his superiors and in 1838 they sent him to a church school in Illinois, where he studied until the fall of 1839 and then returned to Canada. The success of his education is fully demonstrated by the fact that he was the first Canadian Indian to write a book, *The Life, History and Travels of Kah-ge-ga-gah-bow*, published in 1847. His academic and professional achievements had much in common with Peter Jones. Both became Methodist preachers and teachers, both had successful speaking tours in Europe, and both were authors of popular publications.[9]

Another noteworthy Ojibwa student from these early Indian schools was Sowengisik, who later became known as Henry Bird Steinhauer. The origin of his German name sheds some light on how Indian children were used to 'drum up' funds for their education. As donations were required to carry on the work of the schools, William Case, the first elected secretary of the Methodist Conference in Canada, made frequent fund-raising visits to the United States. To gain sympathy for his cause, he took with him the best native boys and girls 'who delighted large and enthusiastic audiences with their Ojibway hymns and specimens of their handicraft.' On one such occasion in Philadelphia, Sowengisik was given the name of a philanthropist who paid for his education. In 1829 Steinhauer was sent to Grape Island, a recently established residential school at the south end of Lake Couchiching. After spending three years there, he was appointed schoolteacher at the Credit Reserve. In 1835 he was sent to Upper Canada Academy, later known as Victoria College, but his education was interrupted by his appointment for a year as teacher at Alderville. His return to college was most successful: 'His ability and industry were seen in the fact that during his last year he stood at the head of his class.' After graduation, Steinhauer became famous for establishing mission schools for Indian children in the Northwest.[10]

Two other successful Ojibwa graduates of this early period should also be briefly mentioned. Pahtahsequa (Peter Jacobs), a student of William Case, taught on reserves throughout Ontario and the West. He wrote a small volume on his travels, which was published in 1852.[11] Nahnebahwequay (later, Catherine Sutton) was also an enthusiastic student. She attended the mission school at Credit River until 1837. Then she accompanied her aunt, Elizabeth, the English wife of Peter Jones, on a year-long trip to Great Britain. She, like George Copway, Peter Jacobs, Peter Jones, and Henry Steinhauer, must have acquired a great deal of British culture during her visit. From 1852 to 1854 she and her English husband, William, supervised the work of a model farm on the Garden River Reserve near Sault Ste Marie. In 1860 she again visited England, but for a different purpose. She was presented to Queen Victoria, who noted in her journal: 'She speaks English quite well and is come on behalf of her Tribe to petition against some grievance as regards their land.'

The Sutton journals, located at the Grey County Museum, demonstrate her thorough and comprehensive exposure to British education.[12]

The academic achievements of these six Ojibwa were impressive. They were generally highly literate by the standards of Upper Canada in the early to mid nineteenth century, when the average pioneer child usually attended only Sunday school. Missionaries and government officials had evidence to conclude that an English education was not wasted on the Indians, when they used these individuals as examples. They created an optimistic mood in which some missionaries believed that the Indian could be transformed in one generation into 'respectable,' industrious, and self-sufficient 'Englishmen.' Did the success of a few individuals justify such an assumption?

This brief survey of some of the first Southern Ojibwa to be given a formal British education in Canada raises several questions. First, what motivated the students? Second, were they in a special situation which permitted them to benefit from such an education while others could not? Was the formal Indian educational system, as it started to develop at this time, acceptable to the majority? Third, what were the characteristics of the teachers, the educational structure, and the school program that the students experienced? Finally, were the methods of teaching and the positive attitudes of the students sustained in the evolution of the system? Since these early achievements were decisive, it is imperative to attempt to answer these questions.

There were basically two major motivating forces acting on the Ojibwa, a repulsion from their traditional education and an attraction to the white man's way of life. The repulsion is evident from general descriptions of Indians at the time and from their personal biographies. There are many examples of parental mistreatment of children caused by the decay of Indian values which resulted from the impact of European traders and settlers. The biography of David Sawyer by the Methodist minister Charles Vandusen illustrates the problem: 'Acts of bloodshed and murder were of too frequent occurrence in those days; and he witnessed many scenes of rapine and dissipation among the Indians when they had free access to intoxicating drink, for which they would make any sacrifice to obtain. On one occasion, while his father was in a pagan state, so insatiable was his thirst for strong drink, that he sold David and another Indian boy to a white man, for two gallons of whiskey.'[13]

The Methodists were opposed to alcohol, not just because of its effects on the Indians, but because it seemed to be threatening the foundation of white society in Upper Canada. It was the enemy of thrift, industry, discipline, and punctuality. Many Europeans considered alcohol indispensable to the enjoyment of life. Uprooted, like the Ojibwa, and forced into a grim struggle with a new and often unfamiliar environment, the immigrant population of Upper Canada had from the earliest days relied on intoxicants as an all-pervasive necessity. The use of liquor was, therefore, the symptom of broader environmental problems that both groups were attempting to solve.

The white man's way of life did, however, provide a solution in the example of the successful pioneer farmer whose sober labours created a surplus of food. The attractions of cultural change for the Ojibwa were both religious and secular, as is evident in a speech given by Chief Kegedonce of the Nawash Reserve in 1830: 'It may be while I stretch out my hands to the Great Spirit for the blessings which my Christian brethren enjoy, I may receive a handful of the same before I die ... Brother! Becoming a Christian I shall desire to see my children read the good book. As for myself, I am too old to learn; and if I can only hear my children read, I shall be satisfied with what I hear from them.'[14] Christianity was considered a viable alternative by some for improving their spiritual well-being, but their life on Earth also had to be considered in relation to the 'material' blessings which Christian neighbours enjoyed. The Indians obviously compared their deteriorating way of life with that of the European Christians in southern Ontario. They were in poverty, while the Europeans were in relative wealth. Christianity was intrinsically seen in the context of prosperity, while traditional Ojibwa religion, in contrast, was failing to bring spiritual, intellectual, or material comfort.

For the Ojibwa, there were few acceptable occupational alternatives to the rapidly disappearing hunting and fishing activities. Almost all the early successful Ojibwa students were attracted to missionary work which, at the time, was inseparable from secular teaching. Both teaching jobs and missionary work were encouraged in the early Indian schools, particularly by the Methodists. People who had acquired missionary and teacher skills in the mid-nineteenth century were held in high esteem in both the white and the Indian communities, particularly if they still retained their native language. They could fill the positions of preacher and teacher on the reserves, and also of writer and interpreter in the increasing need to communicate with the Indian Department. In some cases people holding these positions were given a salary and status equivalent to those of chief. It was an attractive incentive to study. In the mid-nineteenth century in southern Ontario, the educated Ojibwa missionary-teacher replaced the successful warrior-hunter in status.

Each reserve, however, could sustain only a few educated Indians. In the early period, Ojibwa who tried to use their education outside the confines of their own people met with only partial success or failure. A case in point is the career of George Copway. He lectured in Canada, the United States, and Europe, wrote several books, and even founded and edited a short-lived newspaper. Although he demonstrated superior ability, his attempts resulted in financial failure, family disintegration, and spiritual unrest. He was rejected by several Indian bands and expelled from the Methodist church, and his constant movement from one Indian community to the next in both Canada and the United States was indicative of his discontent. Few examples can be found to illustrate the successful integration of early Ojibwa students fully into white society, with the possible exception of Peter Jones.[15]

Jones came to the conclusion that 'a civilized state, even without religion, is far preferable to paganism.' His strong preference for the European way of life was typical of those who received a thorough formal education, but it was not typical of the majority of Ojibwa at the time. Jones had a considerable advantage. Although he had gained a certain degree of independence through learning the trade of brickmaking 'to support himself while at school,' he had the moral and financial support of a rich Welsh father who held the enviable position of provincial land surveyor. Moreover, if the painting of Jones by his half-sister, Matilda, is accurate, he had the additional advantage of being able to pass for either white or Indian. Therefore, the traditional prejudice against the 'Apple Indian' did not apply to him. His English wife also helped to dispel his former 'paganism.' The education he acquired led to a respectable and satisfactory career. As teacher and missionary among the Ojibwa he had gained respect, but his greatest contribution was in raising money in Britain for the establishment of Ojibwa schools. In 1833 his speaking tour raised over £1000 and in 1844 another tour resulted in sufficient funds to build and equip a residential school for the Ojibwa of southern Ontario. The praise and respect given to Jones, particularly by the white community, for such an accomplishment obviously led him to believe that a 'civilized state' was preferable.[16]

As long as their traditional way of life was being threatened and there was a need for Indian missionaries, schoolteachers, writers, and interpreters on reserves, there was a strong demand on the part of some Indians for formal education. In 1844 the Indian agent James Winnett wrote in the *Report on the Affairs of the Indians in Canada* that 'a few years since there was difficulty in getting fourteen Children to attend the Boarding Schools, of the New England institute at the village of the Mohawks, there are now fifty applications in addition to the fifty already there.'[17] Ojibwa villages in close proximity to relatively large white settlements demonstrated the strongest desire for education, first along the shores of Lakes Erie and Ontario. In the less populated shorelines of Lake Huron and Georgian Bay, however, the Ojibwa showed little or no interest in acquiring the European ways until some years later. The farmers in the neighbourhood of the more southerly reserves acted as a stimulus in the educational transition to 'civilization.'

Throughout the 1820s and 1830s there was no uniformity in teacher qualifications, education structure, or school programs for Indian children. Indeed, little uniformity existed for the majority of the white students in Ontario until Egerton Ryerson established the Department of Education in 1875.

In the 1830s the common schoolteacher was considered 'worthless scum.' The Legislative Assembly, addressing Lieutenant-Governor Colborne, claimed that the teachers were 'vulgar, low-bred, vicious and intemperate.' He who 'only knew how to read and write a little or he could "figger," read the Bible without stumbling, mend a pen, and control the pupils with vigor, often found opportunity to teach.' In contrast, the teachers who taught some of the first Indian students were at least more dedicated and sober. Ryerson was one of them, and his ability needs no defence. Some Indian students were also exposed to teachers in white, often upper-class institutions both in Canada and the United States. Cazanovia Seminary, Victoria College, and Upper Canada College were attended by Ojibwa in the mid nineteenth century.

In the absence of expert supervision and centralization in both the Ojibwa and the common schools, local conditions, religious organizations, and the judgment of individual teachers determined the course of study and the textbooks. In the native schools, there was some attempt to teach agriculture and European domestic skills as a means of encouraging sedentary habits and self-sufficiency. Smith's *Canadian Gazetteer* of 1846 is most informative in describing the Alnwick school:

For four years past, a school, on the manual labour plan, has been in operation. This system combines elementary instruction with domestic economy. The girls are taught reading, writing, arithmetic and geography, together with house-keeping, spinning, knitting, needlework, and the management of a dairy: in the latter department are several cows. The boys are taught in the same branches as the girls, and in English grammar, and in the business of farming. For the purpose, a model farm of fifty acres in extent is provided. The Scholars, twelve in number, are boarded and lodged in the mission family, and clothed at the expense of the Missionary Society. They are all clad in cloth spun by the Indian girls. During four years past, thirty-one girls and fourteen boys have received instruction in this school.[18]

This was not the curriculum of the average Ojibwa in the second quarter of the nineteenth century. The vast majority were not in school at all. Some students, such as Jones, Sawyer, and Steinhauer, received a more academic education, similar to that of the privileged white students. The Alnwich school was an experimental project which became the model for industrial residential Indian schools. The Muncey Institute opened in 1849 with the capacity to accommodate 100 girls and 100 boys in two schools. Their subjects were similar to those taught in the Alnwick school.

Peter Jones encouraged the Ojibwa to attend these practical

schools. His first concern was his own Credit River band, which was disintegrating from disease, malnutrition, and drunkenness. In the surrender of even more of their land at the river mouth in 1820, the proceeds of the sale were to go to educating their children and constructing a village on the remaining 200 acres, but three years later nothing had changed. The band seemed destined for extinction. At that decisive time, Peter Jones returned to his people in an attempt to bring material as well as spiritual aid.

His success became legendary. In the preface to his book *History of the Ojebway Indians*, published posthumously in 1861, the author is given credit for introducing Christianity to the Ojibwa Nation. This was justly considered a turning point in their lives: 'But for the influence of "the glorious Gospel of the blessed God," the progress of their decay would have been more rapid, if indeed they would not ere now have become extinct.'[19] By 1826 he had convinced his people to accept the Methodist faith and settle in twenty houses provided by the government from their annuity funds. They built a chapel, which also served as the school house, and began to clear land for intensive farming. Their homes were comfortably furnished: window curtains, boxes and trunks for their European wearing apparel, small shelves fastened against the wall for their books, closets for their cooking utensils, and cupboards for their plates, cups, saucers, knives, and forks; some even had clocks and watches. This settlement established a precedent and provided the government with a model for all future reserves established for the Ojibwa in southern Ontario and beyond. The Methodists, spearheaded by native teachers, soon spread their influence throughout the Ojibwa settlements of the province. By 1830 they had eleven schools and numerous teachers. Of the 400 students, 150 could read. It was generally accepted that Indian children had equal ability with whites to learn.

The British government was quick to see the advantages of these establishments for all aboriginal groups. If Indians could become self-sufficient farmers, the government could eliminate the Indian Department with all its burdensome expenses. Yet, there was one problem. The American-oriented Methodists were often viewed by the government as 'advocates of republicanism' and a threat to the state as well as the established Church of England in Canada. Jones and the Methodists were sometimes frustrated in their attempts to take Christian civilization to the indigenous people of Ontario. The government viewed the civilizing of the Ojibwa as their ideal objective, but with Anglicans, or at least British Wesleyans, as the guiding light to furthering the cause of loyalty as well. Lieutenant-Governor John Colborne was alarmed at the Methodists' great increase in strength, at the fact that the strong Reform assembly of 1828 was often called the 'saddlebag' assembly, and that in 1829 the Methodists were gaining enormous support with their hard-hitting new journal, the *Christian Guardian*. Their influence on thousands of potential warriors was considered by some officials as a threat to the 'peace, order and good government of Canada.' However, Colborne soon advised the Colonial Office that the Church of England, his natural first choice for an attack on the root of Methodist strength, was 'a useless tool; that it was unable, because of what he bluntly termed its "supineness," to effectively "stand their ground against the methodists."' A combined effort of the Anglicans and the British Wesleyans was required. Indeed, the overriding problem of Indian Department expenditures meant that all denominations, even Roman Catholics, were reluctantly welcomed into the civilizing program. [20]

The Methodists continued to be the vanguard. In 1828 Lt-Col. H.C. Darling reported that the Methodist Society had introduced missionaries among the Indians 'in every part of Upper Canada where they have been able to obtain a footing.' The Ojibwa at Rice Lake, the Bay of Quinte, the Holland River, and in the Lake Simcoe region expressed a desire to 'adopt the habits of civilized life.' In the same year that Darling gave his report, Thomas McGee, John Thomas Assance, Alexander Chief, John Thomas Smith, William Herkimer, and Peter Jones, all converted Methodist Ojibwa, went to the remote Saugeen territory as 'native speakers.' Again they met with success by converting the powerful chief Kegedonce (the Orator), who was baptized as Peter Jones, after the leader of the proselytizing group. No other sect could match the devotion, ability, and energy of the native Methodists. Nevertheless, they tried.

The reserves established by the government at Coldwater and the Narrows (Orillia) were to be 'their Anglican models' for reclaiming the indigenous people from their 'wild state.' The Indians who requested the settlement seemed to be predisposed for such a move since, in a petition, they complained that 'white men seize on our furs, and take them from us by force, they abuse our women and violently beat our people. We are poor in lands and have few places for hunting, much of our hunting grounds are covered by white Settlements.'[21] They asked for protection. In 1830 Colborne constructed dwellings, a meeting house, some barns, and even grist and saw mills. Some land was cleared for them and cattle provided. Missionaries looked after their spiritual needs and a white teacher was engaged to instruct them in farming. The cost to settle approximately 500 Ojibwa amounted to £3000, which came out of their annuities from almost 2 million acres they had sold. In the first few years of the settlement both the minister, Samuel Rose, and the Indian agent, T.G. Anderson, were optimistic and gave glowing reports of the progress of Chief Musquakie's band at the Narrows and Chief Snake's band at Coldwater.[22]

The early government-sponsored settlements, however, were not agrarian utopias for the Ojibwa. Even during the movement of the bands to the new location, there were signs that some younger Ojibwa in this more northerly region were not ready to exchange their rifle for the plow. The chiefs informed Colborne that some of the younger men would 'settle along the portage road from Coldwater to Matchedash next spring [1831]. As for us old men, we intend to settle at the village you are building for us, & end our days there, & our children will be kept at school.'[23] During the planting season on 3 June 1833, the Rev. William Case reported that some of the younger Ojibwa were fishing in Matchedash Bay. They were urgently needed in the fields, but preferred the traditional method of subsistence. Old men and children alone could not carry on farming. Yet early success could attract all of the young men back to the settlements if the villages proved to be viable.

Unfortunately the surrounding white farmers, instead of being exemplary Christians and models of agrarian cooperation, were a retarding influence. Even Anderson admitted in 1835 that the Ojibwa were 'obliged frequently to submit to irritating and extremely unjust Treatment on the Part of the Neighbouring White Settlers.'[24] Internal problems also frustrated the government experiment. Religious rivalry between the Rev. G. Archibald, the Anglican teacher, and the Methodist ministers destroyed the unanimity of effort in the project. In 1836 Sir Francis Bond Head considered the enterprise a failure and 'insisted' that the Ojibwa sell their land and move to Manitoulin Island. Chief John Aisance indicated that fraud was committed in the land transaction when he asserted: 'Sir F. Bond Head insisted on our selling this Land ... we were not made sensible of the full purport, so that we knew not the nature of the bargain.'[25] Although there were obvious problems with the experiment, Head had no perspective in judging the Indians' progress there. Anderson's analysis was much more valid. He indicated that hunting was almost entirely abandoned and habitual intoxication unknown. The young people were becoming literate and had a moderate knowledge of mathematics. Barns and stables were being built and lands cleared by the Indians themselves. They were well clothed in European dress and had exchanged the barter system 'for cash' transactions. Moreover, some Ojibwa had even built two large boats, able to hold about a hundred barrels of fish, which they sold to the white population 'for cash.' Rather than remove these Ojibwa to Manitoulin Island from the settlements in which they were beginning to prosper, local problems should have been resolved. Nevertheless, a new experiment was again attempted, but this time in isolation from pioneer settlements.

The Manitoulin project has been studied by several scholars, all of whom have indicated that the experiment was doomed from the start.[26] Even those Indians who had an inclination towards 'civilization' and who had materially advanced at Coldwater and the Narrows refused to go to the new settlement of Manitowaning on the island. Instead they located at Rama, Beausoleil Island, Snake Island, and Colpoy Bay, where they again attempted to become farmers. Few south of Georgian Bay accepted Bond Head's offer. Those who located in that isolated region likely did so to retain their traditional way of life, not to give it up. Yet the Indians cannot be held fully responsible for the failure of the enterprise.

The government contributed to the demise of its own project in several ways. The geographical choice of Manitoulin for the settlement was extremely poor. George Copway described it as 'a lone barren island, suffered greatly by the bleak winds of the lake, the soil, what there was of it, was not good enough to raise potatoes, or any vegetables for their support, – its chief productions being large rocks and small stones.'[27] His analysis was not unique, and most visitors to Manitoulin shared his view. Nevertheless, Head tenaciously held to the belief that all the Ojibwa of southern Ontario should be removed to this barren, isolated location and he forced several surrenders in southern Ontario in an attempt to achieve this end. The Indian attitude against removal to these islands soon reached officers of the Aborigines' Protection Society, who attacked Head's plan of settling the indigenous people of Ontario on '23,000 rocks of granite, dignified by the name of Manitoulin Islands.'[28] But location was not the only problem. 'The Manitoulin Letters' of the Rev. Charles Crosbie Brough, the missionary of the Church of England on the island, exposed sectarian strife, similar to that which existed at Coldwater. Brough, who had almost no knowledge of the Ojibwa language or culture, made the suggestion that Assikinack, the only person who could translate for him, should be removed since he was under the influence of Father Proulx, who had established a successful Roman Catholic mission nearby at Wikwemikong. The bitter rivalry between the Anglicans and the Roman Catholics on the island contributed substantially to dissipating the strength of the project. The local traders were also a major hindrance since they were 'adverse to missionary establishments ... because in their opinion [the Indians'] settlement and civilization would be detrimental to the traders' commercial interests.' The traders encouraged profits, not Indian 'progress.' Hunting discouraged farming and the liquor trade continued to deteriorate the Indian morale.[29] The government could not eliminate the negative influence of sectarianism or the fur trade on land that was generally unfit for cultivation. The Ojibwa, placed in an environment which still provided their basic necessities, saw greater comfort in retaining their ancient traditions of hunting and fishing.

Displaced Indians from the United States and some from the north shore of Georgian Bay settled on the island. With increasing population pressure, sectarian strife, and negative influence from traders, conditions began to deteriorate. By 1854 Superintendent-General Laurence Oliphant, while making an inspection, described the Ojibwa there as 'miserable, poverty-stricken creatures, wretchedly clad in rags and skins ... looking lean and mangy as curs that shared with them their grilled fish-heads ... [Their] papooses with rolling invisible eyes looking like they were in training for mummies.'[30] The experiment in civilization was not only a failure, but the quality of life among the Ojibwa in the area had dramatically declined. Only seventeen years earlier, the adventurous Anna Jameson had described the Indians on the island as healthy, happy, and well fed.[31] Pragmatism dictated that Manitowaning was not a place of refuge for a large number of culturally shocked people.

The failure of the government-sponsored civilizing projects, first at Coldwater and then on Manitoulin Island, was also indicative of the inability of the Indian Department to cope with change by successfully incorporating the expert leadership of Ojibwa such as Peter Jones. There were two major drawbacks to its approach – personnel and finance. Both were inadequate, especially in the 1830s and 1840s when government policy shifted to making farmers out of hunters and fishermen.

The personnel of the Indian Department were ill equipped to deal with the new objectives. In Upper Canada (Ontario), the Indian Department was divided into five superintendencies for the purpose of administration. Most of the five top positions were filled by employees who had been in service for a considerable length of time. Most of their experience with the Ojibwa had been military, not civil. Lieutenant-Colonel James Givins began his career in the 1790s, became agent for York district in 1797, and in 1830 was made chief superintendent. In addition to that position, he retained control of the central superintendency which stretched north from York to Lake Simcoe and west to Georgian Bay and the Bruce Peninsula. Captain T.G. Anderson was superintendent of Coldwater and later Manitoulin Island. Few surpassed his longevity in office, which began in 1815 as agent of Drummond Island, and continued in various superintendencies until 1858.[32] George Ironside, senior, held his post at Amherstburg for ten years until his son replaced him in 1830. George, junior, held his position until he died in office thirty-three years later. Captain Joseph B. Clench, in charge of the London District, served the department for forty-four years.

All of these superintendencies controlled the affairs of the Ojibwa in southern Ontario. The last one, involving the Six Nations Reserve, was held by the deputy superintendent until John Brant took over for the years 1826 to 1832. Minor posts were held by

Frederick W. Keating at Walpole Island and William Jones in the Sarnia area, with headquarters at Kettle Point. Indian Department personnel did not change as a result of the shift to a civilizing program. Because these positions were based on patronage, the government was reluctant to place dynamic, acculturated Ojibwa leaders such as Peter Jones or George Copway within the upper administrative hierarchy. Indeed, at a time when money was scarce, these positions were considered covetous and lucrative appointments. An excellent opportunity was lost.

Most superintendents received their positions because of past military service. Their experience made them ideal in attracting the Indians to the British military cause in America but ill prepared them to instruct the Indians in a sedentary agrarian life. Very few were farmers. All were Tories and most were Anglicans. As J.D. Leighton notes, 'At their worst, such men were corrupt sycophants ... who regarded their positions as little more than sinecures.'[33] Many were related to one another by blood ties. Indeed, many were members of the Family Compact. The connection of the Indian Department with the business and political élite was close and often personal, and frequently resulted in conflicts of interest when the department was attempting to defend the well-being of its wards. Neither the department nor the Indians had any substantial power in formulating government policy, which emanated from Whitehall. The department implemented the policy, and the Ojibwa were expected to accept the paternalism unquestioningly.

Government critics at the time considered the Indian Department as a 'repository of jobbery and corruption.'[34] Their assumptions seemed to be well–founded, especially in the case of Chief Superintendent Samuel Peters Jarvis, who held his position from 1837 to 1845 when he was dismissed. These were financially decisive years for the Ojibwa of southern Ontario because every cent was required for their attempted evolution into the white man's sedentary mode of life. Yet the government controlled their accounts, and a commission of inquiry exposed numerous irregularities in Jarvis's handling of Ojibwa band funds:

Entries for warrants issued eighteen months previously had obviously been made only days before the commission had received the accounts for examination. Jarvis had made large withdrawals of funds in advance as requisitions for tribal funds; these were supposed to be signed by the chief and show the purpose and the amount of the money withdrawn, but Jarvis had simply marked them 'for the use of the tribe,' making it impossible to trace the disposition of these funds. Jarvis' private bank account and his official one, both at the Bank of Upper Canada, indicated some juggling of money back and forth between the two.[35]

The investigation proved that he had stolen more than £4000 of the Ojibwa's money. In addition to his financial mismanagement, his moral conduct in dealing directly with the Indians was also called into question. The Ojibwa from Snake Island charged that the chief superintendent had issued presents to non-Indians and a double issue to Indians who were his friends. They also complained that Jarvis and some of his friends had seduced four Indian women on board their steamer, *Simcoe*, while returning from Manitoulin Island to Toronto. A woman named Harriet, who came from Big Bay (likely the Nawash settlement), had given birth to a son whom she claimed belonged to Jarvis. Jarvis's family connections and wealth contributed substantially to protect him from legal prosecutions in these affairs. Unfortunately, he was not an exception to the rule. The Indian Department in general was obviously not staffed with men who had the interests of the Indians at heart. It was 'notoreously the worst and most inefficient department in the province.'[36]

As a result, the funds available to the Southern Ojibwa during their transition from hunters to farmers were inadequate. Although they had sold millions of acres to the government, many of them still had to go begging. The *Wesleyan Methodist Report* of 1857 clearly stated the problem: 'Though they have many thousand pounds in the hands of others, yet very little is at their own command. The amount of annuities paid to each, is about six to ten dollars a year, which does not supply their real wants one month, the rest of the time they fish, hunt or beg.'[37] Beggars made poor farmers.

A ceiling of £20,000 per year was placed on Indian Department expenditures as the program of civilizing the Ojibwa was developing in the year of 1829. A considerable demand was placed on this fund. Presents, which Whitehall aptly considered partial payment to the Indians for land, consumed half to two-thirds of the budget. The fixed cost of salaries and pensions to the superintendents and other personnel (£4150) left almost no money in the treasury for implementing the departmental projects.

The distribution of traditional presents was diametrically opposed to the stated objectives of the government in its attempts to create sedentary farmers out of nomadic Ojibwa hunters. To receive the presents at places such as Manitoulin Island, some Indians had to come hundreds of miles and stay several weeks, often during the time when they should have been planting or looking after their crops. Even then, officials could 'shortchange a band either through ignorance or to bolster their own incomes illegally.'[38] Most of the presents were for hunting and fishing, which encouraged their 'nomadic habits.' Often clothing and other items were exchanged with the numerous traders who obtained the presents for relatively inexpensive liquor. Anderson suspected that several prostitution rings were conducted each year on Manitoulin Island by the traders. Needless to say, the distribution of presents was not serving any humanitarian purpose, and a better use could be found for the money.

In 1842 Governor General Sir Charles Bagot launched an investigation into Indian affairs. The Bagot Commission's report was intended as a blueprint to reduce operational costs and make Indian people less reliant on the government, but it became the cornerstone in the evolution to greater expense and dependence. While 'progressive' Ojibwa such as Peter Jones wanted more civil rights, legal control over their lands, and financial responsibility for their own funds, the government unwittingly established the means for greater paternalism. Financial concerns were paramount. The government commission advised that the expensive presents should be paid in implements and tools for farming rather than in guns, ammunition, nets and hooks. This was a positive step in supporting the new Indian policy but, unfortunately, there was also a suggestion that the fund for presents be phased out in a short period of time because they 'encouraged their natural indolence and improvidence; kept them a distinct people; fostered their natural pride and consequence aversion to labour and created an undue feeling of dependence upon the crown.'[39] In 1852 the issue of presents in Upper Canada ceased entirely and was commuted to a money payment beginning with three-fourths the value of the equipment and diminishing one-fourth until final extinction in 1857. During this time the government was forcing more and more Indians onto isolated reserves and providing them with an expensive government department which reinforced their separation from mainstream society. At a time when adequate financial assistance was required to make the transition to farming, funds were considerably decreased.

There was some hope that the annuities resulting from the numerous and extensive land sales would be beneficial to the Southern Ojibwa who were struggling to make the transition to a new way of life. While this concept was certainly feasible, it came too late. The early surrenders involving the best land in southern Ontario were made in exchange for presents. Annuity payments which involved later surrenders were insufficient to cover the expenses of the department's program. In 1854 an attempt was made to provide the required funds in the surrender of half a million acres in the Saugeen Peninsula. Superintendent General L. Oliphant established that adequate funds would come from as little as 100,000 acres at a pound an acre, which he claimed would produce an annuity of £6000. Although the treaty dictated that this money was to go exclusively to the Saugeen, Oliphant suggested that it be used to pay all the expenses of the Indian Department so that Britain would be relieved of any financial burden. His plan was partly adopted. Unfortunately the Saugeen annuity could only cover half the cost of the projected expenditures.[40] Other surrenders were obtained in southern Ontario after 1854 to serve the same purpose, but through mismanagement and small returns, they failed to produce the required capital to develop fully the civilizing program.

Such capital could have been obtained through legitimate sales and the proper management of the Ojibwa trust funds in southern Ontario. Unfortunately, Jarvis's mismanagement and embezzlement of their funds was only the tip of the iceberg. One positive sign that was unique in Canadian Indian-white relations at the time, however, was that hundreds of thousands of acres were sold to settlers in southern Ontario, often at public auctions, for the exclusive benefit of the Ojibwa. Just across the border in Quebec the Ojibwa of Kipawa were given no compensation when Europeans acquired their lands. Yet the Southern Ojibwa did not benefit substantially. The greed, incompetence, stupidity, or criminality of the agents involved in the sales prevented the Indians from having adequate finances in their transition to a farming economy. An examination of agent records of land sales and trust funds for Southern Ojibwa bands exposes the problem.

Few bands failed to suffer from their land agents. The Chenail Ecarté and Lake St Clair bands in 1843 had £200 taken from their funds by agent F.W. Keating, officially for their use, 'but it appeared that the money had not been so applied. Keating indicated he had authority from Jarvis.'[41] Later the Chippewa of Walpole Island surrendered a small reserve in the Township of Moore, which was to be sold at £1171 for their benefit. Colonel Joseph B. Clench, their agent, collected £798 from the sale but could account for only £102. Adding insult to injury, Chief Bauzhi-Giezhig-Waeshikum of Walpole Island complained to Jarvis that squatters had killed a hundred of their pigs, stolen their horses, and shot their dogs 'at the very doors of our lodges.'[42] In another case Clench obtained a surrender of 300 acres in the Township of Auderdon (Block c), called the Chippewa Reserve and occupied by Chief Nottee and two other families, his relatives. They were to remove to Walpole Island, and the money from the sales was to go to them to pay for new houses. A person named Ward bought the land and paid £94 for Nottee's improvements and the first instalment of £125. Two years after the sale 'Nottee had not yet received a farthing and the [money from the] sale was never returned to the Department by Clench. Nottee was really in distress, being quite an old man, and most deserving, having served in every action during the war [of 1812].' Clench claimed that land instalments were not collected by him because of the 'poverty of the purchasers generally.'[43] Indian funds were being used to support poverty-sticken whites.

Nor were the rich neglected. In Sarnia, speculators who bought park lots in the town and even the Grand Western Railroad Co. were in arrears of payment to the sum of £5626. The registration date of purchase by the Grand Western could not even be found, thus preventing a payment of interest at 6 per cent to the Sarnia band on the unpaid debt. When Froome Talford took over the superintendency in 1858, he informed Lord Bury, the superintendent general of Indian affairs, that he was 'obliged to take payment of the third installment [of land-sale payments] without any certainty of the second installments being paid and in the case of the last sale (1854) he had to make out a list of the lots sold from memorandums taken of the persons present at the time.'[44] In such cases, the pioneers were more likely to favour the claims of their white neighbours than the Indians. These financial problems did not simply involve disinterested generosity on the part of the agent. Froome Talford's investigation indicated that there was embezzlement involved: 'It is conclusively shewn by these statements [of land sales] that a large proportion of the sales made and installments paid do not appear at all in the Land Account Books now in my possession.'[45] Agents such as Clench legally received 5 per cent of all the money obtained from land sales, but this was not enough. Greed and nepotism dictated that more could be obtained through illegal means. The claim that the pioneers failed to pay their instalments was likely fabricated in some instances to cover Clench's embezzlement. He was eventually removed from office for stealing 'large sums of money' from the Sarnia Indians. Unfortunately for the majority of Southern Ojibwa, this situation was not unique.

The records of the Northern Agency were in a similar deplorable state, as can clearly be seen from an examination of the accounts over a period of sixty years. The Ojibwa in the Bruce Peninsula had much more to lose since they had surrendered almost a half million acres 'to be sold to pioneers for the benefit of their bands.'[46] The account books from the Indian Land Office in Wiarton give ample evidence of a lack of accuracy and a great deal of confusion resulting from the thousands of individual sales. Up to the year 1910 there is no evidence of any detailed auditing of land-sale records, but in the second decade of the twentieth century there was a systematic audit – over fifty years after the sales had commenced. It came much too late to rectify the problem. The auditors' corrections and notations indicate extensive problems in handling the sales of Saugeen Peninsula lots. The date of purchase was often left out of the reports. As a result, it would have been impossible to determine the interest rate charged on the unpaid amount of the purchase. The auditor made notes such as the following: 'Will you please complete your returns in future before sending them in?' 'Arithmetic, divided as price and interest'; 'More care will be required in the preparation of these returns'; 'If you do [sic] not be more careful and keep your sales nos. correct, there will be needless trouble.' As many as five corrections were made on one month's returns. Numerous mistakes were made in names of buyers, dates of purchase, total price of sale, and in simple addition and division involving principal and interest.[47] Incompetent book-keeping, however, was not the only way in which the Ojibwa were cheated out of the money promised them from the land sales.

The government was constantly pressed for concessions by non-Indians who had settled in the Saugeen Peninsula. Most of the pioneers had bought their lots on the instalment plan. They usually paid one-fifth of the money at the time of the sale, with the balance due in four equal consecutive yearly instalments at an interest rate of 6 per cent. These sales were to be cancelled, with loss of the down-payment, if the instalments were not met, and the land resold for the benefit of the Indians. In addition, timber dues were also imposed on the settlers: $4 was charged for a licence to cut timber, and there was a charge for the various classes of timber taken off the land ranging from $30 for 1000 cubic feet of squared oak timber to 20 cents for a cord of soft cordwood. These provisions, if adhered to, would have resulted in millions of dollars flowing into Saugeen band funds. Some farm lots sold for as high as $30 per acre, while some park lots at Southampton were sold at prices as high as $2200 in 1856. Once the speculators' frenzy had subsided, many realized that they had bid beyond their means. The settlers, who had the power of the vote, expressed their views to the government that such moneys were needed more by them than the Ojibwa.

In 1868 the Ontario Provincial Legislature was petitioned by the Bruce County Council to extend the time for payment of arrears on crown lands and to refund 50 cents per acre on 'wild' lands sold to the settlers. In addition, the county made a claim to 'money derived from the sale of lands in the County of Bruce.' A. Sproat, MPP for North Bruce, stated in the parliamentary session of 1869: 'One-third of the purchase money, required at the time of sale, would in most cases represent the value of the lot, and I hope some plan would be adopted to relieve settlers of two-thirds of the price.'[48] Three years later a deputation was appointed by the county to visit Ottawa and confer with the government. Two of their grievances would result in a considerable loss of Ojibwa band funds. They requested the appointment of a commissioner to revalue the unsold land in the peninsula and, in addition. 'to cause to be re-valued such lands as have been sold at an exorbitant price, of lands of inferior quality on which the whole purchase money had not yet been paid.'[49] The traditional European motto, *caveat emptor*, was set aside in their dealings with the Indians.

Such a re-evaluation required the greatest objectivity in balancing the interests of the Indians against the settlers in Bruce County. Unfortunately, an impartial valuator was not found. William Bull, clerk of the Township of Amabel, was appointed to make an objective valuation of the lands and report to the government, but no Ojibwa was involved. Bull's job and his friendship with his neighbours likely biased his decisions, since the settlers in Amabel represented the bulk of the petitioners. His report was acted on immediately. The Hon. David Laird, minister of the interior, announced in 1875 'that he had been authorized to grant such measures of relief at once that shall be just to both the settlers' and the Indians' interests. That each settler's case would be dealt with on its own merits, and that all interest [on unpaid lands] would be remitted up to the end of that year.' At the same time, the timber licence fee was cut in half and the timber dues reduced by an order in council.[50] Recognizing that the wedge was easily inserted to separate the Ojibwa from their land-sale money, the pioneers struck again. Demands were made for a second valuation in 1897–8. Again, 'large reductions were made in favour of the settlers.'[51] Even this did not satisfy the majority. Only token payments would be acceptable. This was achieved in 1901 by another order in council which eliminated tens of thousands of dollars in interest payment and considerably reduced the price of land purchased but not fully paid as well as land that had not yet been sold. The reductions in the sold and unsold lands as well as the timber dues was a flagrant breaking of faith with the Ojibwa, who had surrendered their lands to be sold for their exclusive benefit.

Thousands of acres of land had been sold but not paid for in full. A letter from the Indian Affairs Department to Indian land agent W.J. Ferguson demonstrates how these cases were treated:

I have to inform you that upon reference to your letter of the 4th April, 1906, you state that Alexander Campbell, owner of this Lot 25 Con. 4, w.b.r., St. Edmunds [Township] was notified that the arrears against it were Principal $62.00 and Interest thereon $72.62 or a total of $134.62, but upon reference to the Valuator's Report it is observed that upon their recommendation, the price of this Lot was reduced to 15 cents per acre or $15.60 for the Lot. As Mr. Campbell paid at the time of purchase $16.00, the Lot is therefore paid for in full.[52]

In this particular re-evaluation, Campbell's first instalment on the 104 acres was accepted as more than full payment and he did not have to pay any of the $72.62 interest that had accumulated on the unpaid portion. It must be stressed that people such as Campbell had willingly and knowingly purchased the land under the condition that they would pay the future instalments and the interest or else forfeit their land. Had this British common-law practice been implemented here, the Ojibwa bands would have gained $16 from the first instalment and, when the second was not paid, they could have sold the land to a new buyer at $2.50, rather than 15 cents, per acre. Instead, Campbell obtained the land at one-eighth of the price he should have paid. This unjustifiable government action was repeated in hundreds of similar cases. The Indian Department in these actions demonstrated a pusillanimous paternalism.

Similarly, in the handling of the lands that remained unsold in the peninsula, the department failed to protect the economic future of its wards. Much of the land sold at less than 15 cents per acre. In most cases it was not a question of relief for struggling pioneers at the expense of the Indian. Rich, land-hungry speculators were the benefactors. W.J. Fenton of Hamilton formed land agencies which bought thousands of acres in Albermarle, Amabel, and Keppel townships at low prices in 1882 and later sold them at inflated prices. Even William Bull purchased 705 acres at the reduced price, which was unquestionably a conflict of interest. The re-evaluation in 1898–9 resulted in over 75,000 acres being sold for 5 or 10 cents per acre. Many of these acreages on the lakefront are today being sold for $100,000. Had the Indian Department held onto the land as 'unfit for cultivation' and sold it later as vacation property, no contemporary Ojibwa reserve would be a 'whiteman's welfare albatross.'[53]

As early as 1857 the object of establishing isolated farming communities of Indians throughout southern Ontario was considered a failure. Most Ojibwa had not become independent, prosperous agriculturalists after almost thirty years of experimentation. Had they achieved their objective, the patronage positions of the Indian Department would have been abolished, with a loss of jobs for members of the establishment and their children. While this might have been an additional factor in retarding progress, certainly the lack of money played a major role. Farming at the time, even under the best of conditions, was a precarious occupation subject to the market value of the produce and especially the unpredictable weather. However, faced with starvation as a result of the depletion of their traditional food supply, many Indians did turn to agriculture as a means of survival. Had they not, the prediction of some Indians and many whites – that they would soon be an extinct race – would have come true. Instead, after the first shock of massive European settlement, the Ojibwa population began to grow gradually at first but then more rapidly. Nevertheless, success was defined by the government mainly in terms of economic independence. This was not achieved, partly because the annuities were being unjustifiably depleted.

In 1857 the final solution had been proposed – enfranchisement. In that year the 'Civilization Act' was placed in the statutes of Canada. Government officials and humanitarians alike expected the act to eliminate all of the existing evils. Full citizenship would protect individual rights and property of those Ojibwa who chose to become enfranchised. Those considered educationally and morally capable would receive a deed to fifty acres of the band's land. No longer would a few coerced members be able to surrender all the land, including the improvements of the more progressive band members. Such enfranchised Ojibwa could also borrow money from the bank, using the land as collateral, and they could make use of the courts as full citizens. They could also vote and hold office in parliament. The advantages seemed endless. What more could be expected than to be treated like full British subjects with all their rights and privileges? The humanitarians became complacent with this success, which they considered the end of the battle with Indian equality.[54]

It was not the final solution. Although many acculturated Ojibwa were expected to take immediate advantage of this 'benevolent' act, few did. Indeed, twenty years after its passing only one Indian, Elias Hill, a Mohawk, was enfranchised. Philanthropic expectations had obviously been misplaced. While the Civilization Act seemed to have great advantages for the Ojibwa, in their eyes the disadvantages were considerably greater. First, the Indians considered it a breach of the Royal Proclamation of 1763, which dictated that the Indians were to determine any alienation of their land. They correctly assumed that once the deed of fifty acres was given to an individual band member, it decreased their common lands and could be sold to anyone without their approval or the crown's. This would certainly have led to the territorial disintegration of the band unit and the loss of its social cohesion. Moreover, assuming that the most highly educated and respectable members were eligible for enfranchisement and would accept it, the band would gradually lose its best members as they integrated into white society. Eventually there would be no band identity, no effective band leadership, and no geographical refuge from the alien European society. In a word, the Ojibwa would be assimilated. While enfranchisement was the ideal of European philanthropists, it was not an elixir for the Ojibwa.[55]

Ojibwa protesters immediately attacked the assimilationist policy. The act, according to one chief, was surely an attempt 'to break them to pieces.' When the Ojibwa at Munsey petitioned against the act, Chief Superintendent R.J. Pennefather simply responded: 'The Civilization Act is no grievance to you.' No Europeans came to their side in this battle. As one historian correctly observed: 'In 1857 the civilizer and the Indian began to march to a different drum. The dichotomy of one wanting to retain tribal identity and the other destroy it created insurmountable problems.'[56] In 1861, when the Colpoy Bay Band were forced from their frame houses, barns, cleared fields, and saw mill, no European was prepared to protest. Many Ojibwa felt that their European friends had abandoned them, and that cooperation in the civilization scheme had come to an end. The object of the Ojibwa of southern Ontario became cultural and economic survival in Ojibwa communities on Ojibwa lands in small pockets throughout southern Ontario.

By the middle of the nineteenth century, how much had the

Ojibwa changed in order to survive the influx of white settlers? An accurate demographic analysis of the degree of Ojibwa acculturation is difficult to determine. Information about the communities came mostly from two major sources – government officials and missionaries. Both were biased. Officials in charge of experimental projects seemed to praise the 'advancement' of certain Ojibwa communities to justify the expenditures on their experimental schemes. However, the same communities were described as retrogressive when their lands were coveted by local pioneers who demanded surrenders. The missionary statistics may also be called into question since they wished to justify their labours in order to obtain desperately needed funds to advance their cause. Possibly a more objective observer might be found in W.H. Smith, who compiled the first *Canadian Gazetteer* of Canada West (Ontario) in 1846.

Smith spent two years, in summer and winter, travelling throughout the province south of Georgian Bay gathering statistical information on both the Indian and the white communities. Unlike the bureaucrat and missionary, he had no vested interest in the Ojibwa civilization program. Indeed, he was critical of the reports of both groups. His demographic study tells us much about the survival methods of individual bands.

He reported that the Mississauga settlement at Alderville, fifteen miles northeast of Cobourg, was not hunting and fishing at all. The 233 Indians there lived on farms divided into twenty-five acres. They had large houses, twenty-two frame and fourteen square log, six commodious frame barns, a sawmill, and a large school house. Their stock consisted of eight yoke of oxen, two horses, eleven cows, twenty-one heifers and calves, and a number of pigs and poultry. They also possessed eight ploughs, six harrows, three carts and wagons, and twelve ox-sleighs. Each family had at least half of their lots cleared and in crops, while several had nearly the whole under cultivation. An experimental farm was the focus of the reserve.

The 700 Ojibwa near Sarnia still retained 10,230 acres on the main reserve and three smaller reserves – 2650 acres at the Rivière aux Sables, 2446 acres at Kettle Point, and 2575 acres on the St Clair River. There were forty-two separate farms, sixteen of which had good substantial log houses and the rest small log or bark houses with sheds for their crops. They had a capacious meeting house that was also used as a church and school. Eight ploughs, four harrows, a number of scythes, two fanning mills, and four cross-cut saws were shared by the Sarnia Ojibwa. They also had nine yoke of oxen, eight cows, and some young stock, besides a large number of horses and pigs. They cultivated chiefly Indian corn and potatoes, and a small quantity of spring wheat, oats, and peas. Field work was done by the men, not the women. They seldom hunted, but their income was supplemented by selling fish, bowls, brooms, rush mats, axe handles, and baskets in the nearby white settlements. Many were employed cutting cordwood for the pioneers. An excellent sign of their adjustment to the new way of life was the fact that three children per family were reaching maturity.

Northeast of Sarnia, the 378 Chippawa of the Thames were also doing well on their 9000 acres which were surveyed into 20-acre farms. They had a school house also used as a church, seventy-six log houses and six wigwams, with twenty-five barns. Their equipment included four wagons and carts, nine ploughs, nine harrows, a fanning-mill, a blacksmith's forge, and two-and-a-half sets of carpenter's tools. They possessed fourteen oxen, fifty cows, thirty heifers, fifty-five horses and colts, and 250 swine. The population was increasing at the same rate as the Sarnia band.

At Walpole Island in Lake St Clair, the 319 Chippewa of Chenail Ecarté were being inundated by over 800 Ojibwa, Potawatomi, and Ottawa from the United States. While some were adopted into the band and settled on the island, many were transients moving on to the more northern reserves. The Ojibwa of Walpole Island did very little hunting and fishing, and many were well on their way to becoming farmers. They had nine ploughs and as many yoke of oxen, besides scythes and sickles in abundance. They also had a large number of pigs and horses and the chief had two cows. The number of dwellings was twenty-eight, of which three were framed, with several more in the course of erection, and four log barns. At least one hundred heads of families had commenced to till the land. Six hundred acres were in cultivation. The chief crop was corn, but large quantities of potatoes, some oats, buckwheat, and peas were also grown. Some of the Ojibwa were anxious to have their children educated and become Christians, but the old chief prevented missionaries from proselytising among them. Again, the population increase was the same as the Sarnia Indians except for the 'roving' Potawatomi.

Only those Coldwater and the Narrows Ojibwa who located south after the surrender of 1836 were reported. These involved Chief Yellowhead's band of 184 people who went to Rama, and Chief Snake's band of 109 who settled on Snake Island, both in Lake Simcoe. Those who went to Beausoleil Island, Christian Island, and Colpoy Bay were not included in Smith's statistics. Considering the disruption of resettlement, the Rama band was adapting adequately. Of 1600 acres, they had 300 in cultivation. They had a large school house, and they lived in twenty houses and had four barns. Their potato crop was so abundant in one year that they sold 400–500 bushels to the settlers in Orillia and Medonte, without inconveniencing themselves. On Snake Island the Ojibwa were not as fortunate in their harvests. They had 150 acres under cultivation, but even the superintendent admitted that the soil was stoney and not well adapted for cultivation. They supplemented their income by making and selling maple sugar. They occupied twelve houses and had two barns. A school house there also served as their church. No indication was given of their population rate.

The two settlements at the ends of the ancient portage route across the Saugeen Peninsula had also begun their adjustments to white incursions. The 130 Ojibwa at Owen Sound had a school house which was used as a church, fourteen log houses, and a barn. With two yoke of oxen they ploughed 120 acres of land. Near the growing town of Southampton, 300 Saugeen cultivated 250 acres. They also had a chapel which served as a school house, six log houses, and the rest bark huts or wigwams. Because there were few settlers in the Saugeen territory, they were still heavily dependent on fishing and hunting. Indeed, in 1851 the census taken in Greenock Township alone, thirty miles from their settlement, indicates that thirty Ojibwa were living in the bush. The superintendent noted that the Indians were already being annoyed by white encroachment on their substantial fisheries. While the missionary claimed they were a happy and progressive people, the Indian agent concluded that they were poor and miserable. It appears that Smith did not visit this remote settlement.

Several hundred Ojibwa in a dozen settlements scattered throughout southern Ontario were adapting to an almost completely new environment. Many more were still attempting to carry on their traditional hunting and fishing economy in areas that were less populated. Those who had chosen farming as a way of life were increasing in numbers, while those who gathered their food from the wilderness were often faced with starvation. The sedentary Ojibwa settlements increasingly became refuges for those who found the white population encroaching on their hunting grounds. In the highly populated areas, the Ojibwa settlements had the advantage of selling their surplus food and crafts. They could also work on white men's farms. However, they did not share equally in the Euro-Canadian prosperity that was growing around them, and they were not assimilated.

It is no wonder, considering the strong cultural heritage of the Ojibwa, the inadequate personnel of the Indian Department, the limited financial commitment, and the attitude of European settlers in Ontario, that the policies established at Whitehall were too idealistic and were doomed to failure in the context of their objectives. However, there is little doubt that the Ojibwa in southern Ontario were faced with insurmountable problems if they were not assisted by British authorities. A new mode of life was required to prevent their total extinction. The cry for help first came from the Ojibwa in the most southerly regions of Ontario, and the way out of their chaotic condition was first led by an Ojibwa, Peter Jones. He acted as a catalyst between his people and the missionaries, between humanitarians and government officials. He succeeded in developing a nucleus of native people who encouraged formal white education and the sedentary occupation of farming as a necessary means of survival. The influence of the Wesleyan-Methodists and of the broad humanitarian alliance was essential to raise the policy above politics and finance for a brief period of time. That period was decisive for the survival of the Ojibwa in southern Ontario. Unfortunately, it was not sustained or strengthened, and the Ojibwa quality of life did not generally rise much above the lowest level of existence. The Indian Department, as guardians of the Ojibwa, did little to improve the condition of their people. Indeed, in many cases, departmental officials only frustrated Whitehall's directives. In 1860 the Indian 'problem,' which the British created and attempted to solve, was passed on to the Canadian government.

8

RESERVE STAGNATION
'We Are under a Dictatorship'

Responsibility for Indian affairs was transferred to the Province of Canada in 1860. The relative objectivity that the British had brought to solving problems between the natives and the colonists came to an end. As a result, the noose around the necks of the indigenous peoples was tightened. In the last half of the nineteenth century, public and political attention shifted from the Ojibwa in southern Ontario to the Indians of western Canada as new lands were settled by pioneers. This was evident in the Indian Act of 1876, which consolidated the existing legislation dealing with native people. The Ojibwa, however, were not neglected by the growing bureaucratic structure after Confederation. The Ojibwa on the southern reserves of Ontario came under tighter regulation than ever before. Much greater control was also placed on the Indian children in reserve schools, who were taught almost exclusively by non-Indians. Residential schools were substantially expanded by the various Canadian religious denominations in an attempt to exclude the cultural influence of the parents. Indeed, self-determination was generally taken away from the Ojibwa by government agents who became the overseers of almost every aspect of their lives. The Ojibwa voiced their objections in their grand councils, but internal factionalism and the power of the dictatorial government over them made such protests meaningless.[1] Existence on reserves came more and more under the control of bureaucrats. Yet the main policy objective of the government to assimilate the Ojibwa into mainstream Canadian society failed because of the ways the policy was implemented. Economic stagnation characterized most reserves.

The 1844 *Report on the Indians of Upper Canada* had strongly recommended manual labour schools as the best method of assimilating the Indians. Because parents were considered a negative influence on their children's education, the students were to be placed in boarding schools, isolated as much as possible from their family and elders. But the application of this plan for all Ojibwa education was extremely expensive and far beyond the existing financial capacity of the Indian Department. Some money had been temporarily obtained for the maintenance of the schools by discontinuing the issue of presents to the Indians. Since ammunition made up part of the presents, Governor General Lord Metcalfe concluded that the action would also restrict the 'roaming habit' of hunting. When these funds also proved insufficient, the government unilaterally deducted up to one-fourth of the land-sale annuity money from the more prosperous bands to support residential schools. The churches continued to play the major role in managing the institutions and making financial contributions to them.

The residential school became the ideal method of educating Ojibwa children from the point of view of the dominant white society. This attitude is expressed in a letter from the Rev. Alexander Sutherland, general secretary of the Methodist Church of Canada, Missionary Department, to Laurence Vankoughnet, deputy superintendent general of Indian affairs: 'Experience convinces us that the only way in which the Indian of the country can be permanently elevated and thoroughly civilized is by removing the children from the surroundings of Indian home life, and keeping them separated long enough to form those habits of order, industry, and systematic effort, which they will never learn at home.' He suggested that the department 'fix the term of residency at five years for girls and six for boys, and make attendance for this term compulsory. The return of children to their houses, even temporarily, has a bad effect, while their permanent removal after one or two years residence results in the loss of all that they have gained.'[2]

Numerous residential schools were founded in Ontario for the Ojibwa. In 1842 an industrial school at Alnwick (Alderville) was established, drawing students from the Chippewa of Lakes Huron and Simcoe, of Saugeen and Nawash, and from the Mississauga of Alnwick and Rice, Mud and Scugog lakes, as well as from Garden

River. The Mount Elgin School at Muncey Town was completed in 1851, with children coming from St Clair, Chenail Ecarté, Thames River, and New Credit. The Mohawk Institute was rebuilt in 1859. Shingwauk Home was established at Sault Ste Marie in 1874, eventually just for boys, and Wawanosh Home for girls was built four years later at the same location. In addition to the Protestant schools, there were Roman Catholic residential schools at Spanish which replaced the school which was destroyed by fire on Manitoulin Island. Some Indians also attended St Jerome's 'white' school in Berlin (later Kitchener). As late as 1940, half of the Indian pupil population of 9000 were still in residential schools.[3]

Because a great number of Ojibwa students attended these institutions, they require close examination, especially since the general philosophy of the system remained the same for over a hundred years. The object was to destroy the Ojibwa culture and assimilate the natives into mainstream Canadian society. The deputy superintendent general, Duncan Campbell Scott, clearly reiterated this policy when he stated: 'The happiest future of the Indian race is absorption into the general population, and this is the object of the policy of our government. The great forces of ... education will finally overcome the lingering traces of native custom and tradition.'[4] Insight into the early development of the residential schools can be gained through the examination of the career of Edward F. Wilson, founder and first principal of both the Shingwauk and Wawanash homes. Many southern Ontario Ojibwa attended these more northerly institutions.

Wilson was not typical of nineteenth-century missionary-educators recruited from the ranks of the upwardly mobile lower class. As a member of a renowned evangelical family, he came from the British upper-middle class, where the Wilson family had earned its wealth three generations previously in mercantile and commercial pursuits. Wilson's grandfather, a founding members of the Church Missionary Society in 1799, had established the Wilson clerical dynasty by purchasing 'the livings of Islington, Worton, Walthamstow, and Tooting for his sons-in-law.' It would have been easy for Edward Wilson to attend Oxford and become a clergyman, but he was influenced by his mother to take up missionary work. He wrote: 'When I was a child it was my mother's hope and wish that I should bear the glad tidings of the Gospel to distant lands. She was a Missionary in heart herself, and it was her earnest desire that one of her boys would grow up to devote himself to that most blessed work.' Wilson easily obtained a commission as missionary to the Ojibwa from the Church Missionary Society, and he arrived at London, Ont., on 22 July 1868. From there he was 'to travel around and select what might seem to be the best spot to make the centre for a new mission.'[5]

Wilson examined southern Ontario but found 'a paucity of pagans.' Most of them were either Methodist or Roman Catholic. He tried to establish a mission on the Kettle Point and Sarnia reserves, but ran into opposition from the Methodists when his arrogance created tension with the already established missionaries there. After he made friends among the Ojibwa, particularly the Wawanosh family, he decided to search out groups in a more pagan state. He looked to Algoma in the north.

On his first visit to Algoma, Wilson found the Ojibwa almost all Christians, but he saw another purpose: 'there first entered into my mind the idea of an institution for training the young Indian.' The idea might have been placed there by one of the chiefs who said: 'The time is passing for my people to live by hunting and fishing as our forefathers used to do; if we are to continue to exist at all we must learn to gain our living in the same way as the white people.' The natural resources of timber, minerals, and land were attracting the Europeans to the north shore of Georgian Bay. What had happened in the more southerly part of Ontario to encourage Indian education was also occurring in the Algoma district. Available land in southern Ontario was becoming scarce and the opening of five townships near Sault Ste Marie caused settlers to pour into the free grant lands in the 1870s. Again education was not seen as a choice but a necessity to many Ojibwa. Chief Shingwauk and his brother Bukhwujenene of the Garden River Reserve believed that their old Indian way of life would have to be abandoned, and they set aside a part of the reserve for an industrial school.

Money had to be raised for the construction of the school. Wilson used methods similar to his predecessors a generation earlier, but he had some additional advantages. In 1872 he took Chief Bukhwu-jenene to England to solicit funds for the new venture, and contributions came from several sources. The Colonial and Continental Church Society started an annual contribution, and Wilson also received a letter, likely from a relative, stating that 'a friend will guarantee you one hundred pounds a year if you remain at your post at Garden River.' The Canadian government unilaterally used funds from the Indian land sales once again to help build and support another school. The first Shingwauk Industrial School was built on the reserve at a cost of £1550. The building was completed on 22 September 1873, by which time sixteen pupils had already arrived. They came from Sarnia, Walpole Island, Manitoulin Island, and Garden River. Six days after its completion, it was burned to the ground. It did not have fire insurance. Fortunately, twice the amount of money was obtained for the reconstruction. By 1875 the second Shingwauk School opened, located ten miles away from the reserve to be closer to Sault Ste Marie.

Four years later another school was built two miles from Shingwauk to separate the boys from the girls. While death and sickness of a student could be explained to the parents as 'acts of God,' pregnancy could not. The girls' school was called Wawanosh, after the famous Sarnia Reserve Chief. The construction of the Wawanosh Home involved the same financial problems as the establishment of most Indian institutions, but the students were not simply used as 'show pieces' for the raising of money. Immediately after the purchase of five acres of bush land, the male students were employed to clear the trees, dig the foundation for the school, and gather stones for a two-storey structure with a forty-five foot frontage. During the summer they collected all of the stone that was necessary and were paid twenty cents a cord for piling it. Wilson noted: 'We were anxious as soon as possible to get the new Home into operation. After the summer of 1876 no girls returned to the Shingwauk and we doubled our number of boys. It seemed hard to shut the girls out from the privilege of Christian care and education.' The story of these schools dispels the myth that the Ojibwa had all their schools built for them by the government. It is also debatable whether the Indian boys were given Christian care and education or 'hard time' on a rock pile. On 19 August 1879 the Wawanosh Home was completed.[6]

The principal's objective in the Shingwauk and Wawanosh schools was to 'raise the Indian to a position equal to that of his white brethren.' The Indian was to exchange the bow and arrow for the carpenter's bench, the war-club for the blacksmith's hammer, the net and canoe for the plough. Many aspects of Indian society were diametrically opposed to the European educational system. Their concept of time, freedom, communication, sharing, authority, religion, and learning had few aspects of positive transfer which could help them in a formal classroom situation. In fact, much that they had acquired in their preschool days had to be unlearned. This 'unlearning' alienated them from their family and community.

The school schedule was to create the transition from the Indian to the white way of life. As Wilson explained:

We soon got into regular working order. School hours were from 9 to 12 in the morning, and 2:30 to 5 in the afternoon, every day except Saturday. We had fifty pupils, twenty-five boys and twenty-five girls, varying in age from six or seven years up to seventeen. It was of course a great change for them to commence regular habits, to run when they heard the bell ring, and do all that they were told; and some of them began to pine under a sense of captivity. Some of them, when home-sick, seemed to lose all control over themselves, and made an unearthly noise, others would watch their opportunity and run away. On the whole, however, the children seemed to be wonderfully contented and happy, and all went merrily and cheerfully day after day. The fish-boys used to go out after their nets each morning and bring in plenty of fish; the water-boys had their ... job. The baker-boys made and baked the bread in the brick oven ... All were willing to work, and seemed to enjoy their life, and on Saturday we gave them a few cents pocket-money as encouragement to good conduct. True the matron was sometimes at her wit's end, with so many to provide for and such raw young girls ... the greater number of whom scarcely speak a word of English.[7]

Did the program, which eventually involved seventy-five boys at Shingwauk and thirty girls at Wawanosh, achieve its goal? Wilson himself had his doubts, but his book, *Missionary Work among the Ojibwa Indians*, does not reveal his concern. He continued to give the impression that the children enjoyed the schedule: 'Our apprentice boys work ten hours a day, six days a week, and very rarely ask for holidays. Having once become accustomed to regular work, they like it, and will stick to it as well as any white man.' One may question whether the boys had any choice. Wilson, as founder and principal of the institution, had an understandable bias.

Fortunately, several students have recorded their personal experiences at Indian residential schools, one of whom attended the Shingwauk Home. The students also wrote with a bias, yet, if used with caution, these accounts give an insight into the impact of residential schools on the Ojibwa.

Most students found the systematic eradication of the Ojibwa language a major factor in alienating them not only from their culture but from their friends on the reserve as well. Basil Johnston, who experienced residential school life, thoroughly understood this alienation: 'As long as language exists it enables men to understand and appreciate their ideas and philosophies and to share in their humor, so long do they adhere to their way of life. To prevent the young from retaining their culture, students in schools were prohibited from speaking their language. Once language disappeared men began to forget their former purpose of life and ideas, they could only understand the thoughts of the adopted culture.'[8]

This linguistic transition to the white man's world and the feeling of alienation were clearly experienced by Geniesh (Jane Willis) at the Shingwauk Home. She was a Cree whose culture was very similar to the Ojibwa who far outnumbered any other ethnic group in the residence. In her autobiography, *Geniesh*, she reflects the frustrating transition that most Ojibwa experienced on the reserve after spending several years in the institutions:

Even the language seemed to have changed, I had difficulty understanding it, but I had even greater difficulty trying to make myself understood. It had been a red-letter day when, two months after I had left the Island, I discovered that I no longer thought or dreamt in Cree, but in English. I found myself having to reverse that process once again. When my relatives repeatedly laughed at my 'funny accent,' I refused to speak any more Cree.

The people, too, had changed. Friends I had grown up with not only refused to come near me, but giggled and retreated.[9]

The reserve friends and relatives who did not share her educational experience had changed but little, while Geniesh had changed considerably. In their traditional society, Ojibwas depended on dreams as a guide in their spiritual as well as secular life. Dreaming in English, rather than Indian, undoubtedly changed this perspective. Shingwauk had not only alienated Geniesh from her village but from life in general.

The policy of destroying the children's native language was common in all residential schools. It even extended to the students' correspondence. In a letter written in 1901 to J.A. McCrea of the Department of Indian Affairs who was investigating the complaints of several Ojibwa parents that they had not received letters from their children, Principal W.W. Shephard of the Mt Elgin Institute explained: 'Our custom is to allow each child an opportunity every two weeks for correspondence. This is done in the school room under the supervision of the teacher. All the appliances are supplied by the Institution except stamps [which many could not afford]. The letters both going and coming are under close censorship and of course have to be intercepted at times. We found it necessary to prevent letters written in Indian from going out, and the pupils all understand that all must be in English – or the letter cannot go. It would be an advantage if all parents and guardians were compelled in the same way.'[10] Even today there are Ojibwa in southern Ontario who cannot speak or write English. A hundred years ago most could not. The impact of this language policy on reserve family life was shown explicitly in Ojibwa chief Snow Cloud's (John Roger's) autobiography. When he and his brother returned home after being in residential school for some years, they were greeted by their mother: 'She endeavored to gather us all into her arms at once. She started talking joyously, but we couldn't understand very well what she said, for we had forgotten much of the Indian language during our six years away from home.' Those who attended residential schools for several years quickly became 'Apple Indians,' not only in language but also in their attitude.

Jane Willis's emotional reaction, upon returning to her village, was likely shared by most Ojibwa children:

I was appalled at the shabbiness and seediness that surrounded me. Had I, for fifteen years, lived amid such utter poverty? Had I become a snob

– as my friends had predicted I would – looking down at my own people and their old ways? My outlook and my feelings, I told myself, could not have changed so drastically in a few years.

By the time I got to my grand mother's shack, I felt better. I raised my hand to knock on the door, but remembered just in time that knocking before entering was considered 'white' and snobbish. I barged in.[11]

Willis's psychological transformation, as a result of the residential school, was typical. The children were comfortable neither in the white man's world nor in the Indian's world, and their self-image and self-respect were shattered.

In the years after the establishment of residential schools, Ojibwa communities were divided on their acceptance of such institutions. The proposed construction of a boarding school in the Indian Peninsula (later, Bruce Peninsula) was resisted by the conservative members of the band and they constantly sent in resolutions objecting to their funds being used for such projects. One of the head chiefs at Saugeen, Wahbadick, prevented the Rev. W. Hurlburt, a Methodist, from forcibly taking some children to the school at Alnwick. Ojibwa hostility to this form of education grew. Often the distance of the schools from the reserves and the initial policy of not granting holidays meant that parents were reluctant to part with their children. Reports of the mistreatment of students, the high incidence of death and disease, and the deliberate policy of cultural transformation did little to assuage the Indians of their hostility.

The schools were increasingly used as depositories for children from broken families and for problem children. Traditionally, families had adopted children who could not be cared for by their parents. As their economic and social base deteriorated, some family units showed signs of disintegration. The children from such families became prime candidates for the residential schools, but with a loss of self-respect to the band members who had previously prided themselves on 'looking after their own.' While most former students were critical of the residential schools, some simply stated: 'Where else could we go?' Even teachers at the schools were critical. The Rev. E.E.M. Joblin, after examining residential schools in western Ontario, reported: 'Too large a proportion of the pupils have been delinquents or problem children, which has created many problems for the staff and proven an unwholesome influence on the other children in the school.'[12] This most expensive component of the Indian educational system proved to be a disappointment, since few graduates made the transition to the white wage economy. Most returned to their reserves and their traditional pursuits.

Church-operated residential schools also had a more sinister disadvantage for its wards. Sexual abuse of the children by ministers, priests, nuns, and teachers was widespread, according to recent evidence.[13] Since the abused are inclined to become abusers, reserve life was likely influenced adversely by these experiences. Wilfred Pelletier of Wikwemikong observed that his 'introduction to sex had been very different on the reserve from what it might have been had he grown up in white society ... White society, I know, tends to look on sex with one's blood relations as unnatural. But to me it seems the most natural thing in the world.' Because of the fear and shame that many of the children experienced as a result of the abuse, the perpetrators of the crimes were seldom brought to justice.[14]

Most Ojibwa children were taught on the reserves in day schools because of the hostility to and expense of residential education. The financial statements of the Indian Affairs Department give ample evidence that many bands not only paid for the buildings out of their own funds but also contributed to maintenance and the teachers' salaries. While most of the chiefs and councillors recognized the importance of a formal education for their children, this was not necessarily true of all band members. Attendance was often irregular. In the early period, the demands of trapping, fishing, hunting, maple-sugar making, and wild rice gathering prevented a sedentary family existence conducive to successful classroom teaching. Later, lumbering and fruit and tobacco picking in various locations off the reserves also added to the movement which was necessary for employment and survival. It was this nomadic existence, along with what was considered a negative parental influence, which caused the authorities to encourage the establishment of residential schools and discourage all economic activities except farming. Successful education on the reserves required regular attendance by the pupils as well as able teachers.

In the formative years of education in Canada there was a constant shortage of qualified teachers. This was certainly true on the reserves well into the twentieth century. Unfortunately, there were few inducements for the best teachers to instruct in Ojibwa schools. For non-Indian teachers, there were problems of isolation, culture shock, and poor pay. Many teachers did not stay for a full year, and unqualified instructors were hired. Mary Moffat, for example, taught at the Cape Croker Reserve for many years, 'even if she fails her examinations.' In 1917 she received a salary of $600, while the Indian agent's daughter, also a teacher, was paid $450, and an Indian, Thomas Jones, was paid the least, $400. By white standards the pay was modest, but in most cases it was equal to or better than the remuneration given to the chiefs of the Ojibwa reserves.[15]

In contrast with the early years, it was unusual to find even 'qualified' Indians as teachers on the reserves in the later nineteenth and early twentieth centuries. They filled the positions only if no white person, qualified or not, could be found. Several factors worked against hiring Indians as teachers. Since the philosophy of both the Indian Department and the missionary institutions was to replace Indian with European culture, it was thought that the best teachers would obviously be white. The most blatant example of this view is found in a letter written by an Indian Department bureaucrat in response to a qualified Indian teacher's application for a job at a school on an Ojibwa reserve:

Re. the Indian Student, Clifford Tobias, I beg to say that his academic standing might be sufficient, especially if his term standing in High School were uniformly good. But he could not teach them Horticulture and Agriculture. I would not advise putting any Indian in charge of an Indian School. These children require to have the 'Indian' educated out of them, which only a white teacher can help to do.

An Indian is always and only an Indian and has not the social, moral and intellectual standing required to elevate these Indian children, who are quite capable of improvement.[16]

It is most unfortunate that Indian graduates were not employed on the reserves. Ojibwa teachers would have created positive role models for the students to emulate. Indian students would have taken pride in the fact that they were being educated by their own people; and, as teachers, Indians would have been more sensitive to the numerous negative stereotypes such as simplemindedness, laziness, and drunkenness. They could be explained in or eliminated from the textbooks and lessons, thus creating a more positive self-image in the minds of the students. Moreover, since there were few job opportunities for Indian graduates, the position of teacher on the reserves would have provided both an incentive and a reward for superior scholarship.

The only source of qualified white teachers were the provincial Normal Schools. In 1947 Elgie Joblin, in his analysis of Indian education, recognized some of the deficiencies in teacher training, and suggested modest improvements. In addition to in-service training, he recommended that some attention be given to educational psychology, kindergarten-primary methods, and the aims and objectives of the coming school year. What was considered most innovative was his suggestion that classes be held on 'the historical background of the Indian people.' This was the first time that an educator had proposed that teachers should learn something of the heritage of the people they had been trying to instruct for over one hundred years.[17] Yet the errors and omissions in the prejudicial textbooks which were produced in the two decades following Joblin's report indicate that the classes in Indian history did little to correct the situation.

The Ojibwa day schools offered a similar program to the Euro-Canadian schools. Some 'liberal' Indians in the nineteenth century seemed to be satisfied with this approach. One band, for example, passed a resolution 'that the agent be required to apply to the Indian Department to have our schools classified according to the program used in the common schools.' They wanted to see some results from the considerable amount of their own band funds that were spent on teachers' salaries and accommodation, books, equipment, and buildings. Some of the more affluent reserves took pride in the excellent musical bands which the councils promoted by lending money for the purchase of instruments. The town of Wiarton, which did not have a school band or any band in their community, praised (with some signs of jealousy) the Cape Croker Reserve musicians who provided entertainment in the pioneer town and on excursions by ship on numerous occasions in the 1880s. Some of the reserves

did not have the finances to add such 'frills.'[18] Indeed, the superintendent of education had to arrange that footwear and clothing be
distributed to 'deserving' students and that a 'plain, warm meal' be
provided during the day to attract the children to the day schools.
However, the regular curriculum was expanded with the addition of
games and 'simple calisthenics,' sewing, knitting, and mending as
well as gardening. Even these measures did not entirely counter the
apathy if not active hostility of Ojibwa parents who felt that the
educational system was alienating their children.

To a considerable extent the curriculum in the day schools was
determined by the ability, ingenuity, and energy of the teachers.
Many were ineffective in implementing the curriculum, and some
were as truant as their most reluctant students. One Ojibwa band
council had to pass resolutions to get the teacher to his job: 'Moved
in Motion No. 9, Dec. 4, 1888, That Mr. Allen [agent] be required
to call on Mr. Burr [teacher] and advise him to fill his school hours
more strictly.'[19] Restrictions in the Indian Act, however, prevented
band councils from terminating the employment of such delinquent
teachers.

Not all the teachers were inefficient or insensitive. Mary Moffat
to some extent personified what could be accomplished in curriculum
development under some of the worst conditions. It must be stressed
that she was an exception to the rule in the day schools on the
reserves. Praise of her methodology and course of study came not
from the Indian Department, white inspectors, or the missionaries,
but from her former students. A booklet produced by reserve
students in the summer of 1970 drew on oral tradition to describe
her system: 'In 1904, Miss Moffat of the teaching order of the
Daughters of Mary arrived to teach at the school near the church
which was at the time called St. Joseph's Church. Her kindness,
efficiency and talent as a teacher and a musician have left their mark
on all the pupils who came under her direction during 25 years that
she remained at the mission.'[20] Verna Patronella Johnston had much
more to say about her former teacher and the curriculum. Johnston
loved school and her teacher, who broke from the accepted practice
of physically punishing the students for misdeeds. She used peer
pressure, which was more in keeping with the Indian way. In
addition to the common school subjects, she taught others of

immediate utilitarian value, integrating school activities into the
community in a humanistic manner:

Miss Moffat could make dresses, and knit, and crochet, and make rugs, and
do embroidery. She raised chickens and gave away the surplus eggs. She
had a big school garden where she raised all the teacher's vegetables for the
year. She could read music, and play the piano, and didn't she even send
off for other instruments, such as trumpets, and trombones, and learned to
play those too, and then teach the children how to play them! When she
wanted to learn a skill to pass on to her students, she sat right out in front
of them all and learned it. Just like that. She decided that her boys should
learn carpentry, so she sent away for tools, and got the men on the reserve
to show her how to use them. Then she showed the boys. Together they
built all kinds of things.

Miss Moffat worked hard with her children, and she made sure that they
got a sense of self-worth and accomplishment from what they learned. The
boys got to take home things they made at school, and the school band the
children played in gave Christmas concerts before the whole community at
St. Mary's Church Hall. Whenever any important visitors came, this band
was called on to play in the Council Hall. And she tied in the vegetable
gardens that her girls were encouraged to grow with the teaching of good
nutrition and cooking.

Then, if a boy was interested in raising chickens, Miss Moffat would
allow him to take home a brooding hen and some eggs. He had to build a
hen-house and a yard, and look after the hen and her chicks for a year. The
hen had to be returned to the teacher's flock, but the boy got to keep the
chicks for his own flock.[21]

On the last day of school she made enough strawberry shortcake
for all the students to eat as much as they wanted. 'Can you imagine
a nicer way to end the school year?'

While Miss Moffat was to some extent the personification of the
ideal teacher in the Indian day schools, she was, nevertheless, a
product of her times. Being in a Roman Catholic order, she was
compelled to teach the story of Canadian martyrs. No attempt was
made to put the atrocities into a balanced historical perspective by
illustrating similar inflictions by Europeans on the Indians. To
Verna Johnston, this part of her education made her feel 'shame and

horror at what Indians had been' and 'was in some ways stronger for Verna than the positive feelings her school experience had given her.' Nevertheless, 'today Verna says she has used not only all the skills Miss Moffat taught her, but all the values too.'[22]

Not all schools were as attractive as Miss Moffat's. Attendance in day schools had been a major problem for over a century and the main impetus for the creation of residential schools. To improve attendance, Chief McGregor of Cape Croker suggested at a grand council in 1878 that some coercion be used to force parents to send their children to school regularly, 'since education would have no effect otherwise.' In 1917 truant officers were being paid out of band funds on some reserves. By 1920 the Indian Act was amended to provide for the compulsory attendance at school of all physically fit children from seven to fifteen years of age. Attendance increased. The next year 52.18 per cent of Ojibwa students were in day schools, and by 1943, 69.74 per cent. However, a good education was not guaranteed simply by forcing students to attend schools which they, and some of their parents, found irrelevant and culturally destructive. Indeed, the Ojibwa had little control over the teachers or the curriculum, even though they had been meeting regularly in an attempt to defend themselves against such autocratic control. In the reserve communities themselves they were also severely restricted when the Canadian government took over the Indian Department in 1860.[23]

It had become clear to the Canadian parliament in the 1860s that previous acts relating to the native people were disjointed, contradictory, and generally peripheral in approach to the problems. The first comprehensive Indian Act, completed in 1876, was therefore designed not necessarily to introduce new laws or amend existing ones, but to consolidate the many disparate laws that had already been placed on the statute books. Nonetheless, certain important changes were in fact made. The consolidation indicated that the government was preparing to control the future of its wards.

The Southern Ojibwa were so concerned about the shortcomings of the act that they published the full minutes of their grand council in the local Sarnia newspaper in June 1879. Much more discretionary power had been given to the superintendent general of Indian Affairs, and native input into the formation of the legislation was almost nonexistent. A thorough examination of this council exposes not only major flaws in the legislation but also destructive factionalism among the Southern Ojibwa.

Eighty-five chiefs and delegates from southern Ontario attended the grand council. Thirteen reserves were represented: New Credit, Georgina, and Snake islands; Six Nations of the Grand River, Walpole Island; Lower Munceytown, Rama, Cape Croker, Alnwick, Saugeen, Garden River, Sarnia, Kettle Point, and Sauble. Many of the 'white educated' Indians dominated, or attempted to dominate the proceedings, especially those who had become ministers of the church. The grand president, the Rev. H.P. Chase from Alnwick, indicated there was some discontent in his opening address. None of his own band had sent a representative, and he admitted he was not appointed as an acting delegate. This might have been because of the proposal he advanced for the consideration of the grand council. Chase had been requested by the Lord Bishop of Huron to go to England to solicit funds for the establishment of the University of Western Ontario, and he indicated in his speech that his trip might provide an opportunity also to raise money for his own people who could then attend the university. He had held his position as grand president for the past four years and requested the support of the delegates in running for another term of two years. The position would give him 'considerable influence with the British Government and other officials' in England. The delegates, however, failed to elect him.

Chief John Henry with forty-five votes, having received a clear majority of one, was duly declared president of the grand council of 1878, to hold office until 1880. Chase, against five other candidates, received only thirteen votes. William Wawanosh was nominated to retain his position of first vice-president, and he was accepted unanimously. When Chase was nominated as grand secretary, 'he strongly declined nomination.' His disappointment in not receiving the presidency was obvious. Wawanosh, and especially Chief John Sumner, played a major role in undermining Chase's attempt at a third term in office. Chase himself was defensive:

The President [Chase] said that before going to England three years ago, he had placed all the business of the Grand Council in the hands of the

Superintendent General of Indians Affairs, at Ottawa. His proposed visit this time during the summer may cause suspicions, and this reminds him of the adage that 'An Indian is afraid of his shadow.'

[Wawanosh] ... thought the President had not been very attentive to his duties while in office. He referred to his going to Ottawa without a memorial from the Grand Council. He also regretted the statement made by the President, that if the law of 1876 was defective, the delegation attending its passage was responsible. He (Wawanosh) as one of the delegation, did his best to carry out the wishes of the Grand Council.[24]

Obviously Chase did not envisage the grand council as a spearhead against government attacks on their cultural and group integrity. The fact that he placed the business of the grand council in the hands of the superintendent general of Indian affairs while he was in England is astonishing. Many of his nation viewed him as an 'uncle-toma-hawk,' one who had crossed over into the 'white world' which he unquestioningly supported. Wawanosh, from the Sarnia Reserve, was most critical of Chase's laying the shortcomings of the Indian Act at the feet of the grand council, when in fact they had little opportunity to change the legislation.

If the Ojibwa were afraid of the 'shadow' of the Indian Act, that fear was justifiable. As a deputy minister of the Indian Affairs Branch noted: 'The Indian Act is a Land Act. It is a Municipal Act, an Education Act and a Societies Act. It is primarily social legisla-tion, but it has a very broad scope; there are provisions about liquor, agriculture and mining as well as Indian lands, band membership and so forth. It has elements that are embodied in perhaps two dozen different acts of any of the provinces and overrides some federal legislation in some respects ... It has the force of the Criminal Code and the impact of a constitution on those people and communi-ties that come within its purview.'[25] The act was essentially non-democratic since it favoured government control at every point where there was a potential contradiction between Indian wishes and federal authority. At the time, reserve status Indians did not have the federal vote.

Such a powerful document required a united effort by the Indians of Ontario in any attempt to counter its negative effects, but that unanimity was lacking. Chief John Sumner called on the grand council to discharge its duties 'irrespective of nationality or creed.' The newly elected president raised several sections of the Indian Act of 1876 that required their notice, namely Sections 16 and 12, subsections 12, 79, 16, 88, 91, 83, and subsection 3.[26]

Abel Waucaush began the debate with the statement that the act was still not giving sufficient protection for the Indians. They could not prosecute and get convictions for trespass on their reserves. He was supported by John French in rejecting or altering Section 16 of the act. Chief G.H.M. Johnson indicated that he found no difficulty in enforcing the law, and had, under its provisions, made several convictions. He was satisfied with it and indicated that the 'white people alone who were made to suffer under it, thought it was too stringent.' John French responded with surprise, saying he had been unable to obtain satisfaction because he had to get advice from the superintendent general, and the delay thereby incurred was the means by which the trespassers could get away. Most of the representatives did not find Section 16 a hindrance, if they had the cooperation of the local Indian agent.

A major issue involved the problem of enfranchisement. Enfranchisement is the process by which an Indian gives up both the benefits and burdens of the Indian Act and becomes a full Canadian citizen with the right to vote and hold office. Indians could become enfranchised as early as 1857, but few Ojibwa saw any merit in the move and did not take advantage of the provisions. Some who did, suffered. The Rev. John Jacobs referred to the steps he had taken to avail himself of the franchise set out in Section 86, subsection 1 of the act. He brought the matter before the council because he 'received official letters to say that professional men had no further claim amongst their own people.' President Henry said that the law depriving ministers of their rights was a hardship, and the clause ought to be laid aside. While the Ojibwa supported the motion to eliminate the subsection, the Iroquois of the Six Nations, as represented by Josiah Hill, considered it 'the best law ever made for the Indians, and the Grand Council would commit an act of folly to ask for its repeal. 'Chief Sumner said that the Ojibwa ought to be careful how they considered the act, since it was not all good. William Wawanosh concurred, because he believed that under the act 'no one would try to attain high positions.' Abel Waucaush also spoke of protecting the educated Indians in their laudable efforts to attain high situations. He did not want to see their birthrights taken away from them. Chief William McGregor of Cape Croker recalled that two years previously at Saugeen, the grand council had agreed that those persons who were eligible and willing to avail themselves of the franchise were to do so of their own free will, and if they were unsuccessful in life afterwards, it was not to be blamed on the band. He also indicated that he did not want to lose his educated friends from the reserves. Charles Halfmoon, an Oneida, urged his 'grand children' the Ojibwa to speak in their native tongue so that the uneducated Indians could understand what was going on. He also opposed his people embracing the franchise. The grand council passed a motion to annul subsection 1 under Section 86 of the act. Forty-nine were for the motion and only three against. Although the vast majority at the council agreed that the compulsory enfranchisement should be abolished, the federal government moved in the opposite direction the following year. In 1880 an amendment declared that any Indian with a university degree would *ipso facto* be enfranchised and therefore no longer be an Indian under the act. Even the most highly Europeanized Ojibwas objected to this move. Dr Peter Edmund Jones, who studied medicine at Queen's University and later became chief of the Credit band, was one of them. He did not want to see 'the tribal union' destroyed because the Indians were 'anxious to retain' it.[27]

The grand council moved on to consider Section 63. The representatives from the Six Nations Reserve showed their inconsistency when they requested that this section be revised because they felt it was ineffective. Previously they had made a motion to accept the entire act. Several Ojibwa spoke against a revision. Josiah and Moses Hill withdrew the motion and made another to disperse the grand council. When this was refused, the disheartened Six Nations' delegation left. The second vice-president, Josiah Hill, left a motion to be read in his absence the next day to the effect that the next grand council be held at the Six Nations Reserve. Chief John Sumner was opposed, since he felt that little was accomplished with the Six Nations mainly because of the difference in language. Abel Waucaush agreed and added it was up to the Ojibwa to decide where the meeting should be held. He believed it should be kept in the hands of the Ojibwa. David Sawyer, a Mississauga-Ojibwa living at New Credit Reserve on the Grand River, was in favour of the Iroquois motion. He wanted all the Indians to be on good terms with each other, and begged the delegates to choose the Grand River, 'in order to have the sympathy and good-will of his friends the Mohawks. The great tree of the peace and council had been planted there by his forefathers, and the language used then was very solemn, and should not now be violated.' Peter J. Kegedonce of Cape Croker indicated that past enmity was not dead between the Iroquois and the Ojibwa when he said that 'he felt sorry when the Grand Council was under the control of the Six Nations, and had felt joyful when it was taken away from them.' Charles Bigcanoe became irritated with discussions relating to the next grand council when so much was yet to be done at this one.[28]

The next controversial issue that the grand council considered was Section 3, subsection D, which involved reserve Ojibwa women who had lost their status because of marriages to non-status Indians. David Root and John Kedugegwan moved that the section be expunged from the act. They were supported by Fred Wahbezee of Saugeen, who stated that two women on his reserve had lost their status which was 'a great hardship when the law deprived them of their birthright.' The band council had attempted unsuccessfully to get their husbands admitted into the reserve. Likely they were recent Potawatomi refugees from the United States. Not all agreed that a change should be made. Joseph Wawanosh from the Sarnia Reserve said he, being a status or treaty Indian, liked the law as it stood. There were plenty of instances on his reserve of strangers and outside Indians who had married into the band, and who had been admitted to share all the privileges enjoyed by himself. Those persons, he maintained, had invariably proved to be drunkards and disturbers of the peace, which gave the local Indians a very bad name. He would fight against the motion. David Root from Saugeen said he did not wish to press his motion, but would merely say that if left as it was, it would do a great injustice. David Sawyer saw no harm in the law. Similarly, John Nicolas saw no reason for changing it since he believed that 'it was expected that a man was able to support his wife, and did not marry for the sake of money, and was bound to take his wife to his own home and act like a man. (Great laughter).' Chief John Sumner saw an advantage in that their daughters had a chance of marrying into 'very rich bands' if they chose to do so. H.H. Madwayosh of Saugeen said, although the law gave his daughter some hardship, still he was not opposed to it; but he thought it strange that when a reserve woman married a non-status Indian she was struck off the pay list; however, when she lived common law with a white man, she still drew her annuity payments. The motion was withdrawn. Needless to say, the reserve Ojibwa women were not represented at the grand council. This sexual inequality would last for over a hundred years. The reserve men were permitted to marry non-status women, who then became band members; but if the reserve women married non-status men they lost their legal Indian status.[29]

This stand was taken by Ojibwa men on the reserves partly because of problems related to intermarriage with the white population, but mainly because of the Potawatomi who were seeking a refuge from the United States. The Potawatomi had strong cultural and historic ties with the Ojibwa of southern Ontario. They had played a military role with the Ojibwa in all of the major battles and had some claim to the land of southern Ontario because they participated in driving the Iroquois out of that location in the late seventeenth century. Indeed, their cultural and historic similarities with the Ojibwa were greater than their differences and in prehistoric times they likely formed one cultural unit with the Ojibwa. However, their difficult relations with the United States government, while the southern Ontario Ojibwa continued under British rule, created unique cultural differences. The Potawatomi were forced out of their lands in Wisconsin, Illinois, Indiana, and Michigan as a result of the American policy of removal west of the Mississippi. In contrast, the Ojibwa in southern Ontario had much of their lands taken from them through peaceful means and were permitted to retain reserves scattered throughout their aboriginal homeland. Moreover, many of the Ojibwa had been converted to Methodism, while the Potawatomi were either pagan or Roman Catholic.[30]

Joseph Wawanosh's ambivalent attitude towards these 'foreign' Indians was typical of most southern Ontario Ojibwa. While he wanted to help them, he did not want it to be at too great a cost to

his own band's resources. During the greatest immigration movement of the Potatwatomi to Ontario in the 1830s and 1840s, Sarnia
had been the major crossing point. Thousands fled to Canada at the
time. Wawanosh's reserve was being threatened by the expanding
city of Sarnia, and the additional pressure of Potawatomi could have
exhausted the small annuities of the band if intermarriage with the
'foreigners' was not restricted. In 1845, 120 Potawatomi were
permitted to live on the reserve but not receive annuities. This
parsimonious treatment caused the Potawatomi population to
decrease, from ninety in 1848 to sixty-two in 1851 and twenty-eight
in 1855. On the grounds of bad behaviour and drunkenness,
Wawanosh attempted to have the band council expel some of the
Potawatomi families. They moved to Kettle Point Reserve, still
under the jurisdiction of the Ojibwa Methodist chief, but in isolation
from the main reserve at Sarnia. In 1873 the Ojibwa among them at
Kettle Point voted to admit them as band members. Since this would
have decreased the per capita annuity distribution to the Ojibwa, the
Sarnia band blocked the move. Several decades later many of the
Potawatomi moved to more northern reserves or returned to the
United States.

To the north of Sarnia the Ojibwa of the Saugeen territory were
more receptive to the Potawatomi refugees. Their land resources
during the period of migration were more extensive and their
adherence to Methodism was not as strong as among the Sarnia
band. A considerable number of Potawatomi were adopted into the
two Ojibwa bands in the Saugeen Peninsula when it was considered
a gathering place for those Indians who were invited to immigrate to
Canada. In 1854, however, pioneer land hunger forced a surrender
of most of the peninsula. Three years later the Potawatomi and
Ojibwa on the well-established Nawash Reserve close to the growing
town of Owen Sound were forced to move from their cleared lands
and frame houses. The government estimated that the Potawatomi
had made considerably more improvements on the reserve than
many of the Ojibwa. Compensation for the improvements was given
to individual band members when they relocated at Cape Croker.
Ojibwa chief James Nawash was not pleased with the arrangements:
'I claim something for my improvements on my lot at Owen Sound.
I did not hear my name mentioned in the list which has just been

read to us. I have a lot of land in our former village and large improvements on it for which I claim payment, as it is not fair that I should be deprived of my rights. Many more of my people [the Ojibwa] are not mentioned in the list. They all claim remuneration for their labour.'[31] The rest of the Ojibwa then joined in and complained that few of them were receiving money for land improvements, unlike the great majority of Potawatomi. The Potawatomi argued that it was the Ojibwa's own fault since they did not clear as much land or build as many substantial houses and barns. The Ojibwa were also critical of the government's building houses first for the Potawatomi who had taken up the best land at Cape Croker. Again the Potawatomi replied that the Ojibwa failed to establish themselves there early when the contractors had arrived. The head chief of the Ojibwa, Wahbahdick, was extremely angry and remarked: 'We are not treated like our new friends [the Potawatomi]. It is true that I do not know how to swing about my legs [meaning he did not know how to dance]. I hate this kind of amusement. I fear the Potawatomis are a hard set. Therefore, I and my sons do not wish to live amongst them. I intend, with my sons, retiring from this place [the village of Cape Croker] to a spot which we have chosen for ourselves on the South side of the portage towards Colpoy's Bay, about three miles from here [later known as Little Port Elgin Settlement], and we expect that the Department will build houses there for us.'[32]

The hereditary chief lamented: 'I am a poor old man, not likely to live long. I was once the sole proprietor of the Saugeen Peninsula, and my fore-fathers lived and died here, but times have changed since and now I have not even a place where to shelter myself from the weather.' Wahbahdick could have commanded the Potawatomi already located on the reserve to leave, but he did not. The wound was open and continued to fester in the following decades. The Saugeen chief at the grand council in 1879 did not want to expand their band memberships through female marriages to Potawatomi after such an experience. Nevertheless, the Potawatomi involved in the dispute did not return to the United States as had those who left the Kettle Point and Stony Point reserves controlled by the Sarnia Ojibwa band. Most stayed, but some moved to other Ojibwa reserves in Ontario.

The first year of settlement was most difficult for the Ojibwa and Potawatomi at Cape Croker because they had not planted crops and starvation threatened them. Tension mounted and took on religious overtones, since most of the Ojibwa were Methodist and some Potawatomi were Roman Catholic who had recently come under the influence of the Jesuits. Factionalism split the Cape Croker settlers down the middle, with Chief Wahbahdick representing the Ojibwa and Chief Kegedonce the Potawatomi. Twenty-five band members petitioned the department demanding Kegedonce's resignation as chief. One of the 'foreign Potawatomi,' W. Angus from Milwaukee, attempted to resolve the problem when Kegedonce on his own initiative threatened to leave: 'When I heard that my people or nation heard that our Chief, K., was going away because of our miss conduct [sic] then I began to think, being a foreigner to this Land, that I had more right [sic] to leave this place then the original owners of the soil. I have made up my mind now to go myself ... I have always done what is right and intend to do so still providing justice is shown to Wahbahdick at large and in the following the Rules of the Owen Sound [Jesuit] Fathers ... I know the government will not recognize me as one of the British subjects – but that is nothing. I want to please my friends the Ojibway.'[33]

Those Potawatomi who moved from one Ojibwa reserve to another suffered greatly until they found a permanent refuge. To the east of the Saugeen reserves, they attempted to join the Ojibwa on the islands of Georgian Bay. Again they were not entirely accepted. After spending at least twenty years on Christian Island, the band of Potawatomi there ran into difficulties with the local Ojibwa and moved in 1877 to Parry Island. This location seemed to be a refuge (as in the case of Manitoulin Island and Walpole Island) for displaced Potawatomi who could not obtain acceptance on Ojibwa reserves. Not only had they come there from Christian Island but also from Cape Croker, Shawanaga, Saugeen, Rama, Alnwick, and Mud Lake. Cultural differences as well as economics were major reasons for the rejection of the Potawatomi by the Ojibwa on many reserves. The Beausoleil Ojibwa wanted the Potawatomi to become Christian and give up their intemperate ways. A joint research project by E.S. Rogers and Flora Tobobondung on Parry Island indicated that the Potawatomi there tenaciously retained their indigenous religion well into the twentieth century. Culturally, they were more conservative than the resident Ojibwa. They were still going on vision quests, were concerned about guardian spirits, practised the Midewiwin and shaking-tent rite, used traditional curers and herbalists, and honoured their dead in traditional Potawatomi fashion. While most Ojibwa by the 1870s had been converted to Methodism, the Potawatomi on Parry Island had sixty-two traditionalists and only sixteen Methodists and thirteen Roman Catholics.[34]

Despite these cultural difficulties, many Potawatomi were accepted on over thirty Ojibwa reserves in southern Ontario, most of them in the more isolated Georgian Bay area. It has been estimated that almost 3500 Potawatomi fled to Ontario during their dispersal. While the grand council of 1879 would not protest the section of the Indian Act that excluded the Potawatomi through marriage to Ojibwa women, the Potawatomi women could and did become band members by marrying the status Ojibwa. After years of confusion and moderate conflict, the Potawatomi were eventually accepted and in many cases formally adopted into the Ojibwa reserves. However, the confusion and internal conflict that existed on the reserves in the last half of the nineteenth century distracted Ojibwa leaders from major issues that were adversely influencing their people.

The grand council in 1879 focused on one major concern of the Indian Act: to stabilize band membership. Forced enfranchisement was deplored unanimously. Councilors realized that the loss of intelligent, progressive people from the reserve could be a major detriment. Similarly, flooding the reserve with new band members through marriage to their women was also viewed as a threat to their cultural and economic integrity. However, their analysis of the complex Indian Act in general had major shortcomings. Few if any delegates at the grand council understood the full implications of the act. The more isolated northerly reserves in Georgian Bay did not even consider the act worthy of attention in their grand council of July 1879.

The Grand Indian Council of the District of Algoma met at Garden River for the purpose of tightening 'the knots of friendship between the several tribes known as the Chippewas, Ottawas and Pottewattomies and smoke the Pipe of Peace.' The major item on the agenda involved former grievances rather than potential future conflict. A petition was 'to be sent to the Imperial Government praying to have the presents renewed which were stopped some twenty-five years ago.' While this motion indicated broken promises which they considered should be rectified, it also demonstrated a lack of appreciation for the present political realities. Britain had cut its ties with the Indians of Canada in 1860 and had no jurisdiction or responsibility in the matter. This was especially true after Confederation in 1867, when the dominion government should have taken over responsibility. What the Algoma Ojibwa failed to see were the new political realities of the Indian Act of 1876 which would determine their destiny for over a century.[35]

The implications of the act were much clearer by 1894. Although the Indian agents were discouraging grand councils by not allowing band funds to be used to pay delegate expenses, they continued every second year but became more secret. Factionalism in the grand council, however, became more evident. While 'progressive' Métis chiefs such as William McGregor, who dominated Cape Croker, wished to advance the government's assimilationist policy, other 'conservative' representatives wished to retard it. Finally they were understanding and feeling the main thrust of the Indian Act, and some did not like it. Chief Augustin 'wished to remain an Indian and cautioned the Grand Council against extending the franchise ... He also cautioned the Indians against changing their mode of living, which would become oppressive to them afterwards.'[36]

As the Canadian West opened vast Indian territories for settlement, the expanding Indian Department was shifting its policy from gentle coercion to forced assimilation. In 1884 the Indian Act transformed tribal regulations into municipal laws and tried to introduce a limited system of band self-government based on the Canadian model but controlled by Indian agents. In the same year an amendment to the act imposed two to six months' imprisonment on anyone participating in certain Indian religious acts. The most dramatic change came on 19 March 1885 when the Conservative government under Sir John A. Macdonald extended the franchise to all male reserve Indians who had reached the age of twenty-one and lived east of Lake Superior. Sir John reflected the views of 'progressive' chiefs such as McGregor when he stated that 'the great aim of our legislation has been to do away with the tribal system and assimilate the Indian people in all respects with the other inhabitants of the Dominion, as speedily as they are fit for the change.' McGregor observed that eight years earlier at a grand council held at Saugeen there was an agreement that those persons who were eligible and willing to avail themselves of the franchise were free to do so. Few did, since they were unwilling to give up the advantages of their Indian status.

The Macdonald franchise gave them the vote without forcing them off the reserves or curtailing their communal interest in the band. It was a bold move that was unfortunately tainted four days latter by Indian involvement in the second North-West Rebellion. Louis Riel's Cree ally, Big Bear, and his band had been responsible for the 'massacre' at Frog Lake and the capture of Fort Pitt. These events spread prejudice against all native peoples, including the Ojibwa of southern Ontario. Moreover, the Liberals argued that the Indian Department would interfere with their wards' ability to cast their votes freely, as indeed some did. Agent James P. Donnelly of the Fort William Ojibwa Reserve attempted to remove Father Joseph Hébert, a missionary, because he 'refused to canvass for the government candidate at the general election, which took place 3 March 1887,' even though the father 'had been solicited directly and indirectly by telegrams from members of the Government and their partisans to throw in all his influence and vote in favour of the administration candidate.'[37] Since the Liberals ran on a platform to repeal the Indian vote, it is little wonder that the Indians generally voted for the Conservatives. The Ojibwa at Saugeen would not even provide the Liberal candidate with a translator at the political meeting. The *Wiarton Echo* reported that 'the Cape Croker Indians proved themselves to be as capable of exercising the franchise as the whites; fifteen of them voted for the reformers and the balance went for the Government.' Both Chief McGregor and Secretary Lamorandière spoke at A. McNeill's victory banquet in Wiarton in June 1887. However, when the Liberals gained power eleven years later, the Indians had their federal voting power taken away. They were punished for not voting the right way. A contemporary observed that by temporarily extending the franchise to the Indians, the government had sowed the seeds of discord forever among them. It would take over half a century before their democratic rights were reinstated.[38]

Destructive paternalism continued to increase. In 1889 another amendment to the Indian Act demonstrated a move to greater federal government control over Indian education, morality, local government, and land. For example, the Ojibwa's most valued possession, their land, could be taken without their consent for leasing to non-Indians. Cultural changes were evident in the appearance of many of the members at the grand council of 1894. As Chief Bugwuchenene observed: 'Everyone seemed to him like white people. He did not see any Indians dressed the same as himself. He did not wear his plumes to embellish his person; he did so only in remembrance of his tribe.'[39] All but one Ojibwa at the grand council, which had expanded to include the Indians of Quebec, had taken on at least the outward appearance of the Euro-Canadian.

The inward psychology was also changing. The cohesive traditional sharing aspect of the band was called into question by the delegates from Cape Croker. They objected to the Indian Act's allowing the legal expenses of an individual band member to be paid out of capital funds. In this sense they were actually in advance of the assimilationist policy of the Indian Department since the 'rugged individualism' of nineteenth-century capitalism, which they were advocating, was foreign to traditional Ojibwa culture. They were likely referring to the department's practice of paying liquor offences by using band funds, which diminished the band's capital account without creating a deterrent in the case of individual offenders. The financial integrity of the band took precedence over the individual; and, in this context, specific prison sentences were preferred to band capital deductions.[40]

Fifteen years after the first Indian Act, the grand council began to assess the larger implications of the legislation. The president made this clear when he said, 'I disapprove of the Superintendent-General assuming all and every responsibility and entirely ignoring Indian Councils.' The council generally objected to the government's being 'masters of the Indians' and 'controlling their money.' The grand secretary had been 'dutifully' mailing the minutes and resolution of their meetings to Ottawa every two years. The Department of Indian Affairs politely responded by stating that their proposed changes to the Indian Act would receive due consideration. They did not. The interest that the government and the bureaucracy showed in the grand councils is clearly expressed in the remarks of Superintendent Alex Logan on the council held at Parry Island: 'I do not know whether their meetings are any good, but it seems to please some of them.'[41] His interest did not extend any further.

Life on the reserves of southern Ontario, however, was very different from what the provisions of the Indian Act seemed to imply. While the stated government policy was one of assimilation, which centred on economic self-sufficiency, in actual fact the implementation of that policy retarded the integration of the Ojibwa into mainstream Ontario society. The role of the Indian agent, who was put in charge of each reserve, is crucial to these developments.

The Indian Act was administered in the Indian communities by the Indian agent. He has been described by some Indians as a cork on a bottle, the bottle being the reserve. Nothing entered it or went out from it without the official sanction of the agent. The past president of the National Indian Brotherhood, George Manuel, saw the agent as a usurper of aboriginal power: 'It was the job of these new white chiefs to displace our traditional leaders in their care over our day-to-day lives in order to bring our way of life into line with the policies that had been decreed in Ottawa.'[42] No chief among the Ojibwa ever had the sweeping powers of the Indian agent. All band decisions were void if he did not pass them on to the Department of Indian Affairs for its approval. No council meeting had any power unless he was present. As Harold Cardinal put it: 'If you are a treaty Indian, you've never made a move without these guys, these bureaucrats ... saying yes or no.[43] The development of each reserve hinged on the capabilities of one man, the agent. The tremendous responsibilities thrust on this person by the department and often by the band itself, since he had the power, were impossible to perform thoroughly and successfully. This was true of even the most able men appointed to the position. Their duties involved carrying on all correspondence with the department, even involving the most trivial matters. He bought all supplies, including cattle, seed, and implements, from off the reserve for the band, and sold all farm produce. He was responsible for taking tenders for building construction and overseeing the work. He acted as judge in civil disputes, was responsible for the moral conduct of the band, and was the inspector of education on the reserve. Such a position required a man of great education and ability, but both were often lacking. The 'wisdom' of the appointments was dictated by party patronage.[44]

This was clearly illustrated when the Cape Croker Reserve received its agency appointments specifically assigned to the Nawash band. The first agent was William Bull, who was appointed in 1882. He had previously gained the reputation of favouring pioneers over Indians in his re-evaluation of the Ojibwa land. The newspaper headline involving his appointment was apt: 'Local Pickin's.' When he died a tragic death two years later, the patronage door was opened again. Chief W.B. McGregor at a general band council meeting explained that 'it became the duty of the people [of Cape Croker] to recommend some *fit* person for the vacancy. He, as chief and chairman, would give his support to A.M. Tyson of Wiarton. (Cheers) It was moved by Chief Wm. Angus, seconded by James Toman, that A.M. Tyson get the support of the band. Carried unanimously, amid great applause.'[45] The members of the local political party, which met for the nomination of the agent, were given this band resolution, but they refused officially to read it. J.T. Conway of Southampton was chosen. The Ojibwa were not the only ones irritated with this appointment, as the local newspaper reported:

By the death of the late Wm. Bull, the Indian agency at Cape Croker is left vacant. The applicants for the position are numerous and we understand Mr. McNeill [M.P.] has recommended to the Indian Department Mr. J.T. Conway of Southampton, as the successor of our late esteemed friend. What reasons Mr. McNeill may have for recommending the gentleman are certainly not known by his most intimate friends and strongest supporters in this section [of the riding] ... Mr. Conway may be a valued citizen of Southampton and is no doubt better appreciated there than he would be by the Indians of Cape Croker, as the most intelligent of whom loudly express their dissatisfaction at the anticipation of the appointment which our member has recommended, and have, we understand sent a protest to the Department. Mr. McNeill may have the thanks of a very few of his supporters for this recommendation but he will certainly entail the censure of his supporters on the [Bruce] Peninsula. The appointment is one which should be given to a resident of this immediate neighbourhood. *It is a well-known fact that such offices are awarded men who have rendered their party or*

member some valuable service and this being the case we fail to discover on
what foundation Mr. Conway bases his claims or Mr. McNeill his
recommendation. The office is on the Peninsula and should be given to a
resident of the Peninsula. The Indians themselves have requested that a
man of temperate habits and good moral character be appointed and there
is no necessity of going to Southampton for such a man. There are many
such men in this neighbourhood and men who have strong claims on the
party for services rendered at critical times. Had the vacancy occurred in
the Saugeen Reserve [near Southampton] it is not likely anyone from this
section would have applied for it or secured it if they had. Probably Mr.
McNeill may have acted conscientiously in the matter, but he has certainly
made an error and one which we and his supporters on the Peninsula hope
he will lose no time in rectifying.[46]

McNeill lost no time. He changed his recommendation to J.J.
Jermyn of Wiarton and gave Conway the Saugeen agency. When
constituency votes were weighed, ability to do the patronage job was
not the top priority. The wishes of the band, whose destiny would
be controlled by the appointment, was not considered important.
When the Shawanaga and Parry Island bands suggested a candidate
who was 'prompt, obliging and thoroughly honest in all his dealings
with us and for his knowledge of our people and their wants,' they
were turned down. Indeed, in the context of representative democracy at the time, were the views of any disenfranchised group worthy
of political consideration? The Indians seemed not to be. A former
superintendent even questioned the wisdom of appointing any man
who was suggested by a band and had their confidence.
    Jermyn did indeed receive the patronage position at Cape Croker
Reserve. In addition to his salary, agents such as Jermyn often
utilized the position to satisfy their own selfish economic needs and
the business interests of their family and friends. Since it was illegal
for any Indian agent to carry on business transactions with the band
under his control, because of conflict of interest, Jermyn established
his son, Henry, on the reserve as owner and operator of a general
store. The goods were sold at exorbitant rates and many of the band
members became deeply in debt. The agent used his position to have
the debts paid, not by the individuals, but through the capital fund
of the reserve. The band protested to Ottawa and requested the

removal of the merchant from the reserve. They were successful only after his father had been removed from office as a result of his party's election defeat.[47]

Other reserves had similar financial problems with their agents. At Chippewa Hill during the same period, the band council passed the following resolution: 'We in council assembled do appoint our interpreter to collect the balance due Mr. Gordon (of Indian Rapid Mills) by our people the same being balances due at the time Mr. Conway ceased being our agent. And that our people must pay ... as follows: all sums of ten dollars and under, to be paid in full ... Sums over ten dollars in installments [of ten dollars].'[48] The band felt obliged to pay these debts because the merchant was honest, but their local agent's business transactions with them required a different consideration. He had got into difficulty with the Indian Department by illegally engaging in commerce with his wards. The Saugeen band, 'on application of Mr. John Creighton requesting a resolution of council to the effect that he did not trade with the Indians while he was their agent [responded], moved that no action be taken in reference to Mr. Creighton.' They were not prepared to defend the actions of their former agent.[49]

Conflict of interest was also a factor in the dismissal of an agent in the Parry Sound superintendency. However, the removal of the Conservative agent, Dr Thomas Walton, had political overtones. Walton had requested and received his position directly from Sir John A. Macdonald in 1884. By 1897 the political tide had turned. Wholesale dismissals of Conservative supporters from the Indian Department occurred when Laurier's Liberals took office, and Walton was caught in the squeeze. He was accused of irregularities found in a timber transaction for the Shawanaga band. On complaint from Chief Nebenayanequod, timber inspector Chitty discovered that Walton was about to transact a deal with a lumber company which would result in a monetary loss to the Ojibwa. Walton ignored letters by Indian Affairs to stop the transaction and gave the contract to the company. Although he was exonerated in an investigation because no evidence could be found that he benefited personally from the move, he was dismissed. After contributing thirteen years into a superannuation fund, he was not permitted to make a claim. Had he been a Liberal, the results might have been different. Walton's replacement at Parry Sound was the son-in-law of the newly elected Liberal member of parliament, William Brown MacLean. Certainly if a band wished to have its agent removed, the best if not the only time was immediately after the party in power had fallen.[50]

The problems with agents went well beyond their indulging in conflicts of interest and nepotism. Jermyn at Cape Croker took advantage of the band's supposed ignorance of the Indian Act. He charged $100 from band funds to 'carry out the law in cases coming under his jurisdiction.' He was also 'making timber on Hay Island, with Indian labour, without the band's consent.' However, the most serious problem involving Jermyn centred on his handling of band funds 'which mysteriously disappeared.' After being called to task for these actions, he was asked by the band to define his duties. Some agents had never even read the act, nor did they have a copy of it. Some band councils did.

It would be incorrect to generalize about all Indian agents in charge of the southern Ontario Ojibwa. Many were bad, a few were good. Franz Koennecke's 'The Anishinabek of Moose Deer Point Reserve No 79' does not make any major criticisms of the agents, perhaps because of the relative isolation and poverty of the reserve. Minute books of the more affluent Sarnia Reserve in the closing decades of the nineteenth century also mention no major problems with agents. Was this because they had earlier and more intensive contact with Europeans which familiarized them with the ways of the white man? Certainly one of their chiefs, Aylmer N. Plain, implied this was the case. In his brief *History of the Sarnia Indian Reserve* he said: 'Gradually our Indian people have learned to be vocal and determined to retain the few rights they still have, taking a lesson from every land transaction ... until, to-day, the Chippewas of Sarnia will dare to match wits with the sharpest of negotiators.'[51] However, political appointments on patronage alone can thrust incompetent persons into power. John W. McIver as agent at Cape Croker was one of them.

McIver's activities illustrate the basic problem with policies which put the destiny of a community into the hands of a person with too much authority. A Liberal who obtained his position following a Conservative defeat, he failed to perform his most important function as agent: he did not regularly attend band council meetings. This was most serious because his presence alone gave legality to the resolutions passed by the council. A more unsuitable man could hardly have been found for the position. His attitude towards some of the Cape Croker people is expressed in two letters to the department. In the first he stated, 'I am at a loss to know what to do with such troublesome people ... I cannot see how I am to make such people much better, as it appears to me that they are possessed of the evil one naturally.' Three years later in reference to the women of the Cape, he commented: 'Take them all round they are a hard crowd to do anything with; they take good care that I see nothing, only hear-say.' He was not performing his duties as far as the morality of the band was concerned. The band observed in council that 'representations have been made to our agent that loose women from off the reserve are prostituting themselves to such an extent that everybody is scandalized and no action taken [by the agent].' Both morally and economically, the Nawash band suffered as a result of McIver's appointment as agent.[52]

He prevented the band from taking advantage of the lucrative lumbering industry on the reserve. In order to establish a lumber mill, band members had to obtain capital for the construction of buildings and machinery. Since they were legally considered minors, the only funds available to them were moneys from their capital account. In 1899 Frank Ashkewee, a treaty Indian at the Cape, requested such capital to construct a sawmill. The band council approved, but McIver responded that 'It would be impossible to enter into such arrangements as it would entail a great amount of work to keep records of such transactions.' In the same year, he allowed non-Indians to harvest trees on the reserve while the Ojibwa could not. The next year he again refused to let them cut and sell timber. As he explained to the Department of Indian Affairs: 'I said the Department would do what was right when they were ready to do what was right and they knew perfectly well. Money obtained from timber is to be used in buying cattle and horses. At the last council meeting the question came up that the animals should not be sold for a fixed number of years to anyone who was not an Indian residing on this reserve [but] I notice the Indians are very careful of having themselves bound up in any way, ever.'[53]

McIver was attempting to follow a directive from the department involving the use of moneys from lumbering activities on the reserve. The income obtained by the Indians from this source was to be used for the purchase of cattle and horses, yet the band members needed the money to buy food in the winter since they were not allowed to sell cattle off the reserve or even slaughter any themselves. Indeed, it was not profitable to retain all the cattle for 'a fixed' number of years since there were and still are many variables involved in the appropriate time for marketing. In addition, the moneys from the sale of timber were to be put into McIver's account. Three years after these regulations came into effect, McIver reported that 'this does not agree with the Indian style of living, only the earnest, energetic ones commence work. Only one-quarter of the licenses to cut timber are used.' This was the only work available for them to do on the reserve in the winter.[54]

Why was McIver so diligent in preventing the Ojibwa from working in the woods when he usually neglected his job as agent? Did he want to stop the Indians from logging on the reserve so he could have cheap labour in clearing his own 358-acre farm or those of his friends? There are numerous examples of Indians working on 'white' farms in the reserve area at the time. In any event, the agent's dictate decreased the financial income of individual band members and made many of them dependent on band relief payments from the capital fund, especially during the winter. The Department of Indian Affairs' fixation on agricultural pursuits for the Indians and the elimination of any other work was diametrically opposed to the major objective of the government – to make the Indians self-sufficient.

Another action which destroyed the lumbering initiative among the Ojibwa was the rejection of a band-operated sawmill and the acceptance of a non-Indian-operated mill on the Cape Croker Reserve. The government had refused to grant the band this opportunity to progress and on several occasions tried to convince the band to surrender its rights to the forests on their lands. The Nawash refused. They finally capitulated, however, in allowing a non-Indian the privilege of establishing a mill on their property, but only if he agreed to cut timber for them at a reduced rate.[55] The reserve mill would permit them to build their own houses and barns at a lower cost. Soon after the mill was in operation, difficulties arose as a result of the high rates being charged by the miller. Reaction was swift. The miller was boycotted by the band members, but McIver responded by recommending to the department 'that the Indians only sell to him [the miller, L.M. McCorkindale].' The Ojibwa were already dealing with the four saw mills at Wiarton, even though they were twenty-five miles away from the one on their own reserve. McIver's move established a monopoly. Since they could not sell off the reserve and obtain a fair price, they simply stopped logging. In 1905 McCorkindale claimed that the band had broken a contract with him by not supplying timber for his mill. The council responded by passing a resolution demanding that the miller be removed from the reserve. This was a hollow threat without the support of the agent, but McCorkindale's investment in the mill was unproductive in the standoff that occurred. In the end he capitulated: 'I agree, if allowed to work my saw mill one year, to pay the market price on delivery ... I yield up all claims on the band.' The agreement indicated that he had admitted that the Ojibwa were not being given a fair price for their labour and their logs. On this occasion the Nawash band had gotten the better of the situation. Certainly, the best results for them and Canadian society generally would have been the eviction of the non-Indian owner from the reserve and the commencement of a band-operated mill. This would have permitted them to preserve their capital funds so that in decades to come they would not have to resort to welfare payments. Unfortunately, the agent and the department would not allow band funds to go into this type of enterprise.[56]

However, a considerable amount of the Cape Croker Reserve's capital fund was being spent on non-Indians in Bruce County at the time. The *Wiarton Echo* reported the unjustifiable expenditure of $5000:

It is definitely known that $5000.00 has been granted to the [Bruce] Peninsula as an equivalent for the loss in taxes of the municipalities by the resuming of lands by the Indian Department, the amount to be expended on the leading roads of the Peninsula. The municipalities have been asked to state where they want the amounts expended. A few of them have already replied to this. Amabel will expend their allowance on the county line between Hepworth and Wiarton, excepting $200.00 which will be used

on the county line south of Hepworth. Keppel Township will expend
theirs on the county line between Hepworth and Wiarton and the diagonal
between Hepworth and the gravel road. Wiarton will expend their amount
in improving the hill to the south of the village and straightening out the
rough spots to the north. Albermarle is scarcely decided as to where they
will expend theirs but it is quite probable that it will be expended on the
east road, and whatever can be got from the Ontario Government will be
expended on the west road. Eastnor and Lindsay and St. Edmunds
townships we have not yet heard where they have decided to expend theirs.
The amounts asked by the municipalities of Keppel, Amabel and Wiarton
is [sic] $1200.00 each. This $5000.00 grant comes out of the funds of the
Cape Croker Indian band's funds and further efforts will be made to secure
a like amount from the Saugeen Indians.[57]

The road improvements did nothing to facilitate the links between
the Ojibwa and 'civilization,' and the expenditure was a travesty of
justice by those government officials who claimed to have the
interest of their wards at heart. The loss of taxes resulted from those
white settlers who failed to make their final payments on the lands
they had agreed to buy from the Saugeen Ojibwa. The capital funds
obtained from the actual land sales were established to help the
Indians to 'rise to a civilized state.' In this context, the use of
Ojibwa money off the reserve was an example of gross mistrust.

McIver on a less grand scale was attempting to carry on the same
activity for his personal gain. In a letter to the Indian Department
he observed eight years later: 'No provisions in surveying Albermarle were made for road connections to the reserve. As a result the
Indians should pay for roads going through farms and the whites'
improvements of cutting bush, etc. They resist.'[58] McIver hoped to
benefit financially from these Ojibwa expenditures on the road from
Wiarton to the reserve. He owned 358 acres at the entrance to the
reserve and there was already a rough road through his farm. As he
said somewhat ironically: 'The Indians have acted *liberally* towards
the making and maintaining roads' in the Bruce Peninsula, but in the
case of roads to the reserve, 'everybody is acting liberally except the
Indian's side of it.' By everybody, he meant the Township of
Albermarle, which eventually was willing to pay half the expense of
the road through the township. McIver finally got his way and the

road was constructed partly at the expense of the Nawash band. While his interest was focused on improving roads off the reserve, he neglected roads inside it. Agents had the responsibility to collect fines each year on the non-fulfilment of statute labour, but 'owing to the 'carelessness" of McIver this was not done.'[59]

In addition to his neglect of duty, McIver's integrity was called into question by the band. In 1905 it was 'moved by Stephen Elliot and seconded by E. Keeshig that all moneys belonging to the band be given by John McIver to Chief McGregor now guardian of the funds.' The reason for this action became evident later when all of the council's frustrations with their agent reached a climax. The band in general council sent a petition to the department. It will be quoted in full here since it questions several myths about the Ojibwa at the time and is a definite indictment against the evils of the clientele system:

Moved by James Solomon, seconded by J.W. Keeshig that owing to the constant absence from the reserve of our agent who is attending to the work of his farm six miles away with gross neglect of his duties here as an Indian agent, the interest and welfare of the band suffers in consequence thereof upon the following grounds: First, we have grievances and torts that cannot be settled except by an agent according to the law. Secondly, our moral welfare suffers the most of all other infractions that require quick and immediate action to be exercised by an agent and there is none here and offenders go free and are ready to do worse. Thirdly, our finances also suffer from the fact that collections made by the agent on timber and otherwise are retained by him an indefinite and unnecessary length of time, thereby in loosing the interest that might accrue. Fourthly, the grants of our money obtained from the Department for works to improve the reserve for our benefit are retained by him till such times as it suits his convenience or the business of his farm. Sometimes the work has to be left over till the following year and *he has the use of the money at that time for nothing*. Fifthly, we have repeatedly found him under the influence of liquor, which alone is sufficient to disqualify him from holding the position. Sixthly, the agency house has been occupied by a white man and his family who enjoyed privileges here in taking his fire-wood from our forest and pasturing his cattle, etc., all this was done by the agent. The house is at present deserted and shows a squalid appearance which was at one time to teach the Indians an example of industry and tidiness. Seventhly, the agent trades and barters with the Indians which is entirely prohibited by the rules of the Department. Eighthly, a magistrate has to be imported from Wiarton to administer the law here, a duty that devolves upon the agent. Ninthly, this delinquency of duty has now existed for years so that the band and council are at present completely wearied out by such conduct of the agent. *The band have their all at stake while he has nothing.* Tenthly, having lost all confidence in our agent therefore, we want all correspondence emanating from us to pass though the hands of the secretary till such time as a change is made. Eleventhly, we the Band in Council assembled most earnestly urge upon your Department to remove without loss of time our present Indian agent from his position, as his usefulness is gone, and appoint another of good moral and sober character and competent to hold the office, *having no regard to political supporters.*[60]

This outburst was a clear indication of why the Ojibwa were frustrated in their attempts to improve their settlements. It exposes the growing dependence on one man and the failures resulting from that dependence, particularly when the agent was as incapable an individual as McIver. In addition, the petition exposes the thorough understanding that some band councils had of their legal rights and economic situation. Unfortunately, the almost invulnerable position of the agents often created apathy and killed much of the initiative that existed on Ojibwa reserves. McIver was not removed. Ironically, the following year in his annual report to the department he made a shallow observation about liquor among the Indians: 'A large number of the band are strictly temperate and have temperance societies. A few of them give trouble when they go to town by managing to get whiskey, but they are getting better in this respect. When they have no money, there is no trouble about their getting liquor.'[61] McIver saw to it that the Indians did not have their money and at the same time encouraged drinking by setting a poor example.

Three years after he made this report, the band secretary was paid $400 to perform the agent's task, 'owing to the drunken state of our Indian agent, J. McIver.' The band attempted to rid themselves of this agent by employing a lawyer to investigate him. Finally they obtained the aid of Father Joseph Cadot, the local Jesuit missionary and a friend of Prime Minister Laurier. This outside aid met with success.[62] McIver was replaced by C.E. Parke in 1910.

Agent Parke's tenure in office was short-lived since the Liberals lost the election to the Conservatives in September 1911, and the office was taken over by a party supporter. During his short stay in office, Parke, representing the Indian Department, failed to accept the democratic decisions of the band council when he rejected their resolutions. He would not grant a salary of $150 per year to the chief, even though the council sanctioned the raise. Previously the chiefs were receiving this amount, but it had been reduced to $100. The council also requested that the band be allowed to cut timber on the 'bluff' to retain their economic independence during the winter months. Parke received a letter in response to this band resolution stating that no timber was to be cut there. After attempting to resolve their problems through their agent, the council sent a telegram directly to the department 'asking to grant us permission to cut and sell timber as previously requested and to explain in detail why they overlooked the motion No. 1 passed Aug. 6 council meeting, 1910, asking the Dept. to raise the chief's salary to $150 a year.'[63] There were no positive results. The remuneration of the position of chief was degraded from $200 in 1900 to half that amount ten years later. Moreover, since the Indians had no work lumbering in the winter, they became more dependent on the capital fund of the band in order to subsist.

Because band members had been denied the remuneration resulting from the cutting of timber, some tried to find other means of employment. In 1910 horses were the main means of farming and transportation on the reserves. Adam Chagano attempted to get a loan for the establishment of a blacksmith's shop, so the Cape Croker horses would not have to be shoed by non-Indians twenty-five miles away in Wiarton. In this way, a degree of independence would be attained by Chagano and the band generally. The department responded to his request by saying they were 'not disposed to grant a loan of $60.00 to Adam Chagano to enable him to buy tools with which to start a blacksmith shop. I may say that there are no funds available for the purpose.' If loans could not be obtained from their own funds, the treaty Indians could turn nowhere else since as 'minors' they were not allowed to borrow money from the banks.

This case was typical of how entrepreneurs were discouraged on southern Ontario Ojibwa reserves.[64]

By 1912 A.J. Duncan had taken over the position of agent at Cape Croker. In that year the negative policy of the department, which prevented lumbering at the Cape, underwent a small change. Because 15 million feet of timber had been blown down on Hope Bay and Centre Bluffs, it was necessary to harvest the trees. The Nawash band were allowed to do the work, but they were charged double dues on the timber cut at Cape Croker, half of which went to their funds for the benefit of the unemployed and half to the crown and not to their benefit at all. The department told them that the deduction for the crown was legal according to Section 128 in the Indian Act, but the Cape Croker Council resolved that it 'does not say anything about Crown Dues.' On 12 July 1912 the council bypassed the agent and wrote directly to Robert Rogers, minister of the interior, but nothing developed and the band continued to pay double dues on their unsurrendered reserve timber.[65]

Few Indians wished to pay the substantial crown dues. Once lumbering was permitted on the reserve, however, the forest began to diminish rapidly. Since no provision was made by the department for fire protection, many of the trees and some of the reserve houses were lost as a result of forest fires. The Nawash band did have foresight and passed a resolution which advanced fire protection and a reforestation project, but government officials made no response to their requests. As a result, the valuable Cape Croker forests were eventually exhausted of this natural resource and the Indians lost an important means of retaining their economic independence.[66]

The aboriginal economy had been based on fish – the major food supply for all of the Southern Ojibwa for time immemorial. The Ojibwa in the Toronto area, however, had this means of livelihood all but eliminated as early as 1800, and the Ojibwa in the Sarnia area were also suffering in this respect by the 1890s. They had been forced to make agreements with the Saugeen for the supply of fish. White encroachment on the Saugeen fisheries began as early as the 1830s. Although there seemed to be a limitless supply of fish in the Bruce Peninsula and especially Georgian Bay, almost an endless number of grievances were sent to the department by both the Chippewa Hill and Cape Croker bands protesting that Europeans were fishing on their grounds which had never been surrendered. It is likely that the Southern Ojibwa considered the fishing grounds more important than their lands since they traditionally located at the mouths of rivers and subsisted mainly on a diet of fish.

The loss of this staple food involved several factors. First and most important, non-Indians all but exhausted fishing as a commercial enterprise in the Great Lakes area. Second, the Indian Department periodically decreased the geographical area in which the Indians were permitted to fish and established laws to frustrate the Ojibwa in commercially fishing their waters. Third, the government was not prepared to supply the facilities required by the Ojibwa to enable them to make a viable living from this natural resource.[67]

By far the most critical factor which eliminated fishing as a means by which the Nawash band could retain its independence was the 'overfishing' done by non-Indians in Lake Huron and the waters of Georgian Bay. In 1880, 5 million pounds of whitefish, 4 million pounds of trout, and 209,000 pounds of sturgeon were legally taken in Georgian Bay alone. In that year, the total catch amounted to 12 million pounds. This was commercial production and did not take into consideration local consumption and the numerous poachers, especially from the United States. Just five years later, the official harvest increased to 22 million pounds. By 1894 Indian Affairs report on the Nawash Reserve observed laconically: 'The quantity of fish taken by them was poor. This was an industry, at one time, by which the Indians derived a large income besides getting a plentiful supply for home consumption.' As early as 1890 the Nawash band passed a resolution 'requesting the agent to give a history of the decrease of the Indian fishing at this place.' Even though the fish had tremendously decreased in this early period, the Indians struggled for the next fifty years in their attempt to remain self-sufficient by fishing. To the north of Georgian Bay where the fish were not easily accessible to the white population, fish remained a major stable well into the twentieth century.[68]

On less isolated reserves, commercial band enterprises in competition with the local white settlers were made more difficult by the Indian agent. The Indians were forced to buy fishing licences and pay royalty dues on the fish they caught. In 1891 a delegation was organized 'to interview the Government to have relaxed the fishing laws with regard to closed season.' This had no effect. Two years later a general council of the Saugeen and Nawash bands met to discuss 'the severity and impoverishing fishing laws.' The following year W. McNeill, 'our member of parliament for North Bruce was asked to co-operate in the matter of fishing regulations.' Although the Ojibwa had the vote at the time, their few numbers commanded no respect from the government. By 1913 the Nawash fishermen and other Indians were having their boats confiscated for fishing out of season. The Ojibwa were clearly aware that they had never surrendered their fishing rights to either the British or the Canadian governments. In 1896 they had requested 'protection of their inland fishing "rights" since there is a movement against them.' There might have been some reasoning on the part of the government in charging the Ojibwa royalty dues and expenses involving a licence while restricting their fishing season to prevent depletion of the fish, but the territorial limitations that were put on their fishing grounds were unjustifiable.[69]

In 1897 the white settlers of Hope Bay successfully carried 'a move against' the Nawash band by petitioning the government. Even though the band requested 'the Indian Department to protect them,' the government responded by taking away part of the Cape Croker fishery. Five years later their grounds were again decreased and again they protested:

Having heard read the letter of the Department bearing date 18th July, 1902, and having seen the place showing the territory which the fishing license issued to the Indians is intended to cover, this Band solemnly protests against deminuation or curtailment of their rights and privileges, which from immemorial they have peaceably enjoyed and that the reasons assigned for reducing the area are considered to be insufficient, unaccept-able and unjustifiable; and the band looks for a speedy restoration of their undoubted rights with as little delay as possible through the Department of Indian Affairs their rightful protector and guardian of their rights.[70]

The Ojibwa could put as much trust in a fox looking after a flock of chickens. The 'speedy restoration' of their fishing grounds was not forthcoming from the 'guardian of their right.' In 1903 they were forced to request that they be given permission to cut timber, since their 'fishing grounds being made so small, the best and most sheltered part taken *by law* now they have lost their nets by being exposed to the open lake.' Money from the sale of timber was needed to buy food. For the next two decades they petitioned for their lost fishery to no avail. They were told by the superintendent of game and fisheries in Toronto 'that it is considered inadvisable to extend the fishing grounds already allowed the Cape Croker Band.' Even in the small area that they retained, there was white encroachment. When the fish became scarce as a result of intensive commercialization by non-Indians, the Ojibwa in the Georgian Bay area obtained some revenue by acting as guides for tourists. By the 1950s, however, even this enterprise was discontinued because of the scarcity of fish.[71]

In the early period, 1897 to 1919, when fishing was still relatively lucrative, the Nawash band made frequent requests to establish a dock for their fishing boats. At first the requests went to the Indian Department, but when these failed, they requested the help of 'all interested parties to agitate about a dock.' This approach also proved to be fruitless, so they sent a delegation to Ottawa. They specifically requested $2000 for the purpose of building a wharf, not from the 'public trough' as the local municipalities did, but from their own capital funds. They even solicited the aid of the Bruce County Council. All came up with the same answer: no dock was to be built. Only when commercial fishing was no longer a viable occupation for the local whites, in 1947, did the Ojibwa in the peninsula obtain a dock.[72]

For over one hundred years there had been one occupation for the Ojibwa that was acceptable and encouraged by the Indian Department: the sedentary life of farming. In the minds of nineteenth-century Euro-Canadians, this life was inseparable from 'civilizing' and 'christianizing the savages.' By the second quarter of the century, British authorities recognized they had failed in making the Ojibwa of southern Ontario self-sufficient farmers, but the policy was continued by the Canadian government well into the twentieth century. Certainly almost all of the Ojibwa who were in close contact with white settlers and under the control of Indian agents put forth a tremendous effort in horticulture.

There were several factors which acted as a deterrent to agrarian progress. Traditionally, the men were hunters and fishermen and the women produced the crops. Farming activities were considered 'women's work.' This attitude never seemed to be entirely eradicated. Another factor involved the quality of the land that the settlers allowed the Ojibwa to retain in southern Ontario. In most cases it was not suitable for intensive farming. This negative attitude and poor land, combined with the non-viable structure imposed by the Indian Department and its agents, frustrated the aim of producing self-sufficient farming communities on the reserves.

R.H. Abraham, agricultural representative for the department, reported that Cape Croker 'seems to be going backward instead of forward. Twenty-five years ago they thrashed as high as 25,000 to 30,000 bus. of grain on the reserve; at the present time they thresh none.'[73] After years of cultivation, the shallow top soil was exhausted. Cape Croker soil was never considered agriculturally productive. The Methodist minister in 1873 stated that 'a great deal of the land is unfit for tillage, being rocky and gravelly ridged; these furnish a good range of pasture land. There is not enough [good] land to tempt the white man; therefore, it is a suitable reserve.'[74] From the start, the objectives of the Indian Department to make the Indians into independent farmers was frustrated by the European greed for fertile lands. Nevertheless, as the Jesuit missionary there said: 'The Indians plough for better or worse.'[75] Several Ojibwa even attended agricultural courses at Guelph College to improve their lands. By 1918 it became obvious to the department that the marginal soil on several reserves was only suitable for pasture land. The agricultural representative in that year concluded that 300–400 cattle could be 'finished off' on the Nawash Reserve alone. Duncan C. Scott, deputy superintendent of Indian affairs, believed that it was a worthy 'experiment' and arrangements were made to find the cattle for Cape Croker.[76] Unfortunately, at first there was no move to utilize band funds or Indian labour since the department intended to put white farmers' cattle on the Indian lands. This had been attempted previously on an individual basis at the Sarnia, Kettle Point, and Stony Point reserves in 1900. At a general council, Chief W. Wawanosh was most 'critical of young Indians leasing land to white farmers and then working outside the reserves and drinking.'[77] Ironically, it was the Ojibwa who were against such moves because it discouraged farming among their own people. Their funds and manpower could have been used to the same purpose. The Cape Croker Band Council also objected to such moves, as their 'functionally illiterate' agent reported: 'Delay was caused by [councilor] Stephen Elliot as he don [sic] his best to block the hole [sic] sceam [sic] and would of [sic] only I told them the cattle would be put on anny [sic] weather [sic] thy [sic] ware [sic] willing or not.'[78] Cattle valued at $10,000 were fattened on the reserve lands that summer and sold in the fall. Again an opportunity was missed by the department to create meaningful employment and financial benefit for the men at Cape Croker and other reserves.

The peak of agricultural production was reached in 1912, when fifty-eight days were taken to thrash the crop. From that year on, however, there was a rapid decrease in farm production. This, combined with the department's policy of discouraging lumbering and fishing, resulted in economic stagnation on the reserve. With the exception of the New Credit band, the reserve records of Sarnia, Kettle Point, Alderville, Hiawatha Curve Lake, Stony Point, and Chippewa Hill indicate a similar situation.

The reserves on the north shore of Georgian Bay did not suffer the same fate, since serious agriculture activities were not attempted by agents in the more isolated and less fertile areas. Traditional pursuits of fishing, trapping, and hunting sustained the settlements there long after the Ojibwa in the more southern area attempted to become farmers. Furs were scarce but brought exceptionally high prices. Fishing north of Georgian Bay continued to be a major means of subsistence, and work in the lumber camps added to the income of the Ojibwa in the less populated areas. The larger reserves to the south were less free to pursue such enterprises.[79]

In the last half of the nineteenth and the early twentieth century the Ojibwa of southern Ontario reluctantly agreed that their children should be educated in the white man's world. On the one hand, they wanted their children to acquire the skills of the Euro-Canadian; on the other, they wanted them to have a cultural and linguistic understanding of their people. The 'Apple Indians' who came out of the residential schools and some of the reserve day schools often found themselves in limbo. They were accepted fully neither on nor off the reserves. Their education did little to improve the social, economic, or political life of the bands. Nevertheless, they attempted to retain their independence and establish the viability of the reserve lands they tenaciously held against the intrusions of the ever expanding white population. Grand councils were called regularly every two years to consider common problems and solutions. Internal division resulted from the influx of 'foreign' Potawatomi and especially the conflict between the progressives and conservatives at the councils. This prevented unanimity of effort to counter the negative aspects of the Indian Act. While adaptation to Euro-Canadian culture was recognized as a necessary evil by many, their own cultural identity was still held in high esteem by some. The Indian Department through the Indian Act did everything in its power to assimilate the Southern Ojibwa into mainstream society. Ironically, many of its policies had the reverse effect. Given the choice of enfranchisement or membership in the band, the vast majority chose the latter. Patronage-appointed agents who had sweeping powers on the reserves contributed substantially to economic stagnation in the communities. The misuse of band funds sustained the Southern Ojibwa in a state of poverty and contributed to the creation of apathy found on many of the reserves in the early twentieth century.

Chief Big Canoe attended many grand councils, c. 1880

The Cape Croker band council in the 1880s. Chief William B. McGregor is third from the right, and the secretary-interpreter, Frederick Lamorandière, is at the extreme right. The photograph was taken in a photographer's studio, but the floor has been spread with cedar boughs which the Ojibwa used in ritual purification.

Cape Croker youths, 1880s

Logging reserve timber at the turn of the century

Ojibwa women, c. 1900, illustrating in their dress and carrying boards a blend of two cultures.

Ojibwa camp on Oak Island

Ojibwa missionary Peter Jones led his people from food gathering to farming and from native religion to Methodism.

Some Ojibwa adapted well to a sedentary farm life.

Reverend Robert Steinhauer and family continue their parents' religious traditions in the West.

Manitowaning Anglican Church, 1842

Traditional Ojibwa burial

Cape Croker brass band, 1914. Back row (l to r): Peter Akiwenzie, Wilfred Lamorandière, Enoch Taylor, Peter Waukey, John Akiwenzie Sr, Bill Proulx, Wellington Pendoniquotte, Joseph Akiwenzie (band master), Edward Akiwenzie, Alex Johnston, John Akiwenzie Jr; front row (l to r): Fred Lavallée, Andrew Akiwenzie, Peter Desjardine, Peter Nadjiwon, Charlie Akiwenzie, Resime Akiwenzie

Cape Croker hockey team, 1916. Standing (l to r): Wilfred Lamorandière, Andrew Akiwenzie, Berlyn Lavallée, Gregor Keeshig, Wellington Pendoni-quotte, seated (l to r): Sylvester F. Keeshig, Barney Keeshig, Fred Lavallée

Reserve 'band' member

Ojibwa soldier, First World War

Peter Nadjiwon, 1915

Chief Charles Jones (1856–1956)
of Nawash band wearing a
William IV medal given to his
father Peter Kegedonce

Grand council of Ontario at Curve Lake Reserve, 1926

Dates on this band office sign indicate three major forced land surrenders

St Joseph's residential school, Spanish, Ontario, was attended by many southern Ontario Ojibwa.

Spanish residential school children, 1940s

Laurenda Solomon of Saugeen with a display of her crafts

Valencia Roote with an Ojibwa basket

9

THE RENAISSANCE
'There Is a Strong Spirit of Revival'

The stagnation on the reserves in the late nineteenth and early twentieth century was demoralizing but did not result in complete apathy. While material prosperity in Euro-Canadian terms was deplorable, it began to improve dramatically after about 1950. This change was due partly to a sympathetic public but also to a greater militancy in the native communities. The Ojibwa retained a pride in their culture and heritage which blossomed as the unsuccessful assimilationist policy was rejected. Educational institutions in mainstream society began to appreciate the unique and rich Ojibwa heritage as the Indians increasingly gained control of their own schools. An unprecedented growth of Indian organizations caused the Ojibwa to participate for the first time with Indians across Canada in an attempt to control national Indian policy. They demanded to be treated as 'citizens plus.' To achieve equality, Canada's 'first people' had to be given an advantage in overcoming two centuries of colonial suppression. Improved living conditions, control of education, effective political action, and cultural revival were possible because a glowing spark of self-determination survived the years of paternalism. And this spark was rekindled into a flame as a result of the two world wars.

A hundred years ago, few Euro-Canadians voiced the opinion that the Ojibwas should be given more power and that certain aspects of their culture should be encouraged. After two decades as principal of the assimilationist schools of Shingwauk and Wawanosh, E.F. Wilson came to the conclusion that cultural synthesis and political autonomy were superior to cultural replacement and paternalism. As he said in 1891: 'Surely it were wiser now that a large proportion of our Indians, especially those living in Ontario, are comparatively civilized and educated, and able to converse in English, to take them into our counsels, and learn from their own lips their own Indian views as to their present position in this country, and their prospects for the future. Do they wish to dwell for ever as separate communities? Do they wish to retain for ever their own language?' He went on to raise another point that has only recently been taken seriously by politicians and bureaucrats: 'Would it be any menace to the peace of our country if the civilized Indians of Ontario were permitted to have their own centre of Government – their own Ottawa, so to speak; their own Lieutenant-Governor, and their own Parliament?' Wilson's intimate knowledge of the Ojibwa language and his years among the Ojibwa convinced him that Canadian government policy was wrong. However, only a few missionaries and bureaucrats bothered to read his 'Fair Play' articles in the *Canadian Indian*, and those who did ignored the questions. He was truly an unsung prophet in the Algoma wilderness.[1]

Wilson's questions could only be considered by the dominant culture in an atmosphere of toleration and understanding. The two world wars, with their millions of senseless deaths, shook Euro-Canadian beliefs in their own civilization and 'progress.' No other human societies had killed their own people in such extraordinary numbers. This grotesque experience in the trenches gave native people a greater assurance in their own cultural values and laid the foundation for their assertive action in the future.

The First World War was a turning point in the history of the Ojibwa as well as other native Canadians. The seeds of pan-Indian consciousness were sowed when the war brought Indians from across the nation into contact with each other for the first time. Native people, including the Ojibwa of southern Ontario, enlisted in greater numbers, per capita, than any Euro-Canadian ethnic group. However, they were often refused in the opening years of the war on the grounds that Germans might not extend to them the privileges of 'civilized' warfare. The 160th Overseas Battalion, Canadian Expeditionary Force, induction records indicate that only nine status Indians from the two reserves in Bruce County were enlisted by 1915 but that twice that number signed up the following year. Many more Ojibwa enlisted in places where local prejudice was not so strong. An attempt to put all the Indians into one separate battalion failed partly because some Ojibwa refused to serve with their ancient enemy, the Mohawk. The Ojibwa, therefore, were scattered throughout several military units.[2]

A review of most of the Ojibwa reserves' participation will demonstrate their loyalty to a country which had made them second-class citizens. Rama sent 38 men to the front from a total adult male population of 110; Rice Lake, 43 out of 82; Alnwick, 31 out of 64; Saugeen, 48 out of 110; Georgina and Snake Islands, 11 out of 23; the Thames, 25 out of 110; Walpole Island, 71 out of 210; the Credit, 32 out of 86; Munsee, 11 out of 33; and Manitoulin Island, 50. The Nawash of Cape Croker sent every single man of the class called forth by the Military Service Act. Similarly, Scugog, a little band with only thirty members, sent all of its male population without exception, thereby establishing what is probably an enlistment record unequalled in the annals of the Great War. Of the twenty Ojibwa from Parry Island band, Corporal Francis Pegahma-gabow was the most distinguished. He won the Military Medal and two bars. Enlisting in 1914, he, as a sniper, bears the extraordinary record of having killed 378 of the enemy. After participating at Amiens, he led his company at Passchendaele through an engage-ment with only one casualty, and subsequently captured 300 Germans at Mount Sorrell. He was not the only Ojibwa decorated for bravery. Lance Corporal Johnson Paudash of the Hiawatha band accounted for over forty-two enemy dead, and Francis Misinish-kotewe from Manitoulin won the Cross of Saint George. The Indians' participation in the war effort could have been even greater had it not been for the shortsightedness of the Canadian govern-ment.[3]

Some Ontario native bands wished to participate as 'allies' in the war, but such 'national' recognition was denied. Most Indian groups complained: 'We are not citizens and have no votes, as free men.' Some anti-recruiting Ojibwa followed induction officers to the patriotic meetings and reminded their people of their historic grievances. Others resented recruitment methods in 1916–17, which included intimidation and the enrolment of underage boys. There were even rumours that overseas the Indians would be disguised as

Italians to prevent any recognition of their accomplishments. The reported experiences of the soldiers who had already seen action were most decisive, however. Alleged racial discrimination and inferior treatment in the war deterred young men from enlisting after 1916. Casualties were usually great. All of the hundred plus Ojibwa in the Bull Moose Battalion lost their lives. The Conscription Crisis of 1917 also adversely influenced Ojibwa participation. If this truly was their war as Canadians, it should result in the extension of equality to their people. But rather than grant them equality, an order in council in 1918 exempted Indians from forced military service on the grounds that they had limited citizenship rights and treaty promises.[4]

Nevertheless, the impressive Ojibwa contributions were not confined to personnel alone. Less than two weeks after the declaration of war, the Sucker Creek band at Little Current on Manitoulin Island voted $500 for 'war purposes.' This was multiplied many times by the other bands, by those in Canada who could afford it the least.[5]

During the war, the Grand Indian Council of Ontario kept active. In 1917 F.W. Jacobs, the president, wrote to the Ojibwa Bands of Southern Ontario: 'We as Indians are at a crucial stage of our lives, while our young men are at the Front fighting the battles of our Noble King, and our Country, we cannot say that they are fighting for our liberty, freedom and other privileges so dear to all nations, for we have none; it is our duty to bring forth our requests at this time to the Government ... In looking ahead under our present condition the scene is not very bright and it is plain that something must be done by ourselves and that soon. We Indians, like all humanity, are endowed with the same instincts, same capabilities, and it only remains for the Government to give us a chance to develop those qualities.'[6] In the grand council that the president called at the Chemong (Curved Lake) Reserve in October 1917, attention continued to focus on their lack of political power. Peter Megis of Parry Island bitterly stated: 'The Indian has never had fair play at the hands of the Government.' The council demanded that the government grant the franchise without loss of status. It was partially successful. The Military Voters' Act extended the right to Indians who had enlisted for active service overseas. Since many of the adult males on the reserves had enlisted, Ojibwa veterans could henceforth participate in federal elections.[7]

The government, however, attempted to link the vote with eliminating the Indian status of returning soldiers. In 1920 a new enfranchisement bill proposed that a person appointed by the superintendent general could recommend taking an Indian's status away, even if it was against his will. The Ottawa *Journal* noted that the Indians deserved full citizenship immediately, especially after their efforts during the war. While the Ojibwa wanted the right to vote, they did not want to be forced off their communal lands. In 1919 a new organization, the League of Indians, was formed by one of the veterans to prevent such unilateral government action. The league held its first Congress at Sault Ste Marie and declared as its goal the protection of Indian rights throughout Canada. It campaigned vigorously against enforced enfranchisement. In addition, it proposed that band councils, rather than Indian agents, should be the prime agency through which Indians should deal with the government. The league received no recognition by the Conservative government, and Liberal opposition leader W.L. Mackenzie King attacked the action on the grounds that the Indians should be consulted. Arthur Meighen, who became prime minister in 1920, responded by saying that wards could not be given the same consideration as citizens. The Franchise bill passed. Hostilities increased, and the government, fearful of further antagonizing the Indians, did not force any Indians to become citizens. With the Liberal victory in 1921 the hated amendment was repealed. This issue had galvanized the militancy of the League of Indians. By having the measure repealed, Superintendent General Charles Stewart had destroyed a major focus of the pan-Indian movement. While the league's power continued to be eroded by Indian Affairs and was soon fragmented, it likely played an important role in preventing massive, compulsory loss of Indian status. In addition to eliminating mandatory enfranchisement, the legislation of 1922 confirmed band control of reserve lands 'whether occupied by a soldier settler or any other Indian.'[8]

Although there were numerous attempts to obtain government recognition of Indian organizations which could effectively voice native grievances, little was accomplished. The government always took measures to disrupt or destroy them. One Ontario Indian band, in frustration, took its demands for self-determination to the League of Nations in 1924. Members of the league were told by Britain that they were being impertinent in interfering with the internal affairs of the 'Empire,' and the matter was dropped. While the country was making political and economic gains, the lot of the Ojibwa remained much the same. The sacrifice of their killed and wounded men achieved very little politically, economically, or socially in the years following the Great War.

The decade of the 1920s was progressive neither for Ojibwa veterans nor for their people in general. When the soldiers returned to the reserves in 1919 they wanted to take advantage of their pasture lands. Many requested and received loans to buy cattle, but few were given loans large enough, out of their own band funds, to start a substantial herd. This problem was caused exclusively by the senior administration of the Department of Indian Affairs. Indian agents such as William Moore at Cape Croker demonstrated greater insight and empathy than most bureaucrats in charge of reserves. He clearly defended the Ojibwa point of view:

With further reference to my dealing with the application of certain soldiers of C.C.R. who desire more milch cows to enable them to make a better success at farming and become more self-supporting from the revenues they would derive from such cows.

It is more apparent each year that these Soldier Settlers when given their loans were only supplied with sufficient stock and equipment to be a burden to them in many ways, whereas they only received half the equipment necessary to run a farm and have always to rely on borrowing some neighbor's equipment to complete the work, which has been a very big disadvantage to them and the same case is in reference to the purchase of stock, whereas a farmer when given a loan has only been supplied with one or two cows it has taken the same trouble to look after these animals as it would in caring for a herd of 5 or 6 milkers and whereas it is not expected to get much revenue of one or two, considerable could have been secured of a herd of good milkers. When only having one or two and when in a pinch for food, it has been that the Indian will sell the off-spring and never increase his herd ... It is known that these six soldier settlers here who have herds of 5 or more good milkers and whose sale of cream yields them in all in the vicinity of $300 each year and which rely on their interest moneys like others do and I believe it to be good business to supply cows to those who would ... make themselves self-supporting.[9]

The government as usual did not respond positively by supplying adequate loans from the Ojibwa capital fund, and another opportunity was missed in enabling the Indians to become self-supporting. Such treatment created a negative attitude towards any economic enterprise on the reserves.

The Great Depression aggravated the existing problems. While some Indian workers found employment during the lean years, the previous level of Indian employment off the reserves in the primary resource industries was never again achieved. Indians were the first fired and the last hired. The Indian agents of Parry Sound and Manitoulin Island especially recognized the inferior treatment metered out the Indian veterans during these trying times. Two heroes of the war, Francis Pegahmagabow and Francis Misinishkotewe, were not receiving sufficient relief to support their families adequately. They were not the only ones. During the Depression, status Indian veterans did not receive the $40 per month for a single, or $70 for a married veteran accorded by the Veterans' Allowance Act. Thomas A. Peltier of Wikwemikong on Manitoulin Island, who was wounded in France and permanently disabled, was living on a total income under $688 per year. In 1934 he supported a sick wife and six young children. In writing to C.G. 'Chubby' Power, the minister of pensions, Peltier requested food for his children because he was not able to get help from the Indian agent: 'there is no use asking for help from a man who had never enlisted during the war, and has no sympathy for returned men.' It was the Ojibwa's fellows-in-arms who came to their aid. In 1938 J.C.G. Herwig of the legion's Dominion Command demanded and received equal treatment for Indian veterans on reserves.[10]

The Second World War brought the Great Depression to an end for both the Ojibwa and other Canadians. Enlistment freed the Indians temporarily from reserve poverty. Several Ojibwa were among the first Canadians to see action as a result of their participation in the Dieppe Raid. Mississauga chief Frank King of the Credit band lost one son and another was captured by the Germans there.

Charles Nahwegezhic, a rifleman of the Sheguiandah band from Manitoulin Island, refused to retreat from the Siegfried Line as his platoon withdrew. He alone defended the retreat with a Bren gun. This enabled his platoon to pull back, reorganize, and successfully attack the enemy. One Ojibwa family whose sacrifice received much deserved recognition years later was that of John M. McLeod of the Cape Croker Reserve. John McLeod, a veteran of the First World War, had seen two years of fighting in France. During the Second World War, he enlisted with the Veterans Guard. Two of his sons were killed overseas: Alfred Joseph, a private in the Perth Regiment, in the Ortona salient on 17 January 1944; and John Joseph, a trooper in the 6th Armoured Regiment, south of Caen on 27 July 1944. Two more sons, Charles Donald and Malcolm John, were wounded in action near Buron, France, and two other sons, Max and Reginald, and a daughter, Daisy, also served in the Canadian army. Mrs McLeod was selected as the Silver Cross Mother of the Year in 1972 and laid the wreath at the National War Memorial in Ottawa.[11]

During the Second World War, conditions for the families of Ojibwa soldiers were only slightly better than in 1914–18. Reserve families received the same allowance as those of other servicemen, but claims were made that the Indian wives could not manage the money properly. This reasoning was used by some Indian agents as an excuse to take control of the allowance.[12]

Some reserves suffered more than others as a result of the war effort. The Ojibwa and Potawatomi at Stoney Point Reserve were forced from their village and their 2440 acres of farm lands by the Department of National Defence to make room for Camp Ipperwash. The government used the War Measures Act, rather than a traditional surrender, to take over the reserve. William George of Stoney Point testified later that his people did not consent to the surrender of their reserve for $50,000. Furthermore, an inadequate number of replacement houses were provided for them at Kettle Point, where they were forced to move. In general, however, Ojibwa protests were ignored.[13]

James Fox, who had represented Muncey at numerous grand councils, knew of this injustice when he wrote in frustration:

I will quote Section 4 of the Indian Act which is as follows: 'The Minister of the Interior (Mines and Resources) or the head of any other department appointed for that purpose by the Government in Council, shall be the Superintendent General of Indian Affairs, (Minister), and shall as such, have the control and management of the lands and property of the Indians in Canada'.

You will therefore see from this the uselessness of the Grand Indian Council, as well as the chiefs and council boards on all Indian reservations.

I take the Section 4 of the Indian Act to mean that the Indians are under a dictatorship by the Canadian Government which claims to be democratic in its regime.[14]

Ironically, it was this type of frustration that stimulated interest in Indian leadership and organization after the two world wars. Few Ojibwa could be satisfied with reserve conditions after serving their country overseas. The soldiers returning to the Saugeen Reserve demonstrate this change in mentality. They demanded better housing, telephones, sidewalks, hydro, and tractors. As a result, their land-sale funds, which were used for such improvements, were greatly diminished.[15]

While most soldiers had complained of the food and living conditions in the army, Ojibwa soldiers often considered the standard of living behind the lines superior to conditions on the reserves. At the same time, few Euro-Canadians who served with the Ojibwa could come home without having gained some respect for their Indian brothers-in-arms. It was the combination of these two factors which kindled the spark of change. Active Indian participation in the wars, extensively publicized in the mass media at the time, promoted a new public interest in their plight at home. Nevertheless, events beyond the Canadian borders were necessary to create the atmosphere necessary for a re-evaluation of the treatment of native people.[16]

Changing attitudes among the Ojibwa and the mainstream population of Ontario in the mid-twentieth century must be viewed as a thread in the broader tapestry of decolonization that was unfolding throughout the world. European powers in Asia, Africa, and South America were being forced to give up their colonial domination over the indigenous people. In almost all cases, the success of native people in achieving self-determination rested on the fact that they had superior numbers and a central geographic focus in the power struggle with Europeans. Independence among blacks in the Caribbean, for example, gave birth to demands for equality in the United States. The achievements of blacks south of the border stimulated native groups as well as the French in Canada. The postwar conditions of the southern Ontario Ojibwa must be viewed in this broader context of global change.

A year after the war, some government officials and various organizations in Canada began to urge that the indigenous people should have a greater voice in the management of their affairs. The minister of mines and resources, J. Allison Glen, declared: 'The Indian ... should retain and develop many of his native characteristics, and ... ultimately assume the full rights ... of democratic citizenship.' This statement clearly reflected the views of many of the Ojibwa at that time, but it would be several decades before it was widely accepted and influenced policy. Yet the sympathetic attitude of the administration encouraged the proliferation of Indian organizations across the country, and the Ojibwa began, for the first time, to participate in a nation-wide pan-Indian movement. There was particular interest in the reasons for the failure of Indian education.[17]

In mid-1946 a Special Joint Committee of the Senate and House of Commons was appointed to examine and consider the Indian Act. One of its concerns was the operation of Indian day schools, and testimony from Indians was included in the committee hearings. The North American Indian Brotherhood, with President Andrew Paull, suggested 'the abolition of all denominational schools on reserves.' The Okanagan Society for the Revival of Indian Arts and Crafts proposed a more constructive step, 'recommending that responsibility for Indian education be transferred to the provinces in order to gain some equality for Indians in the places where they live.' The Saugeen band also wanted educational services placed under provincial jurisdiction. The Native Brotherhood of British Columbia supported Paull's suggestion and added 'that the present system be altered to provide greater opportunities for Indians to attend high school and university.' Some Ontario Indian representatives differed on who should have jurisdiction over Indian education. While there was no unanimity on all points, most agreed that the day schools were not satisfying the educational need of the Indians. There was a demand for equality with the non-Indian educational system.[18]

In 1948 the government adopted the policy of educating Indian children in association with other children wherever and whenever possible. In the 1950s, agreements were negotiated with some school boards and the provincial departments of education for training Indian pupils in non-Indian schools. This was not a new idea. Over one hundred years before Ojibwa had been educated in regular schools. The prestigious Upper Canada College, for example, received several chiefs' sons, including Charles Tebisco Keejek, who developed skills as a linguist, and Francis Assikinack, who won first prize in good conduct, map drawing, writing, Greek, geography, and general proficiency. While some, such as the Saugeen chief's son Moses Madwayosh, returned home dejected and rejecting their English education, others graduated. Francis Assikinack demonstrated ability in the late 1840s in integrating himself into his school. His accomplishment in English is demonstrated in three essays he wrote for the *Canadian Journal* on the history, language, and culture of his people. It is unfortunate that he was not permitted by the Indian Department to continue his education in medicine as he desired. Nevertheless, he had a productive life as a teacher on Manitoulin Island and as a clerk in the Indian Department. There were other examples of successful Indian integration into the school system before 1948, but in general neither the government nor the missionaries approved. 'Free education' in the public school system implied that the parents paid taxes, which the reserve Indians did not. Several Ojibwa informants stated that their parents paid $500 a year each for their secondary school education, which they often did not finish because of the expense.[19]

The 1967 study, *A Survey of the Contemporary Indians of Canada*, gave specific attention to the impact of integrating Indians into local schools. H.B. Hawthorn, director of the study, stated, with qualifications: 'School integration has been found to benefit the Indian children who have attended provincial schools.' As early as 1962, 40 per cent of Indians were already being educated in provincial schools. The advantages were obvious. Segregation of minorities in a separate school system generally resulted in inferior teachers, schools, and curriculum, partly because of insufficient funds for their education. Integration into the mainstream of society gave the same exposure to education as the dominant culture received, and, on the surface, appeared to provide equal educational opportunity.

After Hawthorn closely analysed the situation, however, he determined that integration alone would not necessarily bring about equality: 'The integration of Indian children into provincial schools, once so hopefully regarded, has not settled the issue. While it offers an identical education to the Indian child, some of his needs are different from those of most non-Indians and are not met by existing programs. The case ... that the Indians be treated as *citizens plus* because they needed and were entitled to that status becomes stronger for the children.' Neither the cultural background of the students nor their home environment allowed them to compete successfully with Euro-Canadians. As a result, many Indian students dropped out or found themselves in special education classes for slow learners.[20]

Hawthorn's proposal to treat the Indians as 'citizens plus' was taken up by the Indian Chiefs of Alberta and endorsed by the Ojibwa of southern Ontario and other groups. They outlined serious racial problems in the integrated schools. A principal at one of the schools, for example, arbitrarily sent letters to the parents of Indian children saying: 'Your children are not ready for integration, so send them to the reserve day school.' In another school a quota system was established whereby Indian children could be admitted only on the ratio of one to ten. In some classrooms, Indian pupils were segregated by the teachers. Another teacher encouraged overage Indian students to drop out. Students were exposed to such remarks by teachers as 'You're a dumb Indian' and 'Go back to the dirt where you belong.' Similarly, non-Indian children verbally attacked them with such statements as 'Give me that swing, you dirty little Indian.' These were not isolated cases.[21]

There was a large body of knowledge on Indian school integration which substantiated the view that if equality was to be achieved, Indians had to be treated as 'citizens plus.' *The Northian*, a magazine published by the Society for Indian and Northern Education, contained numerous articles supporting this claim. In 1969–71 a House Standing Committee investigated Indian education. Some of the seventeen proposals recommended by the committee had revolutionary implications. One involved a major change in government education policy away from the assimilationist approach which had been the exclusive aim of all educational attempts up to this point. By the middle of the twentieth century the government recognized that Canada had become culturally pluralistic. The Watson Report accepted this reality and applied it to the Indians as part of the mosaic. The report suggested that substantially more Indian history should be taught in public schools, with an emphasis on native contributions to the economy, science, medicine, agriculture, and exploration. Indians should hold positions on county school boards, and universities should encourage Indian studies courses. The government, in turn, should support experimental teaching approaches and training programs designed for Indian people. Parents should be encouraged to become involved in education. Indeed, throughout the report, Indian involvement in education at all levels was stressed. Yet many native organizations, including those of the Ojibwa, felt the report did not go far enough.[22]

The Federation of Saskatchewan Indians and the Association of Iroquois and Allied Indians wanted even greater Indian involvement and a major focus on Indian culture in the education of their children. While they considered that teachers of native ancestry would be preferable, they temporarily accepted non-Indian teachers who were knowledgeable about and had the 'right' attitude towards the Indian. Because they claimed, with justification, that resocializing a child in the early years was tragic, they recommended that elementary school students attend day schools on the reserve. Secondary school integration off the reserves was acceptable. History texts needed revision to eliminate stereotypes, and the history of local Indian communities should be taught. Moreover, all students should be exposed to Indian culture and history not just Indians. In contrast to the years in which students had been punished for speaking their native language, they recommended that indigenous languages be taught in the schools as a credit course. These were all rational suggestions aimed at eliminating some of the problems of the past.[23]

In 1973 there was a radical development in relations between the federal government and the native people when the policy paper *Indian Control of Indian Education*, presented by the National Indian Brotherhood, was approved by the Department of Indian Affairs. In this proposal, the Ojibwa of Southern Ontario joined more closely with other Indian groups across Canada than at any other time in their history. Their unanimity was impressive. The policy paper integrated proposals from the Union of Ontario Indians (who were mostly Ojibwa), Indian Association of Alberta, Manitoba Indian Brotherhood, Union of Nova Scotia Indians, Yukon Native Brotherhood, Federation of Saskatchewan Indians, Union of New Brunswick Indians, and Union of British Columbia Indian Chiefs. Claims that Indian representatives were disunited could not be used against them in this case. The dictatorial policy of the government seemed to have come to an end.[24]

The National Indian Brotherhood called for immediate reform in the areas of responsibility, programs, teachers, and facilities. It demanded that the federal government pressure the provinces to make laws which would effectively provide that Indian people have responsible representation and full participation on school boards. It requested a wide range of programs for Indians, particularly that 'Indian children must have the opportunity to learn their language, history and culture in the classroom. Curriculum will have to be revised in federal and provincial schools to recognize the contributions which the Indian people have made to Canadian history and life.'[25] The NIB also requested the establishment of cultural centres. In the critical area of teacher training, native teachers should be encouraged, but authorities were also urged 'to use the strongest measures necessary to improve the qualifications of teachers' who were non-Indian and 'required courses in Indian history and culture.' Although the NIB emphasized the need to improve substandard facilities on the reserves, it realized that an extension of facilities through integration could not be legislated 'without the full consent and participation of the Indians and non-Indians concerned.' Many educators over the years had tried various ways of providing education for Indian people, but the key to a successful educational experience had not been found. There was one approach which had not been tried before: Indian control of Indian education. The federal government granted the NIB proposal.

The implementation of policy involving segregated reserve schools was feasible, but integrated schools off the reserves presented major problems. Dr Jacqueline Weitz, NIB consultant, clearly stated the difficulties: 'The opportunity to learn in his own way, a way with deep cultural roots and implications, must be provided in the school. We cannot teach Indian children using the educational psychology which dominates today's classrooms. Dependence on the teacher, time blocked activities, programmed learning, are a few practices which violate the learning psychology of the Indian child. Teaching methods, materials, subject matter and goals must conform to the teaching methods of Indian parents and to their goals for educa-tion.'[26] The Ojibwa are beginning to produce curriculum materials which reflect their perspective. William R. Blackbird (Assikinack), as coordinator of the Kirkland Lake Native People's Research Committee, has produced *My People Anishinabe*, for example, which is most useful for Ojibwa children. The vast majority of non-Indian schools across Canada, however, use many of the methods objected to by Weitz. It is doubtful whether they will change to accommodate a small minority.

In 1966, 43 per cent of Indian students were in integrated schools and, by 1979, the proportion had increased to 53 per cent. This trend was evident in every province, reflecting the difficulties in providing more senior and specialized educational facilities in small Indian communities.[27] It has all but negated Indian control of Indian education for these students, unless they have effective representation in the various school boards. But is this cooperation forthcoming?

The answer depends on several factors: available funds, the cooperation of communities involved, and the imagination as well as the progressive nature of the school system. The difficulties encountered are exemplified in the Mahjetahwin project of the Northumberland and Newcastle Board of Education in Ontario. The project planned on developing curriculum units suited to Indian students who had been integrated into Roseneath Centennial School, and on involving the local Indian band in preparing the units. Project coordinator Douglas M. Hall, however, 'soon became aware of the magnitude of his integration programme when he learned of the strong prejudices that existed among both Indian and non-Indian residents of the communities served by the school.'[28] This was the year in which Indians were given control of their education, but the Alderville Reserve had to 'reluctantly agree to this arrangement only after sudden and unforeseen circumstances made this necessary.' The agreement and the circumstances are not detailed, but obviously the band was dissatisfied.

Some Ontario school boards have attempted to accommodate native students at the same time that they educate non-Indians in local reserve histories. The outdoor education centre of Bruce County, under the dynamic leadership of C.E. Birchard, for example, introduced an archaeological/native studies credit course in 1987 at Boat Lake, a portage route which the Ojibwa had used for centuries. In addition to work on the dig, students learned the history of the two local reserves as well as the culture of the indigenous people and contemporary issues of concern to them. The course was offered again in the summer of 1989. In addition, the Ojibwa language is also being taught at the county's elementary and secondary schools by native instructors.

Secondary school education for Indian students in integrated schools showed two trends in the 1970s. From 1969 to 1973 there was an increase in enrolment by 15 per cent, but by 1978 it had dropped to its original position of 60 per cent. The Department of Indian Affairs and Northern Development admitted that the lower 'participation in secondary schools, particularly among the 14–17 age group, may partially reflect the current inability of provincial schools to help Indian students adjust to a new environment.' By 1989 almost half of the native students were in provincial schools at a cost of $200 million. Harvey McCue, the Ojibwa director of education for the Cree School Board, has concluded that little is gained by transferring Indian education from the federal to the provincial government since assimilation will most likely be the result. The Union of Ontario Indians, therefore, has ratified a proposal to establish it own educational system for the province. The Manitoulin Consolidated Education Authority is spearheading the project.[29]

The number of Indian students attending university has increased. Although participation rates are still half the non-Indian level, there had been a ten-fold increase, from just over one hundred students in 1969 to about 10,500 in 1979. Over six hundred of these students are in teacher training to fill the demands for Indian instructors on the reserves.[30] By 1988 there were 13,000 post-secondary students at a cost of $111 million. A year later over 2000 more students were added when Bill C-31 extended the number of status Indians.

The first school turned over to an all-Indian school board was Blue Quills in Alberta in 1970–1. By 1979 there were 100 band schools in operation by Indians, including several Ojibwa schools in Ontario. A further transfer of schools involving about 50 per cent of teaching staff was planned during the following three years. In ten years, 1967 to 1977, native instructors doubled on the reserves. By 1988 band councils were managing 262 of the 395 schools. The teacher/pupil ratio in all provinces was much better than in non-Indian schools except in Ontario, where it was equal. Similarly, educational expenditures per student has been about $400 higher than the national average. In 1979 it was $2600 per Indian student. Capital expenditures on reserve schools also dramatically increased from $10 million in 1969 to $26 million in 1976, but in 1979 it dropped slightly to about $24 million.[31] By 1988, according to the 1990 issue of *Canada Year Book* expenditures had again risen substantially to $58 million. These are all signs that the federal government has finally been active in attempting to improve education on the reserves, but much depends on the economic state of the country. Indeed, the July 1989 issue of *Anishinabek* was almost entirely dedicated to protesting the capping of educational funds for native people. Hunger strikes, sit-ins, marches, and threats of violence have made it clear to the government that the Ojibwa consider education a prime concern.

Numerous native studies courses have been established in colleges and universities across Canada in response to Indian requests. In the last decade, enrolment has grown from 3000 to 15,000. In 1989 there were 220 students from Wikwemikong alone attending post-secondary schools. The Ministry of Colleges and Universities' guide to courses in native studies in Ontario is impressive. All the universities and most of the colleges offer several courses, including oral Ojibwa, Indian identity, and native community development, many of which are specifically tailored to the needs of Indian students.[32]

The educational institutions alone cannot be held responsible for creating incentives to higher learning. There must be a reward in the form of suitable employment at the end of the academic ladder. Many employers, because of age-old prejudices and stereotypes, are reluctant to hire Indians. The federal government has instituted a system of economic incentives to encourage employers to train native people on the job.[33]

Most thoughtful Ojibwa see the need for 'books before bread.' As Basil Johnston from Cape Croker explained, 'before the Indian people can move forward and break down economic, social, and political impediments, the mass of the people must first overcome their want of confidence ... At the political level, they must seize and conduct their own community affairs.'[34] There has been a tremendous increase in native self-confidence in the postwar years and the Ojibwa and other native groups have gradually gained greater control of the in reserves. Some groups have met with success, others with failure, and it is instructive to look at the experiences of a representative cross-section.

After the Second World War the Saugeen seized the opportunity to conduct their own affairs to their financial advantage. The leasing of cottage land at the Saugeen Reserve demonstrates several factors in the changing nature of the Ojibwa's relationship with white society in the decades after the war. The Euro-Canadian population in Bruce County began buying lake-front cottage property on the sandy Lake Huron beaches as early as the turn of the century. By 1945 much of the prime beach land had been purchased, except for the almost ten miles of fine beach property on the Saugeen Reserve. Returning native soldiers were quick to take advantage of the reserve's natural economic asset, and requested numerous location tickets along the lake shore. The band council surveyed a number of subdivisions, opened gravel pits, organized intensive reforestation, and constructed new roads. As the tourist trade increased, it granted commercial leases for gas stations and lunch counters. In the short term, the band's capital account declined sharply, and the 1955 band budget could only be set by waiving the annual interest distribution of $12,000. However, treaty money was less important now that band members were obtaining an income from their leases. James John, for example, was granted a band house loan of $3000 by paying all his 'lease rentals' and using three lots for security until the sum was paid off. In 1963 the leases of 347 communally owned lots were raised to $50 from $30 per year. Strict regulations for size of lot, location of cottage, and health regulations were established a year later. The resulting annual revenue of $17,350 was a good start in the band's attempt to gain economic independence. [35]

Cottage leasing became a major source of income for many Ojibwa bands. As early as 1962, thirteen reserves in southern Ontario rented 2178 cottage sites to non-Indians. The Saugeen in Bruce County had the most, over 850, held collectively and individually with location tickets which permitted each member to use the lots but not own them. The Sarnia Reserve with 180 and the Simcoe bands with 457 were also beginning to capitalize on their major resource, the land. Saugeen band members had invested their time, energy, and band funds in a project that became very successful. The local Township of Amabel hoped to benefit from their achievements. In 1948 H.E. Doubt, clerk-treasurer, wrote to the Department of Municipal Affairs inquiring about the legality of taxing cottagers on the Saugeen Reserve. The deputy minister, W.A. Orr, responded by informing the Amabel Council that 'such persons may be assessed and taxed for the full assessable value of the land (and buildings) he occupies.' The following year the township consulted the Indian Affairs Branch of the Department of Mines and Resources for confirmation, and director D.M. MacKay replied: 'This principal [sic] of taxation has been well established in the Ontario courts ... In practice ... a municipality may tax a lessee of Crown lands despite the fact that the said lands due to their status are not taxable as such.' His answer failed to make sense to the taxpayers and the Saugeen, but the Ojibwa at the time bowed to his decision. After 1960, however, they became more militant. [36]

Taxation of leased Indian land was not an exclusive concern of the Saugeen. Most of the Ojibwa of southern Ontario had a stake in the issue. In 1972 a number of Indian leaders from five Ojibwa bands met to discuss the problem with the deputy of the Department of Municipal Affairs. The bands complained of the inequity of the section of the Ontario Assessment Act which gave most of the financial benefits to the municipalities rather than the native people. Indeed, the Saugeen band estimated that the local municipality collected approximately $35,000 in taxes and returned about $10,000 in services. They had researched the problem in detail and had a strong case.

The Union of Ontario Indians was called upon for support. At a public meeting of over 400 cottagers in Southampton and in front of the news media, President Fred Plain announced: 'The Ontario government will no longer be allowed to enforce the legislation it has passed in violation of the federal Indian Act.' Chief Fred Mason of Saugeen indicated that his people would provide fire protection, garbage collection, road maintenance, and police protection. Moreover, he claimed, it would be '100 per cent better service' than Amabel Township had provided.[37]

The chief's stand was supported by the cottage owners themselves. Walter Menzies, a lessee on Sauble Beach since 1945, told reporters that the township has good roads off the reserve section because of the subsidy paid by cottagers on the reserve. The French Bay Road, one of the main roads through the cottage property, had collapsed because of poor maintenance. Sid Timms of the Cottage Association clearly stated the issue: 'My observations on the whole matter ... are that the whole situation is crazy. Cottage taxes in 1970 were more than five times higher than the rent payable to the Department of Indian Affairs. No wonder the local Indians demand a more equitable distribution of funds. What right does a local municipality like Amabel Township have in taxing an Indian Reserve which is Federal Jurisdiction under an act passed by a Provincial Legislature?'[38] The cottage owners and the Indians mainly objected to the taxes being spent on such items as education and snow removal from which they were not able to receive any benefits. The DIAND lease agreement states that 'the lessee shall not reside on the said lot between October 31st and May 1st.' The cottagers refused to pay $105,000 in taxes and the band raised its rent to $330 from the previous 'token' payment of $40. Because the Indians had been granted the vote in 1960, the government was more willing to listen to their grievances.

The stand taken by Chief Mason was typical of the changing mentality on most of the reserves in southern Ontario. In the past such protests would have stopped at the Indian agent's door. As Mason stated: 'We don't like the parental system we have, the government taking us by the hand. We have to stand on our own feet.' Such a stand added considerably to the band's income and eliminated a number of welfare cases on the reserve by creating jobs in servicing the cottages. However, it also created friction with the nearby white community. Amabel Township was forced to borrow money to pay the Bruce County levies for roads and education since the Ojibwa were no longer subsidizing them.

The close alliance with the reserve cottagers was also not considered sacrosanct. In 1970 Chief Mason engaged a professional appraisal firm which valued lake-front lots at $4000 each. The Saugeen Band Council decided to charge 8 per cent per annum on the appraised value, which translated into an increased rent of 600 to 1000 per cent for many cottage owners. The resulting public outcry was predictable. One newspaper headline shrieked that the 'Indians were Scalping Summer Cottagers.' The reporter, in his ignorance, complained: 'There will come a time when Canadian Indians will have to stand on their own.'³⁹ Indeed, that was what they were doing. Only one uncritical line was devoted to the unfair municipal tax which the non-Indians had been charging for decades. Many cottagers had been making much more money than the Indians from their leases by renting their summer homes at prices above $200 per week. The increased rent was not unfair, it was competitive. Ironically, the agriculturally unproductive sandy beach land that they had been permitted to retain in the 1854 surrender had taken on much greater value, as cottage property, than the nearby fertile farms.

Tens of thousands of tourists flee each year to Sauble Beach to escape the summer heat of the cities. The Saugeen had been generous in freely permitting vacationers with cars onto their beach while the band cleaned up their garbage. Once the band won their case in the tax issue and the increased cottage rents, they examined the economic potential of what is possibly the most beautiful beach in Canada. It was a logical move. They owned the property and were going to the expense of keeping it clean without any economic reward. In the summer of 1979 they closed Sauble Beach to the public.

The negative impact on the tourist villages of Sauble Beach and Southampton was immediate and bitter. Interviews by the *Kitchener-Waterloo Record* with the local white population exposed deep-seated prejudice and ignorance of the culture and history of their immediate neighbours. The owner of a campground which catered to more than 200 people who had freely enjoyed the beach used gutter language to express his feelings: 'They're a bunch of God-damned misfits. No one has the guts to stand up to the damned Indians ... Jimmy Mason (the Indian Chief) is ruining the tourist business in Sauble Beach. There isn't a storekeeper here who won't tell you that ... They're a lower class of Indian. You never hear of anything from the Cape Croker or the Brantford Indians ... they're held in high regard.' Another campground owner suggested a solution: 'Break them up and send them to live with families off the reserve ... You have to get them out of their shell, kick the skids out from under them ... They're on welfare now. They might as well sell their land and spend the money. They'd be on welfare but at least we'd be rid of all these problems. They have no drive, no ambition. Did you ever hear of one studying to be a doctor? They got it pretty good there. Who pays for them? You and I. We're out here – working on Sunday – to pay for the hydro to go there.' The owner-operator of a Southampton grocery store shared the same perspective: 'They should be forced to sell their fricking land and put the money in an account. It has to stop somewhere and once that money's gone, it's gone. The French and the British came in and conquered the Indians and put them on reserves but made promises they couldn't keep ... Now we have fricking [Indian] land claims that mean nothing.' One would suspect that such ignorance of Canadian history, such lack of sympathy for a suppressed minority group, could only come from an uneducated, unrespected, and uninfluential member of our society, yet the grocery-store owner was a member of the Bruce County Board of Education. In that capacity, he had publicly opposed the attempt of the Saugeen to have a band representative on the Bruce County School Board which had many native students in their jurisdiction. He failed, but several local businessmen agreed with his views.[40]

Chief Mason and the Saugeen band were moderate in their methods and demands. To the north in Kenora the Ojibwa Warrior's Society conducted an armed occupation of Anicinabe Provincial Park which they claimed as their own. One of their ten demands was for self-determination and sovereignty over their lands. Local prejudice against them was even more bitter than in Bruce County. Eleanor M. Jacobson produced two racist books, *Bended Elbow*, Parts I and II, in which the American Indian Movement was called 'Assholes In

Moccasins.' This was typical of the book's and the local white community's unsympathetic attitude. Fortunately such views are in the minority and most Canadians see the Indians as people taking increasing initiatives to develop autonomy and improve their own life situation.

Beginning in the 1960s, community initiative was characteristic of most Ojibwa reserves. Throughout southern Ontario, band councils were experiencing much greater vitality and pride. The Sarnia Reserve in the heart of an expanding industrial city, for example, capitalized on its valuable property. The band council was vigilant when the municipalities attempted to tax the lands they leased out. It even supported the distant Rankin Reserve which the city of Sault Ste Marie tried to tax 'without any complimentary services.'[41]

By comparison with more isolated reserves, the Sarnia band is in an enviable financial position with its valuable real estate and close proximity to labour markets. It was one of the first to become a self-governing reserve. In 1970 the band took the initiative by using $125,000 from its capital fund to develop an industrial park. The community's financial benefit from this investment continues to grow, but it is only one part of the band members' income. Most of the heads of families have jobs. Indeed, the general move from rural to urban areas for available work has led the Sarnia band to impose rigid restrictions on visitation privileges there. In 1971 the band's revenue budget was over $100,000, more than most municipalities with an equal population of 600 people. While band members are closely integrated socially, economically, and politically with the City of Sarnia, they provide their own people with extensive recreational and cultural activities. They have typical municipal organizations such as hockey teams, baseball teams, Guides, Brownies, and Air Cadets, and they also provide funds for Indian dancers, a native library, a native art and artifact gallery, and an Ojibwa language school. Band members frequently attend folk schools, leadership seminars, and Indian political meetings.[42]

In contrast, reserves in more isolated areas struggle to develop an economically viable community. Residents of Cape Croker in the Bruce Peninsula have much fewer opportunities for employment off the reserve. Their land has the potential of becoming a tourist paradise, but there are two major obstacles to overcome: first, few cottagers are willing to drive the considerable distance to the reserve, and, second, the attitude of the Nawash band towards the natural beauty of the reserve. Chief Wilmer Nadjiwan reflected the views of many of his people when he said: 'The white man tries to conquer nature and to submit to it his aims; the Indian tries to live with nature and to submit himself to it.' He was not prepared to sacrifice nature for rapid commercial growth. In 1966 the band had an income of only $800 from cottage-lot rentals and had only recently started development of their reserve park. A few people were raising livestock and others were making handicraft, but most obtained part-time seasonal jobs picking tobacco, fruit, and berries. Skilled jobs on the reserve accounted for only $7000 of the band's income and off-reserve skilled jobs, $5000. Their substantial capital fund from numerous land sales had been reduced to $150,000, mainly as a result of relief payments that had increased in the postwar period and more recently from a major housing project. Band councilor Art Jones objected to spending the reserve's funds on houses, since he wanted it spent on industry. Good houses could then come from individual initiative. A rustic furniture factory failed mainly because of insufficient government financing. Other projects have been attempted, but with only moderate success. In 1963 the per capita income from all sources was $667, much below the poverty line. As on many reserves, welfare payments are required to close the gap.

It is possible to argue that economically depressed non-Indian communities in rural Ontario have become ghost towns as a result of migration to the cities, and that Indians on isolated reserves should sell their lands and move to where the jobs are located. Joining mainstream Canadian society was the dominant concept of the 1969 white paper, 'Statement of the Government of Canada on Indian Policy.' In his opening statement, Prime Minister Trudeau said that 'no Canadian should be excluded from participation in community life, and none should expect to withdraw and still enjoy the benefits that flow to those who participate.' The white paper aimed at eliminating legislative discrimination, including treaty rights and the reserve system. Many Ojibwa and most of the Indian organizations, including the Union of Ontario Indians, believed that if they accepted the recommendations of the white paper they would be 'willing partners in cultural genocide.'[43]

Instead, Chief Wilmer Nadjiwon, as president of the union, proposed a crown corporation concept to the Ontario government which would transfer a share of the responsibility for Indian community development to the Indians. His moderate approach gave Indians greater autonomy but fell far short of self-determination. Within months he resigned his presidency on the grounds that he was under too much pressure and because he 'felt he was neglecting his reserve and his Indian Craft and Furniture Factory at Cape Croker.'[44]

He was replaced by Chief Frederick Plain of Sarnia, who filled the position as pro-tem president. Plain's proposal was much more radical. He presented a brief to Ottawa which would give twelve seats in the House of Commons to Indian representatives. Although he expected to be ridiculed with the same type of arguments which 'kept the aboriginal in his place the past three hundred years,' he pointed out that New Zealand already had such a plan in effect for its Maori population.[45] Understandably it was difficult for the government to react to the proposal of the Union of Ontario Indians when it already had several briefs from many other provincial Indian organizations with divergent solutions to the problems.

The Ojibwa of southern Ontario attempted to find the solution in uniting with Indian organizations across Canada in opposing the assimilationist move. The Ojibwa fully supported Harold Cardinal of Alberta as a national Indian leader when he presented the 'red paper' to the prime minister in 1970. The red paper and his book, *The Unjust Society*, advanced the idea of self-determination for native people in the context of the government's honouring the treaties and considering the Indians as 'citizens plus.' When Cardinal's proposals were attacked by the successful native lawyer, William Wuttunee, on CBC-TV and in his book, *Ruffled Feathers*, the Union of Ontario Indians used their newspaper, the *Calumet*, to give Cardinal their full public support. Fred Plain, as president of the union, bitterly criticized Wuttunee and praised the 'true Indian leaders of this country [who] are the leaders such as Mr. Cardinal who sees the plight and the poverty and the actual conditions of the people at the grass-roots level.' The Ojibwa support was not unconditional or long lasting. Waubageshig (Harvey McCue) of the Georgina Island Reserve reflected the traditional attitude of most of his people when he said: 'As an Ojibwa, I know that representation of many people by one or a few voices is not yet a concept accepted completely by my people; indeed perhaps it never will be.' Temporarily they spoke with one voice, and the government was responsive. In 1971 the white paper proposal was officially withdrawn and the government promised not to amend the Indian Act without the agreement of the native people.[46]

The Ojibwa and most Canadian Indians did not automatically assume that the assimilationist policy had ended with this official declaration. Indeed, there is almost conclusive evidence that it did not. David Nicholson, who was assistant deputy minister of Indian affairs in the 1970s and director-general of Indian affairs and northern development for the provinces of Manitoba and Alberta in the 1980s, stated that the 'Canadian government is still deliberately and systematically committed to implementing its 1969 *White Paper* proposals.' He viewed the 1971 federal government economic development program for Indian communities as a superior method to spur the integration of the native economic sector with the Canadian economy.[47]

Nevertheless, in the 1970s and into the 1980s there were real signs that Canada's Indian policy was changing. Some obvious injustices against the Ojibwa were being corrected. The Kettle Point band, for example, which had been forced to surrender its reserve for a military camp at the low price of $50,000, was given $2.4 million in compensation in 1980. The government, rather than discouraging Indian organizations as it had in the past, encouraged them financially. There was also a considerable improvement in the standard of living on many reserves, especially among the Ojibwa in southern Ontario. Unfortunately, in some cases this was not necessarily the result of Indian participation in the productive aspect of an expanding economy. Instead, it 'relates to the increase in transfer payments, prompted by moral outrage at the dismal situation in which the Indian population finds itself, coupled with strong sentiments that Indians because of their history and cultural separateness are entitled to special considerations from the larger society.'[48] Per capita expenditures on reserves increased to $6330 for about 292,700 status Indians in 1982–3, and the total payment for programs such as education, social services, health, housing, and economic development rose to $1492 million. In Ontario, social assistance expenditures were $27 million, more than five times greater than a decade earlier. As Waubageshig said: 'While the lack of funds in the past seriously impeded the social and economic growth of most native communities, the mere injection of monies into native coffers will not solve anything.'[49] Under such conditions, economic dependence might be increasing, not decreasing. Self-determination could become more remote, or, conversely, the increased expenditures could stimulate economic independence through job creation on the reserves. There is historical evidence to conclude that under-financing has retarded progress on the reserves, but it is too early to determine the effect of the substantial increases in transfer payments.

Undoubtedly there was an increase in native confidence. By the 1980s the Ojibwa and other Canadian Indians began to press for Indian self-government in a national sense. Some leaders pointed out that before the Europeans settled in North America, the continent had been inhabited for thousands of years by self- governing Indian nations such as the Ojibwa. Their success is evident in that they were a self-sufficient, powerful, and independent nation when the Europeans first met them almost four hundred years ago. During the colonial period, they recognized neither French nor British sovereignty over their people. Some Ojibwa want to reassert their political independence, which has been eroded through paternalism. The National Indian Brotherhood, led by president Del Riley who had also presided over the Union of Ontario Indians, took over two hundred Canadian Indian chiefs to England to apply political pressure to the Canadian government. In his 1984 article 'What Canada's Indians Want and the Difficulties of Getting It,' he demonstrated a degree of frustration and uncertainty. There had never been an Indian organization that encompassed all the Canadian Indians prior to European contact. Indeed, it is only within the last two hundred years that an Ojibwa in the Great Lakes region has had any knowledge of a Haida on the West Coast of Canada. Non-Indian, international political structures and methods seem to be necessary to accomplish their goals. Riley's major fear is that a consensus on their objectives and approach may not be reached by the various Indian 'nations.' In order to achieve success in Canada, the National Indian Brotherhood must speak with one voice for the majority of its people.

But majority rule and representative democracy have not been acceptable as traditional governing concepts of most Indian groups.[50]

By examining the views of just two Indian nations in Ontario on
aboriginal constitutional matters, the Ojibwa and the Iroquois, the
problem of broader representation becomes clear. Throughout the
1980s there have been several unsuccessful meetings of native leaders
and the first ministers concerning aboriginal involvement in Canada's
new constitution. At Meech Lake, the Province of Quebec was
recognized as having a distinct society and many Ojibwa and other
Indian groups believe that, as the 'first nations,' they should have
preferential treatment as well. This was not achieved. Although most
Indian organizations are pressing the government to consider the role
of aboriginal peoples in the constitution, the Iroquois refuse to
participate. Tom Porter, chief of the Bear clan of the Mohawk,
stated: 'We in the East, the Iroquois, are having nothing to do with
Canada's Constitution ... because the Creator gave us our own
Constitution over one thousand years ago. When Indian leaders seek
Indian government, they take the guidance of the Creator.' Participation, they claim, is tantamount to accepting the federal government
as the dominant political structure. The Six Nations have always
considered themselves allies, not subjects, of Britain and the
dominion. Oren Lyons, another Iroquois, has stressed that the
Western systems of government are diametrically opposed to the
Iroquois political system. While Lyons wants Indians to use
decision-making processes where there is an avoidance of disagree-
ment and possibly a loss of material well-being, Riley wants Indians
to confront the issues and to share in Canada's prosperity.[51]
Centuries of contact between the Ojibwa and the Iroquois resulted
first in war, then in a lengthy neutrality, but it did not produce a
lasting, productive alliance, probably because of the economic,
cultural, and linguistic differences between the two groups. Yet any
possibility of achieving national Indian self-government would
require at the very least the cooperation of most of the fifty Canadian Indian 'nations,' not just a couple of them. Given the diametrically opposed views of the Ojibwa and the Iroquois, unanimity appears
to be remote. Add to this dilemma the historical differences and
objectives of the Métis and the status and non-status Indians, and
unanimity becomes almost impossible.

A major underlying problem facing Canadian Indian leadership is the lack of an acceptable and fundamental definition of 'Indian government.' Most concerned people share anthropologist Sally Weaver's dilemma: 'I am confused about the concept of Indian government. Having read several position papers from Indian associations, I think the notion of Indian government at the moment remains essentially at the level of a "value-notion." It is as yet an unarticulated, vaguely conceptualized ideology or philosophy.' She goes on to say: 'Realistically, I think that the goal of Indian government will ultimately be achieved through band governments asserting their rights to govern at the reserve level.'[52] This form of self-government appears to be the dream of some Ojibwa such as Wilfred Pelletier of Wikwemikong: 'Some day soon, somewhere in Canada, some Indian reserve is going to declare its sovereignty; going to start feeling its way toward independence, toward its own version of freedom, its own laws, its own means of keeping peace, its own answers to survival.'[53] This approach would avoid most of the organizational problems connected with political structures beyond the band level, but at this level, could Ojibwa 'national' self-determination be achieved?

The federal government seems to be moving in the direction of band self-government. In 1986 Bill C-93, The Sechelt Indian Band Self-Government Act, was passed by parliament and the Sechelt Indian band became the first individual band to be recognized by the federal government as self-governing. It also became the first Indian band in Canada to hold fee-simple title to its reserve land. The Sechelt Act is a form of enabling legislation which does not detail every aspect of the proposed form of government, but contains the general authority for the small Sechelt band of 201 adults *to become* a self-governing entity. The act does not list the rights, powers, and duties of the Sechelt government, but establishes it as a legal entity with powers of a 'natural person.' The band constitution, in which the powers and structure of government are set out, is the operative governing document. It sets forth the powers of the Sechelt government in relation to band membership, reserve land, natural resources, expenditures, financial controls, and the law-making procedures which involve non-Indian Sechelt residents as well. Federal funding will continue to remain at the same level through annual federal transfer payments. In 1988, however, the required British Columbia provincial cooperation had not been finalized.[54] Under such conditions, the Ojibwa of southern Ontario have not shown any great interest in this form of autonomy.

The Ojibwa were more concerned with the status of their 'conditionally surrendered' lands, lands that were leased by bands for development purposes but would revert back to them at the end of the lease. The numerous cottage lots or industrial parks held by the Ojibwa of southern Ontario created jurisdictional problems and uncertainty in the areas of taxation, zoning, health, sanitation, and municipal services. Band, municipal, provincial, and federal powers were all involved. On 9 March 1988 the minister of Indian affairs and northern development tabled Bill C-115, a set of amendments to the Indian Act which would implement certain Indian proposals for greater control over their lands. To date, the bill has not received royal assent.[55]

The 1980s have also created considerable uncertainty with regard to the legal definition of a Canadian Indian. In 1970 Jeannette (Corbière) Lavell, a member of the Manitoulin Island band, registered an injunction prohibiting the registrar of the Indian Department from cancelling her status as an Indian because of her marriage to a non-Indian. Using the Bill of Rights clause against sexual discrimination, Lavell demanded, as an Indian student, that the federal government continue paying for her university fees, book costs, and a living allowance of $120 a month. She also wanted to retain the rights of a status Indian to live on the reserve with her family and to be exempt from taxation. Most Ojibwa men did not sympathize with her demands because, they claimed, the continuation of Indian status for women marrying non-status men would jeopardize the per capita economic integrity of every band. Certainly, if the Lavell case were accepted by all bands, the reserve populations would grow dramatically and the economic base would decrease proportionally. The case was won in the lower courts but it was defeated in the Supreme Court. The Indian Act took precedence over the Bill of Rights. Sandra Lovelace, a Malecite from the Tobique Reserve in New Brunswick, took a similar case to the United Nations which, in 1981, found Canada in violation of an international covenant on human rights. The Assembly of First

Nations, however, representing most status Indians, objected to government action without consultation and demanded that the First Nations be allowed to determine their own citizenship. In 1985 the act was rewritten to remove sexual discrimination.

The government action was a compromise. It did not solve the problem on the band level since some Ojibwa bands wished to retain the traditional status qualifications. Changes in the Indian Act, nevertheless, have created a new classification of Indians, those that have status but no rights on a reserve. The government, in keeping with self-determination, has attempted to shift the problem to individual reserves. As of 31 May 1987, control of membership had been transferred to twelve bands; by 16 September, sixty-eight bands had control, with 211 awaiting decisions. By 1990 most bands controlled their membership. Among the Ojibwa, the men continue to give Indian status to their wives while the women increasingly avoid marriage with non-status men to prevent loss of reserve rights. On reserves such as Cape Croker, however, membership has dramatically increased by one-third as a result of the band accepting full sexual equality.[56]

While political and economic activities among the Ojibwa have been developing at a rapid and assertive pace during the 1970s and 1980s, the creativity of the Ojibwa in story telling, poetry, and art has experienced something of a renaissance. Story-telling for the Ojibwa has always been an educational as well as a religious experience. In the past, story-tellers spoke to small groups as they sat around campfires, usually in the winter months. A strong tradition continued through the centuries in this manner, but to involve a larger audience a new vehicle was required – the written word. Generally, writers must have a high degree of literacy, access to a publisher, and a substantial reading audience if they are to be published. These qualifications presented a major problem to native writers because, until recently, they did not use a written language and did not have the financial means to purchase books. The first European-educated Ojibwa authors, such as George Copway, were writing to an almost exclusively non-native audience. Very few books were written by Indians for Indians. Most publishers were interested in native manuscripts only if they satisfied the curiosity of the more lucrative and extensive market of the white population.

Although several generations of Indians have been exposed to an English-Canadian education, only 160 books written by Indians were published before 1969. In a three-year period from 1969 to 1972 almost twice as many books by Indian authors were printed. There is a strong desire on the part of the public to understand the perspective of the indigenous people, and for Indians to know more about their own cultural heritage. Native writers are now issuing books for their own people as well as mainstream Canadian society.[57]

Of all Indian groups, the Ojibwa have produced the greatest number of Indian authors. Among the reasons for this literary output are the large size of their population, their lengthy contact with Europeans, the early attempts at giving them an English-Canadian education, and their close proximity to publishers and a literate population.

One of the most prolific contemporary writers among the Southern Ojibwa is Basil H. Johnston. Born on the Parry Island Indian Reserve and member of the Nawash band, he received his education on the reserve, in the Spanish Indian Residential School, and at Loyola College in Montreal. He is employed at the Royal Ontario Museum as a teacher, researcher, and writer. His books, *Moose Meat & Wild Rice*, *Ojibwa Heritage*, *Tales the Elders Told*, *By Canoe & Moccasin*, and *Indian School Days*, depict the ceremonies, rituals, songs, dances, prayers, and legends of his people, and reveal, with humour and gentle satire, the relationship between Indians and the white population. He was the first Ojibwa to receive the Order of Ontario for his contributions to Canadian literature. Patronella Johnston is another author from Cape Croker who, in *Tales of Nakomis*, carries on the respected Ojibwa elders' tradition of story-telling; in *I Am Nokomis, Too*, she provides considerable insight into contemporary reserve life.[58]

Possibly the best-known Ojibwa poet is Duke Redbird, born Gary James Richardson on the Saugeen Reserve in 1939. Although he was raised in white foster homes from early childhood because of his mother's death and had little experience of reserve life, he strongly identified with the plight of his Ojibwa people. Many contemporary anthologies of Canadian poetry contain some of his works. Indeed, his writing has found its way into books that are prescribed reading for all Ontario secondary schools. 'Banff Indian Seminar,' 'My Lodge,' 'I Am the Redman,' 'Old Woman,' and 'Tobacco Burns' demonstrate his longing for a time long past. In 'The Beaver,' Redbird rejects the assimilationist alternative which he thoroughly experienced. While many of his poems are ethnocentric with limited appeal, others have a universal message.[59]

The Ojibwa have been particularly successful in the contemporary art scene. Norval Morrisseau is best known as founder of the Woodlands Art School, a group of artists who make extensive use of oral tradition in their painting. Daphne Odjig, who was born on the Wikwemikong Indian Reserve on Manitoulin Island, is another famous artist in this school. Both use bold and brilliant colours in their work, though the Ojibwa taboo on depicting legendary figures visually has brought them into conflict with their elders.

Morrisseau's life personifies in many ways the aspirations, frustrations, and achievements of his people in the latter part of the twentieth century. Born on the Sand Point Reserve in 1931 to a French-Ojibwa father and an Ojibwa mother, he attended St Joseph's boarding school in Thunder Bay where he acquired a grade 2 education after six years attendance. At the age of ten, he was sent to a school in Beardmore, Ontario, for two years and then returned to his parents. There he became immersed in Ojibwa culture and language during his formative teenage years. When art dealer Jack Pollock discovered the artist, Morrisseau was living in a makeshift shack of Coca-Cola signs, crates, and logs erected on the garbage dump outside the mining community of Beardmore. Within a decade, Copper Thunderbird (Morrisseau) achieved in art what many Ojibwa leaders hoped to achieve in politics. His works may be found in such prestigious art centres as the Musée du Québec, Glenbow Museum, Winnipeg Art Gallery, Canadian Museum of Civilization, McMichael Canadian Collection, and major collections including Imperial Oil. To celebrate Canada's Centennial, Morrisseau was commissioned to paint a mural large enough to cover one entire wall of the Indians of Canada Pavilion at Expo 67 in Montreal. Millions of people from around the world were exposed for the first time to Ojibwa culture. In 1979 he was awarded the Order of Canada, and a book, *The Art of Norval Morrisseau*, was published. He had become one of the most lauded artists in Canadian history.[60]

While Morrisseau's achievements in art exemplify the spark of creativity that still exists in the Ojibwa people as a whole, the future cultural integrity of his people remains in question. In the two great wars they demonstrated their outstanding ability to fight on the battlefields, but as a small minority in the political arena they are on even more foreign ground. The foundation of their political philosophy has been for centuries their belief in strong individual rights. While they have demonstrated their strength to rise and challenge external forces that threaten their cultural integrity, as in the case of the white paper, they seem unable to sustain an alliance with other Canadian Indian nations. As a result, self-determination, if it is achieved, will likely be obtained at the band rather than the national level. Much has been accomplished in gaining control over the economic resources of the reserves and the education of their children, but a great deal depends on massive and sustained financial aid from the federal government and cooperation from the province. If the Ojibwa continue to be treated as 'citizens plus' by the dominant society, their cultural renaissance may spread to include the economic and political elements which are needed for them to continue as an independent nation.

10

CONCLUSION

'Native Issues Will Come to the Forefront in the 1990s'

When Paudash made his speech to the Ontario Historical Society in 1905 he was optimistic that the 'neglected' history of his people would be written. From their 'importance in the deeds of war' alone, he believed that the Ojibwa of southern Ontario deserved a place in the history of Canada. Over half a century later his wish had not been granted. This study has been an attempt to weave the major events of his people into the historical fabric of the nation. To avoid a Euro-Canadian bias, the Ojibwa perspective of the events has been employed as much as possible. By profuse quotation from native oral tradition and recorded histories, the Ojibwa have been allowed in some part to speak for themselves. Such an approach, with the addition of French and English colonial records, is essential. As E. Palmer Patterson has observed, 'They cannot be understood within the context of "Canadian history" but must be understood as a part of an on-going and long-developing aspect of the colonial parallel, of the Indian as seen consistently and continuously as the centre of his own history.'[1]

This Ojibwa history has proved to be more dynamic than static. As is the case with many indigenous peoples of North America, the Ojibwa heritage has demonstrated an ability to adapt and adjust without loss of identity and self-awareness. Even allowing for the great diversity of social, economic, and cultural characteristics among contemporary Ojibwa life in southern Ontario, it is still possible to identify the Ojibwa as a people.

This study attempts to make a fair examination of the collective past of the Southern Ojibwa, but it makes no claim to being a definitive work. A detailed examination of each of the three dozen unique reserves in southern Ontario would be required to meet this objective. Even then, it would not take into consideration the hundreds of Ojibwa who are found off the reserves in such centres as Toronto, London, and Kitchener. Many are also living in the United States, though they hold location tickets as status Indians in Ontario. The Southern Ojibwa are a widely dispersed and diverse group, yet there are some common denominators which apply to their majority as a result of their shared heritage.

The Ojibwa of southern Ontario, as a broad demographic category, are economically disadvantaged. Many of them live in areas that have been designated overall as economically depressed, and their people as a whole are poorer than the provincial or national average. Ojibwa incomes and standard of living, however, vary from community to community, depending on such factors as proximity to employment opportunities, availability of public services, size of community, and general patterns of relationships with whites. Within each community, moreover, there are wide variations in cash income and material way of life. Each band has members, including families and individuals, who live in poverty by any Canadian standard, but at least a few Ojibwa in nearly every community have a standard of living surpassing median levels for the general southern Ontario population. In the Georgian Bay area many families augment their incomes through the tourist trade, hunting, and fishing, and any blanket characterization of modern Ojibwa 'as poverty stricken' must be regarded somewhat sceptically as a generalization. This should not be taken to mean, however, that the Ojibwa of southern Ontario typically live in affluence.

The traditional culture of the Ojibwa shows the same patterns of variation as in economics. Contemporary Ojibwa culture is different from aboriginal culture, as it has adapted under a variety of social, political, and economic pressures. The 75,000 Ojibwa in Canada (and almost as many in the United States), however, still retain the major factor of their ethnicity – their language. There are 30,000 Ojibwa-speakers in Canada alone. The proportion of native speakers on reserves increases in the more northerly areas, but even in these isolated regions there are those who speak only Ojibwa or English.

There is a similar variation with other traits such as possession of an Indian name, knowledge of folklore, and religious beliefs. Although some young Ojibwa are interested in native medicines, the shaking tent, the traditional dances, and other cultural aspects of their heritage, the elders complain that the influence of mainstream society is rapidly eroding their group identity. In recent years, the elders have been more successful in attracting the youth into native dance groups, language classes, and pow wows.

However, the assimilationist policy of the past has left its mark. Many young Ojibwa know little of native history, language, or lore. They no longer constitute a group culture in the anthropological sense. Their independence as a political entity is severely limited by the dominant culture and by the government. Their lives are mostly bounded by the same social, economic, and political forces that shape the behaviour of Canadians in general. Nonetheless, within the context of national political and economic supremacy and immersion in Canadian mass culture, the Ojibwa can be distinguished on several bases.

Ojibwa social differentiation rests upon, and is in part derived from, the biological descent of the Ojibwa from a discernible aboriginal population. However, there are now few 'full-bloods' and many 'mixed-bloods' on the reserves. This has come about as a result of off-spring from fur traders, especially the French in the early period, and in more recent times from reserve men marrying non-Indians. When the Canadian government established specific lists of band members in the latter part of the nineteenth century, any person with some Indian blood and, most important, those who were accepted by the majority of the band were given legal status as Indians. Traditionally, members were adopted into the band when a majority of the community consented. The processes of white admixture and acculturation have produced a situation in which some individuals regarded as Indians by both whites and Indians may have more European-derived ancestry than Ojibwa. Others can pass for white, but are identified by themselves, their kinsmen, and their associates as Indians. A great many Ojibwa with varying degrees of white ancestry bear key physical characteristics that immediately mark them as Indian in the eyes of both Indians and whites, and they are treated accordingly. They are generally treated differently by both the Ojibwa and the local white community – the former being more friendly and the later more condescending.

More important is the structural separateness of the Ojibwa from other Canadians by national institutions specifically designed to serve Indians, such as the Department of Indian Affairs and Northern Development and the Indian missions of various churches, both on and off the reserves. The general exclusion of Indians from other white organizations, such as social clubs, whether intended or not, also serves to maintain boundaries between whites and the general Indian population. The structural integrity of Ojibwa reserves is maintained in much the same way as that of other communities – through territorial delineation, exclusive rights of political participation, and control of communal resources. Because all of these communities are made up primarily of individuals who are categorized locally as Indians, their separation is interwoven with the maintenance of broad racial boundaries as well. This is especially true since the reserves have been controlled mainly by external forces such as the federal government for most of their history. Paradoxically, the negative aspects of that force have strengthened Ojibwa community identity by creating a united effort to resist the dictatorial actions of a paternalistic government. [2]

The most potent symbol of southern Ojibwa identity is the collective ownership of land. Ironically, the government's assimilationist policy of separating the Ojibwa on these lands has contributed most to the retention of their cultural identity. Historically, land has been the primary issue in the Ojibwa's official dealings with other native groups and especially with Europeans. The many broken treaties connected to these lands have become another important symbol of unity among the band councils. The threat in the 1969 white paper to terminate collective ownership of reserves further stimulated interest in the land. For most Ojibwa land represents the major resource with which their leaders hope to overcome the economic disparity between Indians and whites. It is the locus of Indian social and cultural resources and the home base to which off-reserve Ojibwa can withdraw from the white man's world. It is also the major link between the present and the past, providing the Ojibwa with a sense of historical experience.

In the closing decade of the twentieth century the Ojibwa land base will become increasingly decisive in their struggle for survival. With the dramatic increase in the population of the reserves as a result of the high birth rate and the extension of band membership, their resources will be strained to the limits. This pressing economic situation has already led to sixty-two demands for the settlement of land claims.

The Ojibwa have had moderate success in several areas. The five bands represented by the United Chiefs and Councils of Manitoulin and Cockburn Island were the first to strike a land settlement with the province of Ontario in 1990. In this agreement, the Ojibwa received $4.5 million to buy land and $2.5 million for economic development such as tourism projects, along with $1.62 million worth of crown land near existing reserves. For the Indians of Manitoulin Island, this was not their only claim. They have not yet received compensation for the 23,000 islands in Georgian Bay taken from them in the 1862 treaty. To the northeast of the bay, the Teme-Augama Anishnabai (Ojibwa) band has rejected a provincial offer of $30 million and a 100 square kilometre reserve for their 10,000 square kilometre land claim. South of Georgian Bay, the Saugeen have registered numerous claims. Their struggle to obtain 2.4 kilometres of the valuable Sauble Beach frontage was backed in January 1990 by the federal Department of Indian Affairs and Northern Development, but Amabel Township is strongly resisting their move. Another contentious issue in Bruce County involves the fishing grounds of the Cape Croker band. A former chief and ten band members were given fines of up to $10,000 and jail sentences of up to ninety days for poaching fish from areas that have never been surrendered. While there is no clear trend here, it appears that native issues will come to the forefront in the 1990s.[3]

NOTES

ABBREVIATIONS

AO	Archives of Ontario
BCA	Bruce County Archives
CCA	Cape Croker Archives
CHR	*Canadian Historical Review*
DCB	*Dictionary of Canadian Biography*
DIAND	Department of Indian Affairs & Northern Development
Doc. Hist. NY	*Documentary History of the State of New York*
Hist. of NY	*History of New York*
JR	*Jesuit Relations*
Miss. Val. Hist. Rev.	*Mississippi Valley Historical Review*
NA	National Archives of Canada
NYCD	New York Colonial Documents
OH	*Ontario History*
RG	Record Group
SBA	Saugeen Band Archives

In the notes, items that appear in the Select Bibliography are given in short form only. All other references are given in full at first mention, and a short form is used thereafter.

PREFACE

1 The Ojibwa of southern Ontario are defined in this study to include those who live south of the north shore of the Georgian Bay, in the more heavily populated areas of the province. The Indians called the territory that is now southern Ontario 'Saganan.' During the French period and up to 1791, the Europeans included it as part of Quebec or New France. After that date it became 'Upper Canada.' In 1841 the area was designated 'Canada West,' a

name it retained until Confederation in 1867, when it received its final name, 'Ontario.' To avoid confusion, 'Ontario will be used throughout this book. See Rogers, 'Southeastern Ojibwa,' 767; W.G. Dean, ed., *Economic Atlas of Ontario* (Toronto 1969), plates 8 and 9. Rogers estimates the number of Ojibwa in Ontario at about 10,000, but the Department of Indian Affairs and Northern Development in 1967 indicated that there were about 33,000 in the province. The arbitrary dividing line between north and south makes it difficult to determine the exact number. This is especially true in 1989, since Indian status has been extended to reserve women who have married non-status men. See *Linguistic and Cultural Affiliations of Canadian Bands* (Ottawa 1967), 10–13, 15.

CHAPTER ONE: INTRODUCTION

1 [Hodge, Frederick Webb, ed.], *Handbook of Indians of Canada* (Ottawa 1913), 99–100. Hodge gave his assent to this project, but the actual work was directed by James White. Also see Dunning, *Social and Economic Change among the Northern Ojibwa*, 3.
2 Tanner, *The Ojibway* 1; Smith, 'Who Are the Mississauga?,' 211. Because of the confusion in terminology, there has been some attempt to popularize the name used by the Indians, 'Anishinaubag,' with its various spellings. See Paredes, ed., *Anishinabe*, vii–xi. As the title indicates, this study has complicated the terminology rather than clarify it.
3 Thwaites, ed., *Jesuit Relations* (*JR*), 54: 127. Dablion named 'Outaouaks,' but there are several different spellings for this word which evolved into 'Ottawa.' Confusion of tribal terminology involving the Great Lakes Indians was compounded when the British took control of the area after the Conquest. In 1760 and the following decades, British knowledge of the tribal organizations in the area was incomplete and inaccurate mainly because of lack of competent translators and dependence upon the Iroquois, who were historically their bitter enemies. Even as late as the War of 1812 they did not know the precise affiliation of the chiefs who were allied with them. Neywash (Nawash), for example, who spoke on behalf of the 'Western Indians,' was considered the chief of the Ottawa in 1814, and Kishkiwabik, chief of the Chippewa (Ojibwa). In numerous later sources, however, Nawash is considered chief of the Saugeen-Ojibwas. Ojibwa (Chippewa) and Ottawa were often synonymous terms. See 'Speech of Neywash on the Part of the Western Indians,' 14 June 1814, and 'List of Allied Chiefs,' contained in the letter sent by 'Lieut Gen Drummond to Sec. Freer,' 16 Feb. 1814, in 'War of 1812,' *Michigan Historical Collection* 15 (Lansing 1889): 492, 593; and Schmalz, *History of the Saugeen Indians*, 10, 39, 42, 66, 88.
4 Orr, 'The Mississaugas,' 7–18; Rogers, 'Southeastern Ojibwa,' 761; *JR*, 18: 231, 259; 54: 131–3; Hickerson, *Chippewa Indians*, 35. Peace with the Sioux lasted until 1736. The expansion of the Ojibwa into northern Ontario, as explained by Charles Bishop, has recently been called into question by Greenberg and Morrison in 'Group Identity in the Boreal Forest.' This

article examines the major hypotheses regarding the migration and emergence of the Northern Ojibwa. Documentary evidence is provided which suggests that groups known today as Northern Ojibwa have inhabited the boreal forest at least since contact. Rather than a migration or general population movement, as Bishop, *Northern Ojibwa*, argues, the 'emergence' of the Northern Ojibwa was nothing more than the diffusion of the term 'Ojibwa' to ethnic units known at contact under a host of different names – among them Kilistinon or Cree, Monsoni, Muskego, and Gens des Terres. There is no such problem with the Ojibwa of southern Ontario, since it is well established that the Ojibwa replaced the Iroquoian-speaking people in Ontario. The article contains an excellent analysis of early French names used to describe various bands which became Ojibwa.

5 [Hodge], *Handbook*, 100. There are several spellings: Salteur, Santeaux, Santena, Santeur, Sault Indians, Sautou, to mention only a few. See also *JR*, 54: 129–31; 51: 61.

6 Peter Jones, *History of the Ojibwa Indians* (London 1964), 31. See Landes's introduction to Paredes, ed., *Anishinabe*, viii. Irving Hallowell indicates the importance of their religion in 'The Spirits of the Dead in Saulteaux Life and Thought,' *Journal of the Royal Anthropological Institute of Great Britain and Ireland* 70 (1) (1940): 29–51.

7 Alanson Skinner, 'Bear Customs of the Cree and Other Algonkin Indians of Northern Ontario,' and Paul Radin, 'An Introductive Inquiry into the Study of Ojibwa Religion,' *OH* 12 (1914): 203–9, 210–18, respectively. See also Rogers, 'Part IV – Religion,' *The Round Lake Ojibwa*. Rogers's account indicates that much of the aboriginal religion of the more isolated Northern Ojibwa has been retained, though it has been influenced by Christianity. See also Landes, *Ojibwa Woman*, 124–177.

8 Radin, 'Introductive Inquiry,' 215–16

9 Kinietz, *Chippewa Village: The Story of Katikitegon*, 92. In the war dance, every warrior who had previously killed an enemy, taken a scalp, or secured a prisoner told of his exploit. See also Jones, *History*, 90–1; Warren, *History of the Ojibwa Nation*, 249; and William E. Culkin, 'Tribal Dance of the Ojibwa Indians,' *Minnesota History Bulletin* (May 1915): 1: 83–93.

10 Edwin Seaborn, *The March of Medicine in Western Ontario* (Toronto 1944), 8–10; Jones, *History*, 89–90. The close religious relationship between man and animal is clearly demonstrated in the oral tradition collected by Radin, *Some Myths and Tales of the Ojibwa of Southeastern Ontario*, and A.F. Chamberlain, 'Nanibozhu amongst the Otchipwe, Mississagas, and other Algonkian Tribes,' *Journal of American Folklore* 4 (14) (July-Sept.) 1891: 193–213. The medicine bag was still carried into battle by some Ojibwa as late as the First World War; Kinietz, *Chippewa Village*, 155–6. Metamorphosis was not just confined to warfare and good purposes. As late as 1860 an Ojibwa called Otter-heart explained the abnormal actions of a wife by saying that 'she was converted into a long-haired she-wolf.' See Kohl, *Kitchi-Gami: Wanderings Round Lake Superior*, 99–100.

11 Henry, *Travels & Adventures in Canada*, 73–6, 98–102, 121–54

12 Vecsey, 'Traditional Ojibwa Religion and Its Historical Changes,' 54
13 Perrot quoted in Handy, 'Ojibwa,' 16; Antoine Silvy, 'Letter No. 32, Quebec, 1709: Political Government of the Indians,' *Letters from North America* (Belleville, Ont. 1980), 129
14 Kinietz, *Chippewa Village*, 69; and Kinietz, *Indians of the Western Great Lakes, 1615–1760*, 317
15 George Irwing Quimby, *Indian Life in the Upper Great Lakes, 11,000 B.C. to A.D. 1800* (Chicago 1967), 122–7
16 Harold Hickerson, *Chippewa and Their Neighbors*, 9–13
17 Silvy, *Letters*, describes the Indians and their activities at the Sault in 1710: Letter No. 45, 'Lake Huron, the Amikouas, and the Mississaugas,' 152; Letter No. 46, 'The Saulteaux Indians and Where They Live,' 153; Letter No. 47, 'The Saulteaux Conjurors (Medicine Men),' 154. Warren in the *History of the Ojibway Nation* explains the following terms. *Clan totems*: The Ojibwa as a body were divided into several grand families or clans, each of which was known and perpetuated by a symbol of some bird, animal, fish, or reptile which denominated the totem or *Do-daim* (as the Ojibwa pronounce it) and which was equivalent, in some respects, to the coat of arms of the European nobility. The totem descended in the male line, and intermarriage never took place between persons of the same symbol even if they belonged to different and distinct groups, since they consider one another related by the closest ties of blood and called one another by the nearest terms of consanguinity (34–5). The *Midewiwin Society* was a widespread secret organization with rituals and fellowship similar to those of the Masonic Lodge. An Ojibwa went through many years of training in order to reach the highest level in both medicine and religion (65–7, 77–81). The *Feast of the Dead* was performed every eight to twelve years on average. The Ojibwa would disinter all single burials so that the remains could be placed in a common grave. It was not only a religious ceremony but also an occasion to symbolize tribal unity. The ceremony was probably acquired from the Huron. Conrad Heidenreich, 'Huronia,' in Bruce Trigger, ed., *Handbook of North American Indians*, vol. 15: *Northeast* (Washington 1978), 374
18 Jones, *History*, 108; Copway, *Traditional History and Characteristic Sketches of the Ojibwa Nation*, 144, 146–50; Hickerson, *Chippewa and Their Neighbors*, 40, 52–63; Hickerson, *Chippewa Indians*, 16

CHAPTER TWO: CONQUEST

1 Trigger, *The Children of Aataentsic*, 1: 62–3, 166–76, 243, 351–5, 605–7. The northern Algonquian (Ojibwa) had an essential reciprocal trade relationship with the Huron even before white contact. The Ojibwa exchanged furs, fish, and meat for corn. Trigger points out that it would have been impossible for the large population of Huronia to exist without the high-protein food provided by the Ojibwa, and the Ojibwa, in turn, would not have been able to develop a large population without the necessary supply of

corn in the winter. This economic relationship overlapped to military matters, since the existence of one group depended on the other. Champlain, *Works*, 2: 65–100

2 Champlain, *Works*, 3: 43–4

3 Olga Jurgens, 'Etienne Brûlé,' *DCB*, 1: 130–3. *JR*, 2: 279; Orr, 'The Mississaugas,' 7; Handy, 'Ojibwa,' 12; *JR*, 18: 231

4 *JR*, 33: 149

5 George T. Hunt, *The Wars of the Iroquois* (Milwaukee, Wisconsin 1967), 174. Trigger, *Children of Aataentsic*, 2: 628–33; J.D. Jennings, *Prehistory of North America* (New York 1968), 24, n29. There were obviously factors other than military technology involved in Iroquois success. See Bruce G. Trigger, 'The French Presence in Huronia: The Structures of Franco-Huron Relations in the First Half of the Seventeenth Century,' *CHR* 49(2) (1968): 6.

6 Hunt, *Wars*,

7 Trigger, *Children of Aataentsic*, 2: 729, 838–9

8 Dollier de Casson and de Bréhant Galinée, *Exploration of the Great Lakes, 1669–1670*, ed. and trans. James H. Coyne, Ontario Historical Society, *Papers and Records* 41–7, 78, 81. La Potherie, *Histoire de l'Amérique septentrionale*, 1: 275, 280–1. La Potherie used the term 'Sauteurs' to describe the Ojibwa. *JR*, 1671; [Hodge], *Handbook*, 348; Bruce G. Trigger, 'Tekarikaken,' *DCB*, 2: 624; Perrot, *Memoir*, 150–3; *JR*, 45: 161, 163

9 Perrot, *Memoir*, 194, 193, 181. 'Alexander Henry mentions in his book that he was told a thousand Iroquois died at Point Iroquois (or "Grave of the Iroquois" as he called it) and to this assertion, the editor of his papers (James Bain) simply puts a footnote listing the number as a hundred!' See Eid, 'Ojibwa-Iroquois War,' 312–13.

10 Hickerson, *Chippewa*, 32–3; Eid, 'Ojibwa-Iroquois War,' 312–15; Schoolcraft, *Algic Researches*, 203; Jones, *History*, 118–22; Perrot, *Memoir*, 151. 'Ottawa' is the term used here, but it is safe to assume that these were mainly Ojibwa. Wampum, mnemonic devices made of strings of coloured beads and pictographs on birchbark, were used by the Ojibwa to record arrangements and ideas. See Tehanetorins, *Wampum Belts* (Ohsweken 1983), and Dewdney, *Sacred Scrolls*.

11 Handy, 'Ojibwa,' 31. More efficient hunting also depleted the game in the north and, therefore, made the food supply in southern Ontario more attractive. W. J. Eccles, *Frontenac: The Courtier Governor* (Toronto 1959), 178ff; Kellogg, *French Regime* 212ff; Donald B. Smith, 'Kahgegagahbowh,' *DCB*, 9: 419–21; Copway, *The Traditional History and Characteristic Sketches of the Ojibwa Nation*, 88. Although most Indians do not mention the specific date of these battles, Copway estimates them as occurring nearly forty years after the Huron route. In the context of other evidence, it is safe to assume that the battles occurred in the 1690s (33–4). Another Ojibwa writer from the United States indicated that his nation and their allies 'sent their united forces against the Iroquois, and fighting severe and bloody battles, they eventually forced them to retire from Canada.' Since almost all of the battles occurred in Ontario, the oral tradition of Ojibwa outside the province is considerably less

detailed. See Warren, *History of the Ojibwa Nation*, 146–7. James Masson, the chief (1960s–70s) of the band at Chippawa Hill on the Saugeen River, confirms the tradition of the Battle of Skull Mound. Chamberlain, 'Notes on History, Customs, and Beliefs of the Mississaugua Indians,' 150–60, recorded the oral tradition of Sarnia Ojibwa Allen Salt in 1888, which also substantiates Copway's claim of victory over the Iroquois. Schmalz, *History of the Saugeen Indians*, 33–4

12 Paul Kane, *Wanderings of an Artist among the Indians of North America* (London 1859), 3

13 George Laidler, 'Long Point, Lake Erie: Some Physical and Historical Aspects,' Ontario Historical Society, *Papers and Records* 36 (1944): 56. Laidler puts the Ojibwa victory at 1710, which is likely at least a decade too late. His source for this information is C.W. McCall, 'An Indian Battle off Long Point,' *Simcoe Reformer*, 2 Nov. 1940, which indicates that the informants were Ojibwa who probably participated in the lake battle. Cruikshank, ed., *Correspondence ... Simcoe*, 1: 291–2

14 Wm T. Mitchell, 'Legends of Indian History in St. Clair County,' *Pioneer Collections: Report of the Pioneer Society of the State of Michigan*, vol. 6 (Lansing, Michigan 1884), 416–18. The author indicates that one attack was against the Huron as well as the Iroquois. These could have been the Huron who, after their conquest in 1650, had been integrated into the Five Nations.

15 Oral tradition comes from interviews with chiefs, band councilors, and other leading members of the communities at Saugeen and Cape Croker reserves in the period 1968–89. The informants are from the major families on the reserves, including the Joneses, Akiwenzies, Masons, Johnstons, Elliotts, Nadjiwons, Kahgees, and Kewageshigs. Local archaeologist Fritz Knechtel was also most helpful. See also Rose M. MacLeod, *The Story of White Cloud, Hay and Griffith Islands* (Owen Sound, Ont. 1979), 4; and the *Wiarton Echo*, 3 Aug. 1883, which indicates that a great battle against the Mohawk was conducted at Cabot's Head. The battle on Indian Hill, Lot 22 Concession 15 of Culross Township, is recorded in Marion McGillivray, ed., *All Our Yesterdays: A History of Culross Township, 1854-1984* (Owen Sound, Ont. 1984), 20. Many of these accounts are traditions of the farming community passed on from the early pioneers who received them from the local Indians; see Smith, 'Who Are the Mississauga?' 'The Mississauga, Peter Jones, and the White Man'; Jones, *History*, 112. The location of Skull Island is not specifically given by Jones; however, James White in "Place Names in Georgian Bay," Ontario Historical Society, *Papers and Records* 11 (1913): 70, identifies one location as Skull Island where 'a large number of skeletons were found in a pit in the rock on the island.' J. Hugh Hammond in recording the traditions of the Lakes Huron and Simcoe Ojibwa noted that Wendausum (Lightning) and Mesaquab (getting into the land) believed that a big battle was fought 'on [near?] Manitoulin Island between Ojibwas and Mohawks; you will find some of the skulls there.' The two informants also indicated that the Mohawk were defeated at their villages between Penetan-

guishene and Orillia, Skigawog or Pigeon Lake, near Kingston, and the banks of Lake George. See Hammond, 'The Coming of the Ojibwas,' Province of Ontario *Annual Archaeological Report 1904*, (Toronto 1905), 76–7.

16 William D. Le Sueur, *Count Frontenac* (Toronto 1912), 243–4. At the battle of Sand Point on the Ottawa River, thirty Iroquois were killed; Higgins, *Whitefish Lake Ojibwa Memories*. Higgins accepts the myth that the French were most responsible for the destruction of the Iroquois. Fear of the Iroquois, rather than pride in victory, dominates the memory of the White-fish Lake Ojibwa. Since they did not settle to the south, their participation was probably minor in the aggressive campaigns. The informant from Gogama was Irene Johnson, whose memories of these events were recorded in 1970 when she was eighty-five years old. The Indians in the Gogama area still scold their children by saying, 'the Iroquois will get you if you are bad.' *The Temagami Experience: Recreation, Resources, and Aboriginal Rights in the Northern Ontario Wilderness* (Toronto 1989), 14–26

17 Douglas Leighton, 'Assiginack,' *DCB*, 9: 9–10. Francis Assiginack in *The Report of the Canadian Institute* (Toronto 1856–9) signed his articles, 'A Warrior of the Odahwahs.'

18 See H.G. Tucker, 'A Warrior of the Odahwahs,' *OH* 18 (1920): 32–5; Schmalz, *History of the Saugeen Indians*, 6; Perrot, *Memoir*, 179–81, Milo Melton Quaife, ed., *The Western Country in the 17th Century: The Memoirs of Lamothe Cadillac and Pierre Liette* (Chicago 1947), 65; Donald Chaput, 'Kouta-oiliboe,' *DCB*, 3: 324–5; and Donald Smith, 'Saguima,' *DCB*, 3: 576–7. Joseph Hacques Marest, the Jesuit at Michilimackinac, believed that Saguima 'had more influence over the Ottawa than anyone else.' Smith notes that the name had several spellings: Saguina, Sakima, Saquima, and possibly Saquin. Sahgimah may be added to the list. *Doc. Hist. NY*, 1: 132. This is what M. de Denonville called the territory between Lakes Huron and Erie.

19 J. Hampden Burham, 'The Coming of the Mississagas,' Ontario Historical Society, *Papers and Records* 6 (1905): 7–11. The name 'Gemoaghpenassee' cannot be found in any of the primary sources consulted or the secondary sources beyond the one noted, but this is not unusual since no European seems to have participated in the battles under consideration. It is well established that the Mississauga are part of the Ojibwa. See Smith, 'Who Are the Mississauga?'

20 Smith, 'The Mississauga,' 37; Burnham, 'Coming,' 7–11; NA RG 10, 2331, file 67, 071-4B, 'Commission at Hiawatha Reserve, Rice Lake, Testimony of Johnson Paudash,' 26-5-1923. In presenting evidence to support land claims, Paudash gave more details about the conquest. He claimed that Gemoagh-penassee (Bald Eagle) led 15,000 [more likely 1500] warriors from Nipissing and the Mississauga River to Skull Island [possibly Giant's Tomb Island] at the mouth of the Severn River. He also indicated that 'the Ontario Govern-ment did some digging at Roch's Point and found the skeletons and they were pierced with arrows.' George Monro Grant, ed., *Picturesque Canada: The Country as It Was and Is*, 2 vols. (Toronto 1882), 2: 642; William Canniff, *The*

Settlement of Upper Canada (Toronto: Dubley & Burn. 1869), 407; NYCD, 4: 564ff; Jones, *History*, 113

21 Hale, *Iroquois Book of Rites*, 59, 91; Peter Doyentate Clarke, *Origins and Traditional History of the Wyandotts* (Toronto 1870), 62–6; Eid, 'Ojibwa-Iroquois War,' 319–20

22 Trigger, *Children of Aataentsic*, 2: 838–9; Konrad, 'Iroquois Frontier,' 135, 138; La Potherie, *Histoire de l'Amérique Septentrionale*, 2: 134; Conrad Heidenreich, *Huronia: A History and Geography of the Huron Indians, 1600-1650* (Toronto 1971), 127ff, who indicates that the population size of villages such as that found at Keinte-he in 1670; and review of his book by P.S. Schmalz in *Canadian Journal of History and Social Science* 9 (4) (Summer 1974): 63–4.

23 Jones, *History*, 113. Heidenreich observed that 'the Iroquois abandoned their villages on the north shore, but these villages did not disappear. Their continued appearance on historical maps until after the end of the French regime owes much to the habit of map copying and to the lack of new geographic knowledge of the Lake Ontario area during the eighteenth century. That this occupation was by Algonquian-speaking Indians from the north was not well known. Since the same locations were occupied, the original village names remained on the maps' (141). Champlain, *Works*, plate 81 in the portfolio; NYCD, 4: 693ff; Donald Chaput, 'Kinonge,' *DCB*, 2: 317. The year before, the Ojibwa brought thirty Iroquois scalps to Cadillac at Michilimackinac. See also Leon Pouliot, 'Henri Nouvel,' *DCB*, 2: 221, 500–1; Yves F. Zoltvany, 'Louis-Hector de Callière,' *DCB* 2: 631; NYCD, 498ff. Zoltvany in his biography of Callière notes, 'On 18 July 1700 Tonatakout arrived in Montreal with Aouenano and two other Seneca chiefs and the Onondagas, Aradgi and Ohansiowan. They had come to ask Governor Callière to bring to an end the attacks that the western tribes [mainly Ojibwa] had been making on the Iroquois.' See also Bruce G. Trigger, 'Tonontakout,' *DCB*, 2: 631.

24 Eccles, *Frontenac*, 332. In a later publication, *The Canadian Frontier* (New York 1969), 135, Eccles recognized that this barrier was not achieved. It is most likely that the governor was unaware of the agreements being made by the Ojibwa with the Iroquois involving the Ojibwa's gaining access to Albany's trade. Callière's negotiations with the Indians during the several days of treaty talks focused mainly on the problem of returning the prisoners. The chiefs of the Ojibwa and their allies never seemed to bring up the topic of trade with the English or the fact that the Ojibwa had taken over the Iroquois beaver-hunting grounds in southern Ontario. See Donald J. Horton, 'Chingouessi,' Ottawa Sinango [Ojibwa] chief; 'Chichikatelo,' Miamis chief; and 'Ouenemek,' Potawatomi chief, *DCB*, 2: 143, 144, 503; Yves F. Zoltvany, 'The Problem of Western Policy under Philippe de Regaud de Vaudreuil (1703–25),' Canadian Historical Society, *Report* (1964): 9–24; NYCD, 4: 732ff. A note indicates that the French called all those nations to the west and northwest of Albany, 'Ottawa,' though the English called them 'Dowaganahas.' They would have been mainly Ojibwa. See also NYCD, 3: 778,

which indicates that some Ojibwa had been to Albany as early as 1691, but died of smallpox. See also the French source in NA, France, Archives des colonies, correspondence générale, Canada, serie c11A, 29, 25–102; NYCD, 4: 899.

25 Eccles, *France in America*, 103; Eccles, *Canadian Frontier*, 136. The earlier publications on Frontenac noted in this paper also take this stand. See NA, c11A, 11, Denonville to Seignelay, 314–42; 'Dubuisson, Commanding Officer at Detroit to the Governor General, 1712,' in Thwaites, ed., 'French Regime in Wisconsin, 1634–1727,' 267–87; NYCD, 4: 900–8. Samuel York, an Englishman who had been a prisoner of the French for ten years, escaped and was sent to the Ojibwa by Bellomont in 1700. Bellomont was afraid that the Iroquois were not telling the truth when they said they would allow the Ojibwa to trade at Albany: 'It is much to be feared they will as often as they meet those Indians, rob them of their peltry and then knock them on the head, that they may tell no tales.' NYCD, 4: 728. Samuel York may have given his name to a major Ojibwa chief at Owen Sound where Peter Yorke was leader of the Nawash band. See E.L. Marsh, *A History of The County of Grey* (Owen Sound, Ont. 1931), plate of his picture opposite 32; NYCD, 4: 728, 114, 813.

26 Smith, 'The Mississauga,' 25; and Eid, 'Ojibwa-Iroquois War,' 308–9. For translated French primary sources see Thwaites, ed., 'French Regime in Wisconsin (1634–1727),' 14, 291, 263, 335, 336, 370. Surtees, 'Indian Land claims,' 13. An interesting but somewhat confusing handwritten record on Indian land rights is in the Wawanosh Papers at the University of Western Ontario Library. It was written by Jean Baptiste, 7 March 1850, and states: 'Wamens [?] head chief of whole tract of land comprising Owen Sound, Sauging, Goderich, the Sauble, and Port Sarnia had nine brothers. To one nephew, TrabisanichBang, he gave tract from Owen Sound to Sauging inclusive. Wabitik, the present chief is his son. Another nephew, Trach-Binmin-dji, from the Sauble to Sarnia inclusive. Wawanosh, the present chief, is the same. Wamens reserved to himself from within 20 miles of Sauging to 10 of Sauble.' From this document it is obvious that there was a definite hereditary right among the Ojibwa to specific locations in Ontario. This right became important during the surrender period. See Schmalz, 'The Saugeen Indian Land Surrenders,' in *Saugeen Indians*. For the purchase of land in Ontario for the Iroquois see Johnston, ed., *Valley of the Six Nations*, 46, 49.

27 J.V. Wright, 'A regional Examination of Ojibwa Cultural History,' *Anthropologica*, NS 7 (2) (1965): 218–9; Allen Edwin Tyyska and James A. Burns, *Archaeology from North Bay to Mattawa* (Toronto 1973), which describes rock pictures, an ochre mine, a refinery, and an extensive system of stone structures which may have been used by Midewiwin shamans; Dunning, *Social and Economic Change among the Northern Ojibwa*; Landes, *Ojibwa Sociology*; and Paul Radin, 'Ojibwa of southeastern Ontario,' *American Anthropologist*, NS 30 (1928). An amateur anthropologist in 1895 observed, 'The Iroquois did not

readily give up this territory, according to the current beliefs of the Ojibwas, by more than one of whom I have been assured that the claim was ultimately settled by a great battle, in which the Iroquois were defeated.' See Boyle, 'Notes on Primitive Man in Ontario,' 14; Trigger, 'Indians and Ontario's History,' 246.

CHAPTER THREE: THE GOLDEN AGE

1 Danziger, Jr, *Chippewas of Lake Superior*, 31; Henry, *Travels & Adventures in Canada*, 187–8
2 W.J. Eccles, 'A Belated Review of Harold Adams Innis, the Fur Trade in Canada,' *CHR* 60 (4) (Dec. 1979): 419–41. Eccles indicated that there was little difference between the English and the French prices of furs. On two occasions, however, he notes that no systematic study has been conducted on the topic. See J.B. Brebner, 'Subsidized Intermarriage with the Indians: An Incident in British Colonial Policy,' *CHR* 1 (1) (March 1925): 33–6, in which a white woman or man was to be given a gift of £10 and fifty acres free of rent for twenty years if they married an Indian. There is not one case of this offer being acted upon between the years 1719 and 1773.
3 Severance, *Old Frontier of France*, 1: 278–303; 2: 87
4 NYCD, 4: 981, 990. Preston, ed., *Royal Fort Frontenac*, 241. Marriage records at Fort Frontenac in 1751 indicate that a Sioux, likely an Ojibwa prisoner, was married to a Frenchman at the fort. *Doc. Hist. NY*, 9: 763; Zoltvany, *Philippe de Rigaud de Vaudreuil*, 120; *Doc. Hist. NY*, 9: 758ff
5 See 'Ramezay and Begon to French Minister, 7 Nov. 1715' in Thwaites, ed., 'French Regime in Wisconsin, 1634–1727,' 334–5; NYCD, 5: 659.
6 Zoltvany, *Vaudreuil*, 122ff. Smith, 'Saguima,' *DCB*, 3: 576–7. Zoltvany indicates, 122, that Saguina had 150 warriors. Charles Callender in his article on the 'Fox,' in Trigger, ed., *Handbook of North American Indians*, vol. 15: *Northeast*, 637–8, gives no figures involving the battle and even indicates that the French commander incited a coalition of different groups to attack the Fox who threatened his fort. Kellogg, *French Régime in Wisconsin*, 282
7 Robinson, *Toronto during the French Régime*, 80. NYCD, 5: 541, 695. A footnote on page 86 in *The History of the Five Nations* (Ithica 1964), identified the Aghsiesagechrone as Mississauga, according to Cadwallader Colden. See also Handy, 'Ojibwa,' 35, in which she observes that 'by the 1720s the Ojibwa were at the height of their economic prosperity and cultural fluorescence.'
8 Robinson, *Toronto during the French Régime*, 80–1; NA, Archives des colonies, c11A, vol. 47, 126; NYCD, 9: 1015, 1099; Eccles, 'A Belated Review,' 419–41; Severance, *Old Frontier of France*, 1: 265ff; Henry, *Travels & Adventures in Canada*, 13ff; Arthur Dobbs, *An Account of the Countries Adjoining to Hudson's Bay in the North-west Part of America* (London 1744; reprinted New York 1967), 12ff
9 Kellogg, *French Régime in Wisconsin*, 376ff; NYCD, 10: 34ff; Severance, *Old Frontier of France*, 323 (my emphasis); Adam Shortt and Arthur G. Doughty,

eds., 'The Colony in Its Economic Relations,' *Canada and Its Provinces* (Toronto 1914), 2: 503

10 Severance, *Old Frontier of France*, 323

11 NYCD, 6: 391. The three groups were 'Missesagues, Wawehattecooks and Ockneharuse,' 'who have eight big Castles, the biggest of all the nations, these people are 1500 or 2000.'

12 NYCD, 10: 87

13 Ibid., 157, 161ff

14 Ibid., 181–3; Etienne Taillemite, 'Marquis de La Galissonière,' *DCB*, 3: 28. The loyalty of the Mississauga in the Toronto area to the French in 1746 was also confirmed by Jonquière in 1751. Apaequois, their chief, sent him an English 'collar,' exposing an attempted conspiracy against the French. See 'La Jonquière to the French minister, 5 October 1751,' Thwaites, ed., 'The French Regime in Wisconsin (1743–1760),' 18: 99–104.

15 NYCD, 10: 141–71

16 Ibid., 200–1

17 Ibid., 248

18 Severance, *Old Frontier of France*, 400; Kellogg, *French Régime in Wisconsin*, 411–12

19 *Wisconsin Historical Collections*, 18: 104–8. See also R. David Edmunds, 'Old Briton,' *American Indian Leaders* (Lincoln, Nebraska 1980), 1–20. The Ojibwa, in supporting Old Briton for a short time, killed a few French traders, but soon allied themselves with the French against their traditional enemy, the Miami. Paul Trap, 'Mouet de Langlade, Charles-Michel,' *DCB*, 4: 563; Kellogg, *French Régime in Wisconsin*, 420–2; W.J. Eccles, 'Rigaud de Vaudreuil de Cavagnial, Pierre de, Marquis de Vaudreuil,' *DCB*, 4: 666

20 Guy Frégault, *Canada: The War of Conquest* (Toronto 1969), 96; Trap, 'Longlade,' 563; Kellogg, *French Régime in Wisconsin*, 428

21 NYCD, 10: 372, 561

22 Thomas S. Abler, 'Gaiachoton,' *DCB*, 4: 408; NYCD, 6: 975; 10: 401–511

23 NYCD, 9: 1015. This source indicates numerous Ojibwa attacks.

24 Johnson, *Papers*, 10: 437–41, 445; Frégault, *Canada*, 128, 131; Severance, *Old Frontier of France*, 2: 184–5

25 Robinson, *Toronto during the French Régime*, 135–6; La Rochefoucault-Liancourt, *Travels in Canada, 1795*, 113; NA, c11A, 102, Vaudreuil to the Minister, 272–3. He observed: 'We are so destitute that unfortunately the needs to the service [rather than the Indian trade] become more urgent every day.'

26 NYCD, 10: 605. The specific bands and in many cases their locations are given here. The Fox and Miami also participated in the battle but most of the warriors were Ojibwa. NYCD, 11: 512; Frégault, *Canada*, 153–4; Kellogg, *French Régime in Wisconsin*, 429–34. See also Alanson Skinner, 'War Customs of the Menomini Indians,' *American Anthropologist*, NS 13 (1911): 299–312. It was customary to take scalps for the 'scalp-dance' to prove one's bravery in battle. Officers were special targets since the leader of the party

gave embroidered pack-straps 'as gifts to that warrior who slayed a chief of the enemy.' In addition, the presentation of enemy scalps at French forts were certain to be rewarded with handsome payments. There is a degree of hypocrisy among French writers who criticized the Indians for such actions.

27 NYCD, 10: 704. This shortage was only temporary. A month later, 16 June, the considerable amount of 12,000 barrels of flour arrived at Quebec (717)

28 Severance, *Old Frontier of France*, 2: 187; *Wisconsin Historical Collections*, 19: 152–8; Frégault, *Canada*, 162–3; Kellogg, *French Régime in Wisconsin*, 431–4; Johnson, *Papers*, 9: 412ff. William Williams reported to Johnson that smallpox was devastating the French Indian allies. One hundred Caughnawaga had died, as well as eighty Ojibwa at Niagara and Frontenac. Complete statistics on the deaths are not available. NYCD, 10: 700

29 Frégault, *Canada*, 223–7; Kellogg, *French Régime in Wisconsin*, 383; NA, C11A 103-1, 'Vaudreuil to Messiac,' 175–86; Johnson, *Papers*, 2: 889–90; Preston, ed., *Fort Frontenac*, 262; James Thomas Flexner, *Mohawk Baronet: Sir William Johnson of New York* (New York 1959), 194–9; L.F.S. Upton, *Micmacs and Colonists: Indian White Relations in the Maritimes, 1713–1867* (Vancouver 1979), 56; Robinson, *Toronto during the French Régime*, 136; Johnson, *Papers*, 9: 415, 945ff. The Seneca speaker reported to Johnson on 21 July 1758; 'We delivered this your Belt of Wampum & are now to acquaint you that we did send Messages to all our Allies & have had Negotiations with the Messasagas, Jenundadees & several other Western Nations, and our Head Man your good Friend Tageghsadde – meaning the Drunkard the Chief Seneca Sachem, is still employed in this good Work, and he shortly proposes to come down here & pay you a Visit with a number of his Warriors in order to give you a full & particular relation of all his Transactions' (947).

30 NYCD, 10: 952, 824; Flexner, *Johnson*, 198–319. Severance, *Old Frontier of France*, 317ff. English Captain de Lancey made this report after the battle.

31 Flexner, *Johnson*, 199

32 Johnson, *Papers*, 12: 118–19, 148

33 The major leaders were Messeaghage, a civil chief, and Oulamy, a war chief. Howard H. Peckham, *Pontiac and the Indian Uprising* (Chicago 1961), 53–4. The prisoner is quoted in Croghan's diary, 10 Oct. 1759. NYCD, 10: 1093–4

CHAPTER FOUR: THE BEAVER WAR

1 Henry, *Travels & Adventures in Canada*, 44

2 C.P. Stacey, 'Amherst, Jeffrey, 1st Baron Amherst,' *DCB*, 4: 24; NYCD, 7: 583; *Johnson Papers*, 3: 514. Amherst in 1763 requested information on the population of the Ojibwa from Johnson, who could only report that they were the most numerous of all the Ottawa Confederacy and had many villages about Lakes Superior, Huron, Erie, etc. Peckham, *Pontiac and the Indian Uprising*, 72. Johnson observed that 'the chief thing is, that the Indians expect whoever possesses Posts, or carrys on Trade in their Country must pay them for it, although they make use of other Argument to account for

any act of Hostility.' *Johnson Papers*, 11: 221–2; 13: 221ff; Jane E. Graham, 'Wabbicommicot,' *DCB*, 3: 651; NYCD, 6: 486; 7: 239, 259. Wabbicommicot remained friendly towards Johnson throughout the Pontiac Uprising. *Johnson Papers*, 10: 325; 13: 227–56. NA, Haldimand Papers, vol. A-615, 'Proceedings of a Garrison Court Marshal held at Fort Pitt,' 12 July 1762. A soldier was put on trial for defrauding an Indian, but the case was dismissed because the Indian had not been asked to give evidence. Robinson, *Toronto during the French Régime*, 145

3 *Johnson Papers*, 10: 329

4 Ibid., 9: 37; La Rochefoucault-Liancourt, *Travels in Canada*, 113

5 *Johnson Papers*, 10: 578

6 NA, Archives des colonies, C11A, 45, 45, 'Statement of Provisions, Munitions, and Trade Goods which Have Been Traded at Forts Frontenac, Niagara, the Head of Lake Ontario, and at the Bay of Quinté during the Years 1722 and 1723,' 195–202; *Johnson Papers*, 10: 278–79; Henry, *Travels & Adventures in Canada*, 50; *Johnson Papers*, 8: 'Ferrall Wade to William Johnson,' 6 April 1771, Toronto, 64–5; 'Wade & Keiuser to William Johnson,' 18 June 1771, 149–50; Lajeunesse, ed., *Windsor Border Region*, xcii

7 *Johnson Papers*, 10: 507

8 Ibid., 291, 284

9 W.L. Jenks, 'The Hutchins' Map of Michigan,' *Michigan History Magazine* 10 (July 1926): 358–73; this source contains his journal as well.

10 *Johnson Papers*, 3: 510; Francis Parkman, *The Conspiracy of Pontiac and the Indian War after the Conquest of Canada* (New York 1962); Thomas Guthrie Marquis, *The War Chief of the Ottawas: A Chronicle of the Pontiac War* (Toronto 1964), considered Parkman's study 'the fullest and best treatment of the subject (139); Peckham, *Pontiac and the Indian Uprising*; Clide Hollmann, *Pontiac: King of the Great Lakes* (New York 1968).

11 Andrew J. Blackbird, *History of the Ottawa and Chippewa Indians of Michigan* (Ypsilanti 1887), 7

12 Peckman, *Pontiac and the Indian Uprising*, in an extensive footnote, 15–18, indicates sources which give Pontiac several different nationalities. Graham, 'Wabbicommicot,' 652

13 *Johnson Papers*, 10: 534–5

14 Graham observed: Wabbicommicot complained that is was not proper for the traders to go so far up the lakes among the 'strange' Indians, and that if any mischance might happen by their going so far away it would not be in his power to remedy the situation. It is possible here that Wabbicommicot had the interests of the traders at heart since the Ojibwa beyond his jurisdiction proved to be hostile, but it is also likely that he was attempting to retain the middle position in the fur trade and wished to have his band carry on business with the 'strange' Indians.

15 Graham, 'Wabbicommicot'

16 *Johnson Papers*, 10: 'Jean Baptiste de Cougagne to Sir Wm. Johnson,' 26 May 1763, 684–5; and 'Indian Speech' reported to Henry Bouquet by Robert

Holmes, commanding at the Miamis, 30 March 1763, in 'Bouquet Papers,' *Historical Collection: Collections and Researches made by the Michigan Pioneer and Historical Society* 19: 181–2. Navarre (?), *Journal of Pontiac's Conspiracy, 1763,* 160; Burton Historical Collection Staff, 'Robert Navarre,' *DCB,* 4: 579–80; *Johnson Papers,* 2: 271, which indicates that an unnamed Ojibwa chief, two days' journey from Toronto, received war belts but refused to fight. He was likely the chief of the Ojibwa from Matchedash which was two days' distance from Toronto. Henry, *Travels & Adventures in Canada,* indicated that there were eighty Indians from Matchedash at the Niagara conference to meet Johnson on 10 June 1764 (176); Peckman, *Pontiac and the Indian Uprising,* 182, 210. Parkman, *The Conspiracy of Pontiac,* 248, indicated that 120 Ojibwa warriors also came to the Detroit siege from the 'Grand River.' It is likely that Sekaho's force was composed of Ojibwa from both rivers. Coaugne reported the capture of the traders in Lake Erie. See *Johnson Papers,* 10: 723. Harry Kelsey, 'Wasson,' *DCB,* 4: 761–2, claims the number was 200. According to Navarre's Journal (7) there were 250 Ottawa and 420 Ojibwa. James Cleland Hamilton, 'Famous Algonquins: Algic Legends,' *Transactions of the Canadian Institute* 6 (1898–9): 306

17 Henry, *Travels & Adventures in Canada,* 72–3. Although Henry was at the fort when the attack occurred, his estimation of numbers might have been exaggerated.

18 David Armour in his biography of Minweweh (*DCB,* 3: 452–3) puts the garrison force at thirty-five. See Armour, 'Laurent Ducharme' and 'Pierre Du Jaunay,' *DCB,* 4: 233, 240–1; Henry, *Travels & Adventures in Canada,* 77–149. According to Henry it was Cadotte who prevented the Ojibwa of Lake Superior from joining Pontiac after they took the fort. Certainly another factor was the lack of cooperation between the Ojibwa and the Ottawa in the north. Armour, 'Minweweh,' 452–3; Carl A. Brasseaux and Michael J. Leblanc, 'Franco-Indian Diplomacy in the Mississippi Valley 1754–1763: Prelude to Pontiac's Uprising?' *Journal de la Société des Américanistes* (1982): 59–70

19 Peckham, *Pontiac and the Indian Uprising,* 204–9, 234; *Johnson Papers,* 10: 861–2. It is important to note that there was another chief called Outquandageghte at this location who wanted to use his Mississauga warriors to stop English communications with Quebec. Not all the Indians on the north shore of Lake Ontario were pro-British.

20 See *Johnson Papers,* 10: NA, Haldimand Papers, vol. A-609, Gage to Haldimand, 20 Feb. 1759; Peckham, *Pontiac and the Indian Uprising,* 239–40.

21 *Johnson Papers,* 11: 172, 12

22 Until the Indian Act of 1876 there were traditionally two chiefs, one for war and the other for peace. Several passes and certificates were given to the Toronto chief as an indication of his loyalty to the English. Gage, in writing to Lieutenant Potts, 18 Aug. 1764, observed that 'except for the Hurons, some Mississaugas and some Chippiwas, none of the tribes who had borne arms in the hostility sent deputies.' *Sessional Papers* 23(6) (1890): 70; *Johnson*

Papers, 11: 276ff. Unfortunately, in many cases the name of the chief is omitted; Wabbicommicot is one of the few Ojibwa chiefs specifically noted.

23 W.G. Godfrey, 'John Bradstreet,' *DCB,* 4: 83–4; *Johnson Papers,* 2: 326ff. The Ojibwa requested the inclusion of a person by the name of McCarty, 'who lived several years amongst them & speaks their language very well, 2: 818.

24 *Johnson Papers* (my emphasis) 820. According to Johnson, Wabbicommicot had 150 warriors under his direct control (797). Thomas Gage 'judged it best that Wabbicommicot should be accompanied by some proper White Man on his Journey with the Belts & Messages to Pondiac & the Western Indians' and therefore appointed Jean Baptiste de Couagne to accompany him (831).

25 Ibid., 2: 940, 772, 780. Johnson recognized the Ojibwa as the 'strong people to Westward.'

26 Peckman, *Pontiac and the Indian Uprising,* 288–97

27 Ibid., 322

28 *Johnson Papers,* 2: 370–1, 782. The cost of presents to the Indians in the two years following the war was extraordinary. While no total figure can be found, in November 1764 Johnson had an account of expenses amounting to £5000. In 1763 the British government decreed, through the Royal Proclamation of 7 October, that the lands lying west of the Appalachian Mountains be deemed an Indian territory. The boundaries of that territory included the present province of Ontario south of Lake Nipissing and west of Cornwall. This proclamation 'legally' protected all the Ojibwa lands.

29 Marquis, *War Chief of the Ottawas,* 60–90; *Sessional Papers* 24(5) (1891), Dorchester to Grenville, 27 May 1790, 141; Benjamin Franklin, *Writings,* 10 vols., A.H. Smyth (New York 1905–7), 4: 289–98, 308–14; *Sessional Papers* 23 (6) (1890): 212; 'Gen. Jeffery Amherst to Col. Henry Bouquet,' 25 Sept. 1763, 233–4; Marquis, *War Chief of the Ottawas,* 7; Peckham, *Pontiac and the Indian Uprising,* 170; A.T. Volwiler, ed., 'William Trent's Journal,' *Miss. Val. Hist. Rev.* 11 (1924): 400; Bernhard Knollenberg, 'General Amherst and Germ Warfare,' *Miss. Val. Hist. Review* 40 (June 1954): 489; Wayne E. Stevens, reviewer, '*Pontiac and the Indian Uprising* by Howard H. Peckham,' *Miss. Val. Hist. Rev.* 34 (March 1948): 676, in which Peckham's scholarship is highly praised. *Sessional Papers* 23 (6) (1890): 243; Peckham, *Pontiac and the Indian Uprising,* 238–9, 336; Julian Gwyn, 'Sir William Johnson,' *DCB,* 4: 395–7; *Johnson Papers,* 2: 394–6; NYCD, 10: 1159

30 NA, vol. A-618, Haldimand Papers, Lord George Germain to Haldimand, 25 July 1778; vol. A-617, McKee, Dept. Indian Affairs agent at Fort Pitt to Major-General Haldimand, 3 July 1773; and Haldimand to Colonial Office, 30 Nov. 1773

CHAPTER FIVE: THE PEACEFUL CONQUEST

1 Herbert C.W. Goltz, 'Tecumseh,' *DCB,* 5: 799. Goltz refers to 'Naywash' as

an Ottawa chief, but later both he and his reserve were called Chippewa (Ojibwa). For more details on the confederacy see Goltz, 'Tecumseh, the Prophet, and the Rise of the Northwest Indian Confederacy.'

2 Smith, 'The Missassauga,' 47, 57–8; *Johnson Papers*, 3: 457. This speech was given in 1761 on behalf of his people; Robinson, *Toronto during the French Régime*, 152. See also *Johnson Papers*, 12: 590, which indicates that four Mississauga from 'Le Miscotaigna' to the north of Lake Ontario presented a belt to Johnson. It was the same as or similar to the one received by the Toronto chief who at his death was replaced by Papinass along with Monoghquit. The belt had two white villages joined by a road. The great chief's name in this letter is missing because of this tragedy. However, it possibly was Nanebeaujou, who also was considered a chief of the Grand River by Norman MacLeod of Niagara on 10 May 1769.

3 *Johnson Papers*, 6: 750; 8: 270–3

4 Hickerson, *Chippewa and Their Neighbors*, 76–9

5 Koennecke, 'Wasoksing,' 113. Smith, 'The Mississauga,' 47

6 Owen, *Pioneer Sketches of Long Point Settlement*, 39

7 Peter Jones, *History*, 109

8 *Johnson Papers*, 8: 482–520

9 Ibid. Johnson is communicating the Ramsay affair to Thomas Gage.

10 See also *Johnson Papers*, 8: 1164–5, and 'Sir Frederick Haldimand,' *DCB*, 4: 793–4. The Ramsay murders are not an isolated case since in the same letter to Gage, Johnson reports that two Seneca men and a woman were unjustly killed by some Virginians. Peckham, *Pontiac and the Indian Uprising*, 149, 182, 162

11 *Johnson Papers*, 8: 512, 530, 498–9, 514–15, 519–20, 524, 551, 562, 584

12 Ibid., 963

13 Ibid., 12: 964, 967, 969–70, 976; 8: 496. Smith, 'The Mississauga,' 54. Long, *Voyages and Travels*, 144–7. Smith, 'The Mississauga,' 44ff; and Cruikshank, ed., *Correspondence ... Simcoe*, 4: 114

14 'Gen. Jeffery Amherst to Col. Henry Bouquet,' 7 Aug. 1763, in 'Bouquet Papers,' 223–4

15 'Major Henry Basset to Gen. Frederick Haldimand,' 29 April 1773, in 'Haldimand Papers,' 297

16 Charles E. Lart, 'Fur-Trade Returns, 1767,' *CHR* 3 (Dec. 1922): 351–8. In 1762 Lucas Van Vachten & Co outfitted four Englishmen, two negroes, and twelve Canadians in three canoes carrying forty bales of dry goods, eight nests of trunks, and 200 gallons of rum on a trip to Toronto. This would make six men in each canoe. See *Johnson Papers*, 3: 754, 943. This was reported to Amherst by Major Wilkins. Marjorie G. Reid, 'The Quebec Fur-Traders and Western Policy, 1763–1774,' *CHR* 6 (1) (March 1925): 25, 29

17 Robinson, *Toronto during the French Régime*, 153; and *Johnson Papers*, 4: 573, which indicates that two traders were arrested in 1767; 7: 729, 739; 4: 490–1, 526

18 Lajeunesse, *Windsor Border Region*, lxxii. In August 1776 Lt-Gov. Hamilton at

Detroit wrote to the Earl of Dartmouth that some Ottawa, Chippewa, Huron, and Potawatomi were joining the Six Nations at Niagara under orders of Lt-Col. Caldwell. It was Caldwell's son, with the same name and the rank of captain, who led the 'Lake Indians' into battle. This explains why the Indians later accepted him as a settler in the Windsor area. See map in Lajeunesse, *Windsor Border Region*, opposite cxvi.

19 Jack M. Sosin, 'The Use of Indians in the War of the American Revolution: a Re-assessment of Responsibility,' *CHR* 46 (1965): 101–20. See 'Haldimand Papers,' 9 and 19: 408, 419, where Captain D. Brehm at Detroit justified the most liberal distribution of liquor to retain the alliance of the Indians and also to prevent mutiny in these troubled times.

20 Egerton Ryerson, *The Loyalists of America and Their Times: From 1670 to 1816* (Toronto 1880), 2: 85–122. Unfortunately, the American misrepresentation of the attack on Wyoming has been perpetuated by Canadian 'historians' in current popular history, supporting the American myth of Canadian Indian atrocities. Nick and Helma Mika, *United Empire Loyalists Pioneers of Upper Canada* (Belleville 1976), 112, use a picture from the Chicago Historical Society illustrating a horrible massacre. An Indian is in the centre of the picture scalping a live settler, and to the left a British soldier is shooting another settler who is on his knees. The caption in part reads: 'A battle fought in the valley on July 3rd ended in total defeat for the settlers, many of whom were killed, tortured or scalped in the aftermath.'

21 E. Cruikshank, *Butler's Rangers* (Welland 1893), 45–7; Ryerson, *The Loyalists*, 2: 117–18. The location and way in which they died was supposedly symbolically indicated on the back of the scalp. William L. Stone, *Life of Joseph Brant (Thayendanegea)*, (New York 1838), 1: 230–60; Cruikshank, *Butler's Rangers*, 72; and James O'Donnell, 'Joseph Brant,' in R. David Edmunds, ed., *American Indian Leaders* (Lincoln 1980), 30; Gray, *Wilderness Christians* 73–4

22 Cruikshank, *Butler's Rangers*, 105–8

23 Ryerson, *The Loyalists*, 2: 114. John M. Coleman, 'Robert Land and Some Frontier Skirmishes,' *OH* 47 (2) (1956): 52; Johnson, ed., *The Valley of the Six Nations*, xxxviii and 47

24 Canada, *Indian Treaties and Surrenders from 1680 to 1890*, 3: 196–7; Russell *Correspondence*, 2: 186–7. The chief and headmen who asked Brant to handle their affairs with the government were Wabanip (Fishhawk), Polaquan (Buffalo), Nekuguar (Otter), Wabenos (Eagle), Atchechank (Fishhawk), Debandan (Fishhawk), and Pichea Kea (Buffalo). Sally M. Weaver, 'Six Nations of the Grand River, Ontario,' in Trigger, ed., *Handbook of North American Indians*, vol. 15: *Northeast*, 525

25 Smith, 'The Mississauga,' 81. The government carried on an overt policy of divide and rule, especially with these two groups. Long, *Voyages and Travels*, 77–8; Peter Jones, *History*, 114; Lajeunesse, *Windsor Border Region*, cxx–cxxi; Gray, *Wilderness Christians*, 90, 106ff. It is important to note that the Ojibwa of the Thames River 'were going farther westward' at this time, but the

reason for their move is not given. Cruikshank, ed., *Correspondence ... Simcoe*, 1: 157, 220, 242. See Gray, *Wilderness Christians*, 111 to 122, which contains a good discussion on Brant's refusal to fight the Americans. Cruikshank, ed., *Correspondence ... Simcoe*, 2: 65, 105, 223, 252, 262, 306, 315, 317, 326. There were 180 Ojibwa and Potawatomi who 'heard cannon fired at the fallen Timbers,' which indicates that they were possibly too late to participate in the battle. The Americans were reported to be paying $40.00 per Indian scalp.

26 Gray, *Wilderness Christians*, 124–5; and 'Colonel Matthew Elliott to Major-General Brock,' Amherstburg, 12 Jan. 1812, in E.A. Cruikshank, ed., *Documents Relating to the Invasion of Canada and the Surrender of Detroit, 1812* (Ottawa 1912), 6–11

27 Cruikshank, ed., *Correspondence ... Simcoe*, 4: 304. Smith, 'The Mississauga,' 83. Cruikshank, ed., *Correspondence ... Simcoe*, 2: 73. Statistics do not exist for all the Ojibwa bands at the time.

28 Canniff, *Settlement of Upper Canada*, 615. These figures are only estimates. Rae Stuart, 'Jessup's Rangers as a Factor in Loyalist Settlement,' *Three History Theses* (Ottawa 1961), 59–72. Haldimand estimated in 1783 that there would be more than 2000 soldiers with the 12,350 Loyalists who required well over a million acres of land. Cruikshank, ed., *Correspondence ... Simcoe*, 2: 293

29 Donald F. McOuat, ed., 'The Diary of William Graves,' *OH* 43(1) (1951): 10

30 Russell, *Papers*, 41; Donald B. Smith, 'Kineubenae,' *DCB*, 5: 466–7

31 Henry Adams, *History of the United States of America during the First Administration of James Madison* (New York 1890), 2: 67–9. Richard A. Preston, ed., *Kingston before the War of 1912* (Toronto 1962), cxi, in which an Ojibwa chief by the name of Snake was murdered near Kingston and the culprit put on trial, convicted, but apparently not executed. Copway, *Traditional History and Characteristic Sketches of the Ojibwa Nation*, 33–4

32 Smith, 'The Mississauga,' 66–7

33 La Rochefouchault-Liancourt, *Travels in Canada, 1795*, 42

34 Gray, *Wilderness Christians*, 146; Smith, *Canadian Gazetteer*, 238–9. For example, in the severe winter of 1842 wild turkeys 'in emmense numbers were killed in the farm yards, whither they had ventured in search of food. This was complete murder, as most of them were little better than skin and bone.'

35 La Rochefoucault-Liancourt, *Travels in Canada*, 81; Cruikshank, ed., *Correspondence ... Simcoe*, 3: 24

36 Duncan Campbell Scott, *John Graves Simcoe* (Toronto 1912), 142

37 G.S. Graham, 'The Indian Menace and the Retention of the Western Posts,' *CHR* 15 (March 1934): 46–7

38 Donald B. Smith, 'Wabakinine,' *DCB*, 4: 756

39 Ibid.

40 The Yellow Head (afterwards active in the War of 1812) of Lake Simcoe; Akepatwewe, his brother and war chief in Lake Simcoe; Essence, the chief at

Gloucester Bay (Matchedash); Negasam, chief of Lake Huron; and Omascenascoutewe, chief of La Cloche. Russell, *Papers*, 1: 49

41 Smith, 'The Mississauga,' 71–2; Russell, *Papers*, 2: 278–9
42 Charles M. Johnston, 'Joseph Brant, the Grand River Lands and the Northwest Crisis,' *OH* 55 (4) (Dec. 1963): 267–82; Smith, 'The Mississauga,' 73ff. To date, the best analysis of the War of 1812 is Stanley, *War of 1812*, but it does not give in detail the tribal perspectives of the war. William Wood, ed., *Selected British Documents of the Canadian War of 1812*, (Toronto 1920), 1: 506–9. G.F.G.Stanley, 'The Significance of the Six Nations Participation in the War of 1812,' *OH* 55 (4) (Dec. 1963): 219–20. In the victory at Michilimackinac involving mostly Ojibwa, John Askin observed: 'I never saw so determined a Set of People as the Chippawas & Ottawas were' in the battle. It was this early American defeat which caused many of the Indians to join the British. See 'John Askin to Colonel William Claus,' in Cruikshank, *Invasion of Canada*, 67, 73. For a brief biography of Askin see David R. Farrell's article in *DCB*, 5: 37–9. Letters written by Askin may be found in E. Cruikshank's *The Documentary History of the Campaign upon the Niagara Frontier*, part 1 (1813) (Wellington 1902), 48ff.
43 C.F. Klinck, ed., *Tecumseh: Fact and Fiction in Early Records* (Ottawa 1978) 159; William Hull's 'Proclamation,' 13 July 1812, to the British people in Cruikshank, *Invasion of Canada*, 60–3, 184–9, in which Hull orders that 'no white man found fighting by the Side of an Indian will be taken prisoner. Instead destruction will be his Lot,' which certainly is an indication of his fear of the native warriors. He attributed his surrender to fear of atrocities by the Indians.
44 Klinck and Talman, eds., *Journal of Major John Norton*, 298–301. For some references to Ojibwa participation see Thomas G. Anderson, 'Narrative of Captain Thomas G. Anderson, 1800–28,' *Collections of the State Historical Society of Wisconsin* 9 (1909): 137–261 (reprint of 1882 edition). Anderson became very important as an Indian agent among the Southern Ojibwa during the decisive years of their land surrenders south of Georgian Bay. G.F.G. Stanley, 'The Indians in the War of 1812,' *CHR*, 31 (2) (June 1950): 152
45 Mary Agnes FitzGibbon, *A Veteran of 1812: The Life of James FitzGibbon* (Toronto 1894), 99
46 Klinck and Talman, eds., *Journal of Major John Norton*, 332
47 Cruikshank, ed., *Documentary History of the Campaign upon the Niagara Frontier*, 120–1: FitzGibbon to Kerr, 30 March 1818
48 C.M. Johnson, 'William Claus and John Norton: Struggle for Power in Old Ontario,' *OH* 57(2) (June 1963): 101–8; Reginald Horseman, 'Matthew Elliott,' *DCB*, 5: 301–3
49 For a brief note on Major James Givins and the defeat of York see Firth, ed., *Town of York, 1793–1815*, 36. Klinck and Talman, eds., *Major John Norton*, 334; 'Musquakie, William Yellowhead,' *DCB*, 9: 589–90. The American colonel Cromwell Pearce's account of the battle notes that 200 Indians were

involved, but this is likely an exaggeration. See Firth, *Town of York*, 304. In Murray, *Muskoka and Haliburton, 1615–1875*, 100, there is a footnote: 'Yellowhead and his son served in the War of 1812 and took an active part in the defence of York in April, 1813. After the war he was succeeded by his son as Principal Chief of the Chippewas of Lakes Simcoe and Huron.' It possibly was his son, William Yellowhead, who received the wound, since his 'face was scarred from a wound received in the War of 1812.' Joseph Sawyer's participation is recorded by Donald B. Smith, 'Nawahjegezhegwabe,' *DCB*, 9: 592–3. Schmalz, *History of the Saugeen Indians*, 10, 39, 42, 66, 88. Nawash spoke for all the western warriors.

50 Stanley, 'Indians in the War of 1812,' 163n; Mitchell, 'Legends of Indian History in St. Clair County,' 417; Petrone, *First People, First Voices*, 59; Stanley, 'Indians in the War of 1812,' 158. For an excellent short biography of Assiginack (Jean-Baptiste Blackbird) by Douglas Leighton see *DCB*, 9: 9–10. Blackbird's speech is found in William Kirby, *Annals of Niagara* (Welland 1896), 197–8, 200, 231.

51 NA, MG 19, 'Lt.-Col. William McKay Papers,' F29; Smith, ed., *Canadian Indians and the Law*, 21

52 John Howison, *Sketches of Upper Canada* (Edinburgh 1821), 151, 33. La Rochefouchault-Liancourt, *Travels in Canada*, 41–2, indicates that in 1795, £60,000 per year were being spent on the Indian Department, most of which went to providing presents for the Indians.

53 *Ontario Indian* 3 (12) (Dec. 1980): 25

CHAPTER SIX: THE SURRENDERS

1 Surtees, 'Indian Land Cessions in Ontario, 1763–1862'

2 Canniff, *Settlement of Upper Canada*, 382

3 Norman Robertson, *The History of the County of Bruce* (Toronto 1906), 1. Waubageshig, (Harvey McCue) ed., *The Only Good Indian*. Abler et al., *A Canadian Indian Bibliography, 1960–1970*, especially the section on the Ojibwa (500–36), lists books which expose the injustices of the treaties. Scott, 'Indian Affairs, 1763–1841,' in vol. 4, 703–4.

4 Allan G. Harper, 'Canada's Indian Administration: Basic Concepts and Objectives,' *American Indigena* 4 (2) (April 1945): 129

5 Lajeunesse, ed., *Windsor Border Region*, lviii, contains a map of the specific settlers and locations; see 'Abstracts from the Detroit Notarial Records' from 10 April 1766 to 20 January 1776, 312–34.

6 Cumming and Mickenberg, *Native Rights in Canada*, 108; L.F. Gates, *Land Policies of Upper Canada* (Toronto 1968), 11n6, indicates that there was no official documentation of the land agreement. In the Johnson Papers, however, there is a reference to Sir William obtaining the Niagara surrender from the Seneca before he would restore trade to them. Cumming makes the mistake of considering this purchase on the 'east side' which, of course, is not in Ontario. Canada, *Indian Treaties and Surrenders from 1680 to 1890*, 3: 196–7

7 Cruikshank, ed., *Correspondence ... Simcoe*, 1: 396; 2: 65
8 Russell *Correspondence*, 2: 298–304
9 Surtees, 'Indian Land Cessions in Ontario'
10 Russell, *Correspondence*, 1: 34–5. Canada, *Indian Treaties and Surrenders*, 1: 19. Horseman, *Matthew Elliott*, 110–18. This type of treaty involving the surrender of land for the general benefit of all the Indians would be repeated exactly fifty years later by Sir Francis Bondhead, with the Manitoulin Islands, but conditions had changed considerably by then and a separate surrender had to be made to enable whites to settle on the island. Surtees, 'Indian Land Cessions,' There are several other instances of verbal agreements not being honoured, for example, the Ojibwa's desire for Sally Ainse to retain her property (144–54). Smith, 'Dispossession of the Mississauga Indians,' 67–87; and Surtees, 'Indian Land Cessions'
11 Russell *Correspondence*, 2: 137–8; J.L. Morris, *Indians of Ontario* (Toronto 1943), (my emphasis)
12 Leo Johnson, *History of the County of Ontario, 1615–1875* (Whitby 1973), 20–37
13 Simcoe to Dorchester, 6 Sept. 1794, in Cruikshank, ed., *Correspondence ... Simcoe*, 2: 61
14 Cruikshank, ed., *Correspondence ... Simcoe*, III, 24–5
15 Ibid., 25
16 Murray, ed., *Muskoka and Haliburton, 1815–1875*, 97–9. The first report on the difficulty of the survey is found in a letter from William Chewett to E.B. Littlehales, Newark, 31 Aug. 1794; and the second, involving instructions, on 12 Sept. 1794. Russell *Correspondence*, 2: 161
17 Surtees, 'Indian Land Cessions,' 80–128. Surtees correctly indicates that subterfuge on the local level was prevented by higher British government officials who were not in direct contact with the Indians (58–62).
18 C.G. Fenwick, *International Law* (New York 1924), 299
19 *Report on the Affairs of the Indians in Canada, 1844–5*, EEE, section I, 'History of the Relations between the Government and the Indians' (hereafter *Report, 1844–5*)
20 Jones, *History of the Ojebway Indians*, 39–56; Rogers, *Round Lake Ojibwa*, part 3: C1–C78; Surtees, 'Indian Land Cessions,' abstract
21 See map in Morris, *Indian Treaties and Purchases*.
22 Milloy, 'Era of Civilization,' 165–230. F. Bond Head, *The Emigrant* (London 1847), 139, and *A Narrative* (London 1839), particularly the appendix. For the details of the treaty see Canada, *Indian Treaties and Surrenders*, I, no. 45, 12–13. For the numbers at the treaty see Fred Landon, *Lake Huron* (New York 1944), 184. This surrender was similar to the one made almost fifty years earlier involving the Chenal Ecarté which was to be for the general use of the Indians, but was later sold or given to white settlers.
23 Peter Jacob's letter is found in 'Missionary Intelligence,' *Christian Advocate* (New York), 17 June 1836. I am indebted to Dr Donald Smith for sending me this clipping.

24 G.S. French, 'Pahtahsega,' *DCB*, 11: 660–1; Pahtahsega was the author of *Journal of the Reverend Peter Jacobs*. C. Vandusen (Enemikeese) *Indian Chief*, 8. For Copway's account of the evil influence of the Europeans see his *Running Sketches of Men and Places*, 304–12. For an excellent short biography see Donald Smith, 'Kahgegagahbowh,' *DCB*, 9: 419–21.

25 For details of Copway's large Indian reserve idea see his *Traditional History and Characteristic Sketches of the Ojibwa Nation*, 197ff.

26 John Leslie, 'The Bagot Commission: Developing a Corporate Memory for the Indian Department.' Canadian Historical Association, *Historical Papers*, 1982, 36; Milloy, 'Era of Civilization,' 197, 221, 224, 225, 172, 185, 230; C.B. Sissons, *Egerton Ryerson: His Life and Letters* (Toronto 1937), 2: 436ff; Great Britain, Imperial Blue Book, *Report from the Select Committee on Aborigines*, 500ff

27 Schmalz, *History of the Saugeen Indians*, 61–7; Surtees, 'Indian Land Cessions,' 218

28 Aborigines' Protection Society, *Tract Relative to the Aborigines* (London 1843), 16–20

29 Benjamin Slight, *Indian Researches, or Facts Concerning the North American Indians*, 112; *Annual Report of the Missionary Society of the Westleyan-Methodist Church of Canada*, 1837, xii; University of Western Ontario, Regional Collection, D.B. Weldon Library, Rev. James Evans Papers, no. 39. The petition also had the signature of Ojeebegun, who used a totem (no. 40). There were other chiefs, Wahbahdick and Nawash, in the Owen Sound area whose signatures were also required.

30 Schmalz, *History of the Saugeen Indians*, 67

31 NA, RG 10, 501, Givens to W. Jones; Givens to Wahwahnosh

32 Aborigines' Protection Society, *Further Tracts Relative to the Aborigines* (London 1847), 1–33; Canada, *Indian Treaties and Surrenders*, 1: 111–19

33 Canada, Legislative Assembly, *Report on the Affairs of the Indians in Canada*, section III, 1847, app. T

34 The dispute between Chief Alexander Metegob and T.G. Anderson over the breach in protocol is found in NA, RG 10, Anderson Letter Book, 1845–7, Anderson to Sawyer, 3 Dec. 1845; and 409, Jacob Metegob to Anderson, 4 Dec. 1845; reference to the deed is in 410, civil secretary to Anderson, 4 Feb. 1846, and in *Report, 1847*.

35 See Schmalz, *History of the Saugeen Indians*, chap. 2, and 74–7; NA, RG 10, 160, 'Anderson's Speech to Council at Orillia,' 30 July 1846.

36 Smith, *Sacred Feathers*, 323–4. A full transcript of the two-day meeting appears in *Minutes of the General Council of Indian Chiefs and Principal Men Held at Orillia, Lake Simcoe Narrows, on Thursday, the 30th, and Friday, the 31st July, 1846, on the Proposed Removal of the Smaller Communities, and the Establishment of Manual Labour Schools. From Notes Taken in Short Hand and Otherwise by Henry Baldwin, of Peterborough, Barrister at Law. Secretary to the Chiefs in Council* (Montreal 1846), 28.

37 These were the Proclamation of 1763, the 1836 Surrender, and the Royal

Deed. Arthur G. Doughty, ed., *The Elgin-Grey Papers*, 2: 549, Elgin to Grey, 21 Nov. 1849

38 AO, *Copies or Extracts of Recent Correspondence Respecting Alterations in the Organization of the Indian Department in Canada*, Colonial Office, May 1856, 3, 4 (my emphasis)

39 Ibid., 12

40 NA, RG 10, 541, Anderson to Oliphant, 29 Aug. 1854. Anderson to the Saugeen Indians, 16 Aug. 1854, when he again threatened the Indians by saying that they could not be protected because the Owen Sound Municipal Council had petitioned the government for their removal. His explanation of the problem is found in Anderson to Bury, 26 Nov. 1855.

41 Schmalz, *History of the Saugeen Indians*, 80–96, 148–65

42 C.L. Pacey, 'The Evolution, Rationale, and Operation of the Land Management Fund, 1828–1914' (1st draft), DIAND, June 1979, 37

43 Oliphant expected £15,538 to be realized from the sale of the Saugeen Peninsula. Missions and residential schools were to receive £3744 from the fund. NA, RG 10, 49, Anderson to Givins, 12 Dec. 1831; 51, Curie to Richardson, 16 April 1832; Archbold to Colborne, 23 Aug. 1830; Anderson to Givins, 17 Sept. 1832. For Anderson's glowing report and the Ojibwa's intention to leave the settlements see Murray, ed., *Muskoka and Haliburton*, documents C12 and C17, respectively.

44 Peter Schmalz, 'The History of the Saugeen Indians' (MA thesis, University of Waterloo, 1971), 199–204. More details are found in this thesis than in the publication on the same topic. Donald Smith, 'Nawahjegezhegwabe,' *DCB*, 9: 592–3

45 *Wesleyan-Methodist Report*, 1857, xxiii; Schmalz, *History of the Saugeen Indians*, 98–108. A glance through Canada, *Indian Treaties and Surrenders*, will illustrate the numerous surrenders of small parcels of land between the years 1860 and 1890. Canada, *Indian and Inuit Communities and Languages* (Ottawa 1976), map

CHAPTER SEVEN: EARLY RESERVES

1 Milloy, 'Era of Civilization,' 47ff

2 *Proposal for forming a Society for Promoting the Civilization and Improvement of the North American Indians, within the British Boundary* (London 1806), quoted in ibid., 19. Milloy has successfully attacked the thesis that this was a purely philanthropic movement on the part of the British government. He argues that economy, not humanity, was the motivating force. If the Indians could be made into good 'civilized Christians,' there would be no need for an Indian Department. There were other factors, too, including fear of the Indians and the belief that assimilation would eliminate a socially embarrassing condition. Elma E. Gray, *Wilderness Christians: The Moravian Mission to the Delaware Indians* (Toronto 1956), 183–99

3 Donald Smith, 'Kineubenae,' *DCB*, 5: 466–7

4 Wm H. Smith, *Canadian Gazetteer*, 193, 208. The Credit River, one of the best salmon fisheries on Lake Ontario, had been occupied by white men for a long time. This was a problem on other reserves as well. Arrangements were made in the 1860s by the Saugeen band to allow the Sarnia band to obtain fish because the Sarnia Ojibwa by this time had little supply in their location. See D.B. Weldon Library, University of Western Ontario, Regional History Special Collections, Wawanosh Family Papers, box 4382 (1850–1939).

5 There are numerous accounts of the condition of the Indians by travellers in Upper Canada. For a scholarly work on the subject of cultural disintegration see Smith, 'The Mississauga,' chap. 1; Schmalz, *History of the Saugeen Indians*, chap. 5

6 Smith, *Sacred Feathers*

7 MacLean, *Vanguards*, 11, 12

8 Jones, *Life and Journals of KahKeWaQuoNaBy*, 116–17; Johnston, ed., *Valley of the Six Nations*, 254–8

9 Vandusen (Enemikeese), *Indian Chief*, 1–25; NA, RG 10, vol. 410; Victoria University Library Archives, Peter Jones Collection; Donald Smith, 'Kahgegagahbowh,' *DCB*, 9: 419–20; George Copway wrote three books: *The Life, History and Travels of Ka-Ge-Ga-Gah-Bowh* (Albany 1847); *The Traditional History and Characteristic Sketches of the Ojibway Nation*; and *Running Sketches of Men and Places*.

10 Mrs Frederick Stephenson, *One Hundred Years of Canadian Methodist Missions, 1824–1924* (Toronto 1925), 49; MacLean, *Vanguards*, 103, 8, 4, 9; Krystyna Sieciechowicz, 'Henry Bird Steinhauer,' *DCB*, XI, 848–9

11 MacLean, *Vanguards*, 108

12 Donald Smith, 'Nahnebahwequay,' *DCB*, IX, 590–1. See also her 'Journals' at the Grey County Museum in Owen Sound.

13 Vandusen, *Indian Chief*, 23

14 Graham, *Medicine Man to Missionary*, 19

15 Schmalz, *Saugeen Indians*, chap. 3. Copway was put into prison in Canada because some bands, such as the Saugeen, claimed he had embezzled funds. At Goderich he charged his purchase of food for a 'love feast,' which he held on their reserve, to the Saugeen, but the band had not consented to the purchase.

16 Most acculturated Indians, because they were 'red skinned' on the 'outside,' were not accepted by Euro-Canadians; and, because they were 'white educated' on the 'inside,' they were not accepted by reserve Indians. Smith, 'The Mississauga,' 330–5; Peter Jones, *History*; Stephenson, *One Hundred Years*, 72–9

17 NA, CO, 42, vol. 516, *Report: The Affairs of the Indians in Canada*, 1844, app. 17

18 W. Parkenham, 'The Public School System,' in Adam Shortt and Arthur Doughty, eds., *Canada and Its Provinces*, vol. 17 (Toronto 1914), 292–3, 300–19; Egerton, R. Young, *The Apostle of the North: James Evans* (Toronto 1900). This biography and others demonstrate his great ability. Tucker, 'A Warrior of the Odahwahs.' See Also Richard B. Howard, *Upper Canada*

College, 1829–1979: Colborne's Legacy (Toronto 1979). Howard's book gives an excellent examination of the college during the time in which the Indians attended, but he misses a colourful chapter on their activities at the institution. Wm H. Smith, *Canadian Gazetteer*, 3

19 Stephenson, *One Hundred Years*, 79

20 Smith, 'The Mississauga' and *Sacred Feathers*; NA, RG 10, vol. 790, 125. Smith, 'The Mississauga,' 137, claims that Jones returned to his band to convert them to Christianity. It may be that he was as much, if not more, interested in looking after their secular well-being. Peter Jones, *History*, iv. See also J. Donald Wilson, '"No Blanket To Be Worn In School": The Education of Indians in Nineteenth-Century Ontario,' in Barman et al., ed., *Indian Education in Canada*, I, 64–87; Smith, 'The Mississauga,' 'Nahnebahwequay,' *DCB*, 9: 590. Canada Conference Missionary Society Methodist Church, *Annual Report*, 1829, 5; 1829–31, 3; and 1826, 5; Milloy, 'Era of Civilization,' 123–58; Alan Wilson, 'John Colborne,' *DCB*, 9: 140. Bishop John Strachan was their most energetic antagonist. Milloy, 134

21 H.C. Darling's Report to Lord Dalhousie, Quebec, 24 July 1828, in Murray, ed., *Muskoka and Haliburton*, 103–4; UCA, *Christian Guardian*, 29 Feb. 1832; Schmalz, *Saugeen Indians*, 23; NA, RG 10, vols. 5, 3–6 and 128, no. 545; and 'Musquakie,' *DCB*, 9: 589. For a detailed account see Handy, 'The Ojibwa.' Canada Legislative Assembly, 'Report of the Special Commissioners to Investitate Indian Affairs in Canada,' *Sessional Papers*, 1858, app. 21, 80–5, 286; 'Colborne to R.W. Hay, 15 Dec. 1831, in Murray, ed., *Muskoka and Haliburton*, 107–8; AO, Misc. 1831, 'Rose Papers, 1831–59'

22 T.G. Anderson to Colburne, 24 Sept. 1835, in Murray, ed., *Muskoka and Haliburton*, 109–11

23 NA, RG 10, vol. 5, 577–80

24 UCA, *Christian Guardian*, 17, 24 July 1833; Anderson to Colborne, 24 Sept. 1835 in Murray, ed., *Muskoka and Haliburton*, 111

25 NA, RG 10, vol. 5, Anderson to Mudge, 12 July 1830, in Correspondence Received in Lieutenant-Governor's Office in Various Subjects Respecting Indian Affairs, 1829–30; Anthony J. Hall, 'Aisance,' *DCB*, 7: 11–12; and Hall, 'Red Man's Burden,' 83–115; NA, RG 10, vol. 128, no. 545. In 1842 five chiefs complained that they had not received their money from the surrender and that they wanted to retain the grist mill and saw mill at Coldwater for their benefit. Treaty No. 48, page 117 in volume 1 of *Indian Treaties and Surrenders*, which indicates that the tribe was to receive one-third of the money from the sale of the lands.

26 The origin of the reserves is investigated in R.J. Surtees; 'Indian Reserve Policy in Upper Canada, 1830–1845' (MA thesis, Carleton University, 1966), and in his article, 'Development of an Indian Reserve Policy in Canada,' 87–98. It is the major focus in Ruth Bleasdale, 'Manitowaning: An Experiment,' *OH* 66 (3) (Sept. 1974): 147–57.

27 *Report, 1858*, 80–5. See particularly Schmalz, *Saugeen Indians*, 43–5; Bleasdale, 'Manitowaning,' 156; Copway, *Life*, 88.

28 Aborigines' Protection Society, *Report on the Indians of Upper Canada, 1839*, 23–6

29 Lewis, ed., 'Manitoulin Letters of the Rev. Charles Crosbie Brough,' 66–7. For an examination of the liquor problems in the province see Barron, 'Genesis of Temperance in Ontario,' and for the Ontario Ojibwa specifically see F. Laurie Barron, 'Alcoholism, Indians and the Anti-Drink Cause in the Protestant Indian Missions of Upper Canada, 1822–1850,' in Getty and Lussier, *As Long as the Sun Shines*, 191–202.

30 AO, Strachan Papers, 1794–1891, Elliott to Strachan, 12 Oct. 1837; Landon, *Lake Huron*, 186–7

31 Anna Jameson, *Winter Studies and Summer Rambles in Canada*, vol. 2 (Toronto 1972), 287

32 Mrs S. Rowe (T.G. Anderson's daughter), 'The Anderson Record from 1699 to 1896,' *OHSPR* 6 (1905): 109–35. Anderson lived to be ninety-five years old.

33 Leighton, 'Development of Federal Indian Policy in Canada,' 69–72

34 Leighton, 'Compact Tory as Bureaucrat,' 46–7

35 Leighton, 'Development of Federal Indian Policy in Canada,' 104

36 Christopher L. Pacey, 'The Evolution, Rationale, and Operation of the Indian Land Management Fund, 1814–1914,' DIAND, June 1979, 32, 77. In 1913, when the Indian Land Management Fund was closed, it had £798,551, but the account had been established in 1856 after most of southern Ontario had been surrendered and sold. NA, RG 10, vol. 409, R. Carney to Anderson, 24 March 1850. Captain Anderson was accused by Alexander Madwayosh of Saugeen and John T. Wahbahdick of Nawash of misappropriation of funds. Schmalz, *Saugeen Indians*, 148–65; Leighton, 'Development of Federal Indian Policy,' 90

37 *Wesleyan Methodist Report*, 1857, xxiii

38 Leighton, 'Development of Federal Indian Policy,' 27; Milloy 'Era of Civilization,' 307; Leighton, 'Development of Federal Indian Policy,' 99

39 Duncan C. Scott, 'Indian Affairs, 1840–1867,' in Shortt and Doughty, eds., *Canada and Its Provinces*, vol 5, 342, 100; Franz M. Koennecke, 'Wasoksing: The History of Parry Island, an Anishnabwe Community in the Georgian Bay, 1850–1920' (preliminary draft of MA thesis, University of Waterloo, 1983), 72–89, which gives details of the numerous traders in Georgian Bay during the nineteenth century; Leighton, 'Development of Federal Indian Policy,' 103; Smith, *Sacred Feathers*, 184; and John Leslie, 'The Bagot Commission: Developing a Corporate Memory for the Indian Department,' Canadian Historical Association, *Historical Papers* (1982): 31, 52, 146; and Scott, 'Indian Affairs, 1840–1867,' 342–3

40 Milloy, 'Era of Civilization,' 318; *Saugeen Indians*, chap. 7

41 Moore, *Kipawa*, 35; NA, RG 10, vol. 457, Civil Secretary's Office to Jarvis, 22 Nov. 1844; NA, RG 10, vol. 585, Deputy Superintendent General's Office, Letterbook, 1859–64, 20 March 1860

42 Donald Smith, 'Bauzhi-Geezhig-Woeshikum,' *DCB*, 7: 54–5

43 NA, RG 10, vol. 584, Froome Talford to Pennefather, 24 May 1856. This was not an isolated case. Lot No. 27, 1 cons. Bosauquet, sold to Allen Kennedy for £200, was not recorded.

44 NA, RG 10, vol. 585, 7 Dec. 1859

45 Ibid., vol. 584, Froome Talford to Pennefather, 28 May 1856; ibid., Froome Talford to Bury, 16 May 1858.

46 Ibid., Froome Talford to the Superintendent General, 20 May 1858. Joseph Clench also permitted a relative, H. Clench, to cut timber on the reserves illegally against the wishes of the Ojibwa. See Peter Jones to Indian Superintendent, 17 March 1855, and Schmalz, *Saugeen Indians*, 92.

47 Pacey, 'Evolution,' 35–6; CCA, Land Sale Books, 'Returns Made by J.E. Sutherby, Indian Land Agent, of Land Sales and Payments Thereon, in Bank Deposit on Account of the Indians of Wiarton [sic]'; see Sept. 1912, May 1913, Oct. 1913, April 1917, and Jan. 1917. The auditor's initials on the remarks are J.H.Y. Numerous mistakes on the returns were the rule, not the exception.

48 CCA, Land Sale Records. The instalment plan varied. At first, one-third of the purchase price was required and later it became one-fifth. The interest rate remained at 6 per cent of the unpaid amount. The scale used on timber was set in 1873.

49 Robertson, *History of the County of Bruce*, 197

50 BCA, Bruce County Council Minutes, Dec. 1868, 3, m3; Jan. 1869, 6. Reaction to the Saugeen land prices came late because the county had major problems establishing its incorporation, which came about in 1865. See Peter Schmalz, *The County Town Question* (Wiarton 1983); Robertson, *History of the County of Bruce*, 199; BCA, Bruce County Council Members, 19 March 1872, 5 Dec. 1872, 8, m52.

51 Schmalz, *County Town Question*, 3. As early as 1861 there were 182 settlers in Amabel and only fifty-four in the four North Bruce townships. CCA, Land Sale Records, 1875; and letter, K. Van Koughnet, deputy superintendent general, to Ed. Bellrose, local bailiff, 31 Oct. 1885. Indian-owned timber was also a problem. The local bailiff was paid from the Saugeen timber moneys: $1.50 per day in salary, 75 cents per day travelling expenses, and 4 per cent of all dues paid on timber. His job was a patronage position. K. Van Koughnet to Simpson, Indian land agent, 31 Oct. 1885, in which he stated that the timber was being 'plundered within the Peninsula'; and also J.D. McLean, secretary, to W. Simpson, 21 Oct. 1897. Simpson was informed that on 15 Sept. 1888 settlers' licences were reduced from $4.00 to $2.00 by order in council. J.D. McLean to J. McIver, 30 March 1901

52 Robertson, *History of the County of Bruce*, 201; and Schmalz, *Saugeen Indians*, chap. 4; CCA, Department to W.J. Ferguson, 19 Oct. 1907

53 CCA, Land Sale Register and Ledger and Annual Report on Indian Affairs, 1871; *Wiarton Echo*, 4 Aug. 1882; CCA, Land Sale Ledger, 300–60

54 *The Statutes of Canada* 1857, 20 Vic., 3rd Session, 5th Parliament, 84

55 NA, RG 10, vol. 427, Cape Croker Band Resolution to Bartlett, 4 Sept. 1858.

Several Ojibwa at Nawash lost all their improvements when the 10,000 acres north of Owen Sound was surrendered in 1857. Even though the band objected, many of them were not given compensation for the houses, barns, and cleared lands. This certainly discouraged any Indians who wished to become farmers. NA, RG 10, vol. 245, D. Thorburn to R. Pennefather, 13 Oct. 1858

56 NA, RG 10, vol. 519, Pennefather to Sickles, 10 Nov. 1858; Milloy, 'Era of Civilization,' 234; NA, RG 10, vol. 416, Proceedings of a Council of the Colpoy Bay Band of Indians, 16 Aug. 1861

CHAPTER EIGHT: RESERVE STAGNATION

1 Schmalz, *Saugeen Indians*, chap. 7. Several band council resolutions went to the Indian Department objecting to the forced contributions to residential schools.

2 Quoted from Linda Tschanz, *Native Language and Government Policy: An Historical Examination* (London 1980), 7

3 DIAND, *Indians of Ontario: An Historical Review* (Ottawa 1966), 37. Alnwich was established in 1842, not 1848, as indicated in this publication. George Coldwell, *Indian Residential Schools* (Ottawa 1967).

4 D.C. Scott, 'Indian Affairs, 1867–1912,' in Shortt and Doughty, eds., *Canada and Its Provinces*, vol. 7, 622–3

5 Eugene Stock, *History of the Church Missionary Society* (London 1899), 70; Wilson, *Autobiographical Journal*, 1; Nock, 'White Man's Burden: A Portrait of E.F. Wilson, Missionary in Ontario'; Wilson, *Missionary Work among the Ojibwa Indians*, 13, 14

6 D.M. Landon, 'Frederick Dawson Fauquier: Pioneer Bishop of Algoma,' *Journal of the Canadian Church Historical Society* 11 (4) (Dec. 1969): 76, David Nock, 'E.F. Wilson: Early Years as Missionary in Huron and Algoma,' *Journal of the Canadian Church Historical Society* 15 (4) (Dec. 1973): 88; Wilson, *Missionary Work*, 110

7 See the financial statements of the various reserves in the annual reports on Indian affairs in the Sessional Papers; for example, 29 June 1896, page 469, 'Chippewas of Nawash,' $90.36 for Shingwauk Home; Nock, 'Wilson,' 89; Wilson, *Missionary Work*, 135; *Wiarton Echo*, 17 Sept. 1886, 1: 'Rev. Mr. Wilson with two little Indian boys from Shingwauk Home, Sault Ste. Marie, came down by the last trip of "Athabasca." He was taking them to Montreal, and from thence on a lecturing tour to explain his work among the Indian boys and girls.' Wilson, *Missionary Work*, 219–20, 243, 163–4

8 Nock, 'Wilson,' 89–90; Wilson, *Missionary Work*, 244; Basil H. Johnston, 'The Four Hundred Year Winter,' *The Northian* 9 (1) (1972): 36–42, and *Indian School Days*, which does not have Willis's bitterness.

9 Jane Willis, *Geniesh – An Indian Girlhood* (Toronto 1973), 171

10 NA, RG 10, vol. 6205, file 461, pt 1, 13 April 1901. The censorship of Geniesh's mail in the 1950s at Shingwauk was a major reason for her dropping out of school.

11 Rogers (Chief Snow Cloud), *Red World and White: Memories of a Chippewa Boyhood*, 5. Rogers is from the United States, but the experience was similar in Canada. Willis, 172–3

12 Schmalz, *Saugeen Indians*, 34; NA, RG 10, vol. 3926, file 116, 836–1, A.J. McLeod to Commissioner D. Laird, 10 June 1899; E. Brian Titley, 'Duncan Campbell Scott and Indian Education,' in Wilson, ed., *An Imperfect Past*, 144; Joblin, *Education of the Indians of Western Ontario*, 64–5

13 Lavalee, 'Too Little Too Late,' 26–9, 35; Johnston, in *Indian School Days*, indicates that he and his sister were taken to residential schools because his father had deserted the family. The per capita grant for Indian students ranged from $110 to $145 in 1897. NA, RG 10, vol. 3964, file 149, 874, memo of J.D. McLean, 20 July 1897; and M. Benson to J.D. McLean, 24 March 1904. It has been estimated that 80–92 per cent of reserve people have suffered from abuse. A dormitory supervisor was charged with 650 acts of sexual abuse, as reported by Roy Bonisteel in 'A Circle of Healing,' Canadian Broadcasting Corporation, Jan. 1989.

14 Pelliteer and Poole, *No Foreign Land*, 76–7

15 Indian Affairs Department, Annual reports in *Sessional Papers*; and Jamieson, 'Indian Education in Canada.' In 1919 the white schools had 91 per cent of their teachers qualified, while only 44 per cent were qualified in the Indian schools which, from 1910 to 1920, had a 33 per cent changeover of teachers. During this time, Indian school teachers were paid $500 to $800 per year compared with an average of $1348 for non-Indian schoolteachers. CCA, 'Jesuit Diary,' 38; Indian Affairs Department, Annual Report, *Sessional Papers*, 31 March 1917, H-83

16 Robert J. Surtees, *The Original People* (Toronto 1971), 74

17 Garnet McDiarmid and David Pratt, *Teaching Prejudice: A Content Analysis of Social Studies Textbooks Authorized for Use in Ontario* (Toronto 1971); Jamieson, in 'Indian Education in Canada,' although an Indian himself, was not sensitive to the stereotypes; in fact, he reflected the bias of his white teachers. Joblin, *Education*, 95

18 SBA, *Band Council Minutes*, 1883–95, 3 Jan. 1887, 109. Also see Jamieson on curriculum. The following instruments were purchased on 5 December 1887: one brass silver cornet, six cornets, six alto solo, six brass trombones, six brass bass, small drums, six brass moiters. Reserves which had a relatively substantial amount of money from their land sales used their funds to encourage education in this way. See *Band Council Minutes*, 108, 109, 127, 130, and numerous other references. Sarnia Reserve Band Council Minutes, 1901; *Wiarton Echo*, 25 June and 11 July 1880, 6 July 1883, and others; Titley, 'Scott,' 148–9; and DIAND, *Indians of Ontario*, 38

19 SBA, *Band Council Minutes*, 1883–95, 4 Dec. 1888, 160

20 Jones et al., *History of Cape Croker*, 28

21 Vanderburgh, *I Am Nokomis Too: The Biography of Verna Pateronella Johnston*, 62–7

22 *Wiarton Echo*, 27 June 1878; Indian Affairs Department, *Sessional Papers*, 31 March 1917, H-85; DIAND, *Indians of Ontario*, 38; Joblin, *Education*, 54. See also Jamieson, Indian Education in Canada.'

23 From 1897 to 1921 attendance increased from 42.52 to 50.30 per cent in Indian schools throughout Canada.

24 The band council minutes of Sarnia, Cape Croker, Credit River, Chippewa Hill, and others indicate that the grand councils were held on various Ojibwa reserves usually every two years. Unfortunately there is no central source from which to draw minutes of the meetings. James S. Frideres, ed., *Native People in Canada: Contemporary Conflicts* (Scarborough, Ont. 1983), 23. 'Grand Indian Council of the Province of Ontario,' *Wiarton Echo*, 15 Aug. 1879. The minutes of the council were printed in five consecutive publications of this weekly newspaper. All references to the 1879 Grand Council come from this source. Several Ojibwa attended the newly founded University of Western Ontario in the last quarter of the nineteenth century, and some of Chief Wawanash's children were among them. *Wiarton Echo*, 29 Aug. 1879.

25 *Wiarton Echo*, 22 Aug. 1879; Koennecke, 'Wasoksing,' 263. William Wawanosh from Sarnia, Chief John Henry from New Credit, and the Rev. Allen Salt, missionary at Christian Island, were called to Ottawa in February 1876 to evaluate the Indian Act. They took five days to discuss it and found everything satisfactory. They obviously did not understand the full impact of the document. A.D. Doerr, 'Indian Policy,' in G. Bruce Doern and V. Seymor Wilson, eds., *Issues in Canadian Public Policy* (Toronto 1972), 40

26 Ponting et al., *Out of Irrelevance*, 1–22; Harper, 'Canadian's Indian Administration,' 313; *Wiarton Echo*, 5 Sept. 1879

27 For a contemporary Indian analysis of both the advantages and disadvantages of the Indian Act see Harold Cardinal, *The Unjust Society: The Tragedy of Canada's Indians* (Edmonton 1969); and Waubageshig, 'The Comfortable Crisis,' in Waubageshig, ed., *The Only Good Indians*; *Wiarton Echo*, 19 Sept. 1879; Ponting, ed., *Out of Irrelevance*, 12; [Peter Edmund Jones], *Minutes of the Eighth Grand General Indian Council Held upon the Cape Croker [sic] Indian Reserve, County of Bruce from Sept. 10th, to Sept. 15th, 1884* (Hagersville, ND), 8. Doctor Jones was the son of the famous Peter Jones and secretary-treasurer of the council. *Wiarton Echo*, 10, 17 Oct. 1879

28 *Wiarton Echo*, 10, 17 Oct. 1879

29 Ibid.

30 Diamond Jenness, *The Indians of Canada*, 7th ed. (Toronto 1980), 277ff; Clifton, *Place of Refuge*, 20–33. This is by far the best work on the migration of the Potawatomi. NA, 10, vol. 453, 19 Sept. 1859

31 Clifton, *Place of Refuge*, 95. Their descendants now live in the Hannahville community on the Upper Peninsula of Michigan. NA, RG 10, 541, 'Statements in Council at the Village of Cape Croker, in the presence of Superintendent W. Bartlett, 14 October 1858'; Schmalz, *Saugeen Indians*, especially 191–209.

Religion superimposed on the cultural differences between the Ojibwa and Potawatomi caused factionalism on the reserve, thus destroying unanimity of effort to improve the well-being of the band. Clifton, *Place of Refuge*, 97

32 NA, RG 10, 416, 'Petitioners to Bartlett,' 17 March 1861; 'W. Angus to Bartlett,' 17 March 1861; and 'Schedule of Indians living at Cape Croker, 1869,' which indicates that there were more Potawatomi there than Ojibwa. Specific locations from which they migrated are also noted.

33 Ibid.

34 Koennecke, 'Wasoksing,' 331; McCardle, *Indian History and Claims*, 17. Only four 'good examples of published Indian local histories' are given, including Schmalz, and *Saugeen Indians*, Whetung-Derrick, *History of the Ojibwa of the Curve Lake Reserve*. See also Clifton, *Place of Refuge*, 97; Rogers and Tobobundung, *Parry Island Farmers*, 93; and Koennecke, 'Wasoksing,' 186. Many of the Methodists were so antagonistic to the Roman Catholics that they put them in the category of 'pagan.'

35 Clifton, *Place of Refuge*, 88; James A. Clifton, 'Potawatomi,' in Trigger, ed., *Handbook of North American Indians*, vol. 15; *Northeast*, 739; 'Cape Croker [News],' *Wiarton Echo*, 25 July 1879. A more detailed account of the general proceedings was to appear in the *Pipe of Peace Journal* published by Wilson, their missionary and principal of the Wawanosh Indian School. Koennecke, 'Wasoksing,' 268. The chief was not permitted to use $10 from the band account to attend the 1880 grand council at Saugeen. Similarly, at Cape Croker, the agent refused the delegates band funds to attend the meetings. Money was raised by a variety of methods, including boys bidding for their favourite girl's lunch during Sunday socials.

36 *Constitution of the Grand General Indian Council of Quebec and Ontario*, 1894. This was not published in the newspapers to be viewed by the white population, but printed privately by the Grand Council for the reserves involved.

37 Elizabeth Arthur, ed., *Thunder Bay District, 1821–1892* (Toronto 1973), 201–3, and Malcolm Montgomery, 'The Six Nations Indians and the Macdonald Franchise,' *OH* 57 (1) (1965): 13–25

38 For references to the Saugeen and Cape Croker reserves see *Wiarton Echo*, 24 Sept. 1886, and 25 Feb., 11 March, 17 June, 24 Sept. 1887.

39 Ponting, ed. *Out of Irrelevance*, 12; *Grand General Indian Council* 1894

40 In Leslie and Maguire, eds., *Historical Development of the Indian Act*, researcher Robert G. Moore implied that the 1894 Indian Act was to some extent influenced by the grand Indian council of Ontario and Quebec. However, a major result of the act was to eliminate any influence the band councils had in deciding disputes related to Indian estates. CCA, 'Band Council Resolutions,' 8 May 1898, continues to object to this method of payment.

41 Koennecke, 'Wasoksing,' 392; NA, RG 10, vol. 1994, file 6829, 'Report of the Grand Council Proceedings'; and vol. 1942, file 4103, 'Grand Council at Sarnia, 1874.' Other councils are referred to in Leslie and Maguire, eds., *Historical Development of the Indian Act*. Donald Smith has located several other grand council minutes, as noted in 'The Mississauga,' 339. The councils of

1870, 1882, and 1884 are located in the Ontario Archives. The published record of the 1846 council is in the Baldwin Room of the Toronto Public Library. Schmalz, *Saugeen Indians*, 167

42 Manuel with Posluns, *The Fourth World* 54; George Manuel, 'President's Report to the General Assembly,' National Indian Brotherhood, Ottawa 1972

43 Cardinal, *Unjust Society*, 9

44 Internal problems resulting from factionalism on many reserves caused the band councils to give the agent more decision-making powers. The Civil Service acts of 1882, 1918, and 1919 did not have any substantial positive effect.

45 'Local Pickin's,' *Wiarton Echo*, 13 Oct. 1882

46 'The Indian Agent,' ibid., 24 Oct. 1884 (my emphasis)

47 Ibid., 30 May 1884; Koennecke, 'Wasoksing,' 269; CCA, band Council Resolutions, 1880–1900. Many protests and investigations were noted. One humorous example of overcharging involved an Indian purchasing a ham which, he found, contained a huge bone. After protesting without any results, the Indian kept the bone and later concealed it in a block of maple sugar, which he sold back to the merchant. CCA, Band Council Resolutions, Oct. 1893, Dec. 1894, Dec. 1895 (individual debts must be paid by the individual debtor), April 1896. Mrs Joe Akiwenzie gave a brief history of the store: 'The store was taken over from the agent's son by Willis Keeshig, a band member who had married an English bride. When Keeshig died she married Ben Strapp, the son of the United Church minister. They were bought out by Thomas Jones, who had it until we [Joe and Irene Akiwenzie] leased it from Mrs. Jones some years after Thomas died.'

48 Chippewa Hill Archives, Band Resolutions, 5 March 1884, 5 March 1888

49 Koennecke, 'Wasoksing,' 394

50 As Koennecke observed, 'The lack of information provided by Indian Affairs became ridiculous when the Parry Island Band questioned [agent] Skene about the new Indian Act of 1876, holding a copy of its own, while Skene had never seen the Act before'; 'Wasoksing,' 269.

51 CCA, Band Resolutions, April 1895, June 1895, Dec. 1896. The misused funds involved his purchase of a $50 horse which was never delivered. Koennecke, 'The Anishinabek of Moose Deer Point Reserve No. 79,' paper, University of Waterloo, 1983; Sarnia Reserve Archives, Minute Books, 1890–1910; Plain, *History of the Sarnia Indian Reserve*, 16

52 H. Belden, *Illustrated Atlas of the County of Bruce* (Toronto 1881). McIver settled in Bruce County in 1871. He was a farmer, postmaster, and merchant in Albermarle Township, where he owned 358 acres immediately southwest of Cape Croker. Most band council meetings involved the expenditure of money from the reserve funds and this required the signature of the agent. CCA, McIver to Department, 16 Dec. 1901, 5 Aug. 1904. See also 12 Dec. 1899 in which he remarks: 'It is a snake in the grass attitude instinctively natural to a great number of Indians.' CCA, Band Resolutions, 6 Nov. 1899

53 CCA, Band Resolutions. Earlier, on 4 Jan. 1892 and again 4 Aug. 1894,

resolutions had been passed for the purchase of a band-operated sawmill. They were refused. CCA, McIver to Department, 4 Dec. 1899; CCA, Band Resolutions, 8 Feb. 1899. They also objected to non-Indians fishing on the Cape Croker grounds, but the agent did nothing about it. CCA, McIver to Department, 19 Nov. 1899; Department to McIver, 2 Nov. 1901; McIver to Department, 22 Dec. 1901

54 CCA, Band Resolutions, McIver to Department, 11 Jan. 1902. McIver recognized the Indian need for this money. He stated, 'Indians "illegally" cut their own timber because a great number of these people were very hard up, not having sufficient food for their families.' See also 8 Jan. 1899.

55 CCA, Band Resolutions, 6 Jan. 1898: 'Moved by Moses Kiakaik and Ben Elliot that since the Department has several times refused to grant the building of a saw-mill, but would the Department allow an outsider, a white man to put up a saw-mill on the Reserve who agrees to cut Indian timber *at reduced rates.*' The reason for refusing the Indians their own sawmill was exposed later: 'It has been reported to us that a movement has been set on foot by strong men to bring political pressure on the government to induce them to sell the timber on this reserve. We in council *beg* to enter our most solemn protest.' See CCA, Band Resolutions, 6 Aug. 1903. Attempts by whites to get the timber off the reserve at Cape Croker go as far back as 1862. At that time, when band members were asked to relinquish their claim to the timber, they said that 'they wanted to have it for themselves and their children.' See NA, RG 10, vol. 416, Cape Croker Council to Bartlett, 13 Jan. 1862.

56 CCA, McIver to Department, 4 Nov. 1901. McCorkindale was also a trader to whom the Indians were most often indebted. Band Resolutions, 4 Feb. 1901, 12 May, 6 July, and 12 Dec. 1905

57 'A Grant Made of $5000,' *Wiarton Echo,* 20 April 1893

58 CCA, Band Resolutions, 8 July 1905 and 14 Dec. 1905; McIver to Department, 3 Dec. 1901

59 *Illustrated Atlas for the County of Bruce.* These were lots 12, 13, 14, and 15, con 13, Albermarle Township. See map of Albermarle and CCA, McIver to Department, 7 Dec. 1901. CCA, Band Resolution, 1 July 1905

60 CCA, Band Resolution, 7 July 1905, 4 July 1901 (my emphasis). A resolution involving McIver had been made in this year also when they resolved that the 'agent, having lost the confidence of the band for several causes and that his usefulness is gone – request the secretary to bring this to the attention of the Department,' but the problem had not yet reached the high pitch of 1905. CCA, Band Resolutions, 2 Oct. 1905

61 Annual Report on Indian Affairs, 1906; CCA, Band Resolutions, 6 Aug. 1909

62 AO, Cape Croker Band Records, box 103, Jesuit Diaries, 12 Jan. 1910

63 CCA, J.D. McLean to Parke, 11 July 1910; Annual Report on Indian Affairs, 1885, 1909; CCA, J.D. McLean to Parke, 7 Dec. 1910; Band Resolutions, 12 Nov. 1910; Annual Report on Indian Affairs, 1900

64 CCA, McLean to Parke, 9 June 1910. Money was available for buying stock and repairing houses on loan from the band's capital account. This was

limited to about $50 per adult male, and had to be paid back at the end of three years. Payments were almost impossible because of the reserve economy, and the band account continued to decline. Such loans were temporarily discontinued in 1914. See McLean to Duncan, 11 July 1914.

65 CCA, Duncan to Department, 17 May 1912; Band Resolutions, 12 June 1912. They also had problems in obtaining their own dues for the 'non-workers' (the sick, old, young, etc.). See resolution of 8 July 1905: Special Council, J. Solomon and J.W. Keeshig 'have looked over the financial reports for 1903, 1904, and saw nothing of the dues paid on timber. Therefore, the band *beg* the Department to furnish an account of the collection from those years together with the collection made this last year, 1905.' There was also a request to reduce the dues by $100.00, 'as the men have to undergo a hardship to get the timber out.' See resolution, 6 Dec. 1913.

66 CCA, Band Resolutions, 12 July 1912 and 11 Nov. 1940, in which birch bolt dues were 20 cents. There are several accounts of serious fires. See William Sutton, Journals, vol. 2, located at the Grey County Museum. Oral tradition was also obtained from Joseph Akiwenzie, former chief, and Father LaBelle, Jesuit missionary at the Cape. LaBelle had his house burned in one fire.

67 CCA, Band Resolutions, 20 March 1947. See Art Jones, former chief, at Cape Croker, for the oral tradition which is filled with frustration concerning lack of work on the reserve. The lampreys have been blamed for the decrease of fish in the Great Lakes by some authorities, but Arthur Jones of Cape Croker claims these parasites had always been there.

68 James Barry, *Georgian Bay* (Toronto 1968), 111; Annual Report on Indian Affairs, 1894; CCA, Band Resolutions, 8 Nov. 1890; Higgins, *Whitefish Lake Ojibway Memories*, 74–140

69 CCA, Band Resolutions, June 1881, March 1896, March 1905, Jan. 1923, Jan. 1940, Jan. 1944. The annual fishing licence was $50, but in December 1941 $168.25 was taken from the spring annuity payment for members who were fishing. Band Resolutions, Aug. 1891, Dec. 1894, Feb. 1894, Dec. 1913, Oct. 1896

70 Band Resolutions, May 1897, Aug. 1902

71 Band Resolutions, Nov. 1903, Aug. 1904, June 1910, March 1912, Aug. 1921, and J.D. McLean to A.J. Duncan, April 1912; CCA, Band Council Resolutions, Oct. 1907, June 1938, July 1944, May 1946. See also Art Jones, Cape Croker, for the oral tradition on the subject of fish. Band Council Resolutions, Dec. 1901, March 1910, Aug. 1919, Jan. 1947

72 See also Joseph Akiwenzie, who was forced to sell his tug in the late 1940s because there were no longer sufficient catches to make commercial fishing profitable.

73 CCA, R.H. Abraham to Ass. Deputy Sec. McLean, 2 July 1917. It should be noted that at this time the majority of the able-bodied men from the Cape were fighting in the Second World War.

74 Victoria College Archives, *Wesleyan-Methodist Report*, 1873, xxxiii

75 CCA, Jesuit Diaries, 5 May 1910, 20 Dec. 1913

76 CCA, Abraham to McLean, 19 Feb. 1918. CCA, Scott to Lennox, 11 March 1918
77 University of Western Ontario Archives, Chippewas of Sarnia, Kettle Point and Stony Point, Band Council Resolutions, I, 18 July 1900
78 CCA, Lennox to Department, 31 April 1918
79 The quotations of Indian agent reports have been corrected in several cases to avoid detracting from the main idea, but in the Lennox and McIver cases they are quoted as written to demonstrate the quality of those in charge of the Ojibwa at the time. The Ojibwa at the Cape advanced the idea of using their own funds to buy cattle, but to little effect. See Band Resolutions, Dec. 1898, Feb. and July 1899, May 1900, March 1916, and April 1917. CCA, Crane to Lennox, 3 Oct. 1918. For some reason, possibly because the Ojibwa were not compensated for the pasturing, Crane asked the agent to 'kindly treat this letter as confidential.' CCA, Duncan to Department, 20 Nov. 1912. See the annual reports of the Department of Indian Affairs for the reserves mentioned. Smith, 'The Mississauga,' 296–306, attributes the success of the Credit band in their agricultural activities to the rich soil along the Grand River and the example of the Iroquois with whom they lived. One Mississauga-Ojibwa at New Credit raised over one thousand bushels of grain. Smith gives little indication of the role played by the Indian agent, but he does indicate that before the Indian Act of 1876 came into effect, the vast majority of the band had become 'Christian farmers.' Therefore, in contrast to the other reserves, the agent could do little damage there. Higgins, *Whitefish Lake Ojibway Memories.* DIAND, *Indians of Ontario*, 32

CHAPTER NINE: THE RENAISSANCE

1 Fair Play, 'The Future of Our Indians,' *Canadian Indian* 1 (6) (March 1891); (7) (April 1891); (8) (May 1891); (9) (June 1891). Wilson's respect for the Ojibwa language is well illustrated in his *Ojibway Language* which is now being used to teach children their native language on the reserves. For an excellent analysis of Wilson's thoughts see Nock, *A Victorian Missionary and Canadian Indian Policy.* Ironically, one of Wilson's sons opened another school in Elkhorn, Man., where he perpetuated the assimilationist program. J. Donald Wilson, 'No Blanket,' 82; Patterson, *Canadian Indian*, 27
2 James W. St G. Walker, 'Race and Recruitment in World War I,' 1–26; BCA, 160th Overseas Bn, CEF Induction Records
3 Annual Report of the Deputy Superintendent General of Indian Affairs, *Canada Sessional Paper No. 27 of 1920*, 14–17, 25–6; Gaffen, *Forgotten Soldiers*, 20, 21, 27, 28. While at Valcartier with the 1st Division, Pegahmagabow decorated his army tent with traditional symbols, including a deer, the symbol of this clan. He told his comrades that a medicine bag presented to him by an elder would give him a charmed life overseas. He was right. A picture of Francis, in uniform, may also be found on page 28. War monu-

ments on most of the reserves give information about Indian participation.

4 Walker, 'Race and Recruitment,' 16–20
5 *Globe*, 29 Aug. 1914, 5. See Band Council minutes, 1914–18, of the reserves noted here. For example, Cape Croker contributed $500 in Oct. 1914 and $200 the following month to the Patriotic Fund of Bruce County. CCA, *Band Resolutions*, Oct., Nov. 1914
6 NA, RG 10, vol. 2640, Red Series file 1290–3
7 Ibid. See also Barbara M. Wilson, ed., *Ontario and the First World War*, xciii; Leslie and Maguire, eds., *Historical Development of the Indian Act*, 118–19.
8 Daugherty, *A Guide to Native Political Associations in Canada* (Ottawa 1887), 16; *Ottawa Journal*, 23 March 1920; Titley, *A Narrow Vision*, 50–3
9 Schmalz, *Saugeen Indians*, 183–4, 200–3, 206. The returning soldiers at Cape Croker were attempting to gain economic independence in dairy farming, but as the Indian agent observed, they did not have funds to develop a viable business. The veterans became a political force in band politics. For Indian involvement in the League of Nations see Richard Veatch, *Canada and the League of Nations* 96–8.
10 Rolf Knight, *Indians at Work* (Vancouver 1978), 197; McMillan, *Native Peoples*, 299; Gaffin, *Forgotten Soldiers*, 35–8; NA, RG 10, vol. 6772, file 452-40
11 Gaffin, *Forgotten Soldiers*, 41, 51, 53
12 Ibid.
13 'The Kettle Point Question,' brief prepared by the History Club of the University of Western Ontario for use at its meeting, 17 Nov. 1970
14 University of Western Ontario Library, 'Indian File,' James Fox to J.J. Talman, 28 Oct. 1946
15 SRA, *Council Minutes*, 4 March 1946, 19 March 1951, 3 June 1963, 27 July 1964. In 1958 Saugeen were still requesting hydro to put a line through the reserve; in 1963 the band asked for telephone service in private homes; and in 1964 they requested the first sidewalks on the reserve. Leslie, 'Commissions of Inquiry,' 129, 130. In one of the Saugeen Council minutes, 4 Sept. 1945, letters were received from the National Indian Government and the Indian Brotherhood requesting that they attend the respective meetings. Gaffen, *Forgotten Soldiers*, 72–3
16 For an example of articles about Indian soldiers see M. Porter, 'Warrior,' *Maclean's Magazine*, 1 Sept. 1952; *Regina Leader Post*, 14 Oct. 1939, 10 Oct. 1940, 8 July 1941; Toronto *Globe and Mail*, 31 Jan. 1942. Bruce D. Sealey and Peter Van De Vyvere, *Thomas George Prince* (Winnipeg 1981), is the only biography of a twentieth-century (Saulteaux) Ojibwa war hero.
17 Leslie and Maguire, ed., Treaties and Research Centre, Indian and Northern Development, *Historical Development of the Indian Act* (Ottawa 1978), 134, 135, 138, 139, 140
18 James Cleland Hamilton, 'Famous Algonquins: Algic Legends,' *Transactions of the Canadian Institute*, vol. 6, nos. 11 and 12, parts 1 and 2 (Toronto 1899), 72–81
19 Canada, Department of Citizenship and Immigration, *Indians of Ontario*, 39;

Tucker, 'Warrior of the Odahwahs,' 32–6; Douglas Leighton, 'Francis Assikinack,' *DCB*, 9: 10–11

20 Hawthorn, *Survey of the Contemporary Indians of Canada*, 2: 88, 90, 7
21 Indian Chiefs of Alberta, *Citizens Plus*, 92–3
22 Lionel de Montigny, 'Racism and Indian Cultural Adaptations,' in Waubageshig, ed., *The Only Good Indian*, 111–24; 'Racial Overtones in Native School Board Issue,' *Saskatoon Star-Phoenix*, 16 Feb. 1973; *The Northian* 5 (1) (1968); 5 (2) (1968); (3) (1968); 6 (1) (1969); 9 (2) (1972); 10 (1) (1974); Federation of Saskatchewan Indians, 'Response to the House Standing Committee's Recommendations for Indian Education' (Watson Report), *The Northian* 10 (1) (1974): 1, 2
23 Martin P. O'Connell, 'Canadian Standard of Housing in Indian Reserve Communities,' memorandum prepared for the Indian-Eskimo Association, 1965, 8. In 1962 in southern Ontario, 73 per cent of reserve houses had electricity; 7 per cent had sewage facilities; 8 per cent had running water; 7 per cent had indoor toilets; and 27 per cent had phones. Ontario, Ministry of Education, *People of Native Ancestry*, 36; André Rénaud, *Education and the First Canadians* (Toronto 1971), 1971, 6, 7. Father Renaud set the stage for such changes in his Quance Lecture series in Canadian Education. The Association of Iroquois and Allied Indians, 'Proposal on Education for the Canadian Indian,' *The Northian* 9 (2) (1972): 28–34
24 National Indian Brotherhood, *Indian Control of Indian Education*, 33–4, 27–31
25 Ibid., 29
26 Jacqueline Weitz, 'A Look at Indian Control of Indian Education,' *The Northian* 10 (1) (1976)
27 Canada, DIAND, *Indian Conditions: A Survey* (Ottawa 1980), 50
28 D.H. Hall, *Mahjetahwin* (Cobourg 1973). For an examination of the alienation between Indian and white communities see Yngve George Lithman, *The Community Apart: A Case Study of a Canadian Indian Reserve Community* (Stockholm 1978).
29 P.S. Schmalz, 'A Utopian Social Science Environment,' *Past & Present* (Oct. 1988), cover, 6, 7; DIAND, *Indian Conditions*, 49; Harvey McCue, 'Self-Government in Education: The Case of the Cree School Board,' Notes for a paper presented to the workshop Implementing Self-Government, Kingston: Institute of Intergovernmental Relations, Queen's University, 29 May 1986, 27, 53, 54, 125. DIAND, Indian and Inuit Education, Information Sheet No. 5 (Ottawa, April 1989), 1–8
30 DIAND, *Indian Conditions*, 198; *Annual Report*, 1988 and 1989
31 Ibid. See also *Canada Year Book*, 1990, 4–25.
32 Denise Beeswax, 'Native Schooling System,' *Tribal Reporter* 1 (1) (5 June 1989): 3; Ministry of Colleges and Universities of Ontario, *Native Studies in Colleges and Universities* (Toronto 1976), 28. According to Verna Kirkness, those Indian students who really wanted to go to university could find a way; Bruce D. Sealey and Verna J. Kirkness, eds., *Indians without Tipis* (Winnipeg 1973), 146; *Anishinabek* (7) (July 1989).

33 *Globe and Mail*, 7 Jan. 1982
34 Waubageshig, ed., *The Only Good Indian*, 126
35 SBA, *Minute Books*, 4 Nov. 1952, 6 June 1955, 7 May 1962, 28 March 1955
    (road costs in this year were $5000), 10 Jan. 1955, 1 Nov. 1951 (housing
    costs were $35,000 in this year), 9 July 1962, 6 July 1964. On 4 May 1953
    alone ten requests for the shore subdivision were granted to individual band
    members.
36 Bill 205, *The Assessment Act*, 1968–9 (Toronto 1969), 26–7. The Municipal
    Act of 1937 was passed allowing townships to tax non-Indians residing on
    Indian land. Lyon, 'Economic Development of Cape Croker Indian Reserve;
    SBA, D.M. Mackay to A.E. Robenson, MP, 10 Feb. 1949; William Mckim,
    regional director, Indian-Eskimo affairs, Ontario, to E. Sargent, MPP, Grey-
    Bruce, 8 Feb. 1971
37 '400 Cottagers Promised Better Deal by Indians,' 28 Aug. 1972; and Ted
    McCannel, 'Cottagers May Sue Amabel for Taxes Paid since 1949,' *Kitchener-
    Waterloo Record*, 12 April 1973
38 See also S. Timms to J. O'Drowsky, executive secretary, Block 'B' Cottage
    Association, 27 March 1971, from Timm's personal file on the issue.
39 The Union of Ontario Indians was formed in 1969 with Cape Croker chief
    Wilmer Nadjiwon as president. The union staff was composed of five
    Ojibwa, one Potawatomi, one Ottawa, two Cree, two Delaware, one
    Tuscarora, and one Mohawk. See 'Union of Ontario Indian Administration,
    One Year Old,' *Calumet* 2 (2) (Feb. 1970). See also Saugeen Band Council
    Resolutions, 6 July 1964; interview with Chief Mason; *Kitchener-Waterloo
    Record*, 12 Aug. 1970. C. Timms, a member of the Cottage Association, paid
    $320 for his 1971 lease, whereas for the past ten years he had been paying
    $30. *The Ryersonian*, 22 Jan. 1971
40 Frank Etherington and Anne McNeilly, '"Indian Problem" Stirs Up Strong
    Feelings at Sauble,' *Kitchener-Waterloo Record*, 20 Sept. 1979, and letter to the
    editor by R. Gary Mason, welfare administrator, Saugeen Indian Reserve, 22
    Sept. 1979, who objected to 'racist' remarks being published in the paper.
    Mark Nagler, *Natives without a Home* (Ottawa 1972), 73
41 See booklet *Ojibway Warriors' Society in Occupied Anicinabe Park, Kinora, Ontario
    Aug. 1974* (np 1974); and Eleanor M. Jacobson, *Bended Elbow* (Kenora 1975,
    1976); 'Anicinabe Park 6 Week Armed Indian Occupation,' *Sault Star*, 30
    April 1976. Vogan, *Indian Coverage in Canadian Daily News-papers, 1978*;
    University of Western Ontario Archives, 'Chippewa Indian Reserve,' Sarnia
    Band Minute Books, 1970–9, microfilm 45, 5 Jan. 1971
42 The Sarnia Reserve success is not unique. The Curve Lake Reserve near
    Peterborough developed a $100,000 business in the Whetung Craft Centre
    which has two hundred people manufacturing over one hundred lines of
    native craft in sixty households. Of the 667 people, only nine are on welfare.
    Toronto Telegram, 10 April 1971; Sarnia Band Resolutions, 19 Oct. and 1
    Dec. 1970, 17 Jan. and 23 Feb. 1971; see especially the insert of the detailed
    annual budget. The chief and council were paid $10,680 for their able

services. See also the Saugeen Band Minute Books, 1 April and 2 Dec. 1963, 4 May and 1 June 1964, in which several band members were receiving grants to attend the Indian Leadership Institute at Huron College, University of Western Ontario.

43 Schmalz, *Saugeen Indians*, 214–18; Lyon, 'Economic Development of Cape Croker Indian Reserve,' 4–25. See also 1987 advertisement of 'Cape Croker Indian Park' which is distributed by the band to campers. Federal Government, *Statement of the Government of Canada on Indian Policy, 1969*. Walter Currie, an Ojibwa director of Indian studies at Trent University, published 'Is the Canadian Indian Act "Legislated Discrimination" ?' in *Human Relations* in March 1968, a year before the white paper was introduced. National Indian Brotherhood, 'Statement on the Proposed New "Indian Policy,"' unpublished paper available from Indian-Eskimo Association, 1969

44 The Union of Ontario Indians wanted eighteen changes to the Indian Act, but not its abolition. *Brief* No. 14, 23–4 June 1960, in Committee of the Senate and the House of Commons on Indian Affairs, Canada, 24 Parliament, 3 Session, 359–60; *Globe and Mail*, 5 June 1969; Duran and Duran, Jr, 'Cape Croker Indian Reserve Furniture Factory Project,' 231–42

45 *Toronto Telegram*, 28 April 1969. 'Indian Leaders Speak in Defense of Cardinal and against Policy,' *Calumet*

46 Waubageshig, ed., *The Only Good Indian*

47 Weaver, *Making Canadian Indian Policy*, 204; David Nicholson, 'Indian Government in Federal Policy: An Insider's Views,' in Little Bear et al., *Pathways to Self-Determination* 59–64

48 Waubageshig, ed., *The Only Good Indian*, vi; E. Palmer Patterson II, 'Native Peoples and Social Policy,' in Shankar A. Yelaja, ed., *Canadian Social Policy* (Waterloo 1987) 191

49 Lithman, *Community Apart*, 174–5; Little Bear et al., *Pathways to Self-Determination*, 192, 4; Andrew J. Siggner et al., *Regional Comparisons of Data on Canada's Registered Indians*, Dec. 1982, 41, indicates that only one-quarter of the Ontario Ojibwa had inadequate housing. Ministry of Treasury and Economics, *Ontario Statistics, 1986*, 170

50 Katharin Dunkley, *Current Issue Review: Indian Self-Government* (Ottawa, Library of Parliament, 12 April 1988); Del Riley, 'What Canada's Indians Want and the Difficulties of Getting It,' Little Bear et al., *Pathways to Self-Determination*, 159–63; Beaver, *To Have What Is Our Own*, in which the president of the National Indian Socio-economic Development Committee wrote to Jake Epp, minister of DIAND, stating that the Department must change from an administrative and control agency to a supportive and resource-providing agency for development. Pelletier and Poole, *No Foreign Land*, 145, 147

51 Dunkley, *Current Issue Review*, 13; and Tom Porter, 'Traditions of the constitution of the Six Nations,' in Little Bear et al., *Pathways to Self-Determination*, 21; Titley, *Narrow Vision*, 84

52 Sally M. Weaver, 'Indian Government: A Concept in Need of a Definition,'

in Little Bear et al., *Pathways to Self-Determination*, 65–8. For details on these problems see Ponting and Gibbins, *Out of Irrelevance*, and J.R. Ponting and R. Gibbins, 'Thorns in the Bed of Roses: A Socio-Political View of the Problems of Indian Government' in Little Bear et al., *Pathways to Self-Determination*, 122–35.

53 Pelletier, *Two Articles*, 150

54 McMillan, *Native Peoples*, 302–5; Dunkley, *Current Issue Review*, 7, 8; Peters, *Aboriginal Self-Government Arrangements in Canada*, 8–10; Taylor, *Indian Band Self-Government in the 1960s*, considers self-government of a reserve at a municipal level.

55 Canada, House of Commons, *Indian Self-Government in Canada: Report of the Special Committee and Responses of the Government to the Report of the Special Committee on Indian Self-Government* (Ottawa 1988)

56 Ponting et al., *Out of Irrelevance*, 47–8; interviews with male Ojibwa; Dunkley, *Current Issue Review*, 9; Jamieson, *Indian Women and the Law in Canada*; David Ahenakew, 'Answers to Your Questions about First Nations' Self-government,' *Bridges* 1 (5) (June 1984): 18–9; McMillan, *Native Peoples*, 288–9; interview with Chief Ralph Akiwenzie, Cape Croker, 12 March 1990

57 Schmalz, 'An Analysis of Canadian Indian Writers,' unpublished paper, 1982. Copway's work, printed in 1847, was the first volume of Indian history written by an Indian. Guy Sylvestre, comp., *Indian-Inuit Authors: An Annotated Bibliography* (Ottawa 1974); Arlene B. Hirshfelder, comp., *American Indian and Eskimo Authors* (New York 1973)

58 Basil Johnston was a high school teacher before he accepted the position 'with the Education Dept. of the Royal Ontario Museum, to teach the history of Indians.' See picture and notice of his appointment in *Calumet* 2 (2) (Feb. 1970). Basil H. Johnston, ed., 'View of Life,' *Tawaw*, Nov. 1976, which contains several articles on Ojibwa culture written by Johnston and other Ojibwa. Geoff Johnston, 'Ojibway Author, Western Surgeon Receive Order of Ontario,' *Tribal Reporter* 1 (1) (5 June 1989); Vanderburgh, *I Am Nokomis Too*

59 Dunn, *Red on White: The Biography of Duke Redbird*; R.P. Bowles et al., *Canadian Issues & Opinions. The Indian: Assimilation, Integration, or Separation?* (Scarborough 1972), and Kent Gooderham, ed., *I Am an Indian* (Toronto 1969), are on Circular 14, a list of books prescribed by the Ministry of Education for Ontario. See Bowles et al., *Canadian Issues*, 46–7, 247, for examples of Redbird's creativity as a cartoonist and film maker; and Waubageshig, ed., *The Only Good Indian*, in which his poetry is scattered throughout.

60 Norval Morrisseau, *Legends of My People the Great Ojibway*, ed. Selwyn Dewdney (Toronto 1965); Herbert T. Schwarz, *Tales from the Smokehouse* (Toronto 1976), in which Daphne Odjig has numerous erotic illustrations; Mary E. Southcott, *The Sound of the Drum: The Sacred Art of the Anishnabec* (Toronto 1980); Patterson, *Canadian Native Art*, 33–4; Sinclair and Pollock, *Art of Norval Morrisseau*, 17–49

CHAPTER TEN: CONCLUSION

1 Burham, 'Coming of the Mississauga,' 7; Patterson, *Canadian Indian*, 28
2 Don McCaskill, 'Revitalization of Indian Culture: Indian Cultural Survival
   Schools,' in Barmen et al., eds., *Indian Education in Canada*, vol. 2: 153–79.
   See also McMillan, *Native Peoples*, 112–13; Paredes, ed., *Anishinabe*,
   397–410. This contemporary account of the Anishinabe has been integrated
   with knowledge gained from the oral tradition of several Southern Ojibwa
   reserves.
3 Nancy Wood, 'Indians, Province Strike First Deal in Land Claim Case,'
   Toronto Star, 8 Feb. 1990; Bill Taylor, 'Cleanup Vowed If Claim Upheld,'
   Toronto Star, 24 Jan. 1990; Donald Grant, 'Natives To Resume Logging
   Road Blockades,' 3 Nov. 1989; John Wright, 'Men Get Stiff Penalties For
   Poaching,' *Owen Sound Sun Times*, 12 Oct. 1989. See also Hodgins and
   Benidickson, *Temagami Experience*.

SELECT BIBLIOGRAPHY

There is no comprehensive bibliography of the Ojibwa of southern Ontario. P.S. Schmalz's doctoral thesis, however, contains over 500 references and is available to scholars. Helen Hornbeck Tanner's *The Ojibway: A Critical Bibliography* (Bloomington 1976) is an excellent starting point, but much material on the Ontario Ojibwa is not included. This limitation is to some extent corrected in Robert J. Surtees, *Canadian Indian Policy: A Critical Bibliography* (Bloomington 1982). Also useful are *A Reader's Guide to Canadian History, 1: Beginnings to Confederation*, ed. D.A. Muise (Toronto 1982), and *2: Confederation to the Present*, ed. J.L. Granatstein and Paul Stevens (Toronto 1982). *A Canadian Indian Bibliography, 1960–1970* (Toronto 1972) by Thomas S. Abler et al. demonstrates the tremendous volume of print dedicated to the Indians. Another most useful tool for biographical and bibliographical information is the *Dictionary of Canadian Biography (DCB)*. The best bibliography and book related to the Ojibwa of southern Ontario is Donald B. Smith's recent work, *Sacred Feathers* (Toronto 1987), but its sources are naturally limited to its subject, Peter Jones.

Those students who intend to add to our knowledge of Canada's Ojibwa history must go to several locations for primary unpublished sources. The National Archives of Canada is the major repository. There, the Archives des colonies, C11A, is essential reading for French relations with the Ojibwa. Record Group 10 is a major source for the Chief Superintendency, Upper Canada (c. 1830–45), the Civil Secretary as Superintendent General (c. 1845–61), the Deputy Superintendent General (c. 1862–74), and Field Office Records of the Central Superintendency Toronto (c. 1836–83). The Red Series Headquarters files relate to Eastern Canada (c. 1870–1930). An extensive collection of manuscript sources on the Ojibwa of Ontario is also found in the Archives of Ontario. It contains valuable papers such as the diary of T.G. Anderson, Colonial Office correspondence of the secretary of state, Jesuit diaries, the Rose Papers, and the Rankin survey reports. The Metropolitan Toronto Library houses such valuable materials as the James Givins and the Samuel P. Jarvis papers. For unpublished missionary reports, mission registries, and diaries, such locations as the United Church Archives and Victoria University Library in Toronto are essential. This is especially true when the Ojibwa themselves become missionaries in the 1820s. Each Ojibwa reserve contains valuable oral traditions of the elders as well as unpublished records. Schmalz has coordinated the collecting of over two hundred audio-taped interviews at Cape Croker and Chippewa Hill reserves. Some informal interviews were also recorded from other locations. The types of material that can be found in reserve offices and in the hands of private band members include Indian agent letters, agricultural society minutes, council resolutions, land-claims reports, land-sales records, missionary diaries, pay lists of interest distribution of treaty money, relief voucher books, and community development reports. Preliminary hearings of band members in conflict with the law may be obtained from the magistrate courts. Unpublished manuscripts also may be found in county and regional collections. For example, the Grey County Museum/Archives has the Sutton diaries and the D.B. Weldon Library at the University of Western Ontario has the Wawanosh Papers. If one is to write the history of a specific reserve, these sources are indispensable.

One of the most positive signs of research into Ojibwa history is the number of recent dissertations presented on the topic to universities, especially in Ontario. Over two dozen theses are listed here.

For information related to activities on specific reserves, newspapers are crucial. The *Anishinabek, Calumet, Canadian Indian, Christian Guardian, Christian Advocate, Indian News, Comet, Cape Croker Courier, Tribal Reporter, Wiarton Echo, Kingston Whig-Standard,* and *Owen Sound Sun-Times* are examples of publications which contain numerous articles of interest to Ojibwa students.

There are also several periodicals that contain information related to the Ojibwa of southern Ontario. *Ontario history (OH)* with its *Papers and Records* is the best source. The *Canadian Journal of Industry, Science and Art* contains the oral tradition passed on by F. Assikenack and other articles related to the Ojibwa. The *Canadian Historical Review (CHR)* has several essays involving native people but few related specifically to the Ojibwa. The *Northian* is especially good for Indian education. For legal aspects of Indian life see the *Osgoode Hall Law Journal.* The *Canadian Journal of Native Studies* has many themes related to the Ontario native experience. Studies involving the Ojibwa may also be found in *American Indigena, American Anthropologist, Journal of American Folk-lore, Human Organization, Ethnohistory, Annual Archaeological Report, Indian-Eskimo Association of Canada Bulletin, Journal of Historical Geography, Human Relations, Journal of Economics & Political Science, Michigan History, Indian Education, Revue d'histoire de l'Amérique Français, Mississippi Valley Historical Review,* and *The Beaver.*

While there is no single comprehensive published primary source encompassing the history of the Ojibwa of southern Ontario, there are numerous volumes with scattered accounts. The Aborigines' Protection Society produced many sympathetic reports. Many of the Champlain Society books contain references to the Ojibwa. The editorial work of E.A. Cruikshank, R.G. Thwaites, A.G. Doughty, W.R. Riddell, E.B. O'Callaghan, Milo Milton Quaife, and Emma Blair has made available much that is important to the study of the Ojibwa. Several Ojibwa have also recorded their thoughts: Andrew J. Blackbird, William R. Blackbird, George Copway, Peter Jacobs, Basil Johnston, Patronella Johnston,

Peter Jones, Wilfred Pelletier, and Flora Tabobondung. Through much of Ojibwa history, people in various walks of life have recorded their impressions of this group: James Beaven (mission inspector), Henry Bouquet (British officer), Lamothe Cadillac (French officer), C. Van Dusen (Methodist missionary), Sir Francis Bond Head (governor), Alexander Henry (trader), Anna Jameson (traveller), William Johnson (Indian agent), Paul Kane (artist), Ruth Landes (anthropologist), Pierre Esprit Radisson (explorer), Father Gabriel Sagard (Jesuit), John Graves Simcoe (lieutenant governor), and Edward F. Wilson (Anglican minister), to mention only a few. The Indian Department has also produced numerous publications related to the Ojibwa. The Department of Indian Affairs and Northern Development can provide detailed bibliography, and Canada's *Sessional Papers*, Annual Report of the Department of Indian Affairs, 1880–1917, should be examined. With growing provincial involvement in Indian affairs, the Ontario government, especially the Ministry of Education, should also be approached. In addition, there are numerous but all too brief references to the Ojibwa in provincial, regional, county, township, and town histories of southern Ontario.

Ahenakew, Dr David. 'Answers to Your Questions about First Nations' Self-government,' *Bridges* 1 (5) June 1984

Assikenack, F. 'Legends and Traditions of the Odahwah Indians,' 'Social and Warlike Customs of the Odahwah Indians,' and 'The Odahwah Indian Language.' *Canadian Journal of Industry, Science and Art* 14, 16, 17, 1858

Barman, Jean, et al., eds. *Indian Education in Canada*, 2 vols. Vancouver 1986

Barron, F. Laurie. 'The Genesis of Temperance in Ontario, 1828–1850.' PHD, thesis, University of Guelph, 1976

Beaven, James. *Recreations of a Long Vacation or a Visit to Indian Missions in Upper Canada*. Toronto 1846

Beaver, J.W. *To Have What Is Our Own*. Ottawa 1979

Bishop, Charles A. *The Northern Ojibwa and the Fur Trade: An Historical and Ecological Study*. Toronto 1974

Blackbird, Andrew J. *History of the Ottawa and Chippewa Indians of Michigan*. Ypsilanti 1887

Boyle, David. 'Notes on Primitive Man in Ontario,' *Report of the Ministry of Education for Ontario* (Appendix). Toronto 1895

Brill, Charles. *Indian and Free: A Contemporary Portrait of Life on a Chippewa Reservation*. Minneapolis 1975

Campbell, Maria. *Halfbreed*. Toronto 1973

Canada. *Copies of Extracts of Correspondence between the Secretary of State for the Colonies and the Governor-General of Canada Respecting Alterations in the Indian Department in Canada*. 1860

Canada, Department of Citizenship and Immigration. *Indians of Ontario*. Ottawa 1962

Canada, Department of Indian Affairs. *Annual Reports*. Ottawa 1882–1940

Canada. *Indian Treaties and Surrenders from 1680 to 1890*, 3 vols. Ottawa 1891–1912

Canada (Province), Legislative Assembly. *Report of the Affairs of the Indians in Canada, 1844–5*, app. EEE. 1847
– *Report of the Special Commissioners Appointed on the 8th of Sept., 1856, to Investigate Indian Affairs in Canada.* Sessional Papers 1858
Cardinal, Harold. *The Rebirth of Canada's Indians.* Edmonton 1977
Cason, De Dolier, and De Brehant Galinee. *Exploration of the Great Lakes, 1669–1670*, ed. and trans. James H. Coyne. *Papers and Records*, vol. ix. Toronto 1903
Chamberlain, A.F. 'Notes on the History, Customs and Beliefs of the Missisagua [sic] Indians,' *Journal of American Folklore 1*, 1888
Champlain, Samuel de. *Works*, 6 vols., ed. H.P. Biggar. Toronto 1922–36
Christie, Thomas Laird. 'Reserve Colonialism and Sociocultural Change.' PHD thesis, University of Toronto, 1976
Clifton, James. *A Place of Refuge for All Time: Migration of the American Potawatomi into Upper Canada 1830 to 1850.* Ottawa 1975
Copway, George. *Recollections of a Forest Life.* London 1851
– *Running Sketches of Men and Places in England, France, Germany, Belgium, and Scotland.* New York 1851
– [Kahgegagahbowh]. *The Traditional History and Characteristic Sketches of the Ojibway Nation.* Boston 1850
Coyle, Michael. 'Traditional Indian Justice in Ontario: A Role for the Present?' *Osgoode Hall Law Journal* 24 (3) 1986
Cruikshank, E.A., ed. *The Correspondence of Lieut. Governor John Graves Simcoe, with Allied Documents Relating to His Administration of the Government of Upper Canada*, 5 vols. Toronto 1923–31
Cumming, Peter A., and Neil H. Mickenberg. *Native Rights in Canada.* Toronto 1972
Danziger, Edmund Jefferson, Jr. *The Chippewas of Lake Superior.* Norman 1979
De Mille, Susan. 'Ethnohistory of Farming, Cape Croker: 1820–1930.' PHM thesis, University of Toronto, 1971
Dewdney, Selwyn. *The Sacred Scrolls of the Southern Ojibway.* Toronto 1975
Dewdney, Selwyn, and Kenneth E. Kidd. *Indian Rock Paintings of the Great Lakes.* Toronto 1962
Doughty, Sir Arthur G., ed. *The Elgin-Grey Papers*, 4 vols. Ottawa 1937
Dunkley, Katharine. *Current Issue Review: Indian Self-Government.* Ottawa 1988
Dunn, Marty. *Red on White: The Biography of Duke Redbird.* Toronto 1971
Dunning, R.W. *Social and Economic Change among the Northern Ojibwa.* Toronto 1959
Duran, James A., Jr, and Elizabeth C. 'The Cape Croker Indian Reserve Furniture Factory Project.' *Human Organization* 32 (3) 1973
Eccles, W.J. *French in America.* Toronto 1976
Eid, Leroy V. 'The Ojibwa-Iroquois War: The War the Five Nations Did Not Win.' *Ethnohistory* 24 (4), 1979
Ellwood, E.M. 'The Robinson Treaties of 1850.' BA thesis, Wilfrid Laurier University, 1977

Elston, Georgia, ed. *Giving: Ojibwa Stories and Legends from the Children of Curve Lake.* Lakefield 1988

Firth, Edith G., ed. *The Town of York, 1793–1815.* Toronto 1962

– *The Town of York, 1815–1834.* Toronto 1966

French, Goldwin. *Parsons and Politics: The Role of the Wesleyan Methodists in Upper Canada and the Maritimes from 1780 to 1855.* Toronto 1962

Gaffen, Fred. *Forgotten Soldiers.* Penticton 1985

Getty, Ian A.L., and Antoine S. Lussier. *As Long as the Sun Shines and Water Flows: A Reader in Canadian Native Studies.* Vancouver 1983

Graham, Elizabeth. *Medicine Man to Missionary: Missionaries as Agents of Change among the Indians of Southern Ontario, 1784–1867.* Toronto 1975

Grand General Council. *Minutes of the General Council of Indian Chiefs and Principal Men, Held at Orillia, Lake Simcoe Narrows, on Thursday, the 30th, and Friday, the 31st July, 1846.* Montreal 1846

– *Six Nations and Delegates from Different Bands in Western and Eastern Canada: Minutes, June 10, 1870.* Hamilton, nd

– *The Grand General Council of the Chippewas, Munsees, Six Nations etc., etc., Held on the Sarnia Reserve, June 25th to July 3, 1874.* Sarnia 1874

– *Grand Indian Council of the Province of Ontario, 15 to 22 August 1879, held at Sarnia.* Wiarton 1879

– *Minutes of the Seventh Grand General Indian Council Held upon the New Credit Indian Reserve, from September 13th to September 18th, 1882.* Hagersville 1883

– *Minutes of the Eighth Grand General Indian Council Held upon the Cape Croker [sic] Indian Reserve, County of Bruce from Sept. 10th to Sept. 15th, 1884.* Hagersville nd

– *Minutes of the Thirteenth Grand Indian Council of Ontario and Quebec Held upon the Moraviantown Indian Reserve, from 16th to 20th of October, 1894.* Np, nd

– *Minutes and Proceedings of the Grand General Indian Council of Canada Held at Wikwemikong, 15, 16, 17, Sept., 1936.* Np, nd

Grant, John Webster. *Moon of Wintertime: Missionaries and the Indians of Canada in Encounter since 1534.* Toronto 1984

Gray, Elma E. *Wilderness Christians: The Moravian Mission to the Delaware Indians.* Toronto 1956

Great Britain, Imperial Blue Book. *Report from the Select Committee on Aborigines (British Settlements), with the Minutes of Evidence, Appendix and Index, 1836*

Greenberg, Adolf M., and James Morrison. 'Group Identity in the Boreal Forest: The Origin of the Northern Ojibwa,' *Ethnohistory* 29 (2), 1982

Goltz, Herbert C.W. 'Tecumseh, the Prophet, and the Rise of the Northwest Indian Confederacy.' PHD thesis, University of Western Ontario, 1973

Haldimand, Frederick. 'Haldimand Papers,' *Historical Collection: Collections and Researches Made by the Michigan Pioneer and Historical Society*, vols. IX, XIX, 1892

Hale, Horatio. *The Iroquois Book of Rites.* Philadelphia 1883

Hall, Anthony J. 'The Red Man's Burden: Land, Law and Lord in the Indian Affairs of Upper Canada, 1791–1858.' PHD thesis, University of Toronto, 1984

Hallowell, A. Irving. *The Role of Conjuring in Saulteaux Society.* New York 1971

Handy, J.R. 'The Ojibwa, 1640–1840: Two Centuries of Change from Sault Ste Marie to Coldwater/Narrows,' MA thesis, University of Waterloo, 1978

Hawthorn, Harry B., ed. *A Survey of the Contemporary Indians of Canada: Economic, Political, Educational Needs and Policies,* 2 vols. Ottawa 1966–7

Henderson, Wm B. *Canada's Indian Reserves: The Usufruct in Our Constitution.* Ottawa 1980

Henry, Alexander. *Travels & Adventures in Canada and the Indian Territory between the Years 1760 and 1776.* New York 1969

Henry, George [Maungwudaus]. *Remarks Concerning the Ojibway Indians, by One of Themselves Called Maungwudaus, Who Has Been Travelling in England, France, Belgium, Ireland, and Scotland.* Leeds, England 1847

Hickerson, Harold. *The Chippewa and Their Neighbors: A Study in Ethnohistory.* New York 1970

– *Chippewa Indians.* New York 1974

Higgins, E. *Whitefish Lake Ojibway Memories.* Cobalt 1982

Hogins, George, ed. *Documentary History of Education in Upper Canada, 1790–1830.* Toronto 1894

Horsman, R. *Matthew Elliott: British Indian Agent.* Detroit 1964

Indian Chiefs of Alberta. *Citizens Plus.* Edmonton 1970

Jamieson, Elmer. 'Indian Education in Canada.' MED thesis, McMaster University, 1922

Jamieson, Kathleen. *Indian Women and the Law in Canada: Citizens Minus.* Ottawa 1978

Jenness, Diamond. *The Ojibwa Indians of Parry Island, Their Social and Religious Life.* Ottawa 1935

Joblin, Elgie E.M. *The Education of the Indians of Western Ontario.* Toronto 1947

Johnson, William. *The Papers of Sir William Johnson,* 13 vols. Albany 1933–65

Johnston, Basil. *Indian School Days.* Toronto 1988

– *Moose Meat & Wild Rice.* Toronto 1978

– *Ojibway Heritage.* Toronto 1967

Johnston, Charles M., ed. *The Valley of the Six Nations.* Toronto 1964

Jones, Cheryl, et al. *The History of Cape Croker.* Owen Sound 1980

[Jones, Eliza]. *Memoir of Elizabeth Jones, a Little Indian Girl, Who Lived at River Credit Mission, Upper Canada.* London 1838

Jones, Peter. *Life and Journals of Kahkewaquonaby (Rev. Peter Jones), Wesleyan Missionary.* Toronto 1860

Kellogg, Louise Phelps. *The French Regime in Wisconsin and the Northwest.* Madison 1925

Kidder, Homer H. *The Central Ojibway.* Chicago 1929

Kinietz, W. Vernon. *Chippewa Village: The Story of Katikitegon.* Bloomfield Hills 1947

– *The Indians of the Western Great Lakes, 1615–1760.* Ann Arbor, 1940

Klinck, C.F., and James J. Talman, eds. *The Journal of Major John Norton, 1809–1816.* Toronto 1970

Koennecke, Franz M. 'Life of the Reverend Allen Salt, Wesleyan Missionary to the Anishnabek.' Paper presented at University of Waterloo, 1983
– 'Wasoksing: The History of Parry Island, an Anishnabwe Community in the Georgian Bay, 1850–1920.' MA thesis, University of Waterloo, 1984
Kohl, J.G. *Kitchi-Gami: Wanderings Round Lake Superior.* Minneapolis 1956
Konrad, Victor. 'An Iroquois Frontier: The North Shore of Lake Ontario during the Late Seventeenth Century.' *Journal of Historical Geography* 7 (2) 1981
Lajeunesse, Ernest J., ed. *The Windsor Border Region: Canada's Southernmost Frontier.* Toronto 1960
Landes, Ruth. *Ojibwa Sociology.* New York 1969
– *The Ojibwa Woman.* New York 1971
Landon, Fred, ed. 'Letters of Rev. James Evans, Methodist Missionary. Written during His Journey to and Residence in the Lake Superior Region, 1838–9.' *OH* 26, 1930
La Rochefoucault-Liancourt. *Travels in Canada, 1795,* ed. William Renwick Riddell. *Thirteenth Report of the Bureau of Archives for the Province of Ontario.* Toronto 1917
Lavalee, Mary Ann. 'Too Little Too Late.' *Arbos* 5 (2), 1968
Leighton, James Douglas. 'The Compact Tory as Bureaucrat: Samuel Peter Jarvis and the Indian Department, 1837–1845.' *OH* 73 (1), 1981
– 'The Development of Federal Indian Policy in Canada, 1840–1845.' PHD thesis, University of Western Ontario, 1975
Leslie, John, F. 'Commissions of Inquiry into Indian Affairs in the Canadas, 1828–1858.' MA thesis, Carleton University, 1984
Leslie, John, and Ron Maguire, eds. *The Historical Development of the Indian Act.* Ottawa 1983
Levine, Stuart, and Nancy O. Lurie, eds. *The American Indians Today.* Baltimore 1970
Lewis, Rundall M., ed. 'The Manitoulin Letters of the Rev. Charles Crosbie Brough.' *OH* 47 (2) 1956
Little Bear, Leroy et al. eds. *Pathways to Self-Determination: Canadian Indians and the Canadian State.* Toronto 1984
Long, J. *Voyages and Travels of an Indian Interpreter and Trader.* London 1791
Loram, C.T., and T.F. McIlwraith. *The North American Indian Today.* Toronto 1943
Lyon, N. Adverse. 'The Economic Development of Cape Croker Indian Reserve.' MSC thesis, University of Guelph, 1966
Mabindisa, Kholisile. 'The Praying Man: The Life and Times of Henry Bird Steinhauer.' PHD thesis, University of Alberta, 1984
McCardle, B. *Indian History and Claims: A Research Handbook,* 2 vols. Ottawa 1982
MacDonald, G.A. 'The Saulteur-Oijbwa Fishery at Sault Ste. Marie, 1640–1840.' MA thesis, University of Waterloo, 1978
Maclean, H. 'The Hidden Agenda: Methodist Attitudes to the Ojibwa and the Development of Indian Schooling in Upper Canada, 1821–1860.' MA thesis, University of Toronto, 1978

MacLean, John. *Vanguards of Canada.* Toronto 1918

McMillan, Alan D. *Native Peoples and Cultures of Canada: An Anthropological Overview.* Toronto 1988

Manuel, George, and Michael Posluns. *The Fourth World: An Indian Reality.* Toronto 1974

Miller, J.R. *Skyscrapers Hide the Heavens: A History of Indian-White Relations in Canada.* Toronto 1989

Milloy, J.S. 'The Era of Civilization: British Policy for the Indians of Canada, 1830–1860.' D. Phil. thesis, University of Oxford, 1978

Moore, Kermot A. *Kipawa: Portrait of a People.* Cobalt 1982

Morris, J.M., ed. *Indian Treaties and Purchases in the Province of Ontario: Indians of Ontario.* Ottawa 1943

Morrison, R. Bruce, and C. Roderick Wilson. *Native Peoples: The Canadian Experience.* Toronto 1986

Murray, Florence B., ed. *Muskoka and Haliburton, 1615–1875.* Toronto 1963

National Indian Brotherhood. *Indian Control of Indian Education.* Ottawa 1972

Navarre, Robert (?). *Journal of Pontiac's Conspiracy, 1763,* ed. C.M. and M.A.B. Burton; trans. R. Clyde Ford. Detroit 1912

Nock, David. *A Victorian Missionary and Canadian Indian Policy: Cultural Synthesis vs. Cultural Replacement.* Waterloo 1988

– 'A White Man's Burden: A Portrait of E.F. Wilson, Missionary in Ontario, 1868–1885.' MA thesis, Carleton University, 1972

O'Callaghan, E.B., ed. *The Documentary History of the State of New York.* Albany 1849–51

– *Documents Relative to the Colonial History of the State of New York,* 15 vols. New York 1853–87

Ontario, Ministry of Education. *People of Native Ancestry.* Toronto 1975

Orr, R.B. 'The Mississaugas,' *27th Annual Archaeological Report for 1915. Being Part of Appendix to the Report of the Minister of Education, Ontario.* Toronto 1915

Own, E.A. *Pioneer Sketches of Long Point Settlement.* Toronto 1898

Pahtahsega (Peter Jacobs). *Journal of the Reverend Peter Jacobs, Indian Wesleyan Missionary, from Rice Lake to the Hudson's Bay Territory and Returning: Commencing May, 1852: With a Brief Account of His Life; and a Short History of the Wesleyan Mission to that Country.* Toronto 1853

Paredes, J. Anthony, ed. *Anishinabe: 6 Studies of Modern Chippewa.* Tallahassee, 1980

Patterson, E. Palmer. *The Canadian Indian: A History since 1500.* Toronto 1972

– 'Native and Social Policy,' in Shankar A. Yelaja, ed., *Canadian Social Policy.* Waterloo 1987

Patterson, Nancy-Lou. *Canadian Native Art.* Toronto 1973

Paudash, Chief Robert. 'The Coming of the Mississagas.' *Ontario Historical Society, Papers and Records* 6, 1905

Pelletier, Wilfred. *Two Articles.* Toronto 1969

Pelletier, Wilfred, and Ted Poole. *No Foreign Land: The Biography of a North American Indian.* Toronto 1973

Perrot, Nicolas. *Memoir on the Manners, Customs and Religion of the Savages of North America* in *The Indian Tribes of the Upper Mississippi and the Great Lakes Region*, 2 vols., ed. and trans. Emma Blair. Cleveland 1911

Peters, Evelyn J. *Aboriginal Self-Government Arrangements in Canada: An Overview.* Kingston 1987

Peterson, Jacqueline, and Jennifer S.H. Brown, eds. *The New People.* Winnipeg 1985

Petrone, Penny, ed. *First People, First Voices.* Toronto 1983

Plain, Aylmer N. *A History of the Sarnia Indian Reserve.* Bright's Grove 1975

Ponting, Rick, et al. *Out of Irrelevance: A Socio-Political Introduction to Indian Affairs in Canada.* Toronto 1980

Potherie, Bacqueville de la, Claude Charles Le Roy. *Histoire de l'Amérique septentrionale* in *The Indian Tribes of the Upper Mississippi and the Great Lakes Region*, 2 vols., ed. and trans. Emma Blair. Cleveland 1911

Preston, Richard A., ed. and trans. *Royal Fort Frontenac.* Toronto 1958

Quealey, F.M. 'The Administration of Sir Peregrine Maitland, Lieutenant Governor of Upper Canada, 1818–1828.' PHD thesis, York University, 1968

Quimby, George Irwing. *Indian Life in the Upper Great Lakes, 11,000 B.C. to A.D. 1800.* Chicago 1967

Radin, Paul. *Some Myths and Tales of the Ojibwa of Southeastern Ontario.* Ottawa 1914

Radisson, Pierre Esprit. *The Explorations of Pierre Esprit Radisson*, ed. Arthur T. Adams. Minneapolis 1961

Robinson, Percy J. *Toronto during the French Régime: A History of the Toronto Region from Brûlé to Simcoe, 1615–1793.* Toronto 1965

Rogers, Edward S. *The Round Lake Ojibwa.* Toronto 1963

– 'Southeastern Ojibwa,' in *Handbook of North American Indians*, vol. 15: *Northeast*, ed. Bruce Trigger. Washington 1978

Rogers, Edward S., and Flora Tobobundung. *Perry Island Farmers: A Period of Change in the Way of Life of the Algonkians of Southern Ontario.* Ottawa 1975

Rogers, John (Chief Snow Cloud). *Red World and White: Memories of a Chippewa Boyhood.* Norman 1974

Russell, Peter. *The Correspondence of the Honourable Peter Russell*, ed. E.A. Cruikshank and A.F. Hunter. Toronto 1935

Ryan, Helen. *Survey of Documents Available for Research in the Treaties and Historical Research Centre.* Ottawa 1983

Sagard, Father Gabriel. *The Long Journey to the Country of the Hurons.* Toronto 1967

Sanderson, Charles R., ed. *The Arthur Papers.* Toronto 1943

Schmalz, Peter S. *The History of the Saugeen Indians.* Ottawa 1977

– *People of Native Ancestry Course.* Chesley 1987

– 'The Role of the Ojibwa in the Conquest of Southern Ontario, 1650–1701.' *OH* 76 (4), 1984

– 'The Ojibwa of Southern Ontario,' PHD thesis, University of Waterloo, 1985

Schoolcraft, Henry R. *Algic Researches.* New York 1839

Scott, Duncan Campbell. 'Indian Affairs, 1763–1912,' in Adam Shortt and
    A.G. Doughty, eds., *Canada and Its Provinces,* vols 4, 5, 6. Toronto 1913–14
Severance, Frank H. *An Old Frontier of France,* 2 vols. New York 1917
Shkilnyk, A.M. *A Poison Stronger Than Love: The Destruction of an Ojibwa Commu-
    nity.* New Haven 1985
Sinclair, Lister, and Jack Pollock. *The Art of Norval Morrisseau.* Toronto 1979
Slattery, B.J. 'The Legal Status and Land Rights of Indigenous Canadian People
    as Affected by the Crown's Acquisition of Their Territories.' DPhil., Univer-
    sity of Oxford, 1979
Slight, Benjamin. *Indian Researches, or Facts Concerning the North American Indians.*
    Montreal 1844
Smith, Derek G., ed. *Canadian Indians and the Law: Selected Documents,
    1663–1972.* Toronto 1975
Smith, Donald B. *Sacred Feathers: The Reverend Peter Jones (Kahkewaquonaby) & the
    Mississauga Indians.* Toronto 1987
– 'The Dispossession of the Mississauga: A Missing Chapter in the Early
    History of Upper Canada,' *OH* 73 (2) 1982
– 'Who Are the Mississauga?' *OH* 67 (4) 1975
– 'The Mississauga, Peter Jones and the White Man: The Algonquian's Adjust-
    ment to the Europeans on the North Shore of Lake Ontario to 1860.' PHD
    thesis, University of Toronto, 1975
Smith, W.H. *Canadian Gazetteer.* Toronto 1846
Stanley, George F.G. *The War of 1812: Land Operations.* Toronto 1983
Surtees, R.J. 'The Development of an Indian Reserve Policy in Canada.' *OH* 61
    (2) (June 1969)
– 'Indian Land Cessions in Ontario, 1763–1862: The Evolution of a System.'
    PHD thesis, Carleton University, 1983
Tanner, Helen H. *The Ojibwa: A Critical Bibliography.* Bloomington 1976
Taylor, John Leonard. *Indian Band Self-Government in the 60's: A Case Study of
    Walpole Island.* Ottawa 1984
Thwaites, Reuben G., ed. *The Jesuit Relations and Allied Documents,* 73 vols.
    Cleveland 1886–91
– ed. 'The French Regime in Wisconsin (1634–1727), (1743–1760)' and 'The
    British Regime in Wisconsin (1760–1821).' *Collections of the State Historical
    Society of Wisconsin,* XVI, XVIII. Madison 1902–8
Titley, E. Brian. *A Narrow Vision: Duncan Campbell Scott and the Administration of
    Indian Affairs in Canada.* Vancouver 1986
Trigger, Bruce. *The Children of Aataentsic: A History of the Huron People to 1660,* 2
    vols. Montreal 1976
– *Natives and Newcomers: Canada's 'Heroic Age' Reconsidered.* Kingston 1985
– 'Indians and Ontario's History.' *OH* 85 (4), 1982
Union of Ontario Indians. 'Union of Ontario Indian Administration, One Year
    Old.' *Calumet* 2 (2), 1970
Vanderburgh, R.M. *I am Nokomis Too: The Biography of Verna Pateronella Johnston.*
    Don Mills 1977

Vandusen, C. (Enemikeese). *The Indian Chief: An Account of the Labours, Losses, Sufferings and Oppression of Ke-zig-ko-e-ne-ne (David Sawyer), a Chief of the Ojibway Indians in Canada West*. London 1867

Vecsey, Christopher Thomas. 'Traditional Ojibwa Religion and Its Historical Changes.' PhD thesis, Northwestern University, 1977

Vogan, Peggy. *Indian Coverage in Canadian Daily Newspapers, 1978: A Content Analysis*. Ottawa 1979

Walker, James W. St.G. 'Race and Recruitment in World War I: Enlistment of Visual Minorities in the Canadian Expeditionary Force.' *CHR* 70 (1) 1989

Warren, William W. *History of the Ojibway Nation*. Minneapolis 1957

Watson, D.M. 'Frontier Movement and Economic Development in North-Eastern Ontario, 1850–1914.' MA thesis, University of British Columbia, 1971

Waubageshig (Harvey McCue), ed. *The Only Good Indian: Essays by Canadian Indians*. Toronto 1970

Weaver, Sally M. *Making Canadian Indian Policy: The Hidden Agenda, 1968–70*. Toronto 1981

Wesleyan-Methodist Church of Canada. *Annual Reports*. Toronto 1828–85

Whetung-Derrick, Mae. *History of the Ojibwa of the Curve Lake Reserve and Surrounding Area*. 3 vols. Curve Lake Indian Reserve 1976

Wilson, Barbara M., ed. *Ontario and the First World War*. Toronto 1977

Wilson, Edward F. *Autobiographical Journal*. Sault Spring Island 1903

– *Missionary Work among the Ojebway Indians*. London 1886

– *The Ojebway Language: A Manual for Missionaries and Others Employed among the Ojebway*. Toronto nd

Wilson, J.D., ed. *An Imperfect Past: Education and Society in Canadian History*. Vancouver 1984

Wright, J.W. 'The Application of the Direct Historical Approach to the Iroquois and the Ojibwa.' *Anthropological* 15 (1) 1968

Zoltvany, Yves F. *Philippe de Rigaud de Vaudreuil*. Toronto 1974

PICTURE CREDITS

T. Gilcrease, *Institute of American History and Art* (Tulsa): Amikwa Ojibwa, c. 1700

National Archives of Canada: French portrayal of the Iroquois (3165), French portrayal of the Ojibwa (70664)

Royal Ontario Museum Annual Archaeological Report 1905 (Toronto 1906): Ojibwa victory over the Iroquois

George Copway, *Running Sketches* (1851): Kahgegagahbowh, George Copway

Archives of Ontario: Ojibwa woman (S-16356), George Kaboosa and son (S-16359), Ojibwa of Garden River Reserve (S-16353), Ojibwa chief (S-15218), Ojibwa north of Lake Nipigon (S-15105), Ojibwa with child on carrying board (S-12562), Ojibwa camp (S-15720), Ojibwa in traditional dress (S-16352), Garden River band in Hiawatha pageant (S-16351), Captain Anderson (S-1648), Chief Charles Jones (S-4014), Ojibwa women, c. 1900 (S-2471), Mrs Peter Jones (S-4012), farm life (S-16361), Peter Jones (S-2150), Chief David Wawanosh (S-850), Reverend John Sunday (S-14224), Reverend Robert Steinhauer (S-14229), Manitowaning Anglican Church (S-13099), present giving at Wikwimikong (S-18174), Ojibwa camp on Oak Island (S-8250), Spanish residential school children, 1940s (S-15502), St Joseph's residential school (S-15501), Grand council of Ontario, 1926 (13709-15), Chief Big Canoe (S-4015), logging reserve timber (S-4013), Ojibwa soldier (S-14443), traditional Ojibwa burial (S-16416)

Annual Archaeological Report 1904 (Toronto 1905): wampum as mnemonic device

Moses Nawash: Chief Nawash

Grey County Museum: Nahnebahwequay (Catherine Sutton)

James Cleland Hamilton, 'Famous Algonquins: Algic Legends,' *Transactions of the Canadian Institute* 6 (1889): Francis Assikinack

Irene Akiwenzie: Cape Croker hockey team 1916, Cape Croker band council in the 1880s, reserve 'band' member, Cape Croker brass band 1914, Cape Croker youths, 1880s

Cape Croker Reserve Archives: Peter Nadjiwon 1915, birchbark biting design

Peter S. Schmalz: Laurenda Solomon, Valencia Roote, band office sign

INDEX